ASPEN PUBLISHERS

P9-DCR-953

Basic Contract Law for Paralegals

Fifth Edition

Jeffrey A. Helewitz

City University of New York
School of Law

Lecturer, Continuing Legal Education
Association of the Bar of the City of New York
New York County Lawyers' Association

 Wolters Kluwer

Law & Business

AUSTIN   BOSTON   CHICAGO   NEW YORK   THE NETHERLANDS

Aspen Publishers
Attn: Permissions Department
76 Ninth Avenue, 7th Floor
New York, NY 10011-5201

To contact Customer Care, e-mail customer.care@aspenpublishers.com, call 1-800-234-1660, fax 1-800-901-9075, or mail correspondence to:

Aspen Publishers
Attn: Order Department
PO Box 990
Frederick, MD 21705

Printed in the United States of America
1 2 3 4 5 6 7 8 9 0

ISBN 978-0-7355-6735-1

Library of Congress Cataloging-in-Publication Data

Helewitz, Jeffrey A.
    Basic contract law for paralegals/Jeffrey A. Helewitz. — 5th ed.
       p.cm.
    Includes bibliographical references and index.
    ISBN 978-0-7355-6735-1 (alk. paper)
    1. Contracts — United States. 2. Legal assistants — United States — Handbooks, manuals, etc. I. Title

    KF801.Z9H36 2008
    346.7302 — dc22

                                                                2007013111

About Wolters Kluwer Law & Business

Wolters Kluwer Law & Business is a leading provider of research information and workflow solutions in key specialty areas. The strengths of the individual brands of Aspen Publishers, CCH, Kluwer Law International and Loislaw are aligned within Wolters Kluwer Law & Business to provide comprehensive, in-depth solutions and expert-authored content for the legal, professional and education markets.

CCH was founded in 1913 and has served more than four generations of business professionals and their clients. The CCH products in the Wolters Kluwer Law & Business group are highly regarded electronic and print resources for legal, securities, antitrust and trade regulation, government contracting, banking, pension, payroll, employment and labor, and healthcare reimbursement and compliance professionals.

Aspen Publishers is a leading information provider for attorneys, business professionals and law students. Written by preeminent authorities, Aspen products offer analytical and practical information in a range of specialty practice areas from securities law and intellectual property to mergers and acquisitions and pension/benefits. Aspen's trusted legal education resources provide professors and students with high-quality, up-to-date and effective resources for successful instruction and study in all areas of the law.

Kluwer Law International supplies the global business community with comprehensive English-language international legal information. Legal practitioners, corporate counsel and business executives around the world rely on the Kluwer Law International journals, loose-leafs, books and electronic products for authoritative information in many areas of international legal practice.

Loislaw is a premier provider of digitized legal content to small law firm practitioners of various specializations. Loislaw provides attorneys with the ability to quickly and efficiently find the necessary legal information they need, when and where they need it, by facilitating access to primary law as well as state-specific law, records, forms and treatises.

Wolters Kluwer Law & Business, a unit of Wolters Kluwer, is headquartered in New York and Riverwoods, Illinois. Wolters Kluwer is a leading multinational publisher and information services company.

To Sarah — my first, and best, teacher

Summary of Contents

Contents

Chapter 2
OFFER   31

Chapter 3
ACCEPTANCE   55

Chapter 4
CONSIDERATION   83

Chapter 5
LEGALITY OF SUBJECT MATTER AND
CONTRACTUAL CAPACITY   109

Chapter 6
CONTRACTUAL INTENT   129

Chapter 7
CONTRACT PROVISIONS   149

Chapter 8
THE UNIFORM COMMERCIAL CODE   179

Chapter 9
THIRD PARTY CONTRACTS   227

Chapter 10
DISCHARGE OF OBLIGATIONS   263

Chapter 11
REMEDIES   293

Chapter 12
DRAFTING SIMPLE CONTRACTS   317

Appendix A
SAMPLE CONTRACTS   341

Appendix B
SUPPLEMENTAL CASES   399

Acknowledgments

I have been extremely fortunate to have had the kind assistance of several people in the preparation of this project. Joyce E. Larson, a Legal Assistant Coordinator in the Mutual Funds division of Brown & Wood, generously provided succinct and helpful criticism of the work in progress and continual encouragement throughout the writing of this book. Maria Montgomery, a corporate Legal Assistant and translator of international contracts at Stroock & Stroock & Lavan, spent many devoted hours commenting on and editing the manuscript. Words cannot express my gratitude to these two kind and intelligent women, without whose help this book never would have been possible.

I wish to thank all of the people at Little, Brown and Company who worked on the First Edition of this text, especially Betsy Kenny, Carolyn O'Sullivan, Kerry Vieira, and Lisa Wehrle. In addition, I would like to thank Linda Richmond and Lai T. Moy at Aspen Publishers for their work on the Second and Third Editions, respectively; Troy Froebe for his work on the Fourth Edition; and Katy Guimon for her work on the Fifth Edition.

Introduction

This book provides the paralegal student and practitioner with a quick, simple, and straightforward text on the law of contracts. It helps to clarify this very complex area of law using numerous practical examples of how to draft and interpret different types of contracts. This book is not intended to discuss every nuance of contract law, nor is it designed as a casebook for law students. *Basic Contract Law for Paralegals* is meant to be an easy-to-use, readable reference tool for the legal assistant.

The reader should be aware of the fact that there are two legal sources of law with respect to contract formation and interpretation. The first, and traditional source, is the common law, that law that has developed over the centuries based on judicial precedent (and sometimes codified by specific state statute). The second source of contract law is the Uniform Commercial Code (UCC), a form of which has been adopted by every jurisdiction in the country. The UCC regulates contracts for the sale of goods and contracts between merchants. Contracts for services or between non-merchants are still governed by the common law. Throughout the text the distinction between these two sources, whenever significant, will be specifically addressed.

The most important aspect of all laws is the relationship between the parties in dispute. The law is primarily concerned with relationships between and among individuals. In contract law, the value of the contract in monetary terms is of secondary importance; the relationship between the contracting parties is the most important determining factor. The simple contract for the sale of a morning newspaper and the multipage document for the development of a $20 million shopping center both involve identical legal principles. Because the law is concerned with principles and relationships, the logical starting point for the analysis of any legal problem is the legal relationship of the parties.

The most common problem encountered in analyzing a legal situation is that everyone immediately wants to jump to the end result — "What can I get" — rather than discerning the actual rights and liabilities of the parties. It is more important to identify each element of the relationship to determine whether or not a legal dispute exists.

Contracts is only one area of law that defines particular relations between persons; it is not the exclusive area of law applicable to a given situation. To determine a person's rights and liabilities, first you must determine what area of law — for instance, contracts, torts, bankruptcy — best applies to the problem. Then you must determine that all of the requisite elements of the legal relationship, as defined by that area of the law, exist. You cannot bend the law to fit the facts; if the facts do not fit into a particular legal theory, that theory is incorrect and a new one must be found. Keeping this general principle in mind will help in your analysis of all legal problems.

The role of the paralegal with respect to contracts is multidimensional. A paralegal is often called on to draft the initial agreement for the client and, as negotiations develop, to see that all subsequent changes are incorporated into the document. If a problem arises, the paralegal is generally responsible for making the initial analysis of the contract in dispute to determine all potential rights and liabilities of the client. And finally, the legal assistant will work with the attorney to determine the appropriate remedies available to the client. To perform these tasks, the legal assistant must be conversant with all of the elements of basic contract law and drafting.

Basic Contract Law for Paralegals

1 Overview of Contracts

Learning Objectives

After studying this chapter you will be able to:

- Define a legally binding contract
- Identify the six basic requirements to forming a valid contract
- Explain the concept of offer and acceptance
- Define and exemplify "consideration"
- Classify contracts into bilateral or unilateral agreements
- Understand how a contract is created
- Explain the difference between executory and executed contracts
- Differentiate between valid, void, voidable, and unenforceable contracts
- Discuss various contractual provisions
- Know what is meant by the term "contractual capacity"

CHAPTER OVERVIEW

This chapter discusses the six basic requirements for every valid contract and then indicates the various classifications into which all contracts fall. The chapter is intended to give a general overview of, and introduction to, contract law. The specific details involved in analyzing contractual situations are covered in the following 11 chapters.

The law of contracts is one of the most complex and important areas of substantive law taught in law school. Every law school in the country teaches contracts as part of the first year of required courses because, more than any other course of law, contracts affect everyone's daily existence.

Think of everything that you do each day: You wake up in your home, brush your teeth, dress, eat breakfast, read the morning newspaper, and travel to work or to school. Each of these activities involves contract law. Rent or mortgage payments involve a contract with a landlord or lender; brushing your teeth requires the purchase of a toothbrush and toothpaste; getting dressed is accomplished only after buying the clothes worn; buying the newspaper is a simple sales transaction; and even taking public transportation involves a contract with the municipality. Every aspect of normal life is dominated by contractual principles, but few people realize the extent to which they are, in fact, contracting parties. To the nonlaw professional, a contract is a long and complicated legal document that is drafted by an attorney and involves huge sums of money. Yet, in reality, most contracts involve little, if any, written documentation, no lawyer, and only small amounts of money (if money is involved at all). It is this all-pervasive element of contracts that makes contract law both interesting and challenging.

Contract Defined

A **contract** is a legally enforceable agreement that meets certain specified legal requirements between two or more parties in which each party agrees to give and receive something of legal value. It is distinguishable from a gift in that each party gives and receives something. In a gift situation only one party gives; the other one receives. Also, a contract is more than just an agreement. An agreement may not meet all of the specific requirements needed to create a contract; hence it will not be legally enforceable under a contractual claim.

Basic Contract Requirements

To determine whether a contractual relationship exists between two persons, it is necessary to ascertain that all six of the requisite elements of a valid contract exist. If *all* of these elements are not present, the parties do not have a contractual relationship (although they may have a relationship described by some other theory of law, which, if true, then would have to be addressed). Even if all of the elements are present in the agreement, the contract may be unenforceable because of some other statutory reason, such as the Statute of Frauds or the Statute of Limitations.

The six requisite elements of every valid contract are

1. offer;
2. acceptance;
3. consideration;
4. legality of subject matter;
5. contractual capacity; and
6. contractual intent.

Offer

An **offer** is a proposal by one party to another manifesting an intention to enter into a valid contract. Every valid contractual relationship starts with an offer.

 EXAMPLE:

One student asks another, "Will you buy my used Contracts book for $5?" The student has stated a proposal to sell a particular object (the used book) at a particular price ($5). Without this initial proposition, the two students could not possibly develop a contractual relationship.

The offer defines the boundaries of the potential relationship between the parties and empowers the other party to create the contract by accepting the proposition.

Acceptance

To create the contract, the party to whom the offer is made must **accept** the proposal. If she does not, then no contract comes into existence. The law will not force a person to fulfill an obligation to which she has not agreed.

 EXAMPLE:

The paralegal student in the example above says "OK, I'll take the book." In this case a contract has been created because the student has agreed to the proposal of the seller.

The concepts of offer and acceptance go hand in hand in determining whether a contract exists. The offer and acceptance together form the **mutual assent** of the parties—the agreement that they do intend to be contractually bound to each other. Without this meeting of the minds, no matter what else may exist, there is no valid contract.

Consideration

Consideration is the subject matter of the contract; it is the thing for which the parties have bargained. Most people assume consideration to be the price, but that is not completely accurate. Although money may be part of the bargain, it is not always the complete bargain. Nor is money itself always necessary. The crucial aspect of consideration is that each party both gives and receives consideration. Each must give something of value.

 EXAMPLE:

In the example given above, the consideration is both the $5 and the book itself. The seller is bargaining for the money; the buyer is bargaining for the book.

Consideration is deemed to be anything of legally significant value — monetary worth is not the ultimate determining factor of legal value.

 EXAMPLE:

In the example above, instead of asking for $5, the student says "Will you exchange your used Torts book for my used Contracts book?" If the second student agrees, a contract is formed. In this instance the books themselves are consideration — no money changes hands.

These first three elements — offer, acceptance, and consideration — are the three most important aspects of every valid contract because they form the provisions of the contract itself. Without these three components there can be no contract.

Legality of Subject Matter

To be valid, a contract can only be formed for a legal purpose and must fulfil any statutory regulations with respect to form.

 EXAMPLE:

Acme, Inc., a major producer of automobile tires, enters into an agreement with Goodyear to run Dunlop out of business by fixing prices. Although this contract may meet all of the other contractual requirements, it is not enforceable because it violates U.S. antitrust laws. This contract is not formed for a legal purpose.

Contractual Capacity

Contractual capacity refers to the ability of a person to enter into a valid contract. The most typical examples of capacity (or rather, the lack of capacity) deal with the age of the party and the person's mental condition.

 EXAMPLE:

John, a precocious 14-year-old, wants to buy some woodland for potential real estate development. Although it may be a good idea and may possibly bring in millions of dollars, the law considers a 14-year-old incapable of entering into a contract. His age and presumable lack of experience make him contractually incapable.

Contractual Intent

Contractual intent is the last of the requisite elements of a valid contract, but the one that is all pervasive. Even if the contract meets all of the other requirements enumerated above, if it can be shown that the parties did not subjectively intend to form a contractual relationship, there will be no contract. Many times this aspect of intent is not readily discernible by the words of the parties themselves, and surrounding circumstances must be analyzed to determine whether a contract exists.

 EXAMPLES:

1. Kevin agrees to sell Bruce his house for $50,000. The contract is in writing, describes the house, and specifies the method and terms of payment. On the face of it, the contract appears valid. But what if it were shown that Kevin had been forced to sign the contract at gun point? Under these circumstances, Kevin obviously did not willingly intend to enter into the contractual relationship with Bruce.

2. William agrees to pay Sally $500 a week to be his housekeeper. Once again, on its face, this appears to be a valid contract. However, what if William were 85 years old, and Sally had convinced him that none of his relations wanted anything to do with him? She also told him that if he didn't hire her, he'd be all alone and helpless. Under these circumstances, it would appear that

William was the victim of mental coercion. Consequently, his intent to enter the contract of his own free will is suspect.

The above-mentioned six elements must exist if there is to be a valid contract. Each of these elements will be discussed in detail in the following chapters. The foregoing is intended only as a general overview. However, it is necessary to keep all six of these elements in mind when discussing contracts because each one is necessarily intertwined, regardless of the type of contract created.

Classification of Contracts

All contracts fall into a certain number of classifications, or types. Generally, it is a good idea to classify the contract in question prior to analyzing its validity and provisions. This classification process is like making selections from a restaurant menu. Take one item from each category, and when completed, a meal (that is, a contract) is formed.

Type of Obligation: Bilateral or Unilateral

The type of obligation refers to the kind of duty imposed on the parties to the contract. This category defines every contract as belonging to one of two classifications.

All contracts are either **bilateral** or **unilateral.** A bilateral contract is a promise for a promise. A unilateral contract is a promise for an act. This division into bilateral or unilateral is important with respect to what performance is expected from the parties and at what point the contract comes into existence. With a bilateral contract, the parties are expecting a mutual exchange of promises, with the performance to be carried out only after the promises have been given. Most contracts are bilateral, even though it is rare that the parties actually use the word "promise" (except in the most formal of situations).

 EXAMPLE:

In the situation discussed above, with respect to the sale of the used text book, the actual words used were "Will you buy my used Contracts book for $5"? "OK." These words created a bilateral contract. What the parties legally said were: "Will you promise to pay me $5 if I promise to sell you my used Contracts book"? "I promise to pay you $5 if you promise to sell me your used Contracts book." The contract was created when the promises were given. The performance — the exchange of the book for the money — is intended to take place *after* the agreement has been made.

Conversely, in a unilateral contract, the contract is only created when one side has performed a requested act. Instead of an exchange of mutual promises a unilateral contract is an exchange of a promise for an act.

 EXAMPLE:

Allison promises to pay Tim $1500 if Tim paints her apartment on Wednesday. In this instance, Allison is requesting a specific act: Tim's painting the apartment on Wednesday. Allison does not want Tim's promise that he will do the painting; she wants to see the job done. Until Wednesday arrives, and Tim actually paints the apartment, no contract exists. When Tim does the painting, Allison must fulfill her promise to pay him $1500.

There tends to be a lot of confusion in identifying a contract as bilateral or unilateral, simply because most ordinary contracts are formed and completed simultaneously. Consequently, it is difficult to distinguish between the promise and the act. This determination is crucial, however, because it times the start of the contractual relationship. If the contract is bilateral, the relationship is formed at the exchange of promises. The parties are entitled to contractual remedies if one side does not fulfill his promise. (This is the "What can I get?" as discussed in the Introduction.) On the other hand, if the contract is unilateral, the contractual relationship is only formed when one side actually performs the requested act. Until that time, no contractual remedies are available to the parties. If, in the example above, Tim does not paint the apartment on Wednesday, Allison has no recourse to sue him because he is under no contractual obligation.

To determine whether a contract is bilateral or unilateral, it is necessary to determine the intent and the specified wishes of the parties involved. Courts will generally go along with what the parties could most reasonably expect under the circumstances because that would indicate the true meeting of the parties' minds with respect to the manner of acceptance sought. Note that the law is generally pro-contract; that is, it favors contractual relationships and consequently presumes contracts to be bilateral. This creates the contractual relationship sooner than in a unilateral contractual situation.

Method of Creation: Express, Implied, or Quasi-Contracts

How does a contract come into existence? A contract is formed either by the words or conduct of the parties and is classified accordingly.

An **express** contract is one in which the mutual assent of the parties is manifested in words, either orally or in writing. An **implied-in-fact** contract is one in which the promises of the parties are inferred from their actions or conduct as opposed to specific words being used.

EXAMPLES:

1. Eric leases a house from Lisa. The parties use a standardized written lease purchased at a stationery store. This is an express contract because the rights and obligations of the parties are described in written words.

2. In the previous example of the sale of the used Contracts book, the parties have entered into an express contract. Their promises are given orally.

3. Louise goes to a newsstand to buy her morning paper. She picks up the paper and gives the news agent 50 cents. Louise and the news agent have completed an implied-in-fact contract. The contract was entered into by their actions, and no words were used or necessary.

In addition to express and implied-in-fact contracts, the law has also created another category known as **implied-in-law**, or **quasi-contracts**. As the term "quasi" might indicate, these are situations that look like a contract, but, in truth, are not contracts because one of the requisite elements is missing. However, in the interests of fairness, the law has determined that a party should be entitled to some remedy if injured by such a situation.

Whenever the words "quasi" or "estoppel" are used, terms that will be discussed in subsequent chapters, the court is using its equitable jurisdiction. The difference between law and equity is basically the difference between justice and mercy. There are times and situations in which the legal result might be "just" under the laws of society — that is, reasonable under the circumstances — but it would not be "fair" — a party would be injured without recourse. In these situations, the concept of **equity** takes over. Equity was designed to right wrongs, to prevent unfairness and unjust enrichment. Equity was created specifically for those situations in which the application of the law would result in an injured party still suffering. For a more complete discussion of the equity courts, see Chapter 11, Remedies.

With respect to the classification of contracts, the courts have created the concept of quasi-contractual situations, situations in which the parties do not have a contractual relationship but in which it would be most fair to treat them as though a contract did exist. For a quasi-contractual situation to arise, it must be shown that one party unjustly benefited from the other party under circumstances in which a mutual benefit had been expected.

 EXAMPLES:

1. Joan has just completed her paralegal training, but before she starts work she receives a telephone call from her elderly aunt in the Midwest. Her aunt tells Joan that she is very ill, not long for this world, and needs someone to take care of her. The aunt promises Joan that if Joan comes to the Midwest and looks after her, she'll remember Joan in her will.

Based on the foregoing, Joan moves to the Midwest, and for the next ten years cooks, cleans, and takes care of her aunt. When her aunt finally dies, Joan is simply "remembered fondly" in the aunt's will. All the aunt's cash goes to her cat Fluffy.

Can Joan sue the estate for breach of contract? No. Why? Because no contract existed—the aunt merely said she would remember Joan in the will—there was no mutual benefit, and no consideration given to Joan, despite what Joan might have hoped for.

In this instance, the court will probably apply the doctrine of quasi-contract and permit Joan to recover the value of the services she provided for the aunt. Because Joan never intended to make a gift of her services to her aunt, if the aunt received them without compensating Joan, the aunt would be unjustly enriched. This would be unfair to Joan.

2. Sal opens the door to his house one morning and discovers a newspaper on his doorstep. He picks it up and takes it to work with him. For the next week every morning a newspaper appears at his door. At the end of the week Sal receives a bill from the publisher for the newspapers.

Does Sal have a contract with the publisher? No. However, the court, applying the doctrine of quasi-contract, will permit the publisher to recover the cost of the papers. Sal accepted the benefit of the papers by taking them and reading them, and now must pay. If Sal did not want the papers, it was his responsibility to contact the publisher to stop delivery.

Note that there are laws that would make the outcome different if the U.S. mail were used to deliver the goods. Several years ago a statute was enacted stating that if the mail is used to send unsolicited merchandise, the recipient may keep the merchandise as a gift. Also, many states have consumer protection laws prohibiting the delivery of unsolicited goods.

To apply the concept of quasi-contract, it must be shown that no contract exists because a requisite element is missing and one party is unjustly enriched at the expense of the other.

Type of Form: Formal and Informal Contracts

A **formal** contract is a contract that, historically, was written and signed under seal. The concept derives from a time when few people could read or write, and the solemnity of a seal gave importance to a document. The seal was used as the consideration for the agreement. Nowadays, seals are no longer used, and this term refers to a limited group of contracts that different states have declared valid and enforceable if certain statutory requirements are met. Some examples of formal contracts are negotiable instruments (such as checks, and certificates of deposit) and guarantees.

 EXAMPLE:

Fidelity Bank issues printed checks to its customers, which the customers use to pay their bills. These checks do not contain the words and elements of a contract, but they are enforced as a formal contract because of statutory regulations. The contract is between the bank and its customers.

Informal contracts are, simply put, all non-formal contracts. Despite the terminology, informal contracts are agreements that meet all the requirements of valid contracts; they can be quite specific and stylized in and of themselves.

 EXAMPLE:

The contract for the sale of the used Contracts book is an example of an informal contract. All the contractual requirements are present, and its form is not regulated by a statute.

Timing: Executory and Executed Contracts

One of the most crucial questions for the parties to a contract involves the timing: "*When* are the contractual obligations to be performed?" This timing element indicates when the parties have enforceable rights and obligations. Contracts are categorized by indicating whether or not the parties have uncompleted duties to carry out. An **executory** contract is a contract in which one or both of the parties still have obligations to perform. An **executed** contract is complete and final with respect to all of its terms and conditions.

 EXAMPLE:

When the two paralegal students discussed above agree to the terms for the sale of the used Contracts book, the contract is formed but it is still executory. Once the book and the money have changed hands, the contract is complete with respect to all of its terms, and is now completely executed. (Note that the term "executed" is also used to indicate the signing of a document; in that context the obligations are still executory even though the contract is executed (signed).)

Enforceability: Valid, Void, Voidable, and Unenforceable

Finally, getting to the "What can I get?" element, the law classifies contracts in terms of their enforceability. Can a party to a contract have that agreement enforced in a court of law, and which party to the contract has that right of enforceability.

A **valid** contract is an enforceable contract that meets all of the six requirements discussed above: There is a proper offer and acceptance; legally valid consideration is given and received; the parties have the legal capacity to enter into a contract; the contract is for a legal purpose; and the parties genuinely intend to contract — it is complete under the law. Either party can bring suit for the enforcement of a valid contract.

A **void** contract is, in reality, a contradiction in terms because there is no contract, and therefore the law does not entitle the parties to any legal remedy. The agreement has not met the contractual requirements.

In a **voidable** contract a party to the agreement has the option of avoiding his legal obligation without any negative consequences, but who could, if he wished, affirm his obligation and thereby be contractually bound. A contract entered into by a minor is an example of a voidable contract. Legally, a minor does not have contractual capacity and can avoid fulfilling contracts into which he has entered. (There are exceptions for certain types of contracts. See Chapter 5.) However, if, on reaching majority, the former minor affirms the contract, he will be contractually bound.

 EXAMPLE:

Seventeen-year-old Gene enters into a contract with Bob, an adult, to buy Bob's used car. If Gene changes his mind, he can avoid the contract. However, if, on Gene's eighteenth birthday, Gene affirms his promise to Bob by giving Bob a payment, the contract will be totally enforceable. The option of avoidance is with Gene who is under the disability, not with Bob who is not.

A voidable contract may become valid and enforceable if the party under the disability — a minor, or a person induced by fraud, duress, or like condition to enter the agreement — later affirms his obligation when the disability is removed. A void contract, on the other hand, can never be made enforceable, regardless of what the parties do; any addition to the agreement that the parties attempt in order to meet contractual requirements actually creates the contract at that time; it does not validate what was void.

An **unenforceable** contract is a valid contract for which the law offers no recourse or remedy if its obligations are not fulfilled. For instance, a contract may exist in which one party failed to meet her contractual obligation; by the time the aggrieved party decides to sue, the Statute of Limitations has run, meaning that the law has determined that the proponent has waited so long to bring the suit that the court will not hear the question. Or, parties agree to open a store at a particular location, but before the contract can be fulfilled, the town rezones the area for residential use only. Even though the contract is valid, it can no longer be enforced because of a subsequent change in the law that makes its purpose incapable of being legally performed.

In classifying any given contract, remember that it will consist of elements of each type discussed above. The following chart summarizes these five types:

Type of Obligation	Method of Creation	Form	Timing	Enforceability
Bilateral Unilateral	Express Implied in fact Implied in law (quasi)	Formal Informal	Executory Executed	Valid Void Voidable Unenforceable

Every contract will have one item from each of these five categories; the terms are not mutually exclusive.

SAMPLE CLAUSES

1

Dear Irene,

Pursuant to our telephone conversation yesterday, I hereby agree to buy the pearl necklace you inherited from your Grandmother Rose for $500. Come to my house for dinner next Monday, and I'll give you a check.

Love,
Jeannette

P.S. Don't forget to bring the necklace.

The above letter constitutes an example of a bilateral contract between Jeannette and Irene. Irene made an offer for the sale of her necklace, which Jeannette has acknowledged and accepted in writing. The consideration Irene is giving is the necklace; the consideration Jeannette is giving is the $500. In terms of classification, this is an informal bilateral express contract that is executory until the consideration changes hands. Remember that to be legally enforceable, a contract does not have to take any particular form or include words of overt legality. Even a handwritten note may constitute a valid contract.

| 2 |

This contract dated the _____ day of _____, 20 _____, is made between Samuel Smith, hereinafter Smith, whose address is _____, and Peter Jones, hereinafter Jones, whose address is _____.

Jones hereby agrees to paint the exterior of Smith's house, located at _____, on the _____ day of _____, 20 _____, in consideration for which Smith hereby agrees to pay Jones the sum of $2500, inclusive of all expenses, upon the completion of said painting.

In Witness Whereof, the undersigned have executed this contract the date and year first above written.

_____

Samuel Smith

_____

Peter Jones

The preceding is a more formalized version of a simple bilateral contract, this time for services instead of for the sale of goods. Why is it bilateral instead of unilateral, since services are being requested? The answer is that both parties are making present promises to each other: Jones to paint the house, and Smith to pay for Jones' painting services. The contract is formed on the date indicated; performance is merely delayed until the date specified. Whenever there is a mutual exchange of promises, the contract is bilateral.

Note that Smith has included the cost of all of Jones' expenses in the contract price. This means that the $2500 is all that Smith is liable for, and Jones is responsible for paying for all paints, brushes, and so forth, that are required to do the work. This is a written example of an informal express, executory, bilateral contract.

| 3 |

Dear Mr. Whitson:

This concerns the parcel of land I bought from you last month. On making a personal inspection of the property, I noticed that the drainage ditch was clogged. I will be out of state for the next two months and can't clear it myself. Please clear the ditch for me and send a bill to my office for $500.

Sincerely,
Alfred Brace

The following week Mr. Whitson cleared the drain and sent Mr. Brace a bill for $500.

This is an example of an express unilateral contract. Mr. Brace has requested a service from Mr. Whitson and has agreed to pay Whitson upon completion of the requested task. Mr. Whitson accepted the offer by doing the act requested and now is waiting for payment. The contract is still executory because Mr. Whitson has not yet received Mr. Brace's check.

This example differs from Sample 2 in that here the offering party has requested an act, not a promise, and the offer became a contract when the other party accepted by cleaning the ditch. Once again, the correspondence was more informal than a signed and printed document. This does not negate the fact that it is a binding contract between the parties.

In analyzing information that is presented, always go through the checklist of five contract classifications given above to determine the exact form of the documents you are handling. Do not be put off or swayed by the physical appearance of the materials. Handwritten letters, notes, and typed agreements all may be valid contracts, depending on the substance of the material itself. Remember, the classifications only help to organize the material; they do not determine the agreement's legal effect or the relationship created between the parties. That determination involves a minute examination of the six contractual requirements examined earlier in the chapter.

CHAPTER SUMMARY

The law of contracts is one of the most complex, yet most elemental, of all areas of the law. Contract law forms the basis of most people's daily existence and therefore is of paramount importance as a field of study.

To create a valid contract, the agreement must contain the following six elements: offer, acceptance, consideration, legality of the subject matter, contractual capacity of the parties, and the contractual intent of the parties. Without these elements, the parties are not in a contractual relationship and, if injured, must rely on a different legal relationship to resolve the dispute.

All contracts can be classified according to five different categories, and in analyzing a contractual situation, it is best to classify the agreement prior to determining the rights and liabilities of the parties. The five classifications are: type of obligation (bilateral or unilateral); method of creation (express, implied in fact, or quasi); type of form (formal or informal); timing of obligation (executory or executed); and enforceability (valid, void, voidable, or unenforceable). Once the situation has been appropriately classified, analysis of the specific provisions can begin.

SYNOPSIS

Six requirements of every valid contract
1. Offer
2. Acceptance
3. Consideration
4. Contractual capacity
5. Legality of subject matter
6. Contractual intent

Classifications of contracts
1. Type of obligation
   a. Bilateral
   b. Unilateral
2. Method of creation
   a. Express
   b. Implied
   c. Quasi
3. Type of form
   a. Formal
   b. Informal
4. Timing
   a. Executory
   b. Executed
5. Enforceability
   a. Valid
   b. Void
   c. Voidable
   d. Unenforceable

Key Terms

Acceptance: manifestation of assent to the offer proposed

Bilateral contract: a contract in which a promise is exchanged for a promise

Consideration: the bargain of the contract; a benefit conferred or detriment incurred at the request of the other party

Contract: a legally enforceable agreement between two or more parties in which each agrees to give and receive something of legal value

Contractual capacity: the legal ability of a person to enter into a contractual relationship

Contractual intent: the purposefulness of forming a contractual relationship

Equity: the branch of the law that deals with fairness and mercy to prevent unjust enrichment

Executed contract: a contract that is complete and final with respect to all of its terms and conditions

Executory contract: a contract in which one or both of the parties still have obligations to perform

Express contract: a contract manifested in words, oral or written

Formal contract: historically, a written contract under seal; currently, any contract so designated by a state statute

Implied-in-fact contract: a contract in which the promises of the parties are inferred from their actions as opposed to specific words

Implied-in-law contract: see Quasi-contract

Informal contract: any nonformal contract

Mutual assent: agreeing to the same terms at the same time; the offer and acceptance combined

Offer: a proposal by one party to another manifesting an intent to enter into a valid contract

Quasi-contract: a legal relationship that the courts, in the interest of fairness and equity, treat in a manner similar to a contractual relationship, even though no contract exists

Unenforceable contract: a contract that is otherwise valid but for a breach of which there is no remedy at law

Unilateral contract: a contract in which a promise is exchanged for an act

Valid contract: an agreement that meets all six contractual requirements

Void contract: a situation in which the parties have attempted to create a contract, but in which one or more of the requisite elements are missing, so no contract exists

Voidable contract: a contract that one party may avoid at his option without being in breach of contract

EXERCISES

1. Give three examples of bilateral contracts from your everyday life that are not mentioned in the text.
2. What elements would you look for to determine that an agreement is an enforceable contract?
3. Why would a valid contract be unenforceable? Give examples.
4. Create a bilateral contract for a situation that involves barter.
5. How would you attempt to prove the existence or nonexistence of contractual intent?

Cases for Analysis

To elucidate certain points discussed in the chapter, the following judicial decisions are included. The first case, Villarreal v. Art Institute of Houston, Inc., highlights the difficulty in maintaining an action for breach of a contract that is alleged to be partially written and partially oral. Rohaley v. Compere discusses the requirements to create an enforceable contract.

Villarreal v. Art Institute of Houston, Inc.
20 S.W.3d 792 (Tex. App. 2000)

Daniza Villarreal enrolled in the photography program at the Art Institute of Houston, Inc. ("The Art Institute"). The Art Institute is a technical college which offers various degree programs, but does not offer transferrable college credit courses. Villarreal contends that its representatives made numerous false representations to her regarding the program, the school, and the costs. She took out guaranteed student loans in order to pay for the program. She did not complete the program, and did not repay the loans as required. She sued The Art Institute of Houston, Inc. for fraud and breach of contract.

Her case was tried to a jury. After the close of Villarreal's case, the trial court directed verdict for The Art Institute on the breach of contract claim. The jury found for The Art Institute on the fraud claims, and a take nothing judgment was entered against Villarreal. She appeals this judgment, contending that the trial court erred in directing verdict against her on the contract claims, and that the evidence was legally and factually insufficient to support the jury's finding on the fraud claims.

Breach of Contract

We hold the trial court did not err in directing verdict against Villarreal on her breach of contract claims. Villarreal contends that her contract with The Art Institute was partly written and partly oral, and alleges that The Art Institute breached the contract in three ways:

(1) failing to provide her with unlimited use of its photography department facilities and equipment;
(2) failing to provide her with college credits that could be transferred to another college or university; and
(3) failing to provide her with an associate's degree.

Conversely, The Art Institute contends that its contract with Villarreal — in its entirety — was embodied in one document, the Enrollment Agreement. The Art Institute argues that it did not breach the express terms of that contract, and that parol evidence is not admissible to alter its terms. It appears the trial court granted directed verdict on that basis. . . .

The Nature of a Contract Between a School and Its Students

A few Texas courts have addressed the issue of whether a contract exists between a private educational institution and its students. See e.g., Southwell v. University of Incarnate Word, 974 S.W.2d 351, 356 (Tex. App. — San Antonio 1998, *pet. denied*); Eiland v. Wolf, 764 S.W.2d 827, 838 (Tex. App. — Houston [1st Dist.] 1989, *writ denied*) (holding that school catalogue was not enforceable contract when it contained express disclaimer that it did not constitute an irrevocable contract between any student and the school); University of Texas Health Science Center at Houston v. Babb, 646 S.W.2d 502, 506 (Tex. App. — Houston [1st Dist.] 1982, no writ) (holding that a university's catalogue constitutes a written contract between the educational institution and the patron, where entrance is had under its terms); *Taylor*, 275 S.W. at 1090-1919 (holding that a special verbal contract between a school and parent of student may exist in derogation of the written terms of the catalogue, which constitutes a written contract between the educational institution and the patron, when entrance is had under its terms); *Vidor*, 145 S.W. 672 (school catalogue sets forth terms of contract between patrons and school). The First District Court in Houston has stated that "the relationship between a private school and its student has by definition primarily a contractual basis." *Eiland*, 764 S.W.2d at 837-838. And recently, the San Antonio court stated that "where a private college or university impliedly agrees to provide educational opportunity and confer the appropriate degree in consideration for a student's agreement to successfully complete degree requirements, abide by university guidelines, and pay tuition, a contract exists." *Southwell*, 974 S.W.2d at 356.

At a minimum, an implied contract existed between Villarreal and The Art Institute that The Art Institute would provide Villarreal an educational opportunity and confer upon her a degree in photography in consideration for her agreement to successfully complete degree requirement, abide by the school's guidelines, and pay tuition. The other terms of the contract were partly oral and partly written. We confine our inquiry here to whether Villarreal made out her causes of action for breach of contract with regard to the specific terms she alleges were breached in this suit.

While a valid contract did exist between The Art Institute and Villarreal, Villarreal failed to offer any evidence that the terms of that contract required The Art Institute to perform the acts that she complains it failed to perform. Thus, because she has not proven the existence of a valid contract containing the terms upon which she bases her suit, the trial court was correct in directing verdict against Villarreal on her breach of contract claims.

In order for the trial court to have erred in failing to send her breach of contract claims to the jury, Villarreal must have presented enough evidence to raise a fact issue on each element of her three claims of breach. Her three claims are (1) that the Institute failed to provide her with unlimited access to its facilities; (2) that the Institute failed to provide her with an Associate's Degree; and (3) that the Institute failed to provide her with college credit hours that were transferable into a four-year degree program. With regard to each, she must have produced evidence of: (1) the existence of a valid contract binding the Institute to perform the promised act she claims it failed to perform; (2) her performance or tender of performance given as consideration for that particular promise; (3) nonperformance on the part of the Institute; and (4) damages resulting from the breach. See Garner v. Corpus Christi Nat. Bank, 944 S.W.2d 469, 476 (Tex. App. — Corpus Christi

1997, *writ denied*) (reciting the essential elements of a breach of contract action). Each of her claims fails to meet the first element.

The first element in a breach of contract case is that the plaintiff must prove the existence of a valid contract wherein the defendant promised to perform in the manner the plaintiff alleges he failed to perform. The elements of a valid contract are: (1) an offer; (2) an acceptance in strict compliance with the terms of the offer; (3) a meeting of the minds; (4) each party's consent to the terms; and (5) execution and delivery of the contract with the intent that it be mutual and binding. Copeland v. Alsobrook, 3 S.W.3d 598, 604 (Tex. App.—San Antonio 1999, *pet. denied*); McCulley Fine Arts Gallery, Inc. v. "X" Partners, 860 S.W.2d 473, 477 (Tex. App.—El Paso 1993, no writ). "The determination of a meeting of the minds, and thus offer and acceptance, is based on the objective standard of what the parties said and did, and not on their subjective state of mind." *Copeland*, 3 S.W.3d at 604. Villarreal produced no evidence to show a valid contract existed requiring The Art Institute to: (1) provide her with unlimited access to its facilities, (2) confer an associate's degree upon her, or (3) provide her with college credits that could be readily transferred to another university or college. Because she has not shown the existence of a valid contract containing those terms, her breach of contract claims must fail as a matter of law. We address each alleged promise, in turn.

1. *Promise to Provide Unlimited Access to the Institute's Facilities*

A. No Evidence of a Contract

First, Villarreal failed to offer any evidence that The Art Institute entered into a valid contract to provide her with unlimited access to its facilities. She also failed to offer any evidence that The Art Institute breached that agreement. The only evidence she offered was her own testimony that she was told by an admissions representative that once she received her degree, she would "always" be able to come back and use their equipment. She also testified that one of the teachers at The Art Institute told a story about a student that had gone to school there, became a photographer and after graduating had some problems with her personal equipment. She was able to get the job done by using The Art Institute facilities. The implication, of course, was that all graduates of the photography program would be able to return to the Institute to use the facility if necessary.

However, this evidence does not show that a valid contract existed between Villarreal and the Institute requiring the Institute to allow her unlimited use of its facilities. Villarreal does not contend that the Institute made that promise to her in writing, but only alleges that the oral statements referred to above constitute the binding contract upon which she sues. She did not offer any evidence that The Art Institute intended to be bound by that condition, or that unlimited access to the facility was provided as consideration for her tuition and fees. She did not offer any evidence that there were any conditions on The Art Institute's alleged promise to provide her with unlimited use of its facility. She appears to be arguing that The Art Institute promised her unlimited use, regardless of her academic or enrollment status, and regardless of whether she completed or dropped out of the photography program. Her vague testimony that she was promised she would "always" be able to use the facility does not logically imply that The Art Institute intended to enter a binding contract to allow such use, and we find it insufficient to establish that a valid contract existed that contained that term.

B. No Evidence of a Breach

Moreover, Villarreal offered only vague and scant evidence that any such promise was, in fact, breached by The Art Institute. She testified that at a time when she was not enrolled in classes, she went to the school to use the facility and equipment and was told by another student that Jim Estes, the head of the photography department, had said to tell her the next time she came to the school that she was not to use the facility and equipment anymore. Villarreal testified that upon hearing that, she left, and never inquired further about her ability to use the facility or equipment nor did anything to confirm that the message was legitimate. The head of the department testified that he never told anyone to relay that message to Villarreal.

"Some evidence" is that which would enable reasonable and fair-minded people to differ in their conclusions, but creates more than a suspicion or surmise. Ramirez v. Carreras, 10 S.W.3d 757, 760 (Tex. App. — Corpus Christi 2000, *pet. filed* Feb. 23, 2000). We hold that Villarreal did not present any evidence that The Art Institute made and then breached a contract to allow her unlimited use of its facility, and affirm the trial court's granting directed verdict on that basis.

2. *Promise to Confer an Associate's Degree*

Similarly, Villarreal failed to support her claim that The Art Institute promised to provide her with an Associate's Degree, rather than an Associate's Degree of Applied Science/Art. (The difference in the two is that an Associate's Degree is typically comprised of credits that will transfer into a four-year degree program at a college or university, whereas an "applied" degree is comprised of credits in a specialty area that will typically not count toward another degree.) The Art Institute's representatives testified at length regarding the differences in an "Associate's Degree of Applied Sciences" (or Art) and an "Associate's Degree," and testified that the applied degree was the only one offered for photography at the Institute.

Villarreal's own testimony failed to establish that The Art Institute contracted to provide her with an Associate's Degree. She testified that she was given the impression that she would be earning an Associate's Degree from The Art Institute, but not that she was specifically told that. She testified that during her initial interview with The Art Institute admissions representative, she told the representative that she planned to go to college, and the representative responded that she would be attending college at The Art Institute, the only difference was that she could complete an Associate's Degree in two years at The Art Institute versus four years otherwise. She testified that at the time she signed the Enrollment Agreement, she did not know that the "Associate of Applied Science/Art" degree offered by The Art Institute was different from an Associate's Degree. She was told that after she got her photography degree, she could continue her schooling and get a "master's degree."

However, this claim is in express contradiction of a written agreement between the parties. Villarreal executed a form promulgated by the Texas Education Agency when she enrolled at The Art Institute. This form ensures that the students receive the information the school is required by law to provide prior to enrollment. It is to be completed by the student prior to enrollment and the completed form maintained by the school in each student's file. This document is initialed fourteen (14) times by Villarreal, and signed and dated by her at the bottom.

It states, in relevant part:

> If the school awards credit hours, it has been explained to me that transferability of any credit hours earned at this school may be limited. I have also been provided a list of all known Texas institutions of higher learning and state technical institutions that will accept any or all of the credit hours so earned. If the school has an articulation agreement with an academic college or university, that information has been provided with any limitations. . . .

Villarreal testified that at the time she signed the Enrollment Agreement, she did not know that the "Associate of Applied Science/Art" degree offered by The Art Institute was different from an Associate's Degree. She said she was not told that her credit hours at The Art Institute would not transfer to other colleges. She testified that her whole goal was to continue her education beyond the photography course, and if she had known that the hours would not transfer, she would not have taken it.

However, Villarreal did not testify that anyone directly told her that she would receive an Associate's Degree, and not an Associate's of Applied Science Degree. She did not point to any document wherein The Art Institute promised her an Associate's Degree as opposed to an Associate's of Applied Science Degree. In fact, the documentary evidence implies the opposite.

We do not believe this amounts to any evidence that The Art Institute entered into a contract to provide Villarreal with an Associate's Degree. We hold that all this evidence, taken as a whole, does not create a fact question regarding whether a valid contract existed containing this term. At best, it shows that Villarreal was mistaken in her assumptions when enrolling in the school, and that The Art Institute did not take steps to ensure that she did not make that mistake. We find the trial court was correct in directing verdict on the breach of contract claim insofar as it relates to the breach of a promise to provide Villarreal with an Associate's Degree.

3.   *Promise to Provide Her with Transferrable Credits*

Finally, we believe the same principles apply to Villarreal's claim that The Art Institute contracted to provide her with college hours that would be transferrable to another college or university. This alleged promise is in direct contradiction with the language on the Texas Education Agency form referred to previously. Her only testimony that could be construed to evidence of a contract to provide her with transferrable credits was that she was told by an admissions representative that she would be going to college at the Institute, but it would only take two years for a degree rather than four years. We hold this evidence is insufficient to raise a fact issue regarding whether The Art Institute entered into a valid contract to provide her with transferrable college credits. We affirm the trial court's grant of directed verdict on all breach of contract claims.

Legal and Factual Sufficiency: Fraud Claims [Omitted]

We affirm the judgment of the trial court in all respects.

Questions

1.   What did the court say about the implied contract that might exist between a student and a school?

2.   What is the nature of the evidence, according to the court, that must be provided to demonstrate a breach of contract?

3.   What is the effect that the court gives to the school's catalogue?

Rohaley v. Compere
2004 Alas. LEXIS 116

I. Facts and Proceedings

On April 8, 1954, Donald Rohaley filed a homestead entry for a parcel of land south of Anchorage, comprising approximately 140 acres. Rohaley filed a notice of occupancy with the Bureau of Land Management (BLM), which was recorded on May 24, 1954. In May 1998 Sally Compere purchased forty acres of land adjacent to Rohaley's property.

Compere asked Robert Kean, a surveyor, to investigate the existence of a section line easement on Rohaley's property. On October 22, 1998, Kean reported to Compere that based on BLM records and policy "there is every indication that there is NOT a section line easement between Sections 30 and 31 to your property from Canyon Rd." In May 1999 Compere obtained a permit from the Municipality of Anchorage to construct a 450-foot drive along the section line. On July 27, 1999, after contacting Rohaley and learning that there was probably not a valid section line easement over his property, the Municipality revoked the permit and issued a stop work order. Two days later Thomas Knox, a surveyor for the Municipality of Anchorage, issued a memorandum based on Kean's research opining that there was no section line easement. Rohaley sued Compere in July 2000 for trespass and for trespass by cutting or injuring trees and shrubs, a tort governed by Alaska Statute 09.45.730, which provides that a person who commits trespass by cutting down or injuring trees or shrubs can be held liable to the land's owner for treble damages. Rohaley alleged that Compere caused significant damage to his property by "digging deep gouges through the land and destroying numerous trees and shrubs."

The case was heard before Superior Court Judge Sen K. Tan. Compere moved for summary judgment, asking that the court find that there is a valid public use easement running over Rohaley's property. Judge Tan denied Compere's motion on September 4, 2001, finding that there were genuine issues of material fact surrounding the existence and location of the alleged section line easement.

On September 5, 2001, the parties entered into a settlement agreement in open court providing that Compere would restore Rohaley's property to its previous condition at her own expense and pay Rohaley $16,000. This settlement was supplemented by the parties' April 10, 2002, agreement that Rohaley would provide Compere with an easement over the eastern edge of his property in exchange for an additional $5,000. The parties also discussed what would constitute a reasonable restoration of Rohaley's property. This arrangement was intended to be the "final complete agreement between the parties" and was agreed to by Compere's counsel and Rohaley in open court.

Compere's attorney prepared a written agreement designed to memorialize the parties' oral agreement. In addition to Compere's pledge to pay Rohaley $21,000 and to restore his property, and Rohaley's pledge to grant Compere an easement, the written agreement contained several additional provisions which Rohaley found objectionable. The parties were represented by counsel during both court-mediated settlement conferences.

On October 14, 2002, Rohaley moved to vacate the settlement agreement. First, he argued that the settlement agreement did not contain all of the material terms of the agreement and that the parties did not agree to certain material terms that were included in the written agreement. Second, he argued that the settlement agreement was based on the parties' mutually mistaken assumption that a section line easement already existed over Rohaley's property. Rohaley also expressed his concern that he might have trouble enforcing the agreement against Compere. To support his motion, Rohaley relied on a report by attorney Thomas Meacham which stated that "a valid argument may be advanced" that there was no easement over the section line to Rohaley's property.

Judge Tan denied Rohaley's motion on February 7, 2003. Judge Tan found that Rohaley's argument that the court was led to believe that a section line existed was "patently false." He noted that since the terms of the April 10 settlement granted Compere the easement in exchange for $21,000, it was clear that the parties did not assume that the easement already existed. The court deemed it irrelevant that Rohaley discovered an expert witness to support his claim that no section line easement existed, because the court never made a definitive ruling on whether the section line easement existed. Judge Tan also ruled that the parties had come to an agreement on all terms that were material to their settlement agreement. Rohaley appeals.

III. Standard of Review [Omitted]

IV. Discussion

A settlement agreement is a contract, and its construction and enforcement are governed by the legal principles generally applied to contracts. "Generally, 'sound judicial policy indicates that private settlements and stipulations between the parties are to be favored and should not be lightly set aside.' " "The formation of an express contract requires an offer encompassing its essential terms, an unequivocal acceptance of the terms by the offeree, consideration and an intent to be bound." A settlement agreement satisfying these requirements forms a binding agreement between the parties. When the parties to a case, either individually or through their attorneys, orally agree to settle a claim in open court and there is no dispute as to the material terms of the settlement, the settlement is enforceable against both parties.

Rohaley advances several arguments as to why the settlement agreement should be vacated. First, he argues that the parties entered into the agreement while laboring under a mutual mistake of fact. Second, he argues that he possesses newly discovered evidence concerning the subject matter of the original litigation. Third, he argues that the settlement agreement did not contain all of the material and essential terms of the parties' agreement. Finally, he argues that enforcement of the settlement agreement would result in manifest injustice. We reject each of these arguments in turn.

A.   The Superior Court Did Not Abuse Its Discretion in Refusing to Vacate the Settlement Agreement on the Grounds of Mutual Mistake

Rohaley seeks to avoid the settlement agreement on the grounds of mutual mistake under common law principles and under Alaska Civil Rule 60(b). We have previously held that "when the parties to an agreement share a mistaken belief about a material fact, the agreement may be voidable." Civil Rule 60(b) provides for similar relief when the parties enter into a settlement agreement under a mutual mistake and the mistake destroys a "fundamental, underlying assumption" of the agreement.

Rohaley alleges two mutual mistakes. First, he argues that both parties mistakenly assumed that there was a section line easement over Rohaley's property. This assertion is completely contradicted by the parties' in-court settlement agreement and evidence in the court record. Rohaley clearly did not believe that a section line easement already existed because he sued Compere for trespass. And the record shows that Compere received an expert opinion from surveyor Robert Kean in 1998 which stated almost definitively that there was no section line easement over Rohaley's property. In addition, the agreement provides that Compere would pay Rohaley an additional $5,000 in exchange for an easement over his property. Had the parties believed that a section line easement already existed, this agreement would have been unnecessary. Finally, Judge Tan denied Compere's motion for summary judgment precisely because there were numerous unresolved factual issues concerning the existence of the section line. There is no indication that either party or the court was under the impression that a section line easement existed on Rohaley's property as a matter of law.

Second, Rohaley argues that the parties entered into a settlement agreement under the shared mistaken belief that a trial on the issue of a section line easement would have been lengthy and costly. Rohaley claims that Judge Tan was similarly mistaken. He argues that this assumption was mistaken because Thomas Meacham's affidavit definitively settled the issue of whether an easement existed. This argument is flawed. Meacham's affidavit was quite equivocal, noting that a determination whether an easement exists on homestead land involves complicated legal and factual questions which confound even experienced real estate law practitioners in Alaska. And a party's mistaken assessment of the merits of his case or the likely length and complexity of trial cannot serve as a basis for setting aside an otherwise valid settlement agreement. The superior court was correct in refusing to vacate the settlement agreement on the grounds of mutual mistake.

B. *Thomas Meacham's Affidavit Does Not Justify Vacating the Settlement Agreement*

Rohaley argues that the settlement should be vacated under Alaska Civil Rule 60(b)(2) because he presented the court with newly discovered evidence. Rule 60(b)(2) allows the superior court to relieve a party from a final judgment if the party moves for such relief due to "newly discovered evidence which by due diligence could not have been discovered in time to move for a new trial under Rule 59(b)." The evidence to which Rohaley refers is the affidavit by attorney Thomas Meacham setting forth the basis for Meacham's legal opinion that there was no section line easement over Rohaley's property.

Rohaley did not move for relief in the superior court on the grounds that he had new evidence. Rather, Meacham's affidavit was introduced to support Rohaley's contention that the parties had entered into the agreement laboring under a mutual mistake of fact that Meacham's affidavit tentatively resolved. Rohaley's failure to move for relief in the superior court on the basis of new evidence constitutes waiver of that argument on appeal. Moreover, we note that there is no competent evidence to support Rohaley's contention that Meacham's affidavit was evidence that either party was unaware of before settlement, or that Rohaley or his counsel, exercising the due diligence required by Rule 60(b)(2), could not have discovered during litigation or settlement negotiations. Finally, even if Rohaley had sought relief before the superior court on the grounds of new evidence, we concur with that court's ruling that its failure to definitively resolve the issue of whether a section line easement existed renders Meacham's affidavit irrelevant.

C. *The Settlement Agreement Contained All of the Material and Essential Terms of the Parties' Agreement*

Rohaley argues that the settlement agreement is unenforceable because the written agreement contained several material terms that were not orally agreed to, specifically: a confidentiality clause, a provision for interest on any late payments, and an agreement to restore Rohaley's property. Judge Tan ruled that these terms were not material to the parties' agreement and, with the exception of the restoration claim, were not brought to the court's attention during the in-court proceedings. To be enforceable an agreement must include all material terms, although the parties need not address every possible contingency that may arise because courts can " 'fill gaps in contracts to ensure fairness where the reasonable expectations of the parties are clear.' " Because we agree that Rohaley and Compere came to an agreement on all terms material to their settlement, we affirm the decision of the superior court.

1.   The Confidentiality Clause

The written agreement proposed by Compere's counsel contained the following language: "It is understood that the Parties shall keep the terms of this Agreement confidential except as otherwise required by law and shall neither disclose nor discuss its contents with any third party except those persons necessary to carry out the terms of this Agreement." Because the parties did not discuss such a clause in their in-court settlement negotiations, Rohaley argues that the judgment should be vacated, arguing that "Compere sought to add new terms such as confidentiality" to the agreement. He also argues that the confidentiality clause was an essential term of the agreement on which the parties failed to agree.

Though there is no one test to determine what makes a term essential to an agreement, courts in other jurisdictions have characterized a term as essential when the parties "regard [it], at the time of contracting, as a vitally important ingredient in their bargain," when its rejection could have affected the negotiation of other contractual terms, or when it is necessary to determine the rights and duties of each party. One might also discern the subjective importance of a term by considering the actions and words of each party throughout the course of the parties' interactions.

The issue of confidentiality was not essential to the parties' agreement in this case. Neither party raised this issue before the court during settlement negotiations, nor does settlement of a trespass claim or the grant of an easement implicitly raise any issues of confidentiality. Finally, the general intent of the settlement agreement — to restore Rohaley's property, provide Rohaley with payment, and grant Compere an easement — could be achieved regardless of the confidentiality clause. The parties' failure to agree on the necessity of a confidentiality clause does not void their agreement.

2. Interest on the Installment Payments

At the settlement conference, both parties agreed that Compere would pay $10,500 upon the grant of an easement over Rohaley's property and make a second payment of $10,500 ten months later. Neither party raised the issue of what would happen if Compere was late in making either of these payments. Compere's proposed written settlement agreement provided that if "payments are made pursuant to this schedule, no interest shall accrue on the sums due, but if payments are not made in accordance with this schedule, interest at the rate of 4.25% shall accrue on the unpaid balance from the date any sum came due." Rohaley now claims that he should be allowed to avoid the settlement agreement because "there was no agreement reached as to interest in the installment payments."

The parties clearly agreed that Compere would pay a total of $21,000 in two installments, assuming that payments were timely. The parties' failure to specifically provide for interest charges for late payment does not bar enforcement of the settlement agreement. That the parties have left some issues to be determined in the future does not prevent courts from enforcing an otherwise valid agreement "if some method of determination independent of a party's mere 'wish, will, and desire' exists, either by virtue of the agreement itself or by commercial practice or other usage or custom." Alaska Statute 09.30.070 governs the rate of interest applicable to past-due judgments, and the applicable statutory interest rate could apply in the absence of any agreement to the contrary. If Compere failed to pay the $21,000 according to the agreed schedule, Rohaley could obtain a judgment for the past-due amount, including prejudgment interest. The failure to specifically provide for this situation during the settlement agreement does not void the agreement.

3. Restoration of Rohaley's Property

Restoration of Rohaley's property was a material term of the agreement. Rohaley originally sued for trespass to prevent Compere from cutting down trees and shrubbery on his property and to recover treble damages for the injury that she had already done to his property. Restoration of Rohaley's property was discussed during both open court settlement agreements, and the record indicates that the parties did, in fact, come to a complete agreement concerning Compere's obligations in this regard.

At the first settlement conference, the parties agreed that Compere would restore Rohaley's property to its condition prior to her trespass, and that she would pay him $16,000 in damages. At the second settlement conference, the parties agreed that the restoration would be completed by June 30, 2002, and that it would be "reasonable," which Rohaley defined as filling holes and planting vegetation to prevent further erosion. Because the parties' agreement specifically addressed the restoration of Rohaley's property, his argument that no agreement was reached on this essential term is without merit.

D.   There Is No Other Justifiable Reason to Relieve Rohaley from His Obligations under the Settlement Agreement

Rohaley argues that relief from the settlement agreement is also available under Civil Rule 60(b)(6), which allows a court to relieve a party from a settlement agreement for "any other reason justifying relief from the operation of the judgment." Rohaley contends that Rule 60(b)(6) applies because Compere caused him to incur large litigation expenses and because he was somehow coerced into the settlement agreement. He also contends, as sort of a *quid pro quo*, that since Compere was allowed to amend the original settlement agreement, he should be entitled to amend or avoid the second agreement.

Rule 60(b)(6) applies only in extraordinary circumstances. We have found "extraordinary circumstances" for the purpose of the rule when the parties to a divorce settlement had a mutual misunderstanding about one spouse's eligibility for survivorship benefits and federal regulations rendered enforcement of the settlement impossible; when a paternity judgment was based on a mother's knowing misrepresentation of the paternity of her child to the purported father; and when the mutual intent underlying a judgment, order, or property settlement was destroyed by a subsequent event.

Rohaley alleges no inequity in the settlement that would justify relief under Rule 60(b)(6). The fact that Rohaley incurred legal expenses due to his prosecution of Compere's trespass is not an extraordinary circumstance justifying relief. And Rohaley's argument that he was coerced into settlement by Judge Tan's order denying Compere's summary judgment motion is completely unfounded. The record shows that Rohaley entered into the settlement agreement under his own will. "Relief under Civil Rule 60(b)(6) is inappropriate when a party takes a deliberate action that he later regrets as a mistake."

V. Conclusion

Because Rohaley has provided no valid reason to vacate the settlement agreement, we AFFIRM the decision of the superior court.

Questions

1.   What does the court say about the nature of a settlement agreement?

2.   According to the court, what would be the effect of a mutual mistake on the formation of a valid contract?

3. What is your opinion of the court's discussion of the party's equitable argument?

Suggested Case References

1. For a discussion of express and implied contracts, as well as promissory estoppel, read Tuttle v. ANR Freight System, 797 P.2d 825 (Colo. App. 1990).
2. Can a unilateral contract become a bilateral contract? Cook v. Johnson, 37 Wash. 2d 19, 221 P.2d 525 (1950).
3. To see how the federal court sitting in New York defines consideration, read Banque Arabe et Internationale D'Investissement v. Bulk Oil (USA), 726 F. Supp. 1411 (S.D.N.Y. 1989).
4. Allgood v. Procter & Gamble Co., 72 Ohio App. 3d 309, 594 N.E.2d 668 (1991), provides a brief discussion of the basic elements of a valid contract.
5. For a discussion of express and implied contracts, and their relation to employment law, see Duplex Envelope Co., Inc. v. Baltimore Post Co., 163 Md. 596 (1933).

Offer

Learning Objectives

After studying this chapter you will be able to:

- Define "offer"
- Identify the three conditions necessary to create a valid offer
- Explain the concept of "certainty and definiteness in the terms of an offer"
- List the four required terms in a valid offer
- Briefly define the UCC
- Discuss the impact of the UCC on traditional legal principles of a contractual offer
- Know what is meant by an "output contract"
- Apply basic concepts of an offer to contractual clauses
- Draft a basic offer that would meet legal standards
- Indicate the difference between contracting with a member of the general public and contracting with a merchant

CHAPTER OVERVIEW

This chapter focuses on the creation of the contractual relationship. It describes the process and requirements of the first essential element of every valid contract: the offer. For a contract to be deemed valid, the parties to the contract must manifest to each other their mutual assent to the same bargain at the same time. A contract is the meeting of two minds for one purpose. Therefore, the law expects the parties to indicate to each other that they are of the same mind. Without this mutuality of purpose, the parties would have misplaced expectations.

This contractual process of agreement begins with the party known as the offeror, who first proposes the contractual relationship. It is the offeror's function to initiate the contract process, and to determine the boundaries of that agreement under the common law. The terms of the contract are entirely determined by the words or actions of the offeror except for contracts for the sale of goods between merchants pursuant to the provisions of the Uniform Commercial Code. See infra. It is the offeror who creates all the provisions of the contract.

In order to guarantee that there is, in fact, a meeting of the minds between the offeror and the person to whom the offer is made, the offeree, the common law requires that the offer be definite and certain in all of its relevant terms. The relevant terms are price, subject matter, parties to the contract, and the time of performance of the contractual provisions. The law will not countenance an offer that is so indefinite in its provisions that a reasonable person would be unable to recognize and understand the relevant terms of the contract.

Offer Defined

An **offer** is a proposal by one party, the **offeror,** to a second party, the **offeree,** manifesting an intention to enter into a valid contract. The offer creates a power in the offeree to establish a contract between the parties by making an appropriate acceptance.

The offeror, the one making the proposal, is the creator and the initiator of the contractual process under the common law. It is the offer itself that determines all of the relevant provisions of the contract. The terms of the offer are the terms of the contract. Once the offer has been made, the power or ability to create the contract rests with the offeree. This is the key element of all contractual relationships. The offeror proposes; the offeree disposes. Without the assent of the offeree, no contract can exist.

 EXAMPLE:

Jessica proposes to sell her car to Elizabeth so that she can use the money for a vacation. Jessica's asking price is $1200. Elizabeth, when she hears the price, thinks the price is too high, and declines. No contract exists. Elizabeth, the offeree, has refused to accept the terms of the contract that Jessica has proposed.

Not all proposals are considered to be legal offers. For instance, in the example above, if Jessica did not mention a price for the car, how could Elizabeth accept? Elizabeth would not know the terms of the contract she was accepting. Furthermore, what if Jessica simply said she would sell the car to Elizabeth for $1200, but Elizabeth was not around to hear the proposal? How could someone accept a proposition of which she was unaware?

Consequently, the common law requires that the following three conditions be met for a proposal to qualify as a contractual offer:

1. the offeror must manifest a present contractual intent;
2. the offer must be communicated to the offeree; and
3. the offer must be certain and definite with respect to its terms.

Unless these requirements are met, the proposal may exist, but it will not be considered an offer to contract. It must be noted that contracts for the sale of goods between merchants are now governed by the Uniform Commercial Code (UCC), a statute that has made significant changes to the common law for contracts that come within its purview. Therefore, throughout the text, where appropriate, these differences will be addressed.

Present Contractual Intent

The element of intent is a basic requirement of all contractual relationships. Unlike other aspects of life and law, a contract cannot be thrust upon an unsuspecting person. For the offer to have legal validity, it must appear to an objective, reasonable person that the offeror actually intended to make an offer. How is this element of intent determined? Intent is shown by taking into consideration all of the circumstances surrounding the proposal. The more serious the words and expressions used, the more likely it is that the element of intent can be demonstrated. The court will always attempt to find the most reasonable interpretation of the facts based on the circumstances presented.

 EXAMPLES:

1. Philip is showing a group of friends a valuable watch he inherited from his grandfather. While joking around about how old-fashioned the watch is, Philip laughingly offers to sell it for an inexpensive up-to-date plastic sports watch. If one of his friends attempts to accept by giving Philip a plastic watch, there would be no contract. Under these circumstances, reasonable persons would assume Philip was joking, not making a valid offer.

2. Darren, having constant trouble with his car, kicks the wheels and says out loud that for two cents he'd sell the car. John, overhearing him, gives Darren two pennies and tries to drive off with the car.

There is no contract. Under the circumstances, it is unreasonable to assume that Darren intended to offer his car for sale for two cents. Words spoken in jest or frustration lack the requisite element of intent.

Communication to the Offeree

For an offer to be capable of acceptance, the offer must be communicated to the offeree. It is the offeree who has the power to create a valid contract by making the appropriate acceptance, but that acceptance can occur only if the offeree is aware of the offer.

The precise method of communication is left to the discretion of the offeror. The law supposes that the offerer will use effective means of communicating an offer to the offeree so that a contract can come into existence. Oral, written, telephonic, and mechanical means of communication are all considered legally sufficient methods of communication. The offeror is not limited to making the offer specifically to just one person. An offer can be made to a group, or class, of persons, any of whom is capable of accepting the offer.

The effect of a valid communication is to give the person to whom it was communicated the ability to accept. The method of acceptance is discussed in detail in Chapter 3, Acceptance.

 EXAMPLES:

1. Mildred leaves a message on Kate's answering machine offering to sell Kate a used Real Property textbook for $10. This offer has been validly communicated to Kate, even though the words were not spoken to her directly.

2. Upset at her grade in a Litigation course, Mildred screams out in her room that she'd sell her litigation text for $2. Walter, passing by Mildred's window, hears her scream, and tries to buy the book. There is no contract. Not only is it unlikely that Mildred intended an offer, but the proposal was not effectively communicated. Merely making a statement in the presumptive privacy and solitude of one's own room does not constitute communication of an offer.

3. In the school newspaper, Mildred inserts a notice offering to sell her used Torts book for $10. This is a valid offer that has been communicated to anyone who reads the paper.

Take careful note that although the above example illustrates a valid communication of an offer via the newspaper, not all newspaper advertisements are considered to be offers. Courts have determined that in many instances newspaper ads are merely "invitations" to the public to make an offer, or to patronize a particular establishment. The distinguishing factors between a valid offer and a mere invitation turn on intent of the advertisers and the certainty and definiteness of the terms employed. The more certain and definite the words used by the advertiser, the more likely it is that the ad will be considered an offer.

 EXAMPLE:

An advertisement to sell a particular named product at 25-50 percent below the listed price is not an offer to the public, but is an invitation to the public to negotiate for the item. Why? Because the terms of the ad are not sufficiently definite. The presumed intent of the seller is not to make an offer but to invite the public to bid for the product in a range from 25-50 percent below the listed price.

Certainty and Definiteness in the Terms of the Offer

Because the offeror creates the terms of the contract by what is expressed in the offer, the court carefully scrutinizes the terms specified in the proposal. As previously discussed, the more certain and definite the proposal, the more likely it is that the court will construe the proposal as an offer to create a valid contract.

To determine that the terms are indeed definite and certain, the law looks for the presence of four essential elements:

1. the price of the contract;
2. the subject matter of the contract;
3. the parties to the contract; and,
4. the time of performance for fulfilling the contract.

The more certain and definite these elements, the more likely it is that the proposal will be considered an offer under the common law; conversely, the more indefinite or ambiguous these terms, the less likely it is that the proposal will be considered a valid offer. Because the parties are required to demonstrate mutual assent, it would be impossible to have the assent if the parties did not know or were uncertain as to what they were agreeing.

To ascertain that these four elements exist, the court will examine all the circumstances surrounding the creation of the offer. It will consider all the statements made by the parties, all preliminary negotiations that may have existed, and any other documentation that can indicate the intent, certainty, and communications of the parties.

Essential Terms of an Offer

Contracts are a matter of private concern between the contracting parties themselves, and, unless the contract includes some aspect of life that is governmentally regulated, the law leaves the creation of the contract terms completely up to the parties.

Under the common law, when drafting the provisions of an offer, the offeror must be as specific as possible with respect to price, subject matter, parties, and timing of performance. The law requires that these terms be certain, definite, and capable of being readily understood by a reasonable person. If the offeror indicates terms that are not objectively definite but are vague and ambiguous, the offer will not be considered valid.

As a general rule, the courts will not correct vague terms mentioned in an offer in order to create a valid contract. To uphold contracts, however, and consequently the legal expectations of the parties, the court will, under certain circumstances, apply the concept of "reasonableness" with respect to a contract provision that the parties have neglected to include. On the other hand, the court will not insert "reasonable" terms if the parties themselves have attempted to specify a term but have done so badly. In sum, the court can sometimes correct omissions but can never change the terms the parties themselves have used.

How all this fits together will be analyzed in the following discussion of the four essential terms of an offer.

Price

The price stated in the contract is an example of contractual consideration. **Consideration** is the bargain of the contract; it is the benefit conferred or the detriment incurred. Both sides must give and receive something of legal value to make the contract valid. Price — that is, money — is the most typical example of consideration, but it is not the only one. For a detailed discussion of consideration, see Chapter 4, Consideration.

If the parties are intending the sale of a good or service, usually the good or service is exchanged for cash or a cash equivalent such as a check or money order. Because this forms part of the consideration, a requisite element of every valid contract (see Chapter 1), the law requires that the price be specified in the offer itself. If the parties indicate in the offer that the price will be left for future negotiations, no offer or contract exists, even if every other contractual requirement has been met. Why? Because without knowing an essential term, the parties cannot have mutual assent.

 EXAMPLE:

Sam agrees to sell Hank three roasting chickens, to be delivered Friday morning, for a price to be determined at the time of delivery. There is no contract. Hank might have thought that the price would be 29 cents per pound, whereas Sam might have thought $3 per chicken was fair. There is no mutual assent to this offer despite what the parties might have thought.

Under certain circumstances, the price of a contract can be determined by a court inserting the element of reasonableness and thereby salvaging an otherwise void contractual agreement. If the parties completely neglect to mention a specific price, the court can interpret a "reasonable price," and then entertain evidence as to what the reasonable price would be. The court can only apply the reasonableness rule if the term has not been mentioned at all, or the parties state "reasonable price" themselves. On the other hand, if the parties attempt to state a price but indicate one that is vague or uncertain, as in the example given above, the court's hands are tied; the contract will fail on grounds of indefiniteness. The court cannot vary the terms the parties have stated.

Note that for contracts for the sale of goods covered by the Uniform Commercial Code exceptions to the common law rule have been carved out. For contracts for the sale of goods between commercial traders, the UCC will permit contracts to be formed even if the price is not quoted, provided that the parties have a history of past dealings and some objective standard can be used to determine a price.

The parties do not have to specify a particular dollar amount to have a definite price. If the parties refer to some objective standard by which the price can be determined, then the offer will stand. Should the parties refer to some subjective measure, the offer will fail.

 EXAMPLES:

1. After completing her paralegal program, Rosa starts looking for a job. Rosa remains unemployed for several months. Finally, the firm of Hacker & Slacker agrees to hire her. Nervously, Rosa asks what her salary is to be, and Hacker says they'll pay her what they think she's worth. There is no contract. The determination of "worth" has been left up to Hacker's subjective evaluation; therefore, the offer lacks the essential term of price.

2. In the situation above, when Rosa asks about her salary, Hacker says he'll pay her the average starting salary paid to new paralegals at mid-size law firms in their city. This is a valid offer. Hacker has specified an objective standard for determining price, and that price can be proven by analysis of salaries in the area.

Any attempt by the parties to create a situation in which one side has total discretion with respect to filling in the terms will fail because of vagueness and indefiniteness. What one person considers "fair" may be deemed unjust by the other party. Terms such as a "fair profit," "fair price," or "fair rate of interest" are too uncertain to be enforceable. "Fair" is a subjective term. The court can only interpret "reasonableness." It cannot cure defects created by the specific words of the parties themselves.

Subject Matter

The subject matter of a contract is another example of the consideration for the contract. If one side is providing the price, the other side is usually providing a good or service, such as a textbook or paralegal services, which is that party's consideration for the contract.

Under strict common law principles, if the offer is to be deemed valid, the subject matter of the contract must be specifically described, not only in terms of content but in terms of quantity as well. How many textbooks of which subject are offered for sale? How many hours per week is the paralegal expected to work, and what are her functions? Any description of the subject matter that is inconclusive, vague, or ambiguous will cause the contract to fail.

Some typical problems that are encountered regarding the subject matter are discussed below.

Ambiguity.   If the subject matter is described in terms that are capable of more than one interpretation, the offer is deemed ambiguous and will not stand.

 EXAMPLE:

Celeste offers to sell Bonnie her brooch for $100. Celeste has three brooches and fails to specify which brooch is meant in the offer. No contract exists. The subject matter has been ambiguously described.

As in the example given above, if the subject matter is described in words that are ambiguous, the offer will not stand. The offeror must be sufficiently descriptive in her choice of words so that any reasonable person should be able to determine the subject matter of the contract. Ambiguity destroys the certainty of the terms of the offer.

 EXAMPLE:

Andy offers to sell his house in Los Angeles to Jim for $500,000. Andy has two houses in L.A., one worth $450,000, the other worth $3 million. Which house is meant? Andy may mean the less valuable house; Jim may assume the more valuable one. The offer is too ambiguous to stand.

If neither party is aware that the language is ambiguous, and both intend the same object, the court will let the offer stand because there is a meeting of the minds. Both parties intend the same object. On the other hand, if only one party is aware of the ambiguity, the court may uphold the offer based on the intention of the innocent party. In other words, the court won't let one party "pull a fast one" on the other.

 EXAMPLES:

1. Aaron offers to sell his house in Chicago to Brian for $500,000. Unknown to Aaron, Aaron's uncle has died and left him a house in Chicago worth $5 million. Brian hears of the uncle's death, agrees to the offer, and then sues Aaron to have Aaron convey the more expensive property. There is no contract. Because Aaron, at the time of making the offer, did not know the term was ambiguous (he thought he only owned one house in Chicago), the court will find the offer refers to the less expensive house.

2. In the same situation described above, both Aaron and Brian intend the contract to be for the sale of the less expensive house. Because both parties intend the same subject matter, the offer is valid.

Alternate Offers.   The offeror may offer to the offeree alternative subject matter. Making alternative proposals does not necessarily mean that the offer is uncertain. Provided that each alternative is certain and definite, the offeror is considered to be making two offers. Acceptance of one cancels the other.

 EXAMPLE:

Louise offers to sell Sophie her house in Maryland for $500,000, or her house in Delaware for $350,000. Assuming that Louise only owns one house in each state, the offer is definite in its terms, but gives Sophie a choice. Sophie can agree to buy either house, or neither. This constitutes a valid offer.

Note that in the example above, had either alternative been vague or ambiguous (Louise owns two houses in Delaware), there would have been only one valid offer capable of acceptance.

Output Contracts.   Just as with the element of price discussed above, the offer will stand if the quantity or quality of the subject matter can be sufficiently determined by an objective standard to which the parties have agreed both under the common law and the UCC.

The calculation of Rosa's salary by reference to average salaries in the area is a case in point. Another example of this type of agreement is known as an **output** contract. In an output contract, one party agrees to purchase all of the output of the other party for a specified price. If one party agrees to purchase from a supplier all supplies actually used during a given period, this is known as a **requirements** contract. Even though the exact amount of the product that is the subject of the contract is uncertain, the parties have specified an objective standard that can be used to fill in the uncertain term.

 ## EXAMPLES:

1. A juice manufacturer agrees to buy all of the oranges Farmer Brown grows in a given season at the price of $10 per bushel. This agreement is a valid contract because the amount of oranges can be determined by an objective standard: how many oranges are actually grown during the season.

2. Acme Inc., offers to buy all the coal it will need for its factory furnaces from Ace Mining Company for the next six months at a price of $10 per ton. This is a valid offer because the actual use of the factory furnaces can be mathematically determined.

Just as with the price discussed above, if one of the parties retains the absolute discretion to determine the standard for measuring the quantity or quality of the subject matter, the offer will fail for vagueness. The key is whether the standard used by the parties in the term of description is objective or subjective. Only an objective standard will create a valid offer.

 ## EXAMPLE:

Bijoux Jewelers offers to buy from Beta Diamond Mines for $1000 per carat all of the diamonds Beta cuts from its mines for the next six months that Bijoux finds of an acceptable grade for its customers. The offer is invalid. Bijoux has retained the right to determine which diamonds are acceptable to its customers; it is not purchasing all of Beta's output. The standard used is subjective.

Parties

The requirement that the parties be specifically described in the offer generally refers only to the offerees. Usually the identity of the offeror is readily ascertainable because he or she is making the proposal. In rare circumstances, a particular offeror may wish her identity to be unknown in order to have a better bargaining position, and this will usually not affect the validity of the offer. If the identity of the offeror is a prime concern of the offeree, as in the example of a contract for personal services, then identity must be revealed for the offer to be deemed valid. For example, Pavarotti might wish to accept an offer to sing at the New York Metropolitan Opera, but he might not want to accept an offer to sing at the National Opera of Costa Rica. Here the identity of the offeror is of great importance.

The offer creates a power of acceptance in the offeree. Therefore it is important to determine who is capable of accepting the offer. Only the offeree may accept a valid offer, but the offeree does not have to be particularly identified in the offer, provided that his identity can be determined by an objective standard.

And, unless the offeror expressly identifies the intended offeree, any person or persons to whom the offer is communicated is an offeree. The intended offeree may be an individual or a group of persons known as a **class** and any member of the class may accept the offer.

 EXAMPLES:

1. Sid offers to buy 100 shares of Gamma, Inc., stock for $3 a share from the first shareholder who accepts. He makes this offer to all Gamma shareholders. Gamma shareholders are the class, and the first shareholder to accept creates a valid contract.

2. Rhonda offers to sell her bicycle for $50. She makes the offer in front of three of her friends but specifies that the offer is made only to Sue. In this instance, only Sue is capable of accepting, even though several other people are aware of the offer.

Time of Performance

The fourth essential element of a valid offer is the aspect of the timing of the performance. Offers are not expected to last indefinitely, nor are contracts intended to be performed forever. Some words of limitation must be expressed by the offeror. Only in this manner can the parties know when the contract is to be fulfilled and, conversely, know when the parties have not lived up to their obligations.

Just as with a missing price term, if the parties neglect to mention time, the court will interpret "reasonable time" as the intent of the parties. On the other hand, if the parties attempt to designate a time period but do so imperfectly, the offer will fail.

 EXAMPLE:

Farmer White offers to sell five bushels of apples for $10 a bushel to Anne, time of delivery to be determined later. Anne intends to use the apples to bake pies for a church sale. The offer is not valid. Since the delivery time may be too late for Anne's purposes, unless the time is specified in the offer there can be no meeting of the minds.

If time is an important element for the parties — for example, in a contract involving the sale of perishable goods or involving parties who need the goods for a specific purpose — the element of time must be made a specific term of the offer. Such provisions are known as **time of the essence** clauses. They create a specific enforceable duty on the part of the deliverer to convey the goods by the specified time or be in breach of contract. These clauses are used in circumstances in which "reasonable time" would be too late for one of the parties.

"Reasonable time" is one of those terms that is determined by general custom or usage, and may vary depending on the specific circumstances in a particular area, business, or transaction. The court will consider all the surrounding circumstances to determine what is reasonable for a given situation.

 EXAMPLE:

Jim is having a house built and contracts with Richard to deliver piping so the builder can install it. The builder can only do the work on a specific day, and if the pipe isn't there at that time, Jim will have to wait another two weeks to have the pipe installed. This delay will incur additional expense for Jim. In this instance, delivery time of the pipe would be of the essence and should be specified in the contract as such.

Two Related Concepts

Two specific concepts must be mentioned at this point with respect to all of the foregoing. The first deals with the **Uniform Commercial Code.** The Uniform Commercial Code (UCC) is a model law adopted in whole or in part by each state as a statutory enactment that, among other things, has codified certain contractual concepts with respect to the sale of goods. For the most part, contract law still remains an area of law ruled by common law, but the UCC has made several significant changes to the common law of contracts. A complete discussion of the UCC is found in Chapter 8, but at this point one UCC provision should be noted.

If the contract is a contract for the sale of goods between merchants, the contract must comply with the provisions of the UCC. The purpose of the UCC is to promote commerce. To achieve this end, the UCC states that the absence of one or more of the preceding elements of an offer will not render the offer invalid. This exception is based on the presumption that the merchants intend a contract and, as business professionals, are best able to determine the essential requirements of their contracts. But remember, this exception applies only to contracts for the sale of goods between merchants, *not* for service contracts or contracts between non-merchants. (See Chapter 8.)

 EXAMPLE:

Oscar, a fabric manufacturer, agrees to sell Barbara, a clothing designer, ten bolts of fabric. No mention is made of timing of delivery or price, but Oscar has sold fabric to Barbara in the past. There is a valid contract. Because they are both merchants, and the contract is for the sale of goods, the UCC will let the offer stand. It is assumed that the parties know how to transact business, and time and price can be determined by their past business practices or other UCC provisions.

The second concept worthy of mention is that, regardless of any defect in the terms of the offer, if the parties to the agreement have performed or have started to perform, any defect can be cured by their actual actions. The parties' acts will be construed as creating the specifics of the vague term.

 EXAMPLE:

Return to the example given above involving Rosa and the law firm. If Rosa had gone to work for Hacker, even though the salary was left up to Hacker's discretion, and received a paycheck for $300 at the end of the week, the defect of the offer would have been cured by Hacker's actions. The contract would now be interpreted as providing Rosa a salary of $300 per week.

However, if the parties' performances cure one defect but leave other terms indefinite or vague, the offer will still fail.

SAMPLE OFFERS

| 1 | **For Sale**

One blue 1956 Chevy convertible. Excellent condition. Only used by an elderly man to drive three blocks to church on Sundays. Price: $1200. Nonnegotiable. If interested, call Ray: 555-1234.

This simple notice for the sale of an automobile constitutes a valid offer. All of the essential terms for an offer have been met. Remember, it is the elements of an offer that are paramount, not the form that the offer takes. However, should the advertisement have requested offers or said it would sell for the best price, the notice would not be an offer, but rather would be an invitation to bid or to make an offer. The person who answered that type of ad would, in fact, become the offeror.

| 2 |

To: William Smith

Acme, Inc., hereby offers to sell to William Smith 500 yards of decorative copper piping at the price of $.25 per inch, to be delivered by the 15th of next month. To be effective, acceptance of this offer must be sent via certified mail by _____, 20_____.

> Signature
> President, Acme, Inc.

The above example constitutes a sample offer for the sale of goods in which the offeror, Acme, Inc., has specified the means of acceptance for William Smith. As indicated above, the offeror establishes the terms of the contract, the offeree creates the contract by giving the appropriate acceptance. As will be discussed in the next chapter, the offeree must accept in the manner requested by the offeror in order to make a valid contract.

| 3 | **Offer**

_____, hereinafter Offeror, hereby agrees to sell to _____, hereinafter Offeree, the following items for the price indicated next to each item so mentioned.

(FILL IN ITEMS AND PRICES)

The above constitutes a simple form offer, once again for the sale of goods. If the contract were for the sale of services, the services would be specified in the offer where the items and prices are now. As demonstrated, the wording of an offer may be quite simple, provided that the subject matter of the contract and its price are sufficiently described. Precision of wording, as opposed to any particular words, is the key to drafting a valid offer.

CHAPTER SUMMARY

The first requirement of every valid contract is that the parties manifest to each other their mutual assent to the *same* bargain at the *same* time. The process by which this assent is manifested starts with an offer. An offer is a proposal by one party (the offeror) to the other party (the offeree) manifesting an intent to enter into a valid contract and creating a power in the offeree to create a contract between the parties by making an appropriate acceptance.

It is the offer that establishes all of the terms of the contract. Consequently, the law requires that the offer manifest a present contractual intent, that it be communicated to the offeree, and that it be certain and definite in all of its essential terms. It is only by meeting these requirements that the offeree knows what he is agreeing to, thereby creating the contract between the parties.

There are four essential elements with respect to the terms of an offer: the offer must be certain and definite with respect to the contract price, subject matter, parties, and time of performance. If the offer's terms are indefinite or ambiguous, the offer cannot create a valid contract because the offeree would be uncertain as to what she was accepting. Generally, the courts will not fix terms inaccurately stated by the offeror; however, should the offer fail completely to mention time or price, the courts usually will infer a "reasonable" time and "reasonable" price in order to uphold the contract. Any defect in the terms of the offer can be cured by the actions of the parties themselves. If they begin to perform the contract, their performance creates the certainty of the indefinite term.

Finally, when dealing with contracts for the sale of goods between merchants, the UCC has provided exceptions to the foregoing, permitting the merchants to determine the terms in their own contracts in order to further and advance commercial transactions.

SYNOPSIS

Three requirements of an offer
1. Manifestation of present contractual intent
2. Communication to offeree
3. Certainty and definiteness as to terms

Four required terms
1. Price
2. Subject matter
3. Parties
4. Time of performance

UCC exception: Sale of goods between merchants

Key Terms

Class: group of persons identified as a group rather than as named individuals

Consideration: the bargain of the contract; a benefit conferred or a detriment incurred

Offer: proposition made by one party to another manifesting a present intention to enter into a valid contract and creating a power in the other person to create a valid contract by making an appropriate acceptance

Offeree: the person to whom an offer is made; the one who has the power to create a valid contract by making an appropriate acceptance

Offeror: the person who initiates a contract by proposing the offer

Output contract: an agreement whereby one person agrees to buy or sell the goods produced by the other party

Requirements contract: agreement whereby one person agrees to buy all his supplies during a given period from one supplier

Time of the essence clause: contractual clause in which a specified time for performance is made a key element of the contract

Uniform Commercial Code: statutory enactment codifying certain areas of contract law, specifically with respect to sales contracts between merchants

EXERCISES

1.   Take an advertisement from your local newspaper and argue that it is an offer.
2.   Using the same ad as above, argue that it is an invitation to bid.
3.   What is your opinion of the UCC exceptions to general contract law?
4.   Write an offer to sell a piece of your own personal property.
5.   Draft an offer that is capable of being accepted by a specified class.

Cases for Analysis

The following case, G.B. "Boots" Smith Corp. v. Cobb, discusses a requirements contract. In Phil Watkins, P.C. v. The Krist Law Firm, P.C., the Texas court discusses problems with ambiguity in a contract.

G.B. "Boots" Smith Corp. v. Cobb
2003 Miss. LEXIS 578

Smith is a Mississippi corporation engaged in, among other things, the road construction business. Smith entered into a contract with the State of Mississippi to construct a bypass on U.S. Highway 61 in Coahoma County. The completion of this contract would require Smith to purchase a large amount of fill dirt. Smith entered into a contract with the Cobbs as follows: "The Sellers (the Cobbs) hereby sell to Buyer (Smith) all fill dirt for Project No. SDP-009-4(34) on Highway 61 Bypass South from the Sunflower River West to the end of said project, in Coahoma County, Mississippi." The contract further stated that the quantity of fill dirt needed would be approximately 550,000 cubic yards, and that Smith would purchase the fill dirt at the rate of $.40 per cubic yard.

After Smith had removed 443,716.30 cubic yards from the Cobbs' property, it began purchasing fill dirt from a third party. When the Cobbs discovered that Smith was acquiring fill dirt elsewhere, they filed suit alleging that the contract required Smith to purchase all fill dirt for the project solely from the Cobbs.

The chancery court found that, as a matter of law, the contract was unambiguous, was a mutual contract between the parties, required the Cobbs to provide all the fill dirt for the project, and required Smith to purchase all fill dirt for the project from the Cobbs. The chancery court then allowed the parties to put on testimony as to the amount of damages that the Cobbs suffered as a result of Smith's breach of contract.

The chancery court awarded $105,134.80, which is the contractual value of the amount of fill dirt used on the project that was not purchased from the Cobbs at $.40 per cubic yard. The chancery court further found that, because Smith was receiving monthly checks from the State of Mississippi for supplies for the project, Smith was considered a contractor, and the Cobbs were considered subcontractors, a fifteen percent (15%) damages penalty pursuant to Miss. Code Ann. §31-5-27 (Rev. 2000) should be imposed against Smith. The total judgment entered against Smith was for $120,905.02. Smith appeals.

Discussion

We will not interfere with or disturb a chancellor's findings of fact unless those findings are manifestly wrong, clearly erroneous, or an erroneous legal standard was applied. Pilgrim Rest Missionary Baptist Church ex rel. Bd. of Deacons v. Wallace, 835 So. 2d 67, 71 (Miss. 2003). Questions concerning the construction of contracts are questions of law that are committed to the court rather than questions of fact committed to the fact finder. Parkerson v. Smith, 817 So. 2d 529, 532 (Miss. 2002); Miss. State Hwy. Comm'n v. Patterson Enters., Ltd., 627 So. 2d 261, 263 (Miss. 1993). The standard of review for questions of law is de novo. Parkerson, 817 So. 2d at 532; Starcher v. Byrne, 687 So. 2d 737, 739 (Miss. 1997).

I. Whether the Chancery Court Erred in Finding That the Contract Between Smith and the Cobbs Required Smith to Purchase Fill Dirt Solely from the Cobbs

"In contract construction cases a court's focus is upon the objective fact — the language of the contract. [A reviewing court] is concerned with what the contracting parties have said to each other, not some secret thought of one not communicated to the other." Turner v. Terry, 799 So. 2d 25, 32 (Miss. 2001); Osborne v. Bullins, 549 So. 2d 1337, 1339 (Miss. 1989). Only if the contract is unclear or ambiguous can a court go beyond the text to determine the parties' true intent. "The mere fact that the parties disagree about the meaning of a contract does not make the contract ambiguous as a matter of law." Turner, 799 So. 2d at 32; Cherry v. Anthony, 501 So. 2d 416, 419 (Miss. 1987).

Here, Smith filed a motion in limine to prevent any parol evidence that would add terms to the contract upon which this suit was based. Smith, in essence, requested that the chancellor make his findings on the face of the contract alone. The chancellor then found that the contract was clear and unambiguous on its face and that he did not need to go beyond the text by having the parties testify to what was meant by the contract.

The Cobbs contend that the contract meant that they would sell all the fill dirt needed for the project to Smith and that Smith would buy all the fill dirt needed for the project exclusively from them. This type of contract is called a "requirements contract." A requirements contract requires the buyer to purchase all his "requirements" for goods or services solely from one seller. Requirements contracts are recognized in Mississippi and are not void for indefiniteness. Miss. Code Ann. §75-2-306(1) (Rev. 2002). "An essential element of a requirements contract is the promise of the buyer to purchase exclusively from the seller either the buyer's entire requirements or up to a specified amount." Mid-South Packers, Inc. v. Shoney's, Inc., 761 F.2d 1117, 1120 (5th Cir. 1985) (applying Mississippi law).

A Missouri federal court has found that an express promise by the buyer to purchase exclusively from the seller is not always required. In construing a contract in which only the seller has agreed to sell, a court may find an implied reciprocal promise on the part of the buyer to purchase exclusively from the seller, at least when it is apparent that a binding contract was intended.

Propane Indus., Inc. v. Gen. Motors Corp., 429 F. Supp. 214, 219 (W.D. Mo. 1977). "Thus there is no requirements agreement where the buyer fails to make an express or implied promise to purchase solely from the seller." 67A Am. Jur. 2d Sales §225, at 394 (2003) (footnote omitted). Had the formation of a requirements contract called for an express promise to purchase solely from the seller, then the contract at issue here would not be a requirements contract. The plain language of the contract provides an implied contract. While the contract does not contain the phrase "buyers agree to buy all fill dirt for the Project," the wording that was used in the contract implied exactly that. There would be no reason to include the wording "all fill dirt for project" unless Smith intended to buy all the fill dirt needed for the project from these particular sellers.

The chancellor reviewed the contract and, from the words in the contract alone, found that it was clear and unambiguous on its face and that it was a requirements contract. We agree.

   II.   *Whether Damages Were Appropriate in Light of This Court's*
                  Finding in Issue I [Omitted]

  III.   *Whether a Statutory Penalty Should Have Been Imposed*
                      Against Smith [Omitted]

Conclusion

The chancellor correctly found that the contract was clear and unambiguous on its face, and, through its wording, required Smith to purchase fill dirt solely from the Cobbs. In failing to do so, Smith breached the contract. However, the chancellor erroneously awarded the Cobbs the full purchase price of the unused fill dirt instead of only the profits they may have reaped from the sale of the fill dirt. The chancellor also erroneously awarded a statutory penalty.

We therefore affirm the chancellor's finding that the contract was a requirements contract, reverse and render the imposition of the statutory penalty, and reverse the award of damages and remand for a reassessment of damages in accordance with this opinion.

Questions

1. What was the factual basis that caused the plaintiff to file suit?
2. How does the court define a requirements contract?
3. According to the court, may a requirements contract be implied? Explain.

Phil Watkins, P.C. v. The Krist Law Firm, P.C.
2003 Tex. App. LEXIS 6693

This is a breach-of-contract case in which appellant Phil Watkins, P.C. challenges a summary judgment based on the trial court's determination that a one-page letter agreement between Phil Watkins, P.C. and appellee The Krist Law Firm, P.C. was supported by consideration and is unambiguous. Although we find the agreement was supported by consideration, we hold that it is ambiguous and so reverse the trial court's judgment, and remand this case for further proceedings consistent with this opinion.

I.   Factual and Procedural Background

At issue in this breach-of-contract dispute is the extent, if any, to which Krist can recover attorneys' fees and expenses based on its representation of two former clients subsequently represented by Watkins. Krist represented Kinley Sorrells, Sides, Inc., and other plaintiffs in a lawsuit filed against E.I. DuPont de Nemours & Company, alleging damages to their pecan orchards caused by the Benlate 50 DF (R) fungicide manufactured by DuPont (hereafter, the "DuPont Suit"). Krist claims that, while acting on behalf of these clients, it reached a settlement agreement with DuPont under which each plaintiff would receive $200 per affected acre owned by the clients plus an amount to be calculated under a "most-favored-nations provision." Krist asserts that, under this most-favored-nations provision, Kinley Sorrells and Sides, Inc. (collectively, the "Clients") would have received an additional amount equal to the difference, if any, between the $200 paid and the average per acre value paid by DuPont in the highest 25% of pre-verdict settlements that DuPont paid between the date on which the Clients signed their releases and December 31, 2000, in pecan cases in Texas alleging damage from Benlate (R).

Krist claims that the Clients initially consented to this settlement but then discharged Krist without just cause and without Krist relinquishing its right to reimbursement of expenses plus a 40% fee interest in the Clients' claims. Watkins asserts that the Clients discharged Krist for just cause and that the Clients never consented to any proposed settlement negotiated by Krist. Watkins claims that the Clients assured Watkins they did not owe any obligation to Krist and that Krist had told them to get another lawyer if they did not like the settlement proposed by Krist. In any event, after the Clients approached Watkins about representing them in their claims against DuPont, Watkins asked Krist if the Clients had any financial obligation to Krist. After communications with Kevin Krist, a lawyer employed by the Krist firm, Watkins received the letter dated November 22, 1999, which forms the entire basis for the contract claim in this case. The body of this letter reads in its entirety:

> Thank you for your correspondence of October 12, 1999 relative to Kinley Sorrells and the Sides. [sic] We certainly don't have any problem with you assuming representation of these parties since they have discharged us. Nevertheless, they did discharge us in the context of us having reached a settlement agreement with DuPont to which they initially consented. Our suggestion is as follows: if the cases are resolved by your firm in such a fashion as to allow for a recovery on their behalf when none would have existed under the terms of our proposed agreement, then we will forfeit all of our fees and expenses. On the other hand, if circumstances are such that our proposed settlement agreement would have resulted in the same or greater recovery than you eventually achieve, then we would insist upon a full fee and reimbursement of expenses.
>
> Please let me have your thoughts on this as soon as possible as the judge is pressing for substitution of new counsel in order to keep the matter from stagnating on his docket.

Kevin Krist testified that Phil Watkins expressed agreement to these terms during a telephone conversation. Furthermore, Phil Watkins later wrote to the Krist firm, "I will not forget the agreement in your letter of November 22, 1999." Watkins substituted in the DuPont Suit as new counsel for the Clients and arranged for these claims to be litigated in the counties where the respective orchards are located. Watkins eventually obtained settlements for the Clients in an amount greater than the Clients would have obtained under the settlement proposed by Krist. When

Watkins refused to pay Krist its fees and expenses, Krist sued Watkins and the Clients.

Krist alleged a variety of claims against Watkins and the Clients, and all defendants filed motions to transfer venue. Watkins did not set its venue motion for hearing or obtain a ruling on it. Meanwhile, Krist moved for partial summary judgment alleging that the one-page letter agreement was unambiguous and that, under its terms, Krist was entitled to recover from Watkins $544,411 plus attorneys' fees. The trial court granted summary judgment as to liability and damages on Krist's contract claim but denied the motion as to attorneys' fees. After Krist nonsuited its other claims against Watkins and all its claims against the Clients, and after Krist asked for a final judgment that awarded no attorneys' fees, the trial court signed a final judgment awarding Krist $544,411 plus postjudgment interest.

II. Issues and Analysis

A. Did the Trial Court Err by Not Ruling on the Motions to Transfer Venue Before Granting Summary Judgment? [Omitted]

B. Was There Consideration for the Contract?

In the sixth issue, Watkins asserts the trial court erred in granting summary judgment because there was no consideration for the contract. Watkins argues there was no detriment to Krist in entering into the agreement, and thus no consideration to support it. We disagree. Watkins states that the Clients told him they had no obligation to Krist and that he called Krist to confirm this representation. The contract resulted from the ensuing communications between Krist and Watkins. Although Watkins and the Clients contend the Clients owed Krist nothing after they discharged that firm, the language of the agreement itself shows that Krist was still asserting its rights to recover attorneys' fees and expenses out of any settlement the Clients obtained from resolution of the DuPont Suit. By compromising and limiting its rights to seek attorneys' fees, for example, its right to claim a full 40% fee interest in any settlement reached by Watkins on the Clients' behalf, Krist suffered a detriment, and so the contract was supported by sufficient consideration. See Northern Nat. Gas Co. v. Conoco, Inc., 986 S.W.2d 603, 607, 42 Tex. Sup. Ct. J. 75 (Tex. 1998); Leonard v. Texaco, Inc., 422 S.W.2d 160, 165, 10 Tex. Sup. Ct. J. 462 (Tex. 1967). Accordingly, we overrule the sixth issue.

C. Is the Contract Ambiguous?

Under its fourth issue, Watkins argues that the contract unambiguously requires Krist to forfeit all of its claims to fees and reimbursement of expenses if, as turned out to be the case, Watkins obtained a better settlement for the Clients than the settlement allegedly proposed by Krist. Watkins also urges that, if we disagree with this contention, we should find the contract to be ambiguous. Krist responds by arguing that the contract unambiguously requires Krist to forfeit only its claims to fees in any recovery that the Clients realize in excess of the settlement allegedly proposed by Krist. Krist also asserts that Watkins has waived its right to assert ambiguity on appeal by agreeing in the trial court that the contract is unambiguous.

As a preliminary matter, any agreement in the trial court by Watkins and Krist that the contract is unambiguous does not prevent this court from concluding that the contract is ambiguous. See City of Bunker Hill Village v. Memorial Villages Water Auth., 809 S.W.2d 309, 310-11 (Tex. App. — Houston [14th Dist.] 1991, no writ) (reversing summary judgment because the contracts in question were ambiguous and holding that agreement of parties that a contract is unambiguous does not prevent an appellate court from finding ambiguity under the ordinary rules of contract construction). Therefore, in evaluating the fourth issue, we must first determine if the contract is ambiguous.

If a written instrument is so worded that it can be given a certain or definite legal meaning or interpretation, then it is not ambiguous and it can be construed as a matter of law. Lenape Resources Corp. v. Tennessee Gas Pipeline Co., 925 S.W.2d 565, 574, 39 Tex. Sup. Ct. J. 496 (Tex. 1996). If its meaning is uncertain and doubtful or it is reasonably susceptible to more than one meaning, taking into consideration circumstances present when the particular writing was executed, then it is ambiguous and its meaning must be resolved by a finder of fact. See id. In construing a written contract, our primary concern is to ascertain the true intentions of the parties as expressed in the written instrument. See id. This court need not embrace strained rules of construction that would avoid ambiguity at all costs. See id. If the contract is ambiguous, then the trial court erred in granting summary judgment because the interpretation of an ambiguous contract is a question for the finder of fact. See Coker v. Coker, 650 S.W.2d 391, 394-95, 26 Tex. Sup. Ct. J. 368 (Tex. 1983).

The contract, addressing the issue of Krist's rights against any future settlement by the Clients, states:

> If the cases are resolved by [Watkins] in such a fashion as to allow for a recovery on [the Clients'] behalf when none would have existed under the terms of [Krist's] proposed agreement, then [Krist] will forfeit all of [its] fees and expenses. On the other hand, if circumstances are such that [Krist's] proposed settlement agreement would have resulted in the same or greater recovery than [Watkins] eventually achieves, then [Krist] would insist upon a full fee and reimbursement of expenses.

It is undisputed that the settlement Watkins achieved for the Clients resulted in a recovery for the Clients that was greater than the recovery the Clients would have realized under Krist's proposed settlement agreement. Therefore, the second sentence above cannot apply. Under the circumstances present when the contract was made, the meaning of the first sentence is uncertain and doubtful. The trial court apparently accepted Krist's argument that the contract unambiguously forfeits Krist's fees only to the extent that Watkins's settlement for the Clients exceeds Krist's proposed settlement. This construction is problematic because it conflicts with the ordinary meaning of "[Krist] will forfeit all of [its] fees and expenses." On the other hand, it does not seem likely that Krist would agree to forfeit a claim of more than half a million dollars because Watkins achieved a better settlement than the Clients would have received under Krist's proposed settlement. Though there is a dispute as to whether the Clients discharged Krist with just cause, even if it were determined that they did, Krist still would have a claim against the Clients based on *quantum meruit*. See Rocha v. Ahmad, 676 S.W.2d 149, 156 (Tex. App. — San Antonio 1984, *writ dism'd*). It would be unusual for Krist to have agreed to waive its entire claim simply because Watkins achieved a better settlement. Though we may not rewrite the contract to insert provisions the parties could have included, we must construe the contract from a utilitarian standpoint, bearing in mind the particular business activity sought to be served. See Lenape Resources Corp., 925 S.W.2d at 574; Tenneco, Inc. v. Enter. Prods. Co., 952 S.W.2d 640, 646, 39 Tex. Sup. Ct. J. 907 (Tex. 1996).

If the first sentence required Krist, under certain circumstances, to completely waive its claim to more than $500,000 in fees and cost reimbursement, then it would be important to know under what circumstances this drastic result would occur. However, the language of the first sentence is opaque in this regard, stating that it is triggered "if the cases are resolved by [Watkins] in such a fashion as to allow for a recovery on [the Clients'] behalf when none would have existed under the terms of [Krist's] proposed agreement." It is undisputed that the "terms of [Krist's] proposed agreement" included an unconditional recovery of $200 per affected acre owned by the settling party. Therefore, there could have been no circumstances under which "[no recovery] would have existed under the terms of [Krist's] proposed agreement."

Watkins asserts that the first sentence is triggered if Watkins obtains a settlement for more money than the Clients would have received under Krist's proposed settlement. Krist asserts that it waived its right only as to any recovery in excess of what the Clients would have recovered under Krist's proposed settlement. We presume that the parties did not intend an impossible condition. See Page v. Superior Stone Prods., Inc., 412 S.W.2d 660, 663 (Tex. Civ. App. — Austin 1967, *writ ref 'd n.r.e.*). If we construe the condition in the first sentence to mean "to the extent the Clients recover more than they would have under Krist's proposed settlement," then this language, combined with the phrase "*full* fee and reimbursement of expenses" in the second sentence (emphasis added) might favor Krist's construction. On the other hand, if we construe the condition to mean "if the Clients recover more when represented by Watkins than they would have under Krist's proposed settlement," then Watkins's construction might be favored. Given the uncertain and doubtful meaning of the contract, we hold that it is ambiguous. See *Lenape Resources Corp.*, 925 S.W.2d at 574 (holding contract provision to be ambiguous); *Coker*, 650 S.W.2d at 393-94 (holding that contract language was unclear and ambiguous); A.W. Wright & Associates, P.C. v. Glover, Anderson, Chandler & Uzick,

L.L.P., 993 S.W.2d 466, 470 (Tex. App.—Houston [14th Dist.] 1999, *pet. denied*) (holding that language in referral contracts between attorneys was uncertain and doubtful and therefore ambiguous); Gibson v. Bentley, 605 S.W.2d 337, 338-39 (Tex. Civ. App.—Houston [14th Dist.] 1980, *writ ref'd n.r.e.*) (holding that condition triggering provision for sharing amounts to be recovered in lawsuit was susceptible of two irreconcilable interpretations and was ambiguous). Accordingly, we sustain the fourth issue to this extent, overrule the remainder of the fourth issue, reverse the trial court's judgment, and remand this case to the trial court so that the trier of fact may determine the true intent of the parties. See *Coker*, 650 S.W.2d at 394-95.

III.   Conclusion

Watkins waived its motion to transfer venue by failing to set it for hearing before the trial court's ruling on Krist's motion for summary judgment. The contract, though supported by sufficient consideration, is ambiguous. Therefore, we reverse the trial court's judgment and remand this case to the trial court so that the trier of fact may determine the true intent of the parties.

Questions

1.   What is the ambiguity in the contract that the court discusses?
2.   According to the court, what is the primary concern of the courts in interpreting contracts?
3.   How was the alleged contract accepted?

Suggested Case References

1.   In a newspaper advertisement, a department store advertised mink coats for sale for $150. The ad is a misprint; the store meant to say $1500. A customer came into the store and agreed to buy the coat for $150. Is there a valid offer and acceptance? Read the Georgia court's opinion in Georgian Co. v. Bloom, 27 Ga. App. 468 (1921).

2.   A judicial interpretation of the concept of good faith in making a valid offer is discussed by the court in Phoenix Mut. Life Ins. Co. v. Shady Grove Plaza, Ltd., 734 F. Supp. 1181 (D. Md. 1990).

3.   For an analysis of the terms necessary to create a valid offer read Patton v. Mid-Continent Systems, 841 F.2d 742 (7th Cir. 1988).

4.   In Rogus v. Lords, 804 P.2d 133 (Ariz. App. 1991), the Arizona court discusses how membership in a professional association might be considered as creating a contractual relationship.

5.   To see how a court would construe contract terminology, read Sheridan v. Crown Capital Corp., 251 Ga. App. 314, 550 S.E.2d 296 (2001).

3

Acceptance

Learning Objectives

After studying this chapter you will be able to:

- Define "acceptance"
- Differentiate between an acceptance and a counteroffer
- Discuss the mirror image rule
- Indicate the effect of silence on an offer
- Explain who is capable of accepting an offer
- Discuss the methods of accepting a bilateral offer and a unilateral offer
- Discuss the impact of the mailbox rule on the acceptance of a contract
- Explain the effect of the rejection of an offer
- Define "revocation"
- Discuss the effect of the termination of an offer on the parties' ability to create a valid contract

CHAPTER OVERVIEW

As discussed in the preceding chapter, the offeror creates a power in the offeree to establish a valid contract by giving the appropriate acceptance. The acceptance is the second major component of every valid contract, and the offer and acceptance together are what constitute the mutual assent.

This chapter discusses the actual formation of the contract when the offeree gives the appropriate assent. To be valid under the common law the acceptance must correspond exactly to the terms established by the offeror in the offer; any variance in these terms may prevent the creation of a contract between the parties. For contracts covered by the Uniform Commercial Code different legal rules apply.

The manner of the acceptance is dependent on the nature of the contract contemplated: bilateral or unilateral. For bilateral contracts, the offeree must manifest a promise to perform; for unilateral contracts, the offeree must actually perform the requested act.

However, the offeree cannot wait indefinitely to accept or reject the offer. Each offer must be either accepted or rejected in a reasonable time or before circumstances make fulfillment of the contract unlikely or impossible. Unless the offeror has accepted something of value to keep the offer open, the offeror may terminate the offeree's power of acceptance by revoking the offer.

Acceptance Defined

The law is concerned with relationships between persons, and the threshold question in analyzing every legal problem is to determine the exact legal relationship between the parties. Therefore, if a party is attempting to assert a contractual claim, one must be certain that a contract does in fact exist. By giving an appropriate acceptance, the offeree not only creates the contract, but also establishes the moment at which the parties to the contract have enforceable rights and obligations, provided all other elements of a valid contract exist. This element of the acceptance cannot be stressed too strongly; it determines whether the parties have a contract claim against each other, or whether the injured party must seek remedies under a different legal concept.

What is an **acceptance**? Legally defined, acceptance is the manifestation of assent in the manner requested or authorized by the offeror. In making the offer, the offeror may specify exactly how he or she wishes to receive a response. Acceptance requires the offeree to make some affirmative gesture, either by words or actions, depending on the nature of the prospective contract. For the acceptance to be valid, the acceptance must be both unequivocal and unqualified. In other words, the offeree must respond to the *exact* terms stated by the offeror.

Varying the Terms of the Offer

The typical method used to accept an offer is to restate the exact words of the offer or merely to say "I accept." Any change in the terms of the offer or any conditioning of the acceptance on another event ("I accept, provided that I have enough money by the date of the sale") will be interpreted as a counteroffer (or **cross-offer**). A **counteroffer** is a response by an offeree that so significantly changes the terms of the original offer that the roles of the parties are reversed; the offeree becomes the offeror of the new terms. A counteroffer, in effect, rejects the original offer and terminates the original offeree's power of acceptance. A new power of acceptance is created in the original offeror to agree to the terms of the offeree's counteroffer.

 EXAMPLES:

1. Peter offers to sell Rob his home in downtown Los Angeles for $350,000, and Rob attempts to accept by saying "I agree to buy your home in Los Angeles for $325,000." Rob has not accepted the original offer but has made his own offer for the house at a lower price.

2. In the situation above, if Rob says to the homeowner, "I will think about your offer, but do you think you might be willing to accept less than $350,000," Rob has not made a counteroffer but has merely inquired as to whether the offeror would consider changing the terms while still keeping the original offer open.

3. In the same situation, if Rob had responded by saying "I accept your offer to sell me your house in Los Angeles for $350,000, provided that you have a title sufficient to transfer to me a good title to the property," once again this is not deemed to be a counteroffer because having title sufficient to transfer the property is an implicit condition of the homeowner's ability to make the offer.

What can be gleaned from the foregoing? *First*, to be valid, the acceptance must parrot exactly the terms of the offer. This is known as the **mirror image rule**. *Second*, any variance in the terms of the offer creates a counteroffer, which rejects and therefore terminates the original offer. On the other hand, a mere inquiry, couched in terms of a hypothetical proposal, does not create a counteroffer. *Third*, if the variance is merely a term that is implicit in the original offer, that variance will not constitute a cross-offer.

An exception is made under the Uniform Commercial Code for contracts for the sale of goods between merchants. Because the purpose of the UCC is to promote commerce, the Code permits merchants to vary the terms of the offer in their response without falling into the category of counteroffer. Under the UCC, if the merchant offeror wishes to have the offer accepted exactly as stated, he or she must state that it is an "ironclad offer, take it or leave it." Under these circumstances the common law rules apply. Absent such a restriction on the part of the offeror, the offeree may vary the terms and that variance will form a part of the contract unless its provisions materially change the offer. If the offeror does not wish to have the new terms made part of the contract, he or she must object within ten days. What constitutes a "material" alteration is determined on a case-by-case basis. The terms that appear in the last communication between the merchant traders become the contractual provisions. The situation is sometimes referred to as the battle of the forms. (See infra.) For a complete discussion of the UCC provisions, see Chapter 8.

Although the preceding section involved bilateral contracts (a promise for a promise), the same rules apply to unilateral contracts. If the offeree attempts a performance that varies from the requested act, no contract is formed.

 EXAMPLE:

Jack offers Jill $2 if she will bring him a cup of coffee. Jill brings tea. Jill has not accepted this unilateral offer.

Silence as Acceptance

If making changes in the terms of the offer constitutes a counteroffer (except under the UCC, as noted above), what is the effect of silence on the part of the offeree? The basic rule is that silence is not an acceptance, even if the offeror says that silence will constitute acceptance.

 EXAMPLE:

Jeff writes to Brittany offering to sell his used answering machine for $30. In the letter, Jeff says that if he does not hear from Brittany to the contrary within two weeks, he will send the machine. Jeff cannot assume acceptance by Brittany's silence. As the recipient of an offer, Brittany has the right to speak but not the obligation.

However, silence may constitute an acceptance in two situations:

1. if the offer was solicited by the offeree; or
2. the contract is implied in fact (Chapter 1).

Also note that under the UCC a merchant trader may accept simply by shipping the goods ordered. No actual words of acceptance are required.

 EXAMPLES:

1. Imogene admires Jane's antique ring and says, "Will you offer to sell me that ring for $100?" In this example, the offeree has asked

Jane to make her an offer she couldn't refuse. Response becomes superfluous, and the contract is created. This is an example of a solicited offer.

2. Sal goes into the grocery store to buy a can of peas. He places the can on the counter, and the clerk rings up the sale. No words were spoken by either party, but their actions created an offer and acceptance. The contract is implied in fact.

Who May Accept

While at first glance it may appear that only the person to whom the offer is made, the offeree, may accept the offer, this is not always the case. The offer need not specifically identify an individual as the offeree. It may refer just as easily to a class or group of persons, any of whom is capable of accepting the offer. The most typical example of this type of offer is a catalog sale. The "person" who is capable of accepting is anyone who is cognizant of the catalog, subject to any limitations the offeror might have made (for example, offer available only to the first 100 customers).

EXAMPLE:

Howard sees a J. Crew catalog on the lobby floor of his apartment building. He looks through the catalog and decides to order a shirt. Even though the catalog was addressed to Howard's neighbor, Howard is capable of accepting because J. Crew is making an offer to anyone who sees the catalog, not only to the specified addressee.

There are two exceptions to this rule. The first exception relates to options. An **option** is a situation in which, for consideration, an offeror agrees to hold the offer open exclusively for the option holder, or his transferee, for a specified period of time.

EXAMPLE:

Rashid wants to buy Clio's house and gives her $1000 as a binder for one month. During this time period, Clio is prohibited from selling her house to any other person. However, Rashid, as the option holder, can transfer his right to purchase to someone else. The option only binds the person who has received the tangible consideration.

The second exception to the general rule that only the person to whom the offer is made may accept the offer is the case of the **undisclosed principal**.

To understand the undisclosed principal, first you must understand the **principal-agent** relationship. Briefly, an *agent* is one who acts for and in the place of another, known as the *principal*, in order to enter into contracts with third persons on the principal's behalf. The consequence of these contracts is to bind the principal to the third person. The agent is merely the conduit for the negotiation and completion of the contract. Consequently, when a third person makes an offer to an agent, it is in fact the principal who has the power to accept. Even when an agent does not disclose to the offeror who the principal is, it is still only the principal who has the ability to create the contract.

 EXAMPLE:

A famous actress wants to buy a Van Dyke painting; however, she knows that the price will go up if the current owner finds out that she is the buyer. She has her sister Lee go to the owner as her agent to negotiate the sale. Lee tells the owner she represents someone who doesn't want her identity known. When the owner makes an offer to Lee as the agent, the actress is actually the purchaser. Only the actress has the power to accept the offer.

Method of Acceptance

The appropriate method of acceptance depends on the type of contract contemplated: bilateral or unilateral. As stated in Chapter 1, a **bilateral** contract exchanges a promise for a promise, and a **unilateral** contract exchanges a promise for an act. To accept a bilateral contract, the offeree must make the promise requested. In contrast, the only way that a unilateral contract can be accepted is by performing the act requested.

The preceding idea may seem quite simple, yet it is extremely important because it is the acceptance that creates the contract. All contract rights and obligations flow from and are dependent on the existence of a valid contract. Consequently, the timing of the acceptance is crucial to the determination of the rights of the parties.

Acceptance of a Bilateral Contract

Whenever the offeree gives the promise requested, the bilateral contract comes into existence (assuming all other contractual requirements are met). As long as the offeree outwardly manifests an intent to accept the offer, the contract is formed, regardless of the offeree's subjective intent. Even if the offeree is not serious in her intent, as long as her outward appearance gives no indication to a reasonable person that she does not intend to accept, she will be bound by the contract. If all the circumstances lead the offeror to reasonably believe that the offeree was manifesting contractual intent, then the offeror's expectation that a contract exists is usually given full weight. Of course, the "reasonableness" of the situation is crucial to this determination and can only be ascertained by particular facts in a given circumstance.

Not only may a bilateral offer be accepted by giving the requested promise, it may also be accepted impliedly by *doing* the act promised. Action, as well as words, may be used to create a binding contract. See the above reference to the UCC.

 EXAMPLE:

A customer sends an order for buying goods. The seller may respond either by promising to sell the goods at the offered price or by shipping the goods, thereby implying his promise by fulfilling his obligation. In either instance, it is a bilateral contract that is formed.

To give the appropriate acceptance, the offeree must be conversant with all of the terms of the offer. The offeree's incomplete knowledge of the terms of the offer would preclude his ability to give a valid acceptance. How can one accept what he doesn't know? There would be no mutual assent in this situation.

As indicated above, the timing of this manifestation of assent is imperative in determining whether a contract has come into existence. Obviously, if the offer and acceptance are made verbally by each party to the other, there would be no question whether the contract was formed; the parties were face to face at that moment. However, what if another method of communication is used? How are the parties to know at what precise moment in time the contract was created?

Mailbox Rule

Back in the days before the telephone, telegram, and fax machines, the postal service was the typical method of communication used by persons living some distance from each other. From those times a rule was formulated to help determine the moment of the creation of a contract. The **mailbox rule** states that the acceptance of an offer of a bilateral contract is effective when properly dispatched by an authorized means of communication. The moment the acceptance is dropped in the mailbox, the contract is formed.

The mailbox rule requires that the letter be "properly dispatched" and that the means of communication be "authorized." If the letter is incorrectly addressed or does not contain sufficient postage, it would not be "properly dispatched." Also, if the offeror specifies an answer by letter only, an attempt to answer by telegram would not be an authorized means of communication. In these instances, the acceptance would only be effective when actually received by the offeror, and only if he agreed to the variance.

 EXAMPLE:

On Monday Janet offers to sell Brenda her Ming vase for $10,000, provided that Brenda accepts in writing by Friday. At 11:00 on Friday morning, Brenda mails a letter to Janet accepting her offer. On Saturday, Janet agrees to sell the vase to someone else. Does Brenda have a contract with Janet? Can Brenda force Janet to convey the vase to her? The answer to both questions is yes. Even though Brenda's letter doesn't reach Janet until Monday, because she dispatched the acceptance on Friday according to the terms of the offer a contract was formed.

There is an exception to the mailbox rule for option contracts. Acceptance of an option is only effective on receipt. This exception exists because of the nature of an option — a contract to limit the offeror's ability to sell the item to someone else, even though the offeree has not yet accepted the sale itself. Because of the limiting nature of the option, the offeror must actually receive the acceptance to be bound.

Rejection of a Bilateral Contract

If a person is not interested in accepting a specific offer, the offeree has the ability to reject. Be aware, however, that the offeree's rejection terminates the offeree's ability to accept, thus ending that particular offer.

 EXAMPLE:

Jaime offers to sell his used Contracts book to Mitch for $10. Mitch thinks he can get a better price at the bookstore and turns Jaime down. Later, realizing that Jaime's offer was a bargain, Mitch attempts to accept. He cannot. Once rejected, the offer cannot be revived. Mitch's attempted acceptance to Jaime constitutes a counteroffer.

The general rule with respect to the rejection of bilateral contracts is that rejection is effective only when actually received. The offeror does not actually have to have read the rejection for it to be effective. Only receipt is required.

Rejection and the Mailbox Rule

Historically, the mailbox rule and the rule of rejection under contract law have created certain conflicting situations.

EXAMPLE:

In the example posited above with Brenda, Janet, and the Ming vase, what if Brenda decides that she really didn't need a Ming vase? On Friday morning at 9:00 she writes to Janet rejecting her offer. However, at 10:00 A.M. her neighbor mentions to Brenda that he is in the market for a Ming vase and will pay $15,000 for one. Immediately Brenda writes to Janet accepting the offer, mailing the acceptance at 11:00 A.M. The rejection arrives at Janet's on Monday morning; Monday afternoon she sells the vase. Tuesday morning Brenda's acceptance arrives. Does Brenda have a contract right against Janet?

Under the historical interpretation, Janet would be in breach of contract because the contract was formed on Friday at 11:00 A.M. when Brenda dispatched the acceptance. The rejection is effective only on receipt — Monday — so clearly the acceptance occurred first. Therefore, Janet and Brenda have a contract, which Janet breached by selling the vase on Monday afternoon.

Under modern standards, however, this solution would not be fair to Janet. Consequently, the modern approach to the problem is to determine the reasonable expectations of the offeror. In this situation, it is reasonable that Janet would have assumed that Brenda rejected her offer, and so the rejection would take precedence over the mailbox rule.

What if Janet still had the vase on Tuesday, not having agreed to sell it to anyone else. Would Brenda then have a contract with Janet? Probably, because Janet had not changed her position in reliance on Brenda's rejection.

Acceptance of a Unilateral Contract

Unlike bilateral contracts, where the contract is formed before either side has performed any of the promised acts, a unilateral contract may only be accepted by the offeree by actually performing the act requested. Only when the requested act has been performed is the contract accepted.

EXAMPLES:

1. Hillary promises to pay Lorraine $75 if Lorraine types Hillary's term paper this afternoon. If Lorraine does not do the typing, Hillary has no legal recourse. She requested an act, not a promise, and until the act is performed no contract exists.

   2. Jeanne's mother promises to give Jeanne $1000 if Jeanne quits
       smoking for two years. Until Jeanne completes two smoke-free
       years, no enforceable contract exists.

Usually, the law imposes no duty on the offeree to notify the offeror
that the act has been performed. However, there are three exceptions to this
general rule with respect to notification.

   1. The offeree must notify the offeror if the offeror has requested
       such notification as part of the offer.
   2. The offeree must notify the offeror of the performance if the offeror
       would have no other way of knowing that the act has been
       performed.

EXAMPLE:

Sara, who lives in Illinois, offers Frank $1500 to paint her summer
house in Vermont. If she weren't told that the house had been
painted, she wouldn't know the contracted had been accepted.

   3. The offeree must notify the offeror in a reverse unilateral contract.
       In a **reverse unilateral contract** the performer makes the offer
       rather than the promisor.

EXAMPLE:

Eric says to Jeff, "I will paint your house if you promise to pay me
$1500." The offer proposes that an act be exchanged for a promise,
and the offeree must accept by giving the promise (the giving of the
promise constitutes the "notice"). This is an unusual situation, but it is
interesting to note.

Because unilateral contract offers are only accepted by performance of
the act, they are much easier to analyze than bilateral contract offers. One
must merely pinpoint the moment at which the act was completed to determine the moment the contract is formed.

Termination of the Ability to Accept

The ability of the offeree to accept the offer exists only for as long as the
offer remains open. The law does not anticipate that offerors will keep their

offers open indefinitely. Therefore, either by an act of the parties or by operation of law, every offer will have a finite period during which it is capable of acceptance. After that period, the offer is viewed as terminated, and any attempt on the part of the offeree to accept constitutes a counter-offer. A terminated offer cannot be revived unless *both* parties agree to the revival.

To terminate an offer by an act of the parties, either the offeree must reject the proposal or the offeror must **revoke** the offer. An offeror may revoke an offer anytime prior to acceptance by the offeree. Once the offeree has accepted, a contract is formed, and any attempt by the offeror to revoke could be construed as a breach of his contractual obligations (see Chapter 10).

Revocation of Bilateral Contracts

For bilateral contracts, the offeror may revoke any time prior to the offeree giving her promise, the acceptance. However, there are four situations in which the offeror may not revoke an offer prior to acceptance by the offeree.

First, an offeror may not revoke an offer prior to acceptance in the case of an option contract. As discussed previously, one of the peculiar elements of an option is the obligation of the offeror to keep the offer open for a specified period of time. Because the offeror has received consideration for this promise, he is automatically bound to fulfill it.

Second, an offeror may not revoke an offer prior to acceptance if the offeree has detrimentally relied on the offer, even though he has not yet accepted.

 EXAMPLE:

Lil offers to sell her house to Isobel, and gives her two weeks in which to accept. During this time Isobel receives an offer for her own house, and sells it based on Lil's offer. If Lil were to revoke her offer within this two week period, Isobel would be homeless, and consequently, the court would not permit Lil to revoke.

Third, an offeror may not revoke an offer prior to acceptance in an auction without reserve. An **auction without reserve** is a situation in which the property owner agrees to auction her property and specifically to accept as selling price whatever is the highest bid. Because of the specific promise on the part of the property owner and the expectations of the auction dealer and the bidders, the parties are precluded from revoking. Note that this is not the case if the property is put up at an **auction with reserve**, which gives the parties the right to revoke at any time before the gavel finally comes down.

Fourth, under the UCC a merchant offeror may not revoke a **firm offer** for a period of 90 days, even if such offer is not supported by consideration.

Revocation of Unilateral Contracts

The general rule true for bilateral contracts — that the offeror has the power to revoke an offer any time prior to acceptance by the offeree — is just as true for unilateral contracts. However, the time element is different with a unilateral contract because an act must be completed rather than a promise given. Only when the offeree completes the act is the offer considered accepted and a contract created.

EXAMPLE:

On Monday, Steven offers to pay Cal $2000 if Cal will paint his house on Friday. Steven is to supply all the paints and brushes. On Wednesday, Steven revokes the offer. No contract exists between Cal and Steven because the requested act has not yet been performed, and neither party has suffered any damages. But what if Steven revokes on Friday afternoon, after Cal has already painted half the house? What if Cal were supposed to buy the paints and brushes, which he did on Monday afternoon, and Steven revokes on Wednesday? In these instances, would Cal have a cause of action against Steven?

To resolve the questions in the above example, it would help to know about a case decided many years ago that addressed similar problems: the case of Jimmy the Human Fly.

EXAMPLE:

As an advertising gimmick, a store owner put an ad in the newspaper offering "Jimmy the Human Fly" $10,000 if he would climb to the very top of the Washington Monument on a particular day and time. Jimmy was a performer for the circus who claimed he could climb any surface.

On the day in question, a large crowd gathered, and the store owner handed out circulars about a sale at his store. At the appropriate moment, Jimmy arrived and started up the edifice. Just before he reached the very top of the monument, the store owner screamed, "I revoke!"

Jimmy sued the store owner for the $10,000, and won. The court held that because Jimmy had made a *substantial beginning* on the performance, the offeror no longer had the ability to revoke. Although Jimmy hadn't completely accepted at that point (because he had not reached the very top), it would be unfair to him if the offeror could terminate the offer at that point.

Back to Cal and Steven. Based on the foregoing, it would appear that after Cal had painted half of Steven's house, Steven would no longer be able to revoke his offer. If he revoked after Cal bought the paints and brushes but before he started painting, the purchase of the equipment would probably not be considered a "substantial beginning," and therefore there would not be a contract. Would Cal lose the money he spent on the paint and brushes? Probably not, because he only made these purchases in reliance on the offer. Steven would most probably have to reimburse Cal for the purchases. If Cal could prove that the paints and brushes could only be used for Steven's project, and that he had no other need for the materials, it would be unjust to Cal not to have Steven reimburse the money Cal had expended in reliance of the proposed contact with Steven.

Termination by Operation of Law

An offer may also be terminated by operation of law. **Operation of law** is a legal term for the circumstance in which one event has a legal effect on a second, unconnected event. With respect to the law of contracts, there are four circumstances, or events, that terminate offers by operation of law:

1. *Lapse of time.* If the offeree takes an unreasonable length of time to respond, the offer is considered terminated by operation of law. The courts do not expect offers to be kept open indefinitely, and the offeree's attempt to accept after a long delay constitutes a new offer to the original offeror.
2. *The death or destruction of the subject matter.* For example, it is impossible to sell a horse to stud if the horse has died, and substitution in this instance is not possible.
3. *The death or insanity of the offeror or offeree.* Death would appear to be self-explanatory, and insanity falls under the capacity of the parties to enter into a valid contractual relationship (see Chapter 5).
4. *Supervening illegality.* **Supervening illegality** means that the contract was legal at the time of the offer, but prior to acceptance a statute or court decision makes the subject matter illegal.

 EXAMPLE:

Dot is offered a contract to operate a gambling casino in Atlantic City, New Jersey. Prior to acceptance, the town officials of Atlantic City decide that having gambling on the boardwalk is not a good idea and rescind the ordinance permitting gambling in the city. Dot would no longer be able to accept such an offer because the subject matter of the contract, managing a gambling casino, is now illegal.

Effect of Termination of Offer

Once an offer has been terminated, either by act of the parties or by operation of law, it can no longer be accepted. Any attempt on the part of the offeree to accept after that point constitutes a new offer to the original offeror. The roles of the parties are then reversed, and all of the rules with respect to offers and acceptance apply in reverse. The original offeree is now the offeror and must make her offer according to the dictates of the law with respect to offers. The power of acceptance now rests with the erstwhile offeror, who must follow the guidelines of this chapter. This is an important concept because it relates to the issue of whether, and when, a contractual relationship has been created between the parties.

The entire series of events must now be analyzed. Was the original offer valid? Was it terminated before acceptance? Does the acceptance, after termination, convey sufficient precision so as to constitute a valid offer? How can the new offer be accepted? Always remember that every action and word of the parties in a contractual situation has specific legal meaning and ramifications. Never assume a result until a full analysis has been made.

SAMPLE CLAUSES

Unlike other sections of contractual negotiations, there are no specific clauses that one can point to and say, "That is an acceptance!" As a general rule, the offer and acceptance merge into the basic terms of the contract. The offeror creates the contract terms; the offeree merely agrees to those terms. This agreement can take the form of signing the completed contract, agreeing to the terms orally, or, for a unilateral contract, performing the act. No words other than the ones used by the offeror can be used to accept. Any variance in the offeror's stated terms may constitute an offer to the offeror and thus do not form an acceptance except for contracts between merchants for the sale of goods covered by the UCC.

CHAPTER SUMMARY

Acceptance is the manifestation of assent in the manner requested or authorized by the offeror under the common law. To be effective, the acceptance must be unequivocal and unqualified; any variance in the terms, except those implicit in the offer, may constitute a counteroffer (or cross-offer). This common law rule has been changed significantly for contracts for the sale of goods between merchant traders where changes in the offeree's terms, except for an ironclad offer, act to modify the original offer. Acceptance requires an affirmative act, either in words or deeds. Silence, except in solicited offers or implied-in-fact contracts, is never deemed to be assent. The offer and acceptance together constitute the requisite mutual assent to form a contract.

An offer may be accepted only by the person or group to whom it has been made, and the offeree must know all the material terms of the offer to make a valid acceptance. A bilateral contract is accepted by giving a promise or by implying the promise by performing the promised act. A unilateral contract is accepted by performing an act. At the moment acceptance is validly given, the contract is formed, and the parties are thereby obligated to its terms.

Bilateral contracts are accepted when the acceptance is properly dispatched by an authorized means of communication (the mailbox rule). Rejection of a bilateral contract is only effective when actually received by the offeror. But, in any event, the court will uphold the reasonable expectations of the parties as determined by the particular factual situation.

Unilateral contracts are accepted whenever the offeree performs the act requested. The offeree of a unilateral contract, except in special circumstances, has no duty to communicate with or notify the offeror of his performance of the requested act. The act itself is sufficient acceptance.

An offer may no longer be accepted if it is terminated by the parties. An offeree terminates his ability to accept by rejecting the offer. An offeror terminates the offer by revoking the offer prior to the acceptance. In unilateral contracts, the offeror may not revoke once the offeree has made a substantial beginning on the requested performance.

An offer may also terminate, not by act of the parties, but by operation of law (lapse of time, destruction of the subject matter, death or insanity of the parties, or supervening illegality). Any attempt to accept an offer after it has terminated does not revive the offer but creates a new offer extending from the original offeree to the original offeror.

The key questions with respect to acceptance are:

1. Is the acceptance timely and valid?
2. At what point does the contract come into existence?
3. Has the offer terminated?
4. What are the reasonable expectations of the parties?
5. Is the contract covered by the UCC?

SYNOPSIS

Acceptance
1. Must be unequivocal and unqualified
2. Must be in the exact manner and form indicated by the offeror
3. Any variance in terms of the offer is a counteroffer
4. Silence is not an acceptance

Method of acceptance
1. Bilateral
    a. Give promise
    b. Mailbox rule
2. Unilateral
    a. Do act
    b. Substantial beginning

Termination of offers
1. Rejection
2. Revocation
3. Varying terms
4. Operation of law

Key Terms

Acceptance: manifestation of assent in the manner requested or authorized by the offeror

Auction with reserve: parties have the right to revoke any time before gavel comes down

Auction without reserve: property owner relinquishes the right to revoke

Bilateral contract: a contract that exchanges a promise for a promise

Counteroffer: a variance in the terms of the offer that constitutes a rejection of the original offer and a creation of a new offer

Cross-offer: see Counteroffer

Firm offer: offer made under the UCC that remains open for a reasonable period of time but in no event more than 90 days

Ironclad offer: under the UCC, an offer whose terms may not be altered by the offeree

Mailbox rule: rule stating that the acceptance of a bilateral contract is effective when properly dispatched by an authorized means of communication; formulated to help determine the moment of creation of a contract

Mirror image rule: to be valid, the acceptance must correspond exactly to the terms of the offer

Operation of law: the manner in which one event has a legal effect on a second, unconnected event

Option: a contract to keep an offer open for a specified time that is secured by consideration

Principal-agent: an agent is one who acts for and on behalf of another, the principal, for the purpose of entering into contracts with third persons

Rejection: to refuse an offer

Reverse unilateral contract: a contract in which the performer, rather than the promisor, makes the offer

Revocation: to recall an offer

Supervening illegality: a law that renders a once-legal activity illegal

Undisclosed principal: a person, represented by an agent, who is party to a contract but has not revealed his or her identity to the other party

Unilateral contract: a contract that exchanges a promise for an act

EXERCISES

1. What elements make an attempted acceptance a counteroffer?
2. Give two examples in which the actions of the offeree reject a written offer.
3. Compose an offer that specifically limits the offeree's ability to accept.
4. Using the example of Jimmy the Human Fly, argue the case for the store owner.
5. Discuss the circumstances that would terminate a person's ability to accept a valid offer.

Cases for Analysis

The first case summary that follows, Speedy Ketcherside v. McLane, highlights the concept of how a unilateral contract can be formed. The second, Cook's Pest Control, Inc. v. Rebar, discusses the difference between a counteroffer and an acceptance.

Speedy Ketcherside v. McLane
2003 Mo. App. LEXIS 1732

Facts

Defendant owned and rented property in Poplar Bluff, Missouri, when the tenant, SuperValue (a grocery store), decided to "quit possession." Defendant then bought back the equipment in the store for $25,000. A new tenant was moving in shortly, and Defendant wanted to sell the old grocery store equipment via an auction. Consequently, during early July 2000, Crystal Walker ("Walker"), Defendant's agent, contacted Plaintiff (an auctioneer) to conduct the sale.

Walker told Plaintiff that Defendant wished to sell everything in the store. Walker stated that the auction needed to be conducted "as soon as possible[]" because the new tenants would be moving into the store. Plaintiff claimed that Walker told him to "proceed with the auction and get it going." Plaintiff told Walker that his commission would be ten percent of the total sales made the day of the auction. Walker told Plaintiff, "I want you to handle the auction." The pair also discussed advertising and agreed that a limit would be placed on it before spending any money.

As instructed, Plaintiff proceeded with the preparatory aspects of the auction. In much detail, Plaintiff inventoried the entire store because the list provided by Defendant's employee was outdated. Plaintiff photographed the equipment and made detailed lists so as to advertise the make, model, and features of the equipment. Plaintiff used this information to construct a preliminary proof of the sale bill, which would advertise everything offered at the auction. Plaintiff also promoted the sale at other auctions he was conducting during that interim. Summarily stated, Plaintiff testified he "had everything ready to go," and his "work was done all except the actual auction . . . and delivering the sale bills." He claimed that "the actual auction itself is not the biggest deal."

Sometime thereafter, however, Plaintiff was informed that Defendant "elected to go with another auction company." From early July to July 14, Plaintiff was never told that other auction companies were being considered for the sale. It was on July 14 that Plaintiff was first told to submit a proposal in writing (contract or bid). A few days later, Plaintiff was informed that another auctioneer received the job.

Plaintiff then filed his breach of contract lawsuit. The trial court entered detailed findings of fact and conclusions of law, ultimately entering judgment in favor of Plaintiff. The court found, *inter alia*, that "the contract entered into by the parties was by its nature, a unilateral contract and when Plaintiff began performing pursuant to the directions of . . . Walker, the unilateral contract became enforceable." The court awarded Plaintiff $5,516.75 (ten percent commission of total sales at the auction). This appeal followed.

Discussion and Decision

In Defendant's first point, she alleges the trial court committed reversible error in holding that Defendant breached a contract with Plaintiff "because a contract was never formed, due to the lack of mutual assent, in that the parties never agreed to essential terms, never moved past the negotiation stage and there was never a meeting of the minds." In the argument section of Point I, Defendant claims the parties never agreed to the following terms: (1) the commission Plaintiff would receive, (2) the date of the auction, (3) which equipment would be sold, and (4) the method of advertising to be used. As such, Defendant argues that the conversations between Plaintiff and Walker were mere negotiations.

In her second point on appeal, Defendant alleges the court erred in finding a breach of contract occurred because "a contract was never formed, due to the absence of acceptance by performance in that . . . [the] offer was rescinded before [Plaintiff] began to perform." In this argument, Defendant claims that a unilateral contract was contemplated, but Plaintiff failed to substantially perform before Defendant rescinded, i.e., he did not timely accept the offer. Because both points are interrelated, we discuss them in conjunction.

"The essential elements of a contract are: (1) competency of the parties to contract; (2) subject matter; (3) legal consideration; (4) mutuality of agreement; and (5) mutuality of obligation." Baris v. Layton, 43 S.W.3d 390, 396 (Mo. App. 2001). The term "mutuality of agreement" implies a mutuality of assent or a meeting of the minds to the essential terms of a contract. Smith v. Hammons, 63 S.W.3d 320, 325 (Mo. App. 2002); Baris, 43 S.W.3d at 397. Negotiations or preliminary steps towards the formation of a contract do not satisfy this element. Hammons, 63 S.W.3d at 325.

"A unilateral contract is a contract in which performance is based on the wish, will, or pleasure of one of the parties." Cook v. Coldwell Banker, 967 S.W.2d 654, 657 (Mo. App. 1998). The promisor receives no promise in return as consideration for the original promise. Id. at 657. The contractual relationship arises when the conduct of the parties supports a reasonable inference of a mutual understanding that one party perform and the other party compensate for such performance. Commercial Lithographing Co. v. Family Media, Inc., 695 S.W.2d 936, 939 (Mo. App. 1985). "An offer to make a unilateral contract is accepted when the requested performance is rendered." Cook, 967 S.W.2d at 657. The offer cannot be revoked where the offeree has made substantial performance. Id. at 657.

In Point I, Defendant claims that Walker and Plaintiff were merely negotiating, and they lacked mutuality of agreement because they had not agreed upon many essential terms (the commission, the date of the auction, the equipment to be sold, and the method of advertising). Apparently, Defendant misconstrues our standard of review because this record provides ample evidence to support the judgment.

Plaintiff informed Walker that his commission was ten percent of the total sales made at the auction, and she told him to "get it going" and "I want you to handle the auction." The auction was to be conducted as soon as possible, but before the new tenants were to take possession of the premises. Walker also stated that everything in the store was to be sold. The two further discussed advertising and agreed a limit would be set before spending any amounts on it.

It was reasonable for the court to conclude a contract was formed. Walker told Plaintiff to conduct all steps necessary to get the auction started and that everything was to be sold. Plaintiff told Walker that his commission was ten percent. This disposes of Defendant's contention that the contract lacked two essential terms (price and equipment). Mutuality of agreement is determined by looking to the intentions of the parties as expressed or manifested in their words or acts. Hammons, 63 S.W.3d at 325.

As to the date of the auction, although no set date was *at that time* agreed upon, Plaintiff explained that he generally set the date when he obtained the seller's approval of a sale bill. Specifically, Plaintiff testified:

> I had everything ready to go. The sale bills was [sic] to be approved by the sellers. I always let them finalize before I go to print. And then at that time, I'd go and we'd set a date at that time of what date the auction would be. . . .
>
> Once we had the sale bill completed, we was [sic] going to pick out a date that was desirable for all parties involved.

Plaintiff also stated that he and his staff "were sitting on go," and that he was prepared to do the advertising, such as television, when he was "shut down." From this, it was reasonable for the trial judge to infer that Plaintiff was ready, willing, and able to conduct the auction before the new tenants moved into the building. This inference is further strengthened by the fact that the auctioneer, who eventually conducted the sale, prepared the auction within the same time frame that Plaintiff faced, and Plaintiff testified that the only advertising difference was that he would have advertised on television rather than the Internet.

Essential terms of a contract must be certain or capable of being rendered certain via application of ordinary canons of construction or by reference to something certain. Burger v. City of Springfield, 323 S.W.2d 777, 783 (Mo. 1959). "That is, terms of agreement must be sufficiently definite to enable the court to give it an exact meaning." Id. at 783. Uncertainty or indefiniteness in contracts, however, are matters of degree. Shofler v. Jordan, 284 S.W.2d 612, 615 (Mo. App. 1955). In determining whether a term is too uncertain to be enforced, a court is guided by general principles of law applied "with common sense and in the light of experience." Id.

Here, the actual day for the auction was not an essential term of the contract. The essential time factor was for the auction to be held before the new tenants took possession of the premises. As stated above, there was sufficient substantial evidence to establish that the Plaintiff was capable of performing within the essential period, i.e., after the preparatory stages were complete and before the tenants moved in. Consequently, this argument lacks merit.

As for the advertising, Plaintiff and Walker agreed on at least one form of advertising, i.e., a sale bill, but it is reasonable to infer that this was not an essential term of the contract. This follows because Defendant admitted that the contract she eventually signed with another auctioneer contained no provisions for advertising.

In sum, by relying upon these four terms of the contract to support the argument that the contract lacked mutuality of agreement, Defendant has failed to demonstrate any error in the trial court's finding that a contract was formed. Point I is denied.

Turning to the second point, Defendant claims that Plaintiff failed to accept the offer because he did not substantially perform. We dispatch with this argument by noting that Plaintiff testified he "had everything ready to go," and his "work was done all except the actual auction . . . and delivering the sale bills." Moreover, he testified: "The actual auction itself is not the biggest deal. You have more hours spent prior to." He also testified as to the details of his preparatory work. The trial court was free to believe this evidence. *Sanders*, 42 S.W.3d at 8. There was sufficient evidence to support a finding that Plaintiff substantially performed before Defendant attempted to rescind the offer; consequently, Defendant was not entitled to revoke the offer. *Cook*, 967 S.W.2d at 657. Point II is denied.

In this record, we find substantial evidence to support the trial court's judgment that Defendant breached a unilateral contract with Plaintiff. The judgment of the trial court is affirmed.

Questions

1. Which are the essential terms of the contract to which the Plaintiff claims there was no mutual assent?
2. What is the source of the court's definition of a unilateral contract?
3. What evidence substantiated the claim of substantial performance?

Cook's Pest Control, Inc. v. Rebar
852 So. 2d 730 (Ala. 2002)

On August 28, 2000, Cook's Pest Control and the Rebars entered into a one-year renewable "Termite Control Agreement." Under the agreement, Cook's Pest Control was obligated to continue treating and inspecting the Rebars' home for termites during the term of the agreement, which, with certain limited exceptions, continued so long as the Rebars continued to pay the annual renewal fee. The agreement contained a mandatory, binding arbitration provision.

When the initial term of the agreement was about to expire, Cook's Pest Control notified the Rebars and requested that they renew the agreement for another year by paying the renewal fee. On August 16, 2001, Mrs. Rebar submitted a payment to Cook's Pest Control; with the payment she included an insert entitled "Addendum to Customer Agreement" (hereinafter referred to as "the addendum"). That addendum provided, in part:

Addendum to Customer Agreement:

To: Cook's Pest Control, Inc. . . .

Please read this addendum to your Customer Agreement carefully as it explains changes to some of the terms shown in the Agreement. Keep this document with the original customer Agreement. . . .

Arbitration

Cook's [Pest Control] agrees that any prior amendment to the Customer Agreement shall be subject to written consent before arbitration is required. In the event that a dispute arises between Cook's [Pest Control] and

Customer, Cook's [Pest Control] agrees to propose arbitration if so desired, estimate the cost thereof, and describe the process (venue, selection of arbitrator, etc.). Notwithstanding prior amendments, nothing herein shall limit Customer's right to seek court enforcement (including injunctive or class relief in appropriate cases) nor shall anything herein abrogate Customer's right to trial by jury. Arbitration shall not be required for any prior or future dealings between Cook's [Pest Control] and Customer.

Future Amendments

Cook's [Pest Control] agrees that any future amendments to the Customer Agreement shall be in writing and signed by Customer and [an] authorized representative of Cook's [Pest Control].

Effective Date

These changes shall be effective upon negotiation of this payment or the next service provided pursuant to the Customer Agreement, whichever occurs first. . . .

Acceptance be [sic] Continued Use

Continued honoring of this account by you acknowledges agreement to these terms. If you do not agree with all of the terms of this contract, as amended, you must immediately notify me of that fact.

The addendum proposed new terms for the agreement and notified Cook's Pest Control that continued service or negotiation of the renewal payment check by Cook's Pest Control would constitute acceptance of those new terms. After it received the addendum, Cook's Pest Control negotiated the Rebars' check and continued to perform termite inspections and services at the Rebars' home.

On August 30, 2001, the Rebars filed this action against Cook's Pest Control. The Rebars alleged fraud, negligence, breach of contract, breach of warranty, breach of duty, unjust enrichment, breach of the duty to warn, negligent training, supervision and retention of employees, and bad-faith failure to pay and bad-faith failure to investigate a claim. Those claims were based upon Cook's Pest Control's alleged failure to treat and control a termite infestation in the Rebars' home and to repair the damage to the home caused by the termites.

Cook's Pest Control moved to compel arbitration of the Rebars' claims. In support of its motion, Cook's Pest Control relied upon the arbitration provision contained in the agreement; Cook's Pest Control also submitted the affidavit testimony of the president of the company, who testified regarding the effect of Cook's Pest Control's business on interstate commerce.

The Rebars opposed the motion to compel arbitration, asserting, among other things, that a binding, mandatory arbitration agreement no longer existed. The Rebars asserted that a binding, mandatory arbitration agreement no longer existed because the agreement between the parties had been modified when it was renewed in August 2001. The Rebars presented to the trial court a copy of the addendum and a copy of the canceled check they had written to Cook's Pest Control in payment of their renewal fee, which Cook's Pest Control had accepted and negotiated. The Rebars also submitted the affidavit of Mrs. Rebar, who testified that after Cook's Pest Control had received the addendum and had negotiated the check for the renewal fee, Cook's Pest Control inspected the Rebars' home.

On December 18, 2001, the trial court denied Cook's Pest Control's motion to compel arbitration. In its order, the trial court stated:

> The Motion to Compel Arbitration, filed by [Cook's Pest Control] on October 10, 2001, came before the Court on December 7, 2001 for hearing and was taken under advisement.
>
> The Motion is submitted upon the Motion, together with the "Subterranean Termite Control Agreement Sentricon Colony Elimination System" dated 8/28/00, which was in effect for one year. [The Rebars] have filed, on November 14, 2001, Plaintiff's Opposition to Cook's [Pest Control's] Motion to Compel Arbitration with documents attached thereto, which includes Exhibits 1, 2, A, B, C, D, E, and 3.
>
> The contract that was entered into on August 28, 2000, which is Exhibit B to Plaintiff's Opposition to Cook's [Pest Control's] Motion to Compel Arbitration, was for a period of one year and contained an arbitration clause. Thereafter, the same expired and the [Rebars] paid for a termite bond and at the same time made an addendum to the termite agreement, which is Exhibit C to Plaintiff's Opposition to Cook's [Pest Control's] Motion to Compel Arbitration. In said Exhibit C, under "Arbitration," the language reads as follows:
>
> > Cook's [Pest Control] agrees that any prior amendment to the Customer Agreement shall be subject to written consent before arbitration is required. In the event that a dispute arises between Cook's [Pest Control] and Customer, Cook's [Pest Control] agrees to propose arbitration is [sic] so desired, estimate the cost thereof, and describe the process (venue, selection of arbitrator, etc.). Notwithstanding prior amendments, nothing herein shall limit Customer's right to seek court enforcement (including injunctive or class relief in appropriate cases) nor shall anything herein abrogate Customer's right to trial by jury. Arbitration shall not be required for any prior or future dealings between Cook's [Pest Control] and Customer.
>
> The defendant Cook's Pest Control, Inc. accepted said premium with said addendum by the plaintiffs. However, at this hearing, Cook's [Pest Control] does not wish to be bound by the provisions of the addendum made by the [Rebars].
>
> Cook's [Pest Control] could have canceled the termite agreement, but no cancellation was made. The addendum provides in effect that arbitration is not enforceable and is not required unless [the Rebars] agree thereto, and nothing shall limit the right of [the Rebars] to seek court enforcement nor shall anything herein abrogate the [Rebars'] right to trial by jury. (The provision actually reads "customer"; and in this case, [the Rebars] are customers.)
>
> The agreement having expired, and the defendants Cook's Pest Control, Inc. having accepted the premium, changing the terms of the prior agreement, which had expired, the said defendant Cook's Pest Control, Inc. became bound by the provisions provided in the addendum, which is

[the Rebars'] Exhibit C to Plaintiff's Opposition to Cook's [Pest Control] Motion to Compel Arbitration.

Therefore, the Motion to Compel Arbitration, filed by the defendants is OVERRULED AND DENIED.

Cook's Pest Control filed a "motion to reconsider"; that motion was denied by operation of law.

Cook's Pest Control appeals, asserting the following arguments:

I. The trial court erred by incorrectly assuming that Cook's [Pest Control] could have cancelled its ongoing obligations of the termite agreement with [the Rebars] and in interpreting Cook's [Pest Control] continued inspection and retreatment of the [Rebars'] home as acceptance of the [Rebars'] attempted unilateral modification of the contract.

II. The trial court erred because, as a matter of law, Cook's [Pest Control] is entitled to arbitration.

A. The trial court erred in failing to recognize that there was no previous agreement between the parties which contemplated future amendments to the contract.

B. The trial court erred in failing to take into account that an at-will, unilateral business relationship cannot be fundamentally altered by the customer, as the promisor.

Analysis

Cook's Pest Control argues that the trial court incorrectly found that it accepted the terms included in the addendum by continuing to inspect and treat the Rebars' home after it received the addendum and negotiated the Rebars' check for the renewal fee. Cook's Pest Control argues that, under the terms of the agreement, it was already obligated to continue inspecting and treating the Rebars' home. Cook's Pest Control also argues that the addendum was an improper attempt to unilaterally modify an existing contract. We reject those arguments.

First, we reject Cook's Pest Control's argument that the Rebars were attempting unilaterally to modify an existing contract. We note that the parties' original agreement was due to expire on August 28, 2001; Cook's Pest Control had already sent the Rebars a notice of this expiration and had requested that the Rebars renew the agreement by submitting the annual renewal fee.

Upon receiving notice that the agreement was up for renewal, the Rebars responded to Cook's Pest Control's offer to renew that contract with an offer of their own to renew the contract but on substantially different terms. This response gave rise to a counteroffer or a conditional acceptance by the Rebars:

If the purported acceptance attempts to restate the terms of the offer, such restatement must be accurate in every material respect. It is not a variation if the offeree merely puts into words that which was already reasonably implied in the terms of the offer. But the very form of words used by the offeror is material if the offeror so intended and so indicated in the offer. An acceptance using a different form makes no contract. A variation in the substance of the offered terms is material, even though the variation is slight. . . .

In the process of negotiation concerning a specific subject matter, there may be offers and counter-offers. One party proposes an agreement on stated terms; the other replies proposing an agreement on terms that are different. Such a counter-proposal is not identical with a rejection of the first offer, although it may have a similar legal operation in part. In order to deserve the name "counter-offer," it must be so expressed as to be legally operative as an offer to the party making the prior proposal. It is not a counter-offer unless it is itself an offer, fully complying with all the requirements that have been previously discussed. This does not mean that all of its terms must be fully expressed in a single communication. Often they can be determined only by reference to many previous communications between the two parties. In this, a counter-offer differs in no respect from original offers. But there is no counter-offer, and no power of acceptance in the other party, unless there is a definite expression of willingness to contract on definitely ascertainable terms.

If the party who made the prior offer properly expresses assent to the terms of the counter-offer, a contract is thereby made on those terms. The fact that the prior offer became inoperative is now immaterial and the terms of that offer are also immaterial except in so far as they are incorporated by reference in the counter-offer itself. Very frequently, they must be adverted to in order to determine what the counter-offer is. Often, the acceptance of a counter-offer is evidenced by the action of the offeree in proceeding with performance rather than by words.

. . . If the original offeror proceeds with performance in consequence of the counter-offer, there can be no successful action for breach of the terms originally proposed.

The terms "counter-offer" and "conditional acceptance" are really no more than different forms of describing the same thing. They are the same in legal operation. Whether the word "offer" is used or not, a communication that expresses an acceptance of a previous offer on certain conditions or with specified variations empowers the original offeror to consummate the contract by an expression of assent to the new conditions and variations. That is exactly what a counter-offer does. Both alike, called by either name, terminate the power of acceptance of the previous offer.

Joseph M. Perillo, Corbin on Contracts §3.32 at 478-80; §3.35 (rev. ed. 1993) (footnotes omitted).

In this case, the Rebars did not accept the terms proposed by Cook's Pest Control for renewal of the agreement but instead proposed terms for the renewal of that contract that were materially different from the terms of the agreement. See, e.g., Hall v. Integon Life Ins. Co., 454 So. 2d 1338 (Ala. 1984) (where a party to whom an offer is made changes the material terms of the offer, the response is deemed a counteroffer); Smith v. Chickamauga Cedar Co., 263 Ala. 245, 82 So. 2d 200 (1955) (to be effective, the terms of the acceptance must be identical to the terms of the offer). The Rebars did not accept the arbitration provision proposed by Cook's Pest Control; they countered with an arbitration provision of their own.

In addition, the Rebars specified in the addendum the method by which Cook's Pest Control could signify its acceptance of those different terms. Had Cook's Pest Control wished to reject those terms, it could have refused to renew the agreement and forgone receipt of the Rebars' renewal check.

In response, Cook's Pest Control argues that it was obligated under the terms of the original agreement to continue servicing and treating the Rebars' home and that its continued service and treatment should not be regarded as acceptance of modifications to that agreement proposed by the addendum. We disagree.

Because the Rebars did not unconditionally accept the renewal contract as proposed by Cook's Pest Control but rather countered with terms that differed materially from those proposed by Cook's Pest Control, Cook's Pest Control had three options upon receipt of the addendum: (1) reject the Rebars' counteroffer and treat the agreement as terminated on August 28, 2001; (2) respond to the Rebars' counteroffer with a counteroffer of its own; or (3) accept the Rebars' counteroffer. Cook's Pest Control did not reject the counteroffer and treat the agreement as terminated; nor did it respond with its own counteroffer; rather, it deposited the Rebars' check and continued to inspect and treat the Rebars' home — the exact method specified by the Rebars for acceptance of the proposed modifications to the agreement. Those actions constituted acceptance of the Rebars' counteroffer.

Cook's Pest Control also argues that the addendum had no effect upon the renewal of the agreement because none of the employees in the office where the Rebars' payment was processed had the authority to enter into a contract on behalf of Cook's Pest Control. Thus, Cook's Pest Control argues, a properly authorized agent never assented to the modifications proposed by the Rebars. Again, we disagree.

"It is well settled that whether parties have entered a contract is determined by reference to the reasonable meaning of the parties' external and objective actions." SGB Constr. Servs., Inc. v. Ray Sumlin Constr. Co., 644 So. 2d 892, 895 (Ala. 1994). See also Deeco, Inc. v. 3-M Co., 435 So. 2d 1260, 1262 (Ala. 1983) ("The existence vel non of a contract is determined by reference to the reasonable meaning of the parties' external and objective manifestations of mutual assent."). "Conduct of one party to a contract from which the other may reasonably draw an inference of assent to an agreement is effective as acceptance." Merrill Lynch, Pierce, Fenner & Smith, Inc. v. Kilgore, 751 So. 2d 8, 11 (Ala. 1999). It is also well settled that an agent with actual or apparent authority may enter into a contract and bind his or her principal. See Lee v. YES of Russellville, Inc., 784 So. 2d 1022 (Ala. 2000). "Furthermore, a principal may vest his agent with apparent authority to perform an act by omission as well as commission, and such authority is implied where the principal passively permits the agent to appear to a third party to have the authority to act on his behalf." Treadwell Ford, Inc. v. Courtesy Auto Brokers, Inc., 426 So. 2d 859, 861 (Ala. Civ. App. 1983).

We note that if Cook's Pest Control wished to limit the authority of its employees to enter into contracts on its behalf, Cook's Pest Control, as the drafter of the original agreement, could have included such limiting language in the agreement. We find nothing in the agreement so limiting the authority of employees of Cook's Pest Control; we find nothing in the agreement requiring that a purported modification to the agreement be directed to any particular office of Cook's Pest Control, and we find nothing in the agreement stating that, to be effective, such a modification must be signed by a corporate officer or by a duly authorized representative of Cook's Pest Control.

Based upon the fact that Cook's Pest Control received the Rebars' proposed modifications to the agreement and that Cook's Pest Control, for some two months thereafter, acted in complete accordance with the Rebars' stated method of accepting those proposed modifications, we conclude that Cook's Pest Control's external and objective actions evidenced assent to the Rebars' proposed modifications. It was reasonable for the Rebars to rely upon those actions as evidence indicating that Cook's Pest Control accepted their proposed changes to the agreement.

We agree with the trial court's conclusion, i.e., that, after receipt of the Rebars' addendum, Cook's Pest Control's continuing inspection and treatment of the Rebars' home and Cook's Pest Control's negotiation of the Rebars' check constituted acceptance of the terms contained in that addendum. Upon acceptance of those new terms, the binding arbitration provision contained in the agreement was no longer in effect. The parties' agreement regarding arbitration had been amended to state:

> Cook's [Pest Control] agrees that any prior amendment to the Customer Agreement shall be subject to written consent before arbitration is required. In the event that a dispute arises between Cook's [Pest Control] and Customer, Cook's [Pest Control] agrees to propose arbitration if so desired, estimate the cost thereof, and describe the process (venue, selection of arbitrator, etc.). Notwithstanding prior amendments, nothing herein shall limit Customer's right to seek court enforcement (including injunctive or class relief in appropriate cases) nor shall anything herein abrogate Customer's right to trial by jury. Arbitration shall not be required for any prior or future dealings between Cook's [Pest Control] and Customer.

Because the Rebars oppose arbitration of their claims against Cook's Pest Control, the trial court properly denied Cook's Pest Control's motion to compel arbitration. Because of our resolution of this issue, we pretermit any discussion of the other issues raised by Cook's Pest Control on appeal.

AFFIRMED.

Questions

1. Which contractual provision was called into question by this lawsuit?

2. What does the court say about the effect of a counteroffer on a prior offer?

3.   What was the court's rationale for determining that the arbitration clause was no longer operative?

Suggested Case References

1.   The case that established the mailbox rule is Adams v. Lindsell, 1 B & Ald. 681 (1818). Read and analyze the case. Do you agree with the court's decision? What factors did the court consider determinative to its final conclusion?

2.   You are staying at a hotel and, while unpacking your clothes, you find a diamond brooch in the closet. Being honest, you inform the front desk and discover that a reward was offered by the guest who lost the brooch to anyone who found it. Are you entitled to the reward? Is this an example of a unilateral contract? Can you accept terms of which you are unaware? Read Vitty v. Eley, 51 A.D. 44, 64 N.Y.S. 397 (1900).

3.   To see how a New York court interpreted silence as acceptance (or not), read Joseph Schultz & Co. v. Camden Fire Ins. Co., 304 N.Y. 143 (1952).

4.   For an additional discussion of the ability to revoke a unilateral contract, read Marchiondo v. Scheck, 78 N.M. 440, 432 P.2d 405 (1967).

5.   University Emergency Medicine Foundation v. Rapier Investments, Ltd. et al., 197 F.3d 18 (1st Cir. 1999), poses an intriguing variation on the mailbox rule.

4 Consideration

Learning Objectives

After studying this chapter you will be able to:

- Define contractual consideration
- Discuss the concept of mutuality of consideration
- Differentiate between a benefit conferred and a detriment incurred
- Exemplify what is not considered to be legally sufficient consideration
- Explain the "preexisting duty rule"
- Discuss the impact of the UCC on traditional concepts of consideration
- Explain what is meant by the "sufficiency of the consideration"
- Define "promissory estoppel"
- Discuss "accord and satisfaction"
- Indicate how one becomes a guarantor

CHAPTER OVERVIEW

Consideration is the third essential element of every valid contract. It is the bargain that supports the entire contractual relationship. Without consideration no contract can exist. An agreement unsupported by consideration may legally bind the parties to each other, but the parties' legal relationship is not a contractual one.

What is "consideration"? Consideration is the subject matter of the agreement over which the parties have negotiated. It is the used textbook the student wants to sell, the paralegal services the attorney wants to employ, the land that the developer wants to buy. For a contract to be valid, both parties to the contract must give *and* receive consideration. If consideration flows only to one person, then it most probably is intended as a gift. The basic premise of a contractual relationship is a bargain, an element lacking if both sides do not receive something of value.

The monetary value of the object of the contract is, for the most part, irrelevant to the law. A 5¢ piece of gum may have as much legal significance as a $5 million piece of real estate, whereas, under certain circumstances, a $1 million diamond necklace may not be considered sufficient to support a contract. (The adequacy of the consideration may involve questions of capacity. See Chapter 5.) The law is looking for proof of the bargain: It must be evidenced that the parties truly wanted and bargained for the object or service in question.

Consideration Defined

Consideration is something that has legal value. It is generally defined as a benefit conferred or a detriment incurred at the behest of the other party. Because consideration is the subject matter of a bargain, there must be **mutuality of consideration** — each side must give and receive something of legal value (the **quid pro quo**).

In bilateral contracts, the mutuality of the consideration is evidenced by the promise each side makes to the other. Mutuality of consideration in unilateral contracts is evidenced by giving the promise and performing the act. The act is consideration, and its performance creates a duty to perform on the part of the promisor.

The monetary value of the consideration is of little importance. Because the law is looking for the bargain, the only requirements are that the consideration have legal value (benefit or detriment) and be valuable to the person requesting it.

Benefit Conferred

The benefit-conferred concept of consideration is the easier of the two to understand. Simply stated, it is the exchange of the exact object or service described in the contract. Usually it is a good or service that one side is selling and the other side is purchasing. The exchange of goods or services is the most typical type of consideration encountered in everyday contracts.

EXAMPLES:

1. Ted offers to sell, and William agrees to buy, a used textbook for $10. The consideration is both the book and the money. Ted gives the book and receives the $10. William gives the $10 and receives the book. There is a mutuality of consideration.

2. Irene offers to exchange her gold earrings for Denise's pearl earrings, and Denise agrees. Each side gives and receives something of value. Each party has conferred "benefit" (earrings) on the other. The consideration is valid.

3. Leroy is employed as a legal assistant by the law firm of Smith & Jones, P.C., for a salary of $300 per week. Leroy is conferring on the firm his paralegal services, and the firm is conferring on Leroy a salary. There is mutuality of consideration.

Detriment Incurred

Conceptualizing consideration as a detriment incurred at the request of the other party is generally more difficult to comprehend. Most people look for objects, services, or money as consideration because these things are tangible and easily identified as having value. But of what value is a detriment?

For a "detriment" to qualify as consideration, the person incurring the detriment must

1. give up a legal right,
2. at the request of the other party,
3. in exchange for something of legal value.

All three elements must coexist for the detriment to qualify as consideration.

EXAMPLES:

1. Maria's mother is worried about Maria's smoking. Mom offers Maria $1000 if Maria quits smoking for a year, and Maria agrees. There is a contract. This is an example of a detriment incurred. Maria is giving up her legal right to smoke at her mother's request in exchange for $1000. On the other hand, if Maria quits smoking for her own health concerns or simply to please her mother, there would be no contract because she would bargain nothing of legal value for her forbearance.

2. Lisa's mother is worried about Lisa smoking marijuana. Mom offers Lisa $1000 if she quits smoking marijuana for a year. Lisa agrees. There is no contract. This is not an example of a detriment incurred because Lisa has no legal right to smoke marijuana. Consequently, Lisa is not giving up a right at the request of the other party in exchange for something of value. Because no legal right exists, it cannot be offered as contractual consideration.

Usually consideration is specifically noted in the contract. The important factors to ascertain are that the consideration mentioned has legal value and that both parties give and receive consideration.

What is Not Consideration

Far more difficult than determining what is consideration is determining what it is *not*. In making this determination, the court uses the following rules and guidelines.

"Past consideration is no consideration." Even if the object or service mentioned by the parties has legal value, it must be shown that it was meant to be exchanged as part of the present contract. Former gifts or consideration given in prior contracts cannot be consideration for a current contract simply because the parties wish it. It must satisfy legal principles as well. In some jurisdictions past consideration may be deemed sufficient consideration if that fact is put in writing by the party to be charged. Each state's law must be analyzed to determine whether this situation is available for a given contract.

 EXAMPLES:

Three years ago John gave Dorothy a mink coat. Two years ago he gave her a trip around the world. Last year he gave her a diamond watch. Now he wants to use these items as consideration for Dorothy's current domestic services as his housekeeper. The law says no. John must offer new, current consideration.

"Moral consideration is no consideration." Simply because someone feels morally obligated to another person it does not follow that the moral obligation is sufficient to form the consideration of a contract. The parties must demonstrate that they bargained with each other, not simply that one felt indebted to the other.

 EXAMPLES:

1. Hassan's parents pay for his school tuition. When he graduates, Hassan says he will repay his parents with interest. There is no

contract. Hassan's parents did not intend to loan the money to Hassan, and the fact that he feels morally obligated to promise to repay them does not mean that they have a contractual relationship. They did not bargain with each other.

2. Leslie cannot afford school tuition and so gets a job to save money, thereby delaying her schooling. Leslie's parents offer to loan Leslie the tuition, with repayment to be made after graduation at 5 percent interest. This is a contract. Even though Leslie may feel morally obligated to repay her parents, more importantly she is legally obligated to them because the tuition was bargained for, and Leslie's parents expect its return with interest.

"A gift can never be legal consideration." Just because the parties use words that, on their face, would appear to represent consideration, no contract will be formed if it can be shown that under the circumstances the true intent of the parties was to confer a gift. The courts will review all the surrounding circumstances to ascertain that the element and intent of a bargain exist.

 EXAMPLE:

Mr. and Mrs. Jones offer to sell their four bedroom house to Mr. and Mrs. Smith for $10,000, and the Smiths agree. Is there a contract? That would depend on the surrounding circumstances. Consider two different scenarios:

1. The Joneses are the parents of Mrs. Smith. The house has a market value of $450,000.
2. The Joneses have to move to another state for job reasons. They have to sell the house as quickly as possible, and their employers have agreed to compensate them for any loss they incur on the sale. The Joneses have never met the Smiths prior to the sale.

In the first example there would be no contract. It would appear that Mrs. Smith's parents intended to make a gift of the house but used words of consideration to make it appear like a contract (probably for tax advantages).

In the second example, although it may appear the Joneses have made a bad deal, a mutual exchange of bargains has occurred. A contract has been created.

"Illusory promises are never consideration." Recall Chapter 2, Offer, in which the concept of the certainty and definiteness of the terms of an offer was discussed. If a party to the contract retains the discretionary right to determine the subject matter of the contract, the offer will fail. This is an

example of an illusory promise. Even if words of consideration are used, the "consideration" is legally inadequate because it cannot be objectively determined what is to be given.

 EXAMPLE:

The law firm of Smith & Jones, P.C. agrees to pay Emmet what they think he's worth in consideration for his employment as a paralegal. The firm's promise is illusory. There is no determinable consideration, and so there is no valid offer or contract.

To prove an illusory promise, it must be shown that one party has subjective control over its terms. If the term can be objectively determined, like an output contract discussed previously, and can be objectively quantified, it is not illusory.

"Promises to do that which one is already bound to do are not consideration." If one is under a preexisting duty to perform, either because of a contractual or other obligation, a promise to fulfill that obligation is insufficient consideration. The other party has received nothing of value. This is known as the **preexisting duty rule.** However under certain circumstances, a preexisting duty may be consideration for a new agreement:

1. if new or different consideration is given
2. the purpose is to ratify a voidable obligation
3. the duty is owed to a third person, not the promisee
4. unforeseen circumstances make the duty more difficult to fulfill

EXAMPLES:

1. Officer Green promises to catch the burglar who robbed Mr. White's house in exchange for Mr. White's promise to give her $300. There is no contract. The police officer is already obligated by virtue of her job to find the thief and has given nothing of additional value to induce Mr. White's promise. She has a preexisting duty to assist Mr. White.

2. Chris owes Fred $200. Chris asks Fred to accept $100 in full payment of the debt. There is no consideration for Fred to take less than he is already owed. However, if Chris asks Fred to accept $100 now and $110 at a later date, the compromised agreement would be valid because Fred received something of value in addition to what he was previously entitled.

3. Phyllis and Lupe have a contract for the sale of Lupe's computer for $300. After the contract is signed, Phyllis tries to change the

contract to include Lupe's computer programs for the same price. The second agreement is invalid. Lupe received no new or additional consideration for giving Phyllis the programs. Every contract must be individually supported by consideration, and any modification to an existing contract must be supported by additional consideration.

Under the UCC merchant traders may modify their prior contractual obligations without new or different consideration provided that the modification is made "in good faith." This rule substantially changed the common law concepts for contracts for the sale of goods between merchants.

Sufficiency of the Consideration

The concept of the **sufficiency of the consideration** concerns itself, once again, with the element of the bargain. The law is only interested in the legal value of the bargain, not its monetary worth. For this reason, not only must the object, service, or detriment itself be analyzed, but it is also necessary to analyze all of the circumstances surrounding the making of the agreement to determine that a bargain, not a gift, was intended. So, although the value of the consideration per se is not important, it remains a factor in determining whether a bargained-for exchange has occurred.

Does it matter that a party to a contract makes a "bad" bargain — that she does not receive consideration monetarily equivalent to what was given? No. The law does not concern itself with insuring the fairness of every contractual relationship. Obviously, persons only enter into a contract because each thinks he is making a good deal. Unless some other factors exist that would make the contract invalid (see Chapter 6), the law applies the doctrines of **caveat emptor** and **caveat venditor** — "Let the buyer beware" and "Let the seller beware." The only factors that the law looks at are the legal value of the consideration, the mutuality of the consideration, and the element of the bargain.

 EXAMPLE:

Horace offers to sell an old trunk for $25. The trunk has been around for years, Horace doesn't like it, and he wants the space it takes up in the attic. Joanne agrees to buy the trunk, which she needs for storage. Later, Joanne finds out the trunk is an antique worth $1000. The contract is valid, and Joanne has made an exceptionally good purchase. Both Horace and Joanne received what they wanted for the contract; Joanne just made a better deal.

Nominal consideration, consideration that has such an obviously small monetary value relative to the consideration for which it is exchanged, is always immediately suspect by the law. Even though the monetary value is never a primary concern of the law, and the courts usually leave the parties to their own devices when it comes to bargaining powers, the law wants to make sure that a bargain does exist. Consequently, the courts will usually inquire into the surrounding circumstances if the bargain, on its face, appears to be overly one-sided. If a bargain can be proved, however, the contract will stand.

 EXAMPLE:

An advertisement in the newspaper offers one mint condition Rolls Royce for $1 to the first person who presents the cash to the seller at a given day and time. Is the $1 legally sufficient consideration for a Rolls Royce?

   The background of the notice is this: A wealthy man dies, and his will names his wife as executrix. All of the deceased's property is left to his wife, except for the proceeds of the sale of his Rolls Royce, which was to go to his mistress. In this instance, the consideration is sufficient. The widow truly wants the least amount of money possible for the car. She may have violated a fiduciary obligation to the mistress, but the person who bought the car has a valid contract.

Sham consideration is consideration that, on its face, appears to have no true value at all. The concept typically applies to gifts. One party intends to make a gift to the other but phrases the exchange in words of contract for some private purpose. For example, a statement such as "In consideration of $1 plus other good and valuable consideration" represents sham consideration. Terms such as "good and valuable consideration," without being specifically defined, are legally insignificant and tend to indicate lack, rather than presence, of consideration. The circumstances surrounding the contract, not just the words used, may also indicate sham consideration.

Conditional promises are not necessarily insufficient simply because they involve an element of doubt. A conditional promise is dependent on the happening, or nonhappening, of some event that would trigger the obligation. (See Chapter 7, Contract Provisions.) Provided that the consideration promised has legal sufficiency, the contract will be valid.

 EXAMPLE:

Shirley agrees to buy Pam's house for $250,000, provided that she can get financing within 30 days. This is a valid contract. Both the house and the money are legally sufficient; simply because Shirley's obligation to pay is conditioned on her getting a mortgage does not mean the consideration is not sufficient, only that the right to receive the money may not come to Pam.

Promissory Estoppel

Promissory estoppel is a doctrine originally established by the courts of equity. Equity courts, as opposed to law courts, were designed to remedy situations in which the "legal" result might be just but was unfair or unduly hard on one of the parties. Equity provides "mercy" to persons when the legal result appears unfair. (See Chapter 11, Remedies.)

The doctrine of promissory estoppel arises in certain situations in which a person reasonably believes that he has entered into a contract, even though no contract exists. Relying on this reasonable belief that there is a contract, the promisee materially changes his position. This circumstance arises when the promise made by the presumptive offeror is illusory — what has been promised cannot be objectively defined or is left to the discretion of the promisor. These are not contractual relationships, even though at first glance it might appear that a contract was intended. If it can be shown that the promisee has materially changed his position in reasonable reliance on the promise, the law will not allow him to suffer. The promisor will be obligated to compensate the promisee. The promisor is barred, or estopped, from avoiding a promise because to do so would be unjust to the promisee.

The concepts of promissory estoppel and gifts are very closely related; however, with promissory estoppel the element of donative intent is lacking. For a gift to exist, it must be shown that a gift was intended. For promissory estoppel to exist, it must be shown that the promisee detrimentally relied on the promise, and that the promisor never intended to give the promisee a gift.

 EXAMPLES:

1. Simone promises to give Loretta $100,000, so that she will not have to work anymore. Based on this promise, Loretta quits her job. Here there is no mutuality of consideration because Simone did not promise the money in exchange for Loretta's promise not to work; she simply promised the money so that Loretta would not have to work.

    But because Loertta quit her job based on Simone's promise, she can sue Simone under the doctrine of promissory estoppel to recover her lost wages. The court will not give her the full $100,000, but will compensate her for her actual loss based on Simone's promise.

   2. Simone promises to pay for Loretta's college education. Based on
        this promise, Loretta enrolls in school. There is no contract. Simone
        didn't exchange her promise for Loretta's promise to go to college,
        but based on her promise Loretta has incurred the expense of
        tuition. The court will permit Loretta to recover her tuition from
        Simone because she acted in reliance on Simone's promise.

   3. Simone promises to convey her farm in Vermont to Loretta so that
        Loretta won't have to live in the city anymore. Based on this promise,
        Loretta sells her house in the city, packs her belongings, and moves
        to Vermont. The court will enforce Simone's promise. Even though
        there was no mutuality of consideration, and thus no contract,
        Loretta has detrimentally relied on Simone's promise by changing
        her entire living condition. It would be unjust to let her suffer.

   In each of the foregoing situations, Loretta has changed her position
based on her reasonable belief that Simone would adhere to her promise.
There is no specific indication that Simone intended a gift, and in no
example did Simone receive anything of legal value, so there is no contract.
However, under the court's equitable jurisdiction, these types of promises
will be enforced to prevent injustice. Be aware, though, that under the
doctrine of promissory estoppel, even though the promise is enforced, it
is only enforced to the extent the promisee relied on the promise. Take note
of the fact that if the promise is not relied on by the promisee to her detriment, the doctrine of promissory estoppel will not apply. It is an equitable
doctrine designed to prevent injustice. If the promisee cannot prove
detrimental reliance on the promise, it would be unfair to the promisor
to force him to fulfill his promise when no injury was sustained.

   To determine whether contract law or promissory estoppel exists, look
for the mutuality of consideration, the intent of the offeror, and the possible
illusory nature of the promise. If mutuality or legally sufficient consideration and contractual intent can be shown, a contract exists. It is not a
situation to which the theory of promissory estoppel applies.

Special Agreements

   There are several other types of agreements that ordinarily would fail
as valid contracts for lack of consideration but that, because of the formality
of the circumstances and the dictates of public policy, stand as enforceable
obligations.

Accord and Satisfaction

   An **accord and satisfaction** is a very particular type of agreement that
results from a disagreement between the parties to an existing contract.

One (or both) of the parties disputes that he has received the consideration promised in the contract; however, rather than litigating to have the court decide the parties' respective rights, they agree to modify their original agreement. Ordinarily there would be no consideration for the parties to rewrite an existing obligation; however, both sides have agreed to forgo their legal right to sue in court. This mutual detriment (forbearance of the right to sue) constitutes sufficient consideration for the new agreement.

EXAMPLE:

Farmer Green has a contract to sell 1,000 bushels of Grade A oranges to Ace Supermarkets for $10 a bushel. On delivery day, Ace claims the oranges are Grade B, and is unwilling to pay more than $8 a bushel. Rather than sue, Green and Ace enter into an accord and satisfaction, and agree to a price of $9 per bushel, making no comment about the grade of the oranges.

In the example above, each side could have sued under the original contract, and, presumably, the accord and satisfaction gives each party less than he was promised under the original contract. But because each has forborne the lawsuit and has saved the expense of litigation, the accord and satisfaction will stand.

The requirements for a valid accord and satisfaction are

1. a valid contract;
2. a dispute between the parties with respect to that contract; and
3. an agreement to compromise the dispute rather than sue.

Accord and satisfactions are typically entitled as such on the top of the agreement.

Charitable Subscription

A **charitable subscription** is a pledge made to a charitable organization. Under most theories of law, it should be identified as a gift. However, as a matter of public policy, the law has mandated that these pledges are enforceable by the charities. Unlike the promisee in promissory estoppel who is limited to his actual loss, the charity will get the full pledge, not just what it lost in reliance on the promise.

EXAMPLE:

Every year the Muscular Dystrophy Foundation has a telethon to raise money. In the heat of the moment, Vivica calls in a pledge of $250.

When the charity moves to collect the money, Vivica says she has changed her mind. The foundation can sue Vivica to redeem her pledge because it is a charitable subscription.

Debtor's Promises

A debtor who has been discharged of his obligation by the legal system is under no further duty to repay his creditors. A person can be legally discharged from his debt by going through bankruptcy or because the statute of limitations on the claim has expired.

If a debtor, under the above circumstances, voluntarily agrees to repay the debt, this gratuitous promise is enforceable against her even though the promise is not supported by consideration. Again, the law has determined that, as a matter of public policy, it is beneficial to encourage people to repay their debts. Therefore, even though the consideration is only moral consideration, the law will hold the debtor to her promise.

If the debt has been deemed unenforceable due to bankruptcy, the Bankruptcy Act imposes certain additional requirements to make the promise enforceable. The act requires the debtor to reaffirm the promise prior to final discharge by the court and to receive the court's consent. On the other hand, if the debt is barred only by the statute of limitations, the promise itself is generally considered sufficient to make the contract enforceable.

 EXAMPLE:

Floyd has been judicially declared bankrupt, and his creditors are being paid 50¢ on the dollar. Feeling very guilty about his creditors' losses, Floyd promises Jennifer, one of his creditors, that he will pay her back all that he owes her within six months. He gets the court's approval. Jennifer now has a legally enforceable claim against Floyd for the amount.

Guarantees

A **guarantee** is a written promise to answer for the debts of another that is enforceable against the **guarantor**. The guarantee is given at the same time the debtor receives the subject consideration.

Under general contract law principles, it would appear that the guarantor is not legally bound because she has not received any benefit from the promise. However, this is an example of a statutorily created *formal contract* designed to promote business and industry.

For the guarantee to be valid, the following requirements must be met:

1. a valid contract is entered into between two or more parties;
2. the guarantor creates the guarantee at the time the contract is executed; and
3. the guarantee is in writing.

EXAMPLE:

Joanne wants to buy a house, but her credit record is poor. The bank agrees to give her a mortgage if her parents guarantee the loan. When Joanne takes out the loan, her parents sign the mortgage contract as Joanne's guarantors. This is a valid guarantee.

Note that in the example given above, Joanne's parents are merely agreeing to answer for Joanne's payments *if* Joanne does not pay. This is to be contrasted with **co-signers.** Co-signers are persons who agree to be *equally* bound with the obligor, and the creditor can go after a co-signer *instead* of the actual obligor because each is equally liable. With co-signers, a joint and several liability is incurred: The mortgage can sue either Joanne, or her parents, or all three of them together.

For the guarantee to be valid, the obligor must receive consideration at the time the guarantee is given.

EXAMPLE:

In the circumstances given above, assume Joanne has an excellent credit history, and the bank loans her the money on her own signature. Two years later, Joanne loses her job, and the bank, worried about the mortgage payments, asks Joanne to have her parents come in to guarantee the loan. Joanne's parents agree to sign the mortgage. However, because Joanne already received the consideration and became obligated prior to the guarantee, the guarantee is not enforceable against her parents.

For the above guarantee to be enforceable against Joanne's parents, the bank must give Joanne some additional consideration at the time the guarantee is given, such as extending the time for payments, reducing the interest rate, or giving her additional money to increase the overall mortgage. Unless the guarantee is given at the time the obligation is incurred, the guarantee will not be enforceable.

Formal Contracts

A **formal** contract is a contract that meets special statutory requirements and as such is valid even though no consideration is mentioned. The statutory formality of these agreements gives them special status under the law and creates a special situation with respect to consideration. (See Chapter 1.) Each state's statutes indicate what is to be deemed a formal contract.

SAMPLE CLAUSES

| 1 | **Accord and Satisfaction**

In Accord and Satisfaction of all claims arising out of the contract between Farmer Green and Ace Supermarkets dated _____, 20 _____ (Copy affixed hereto), the parties agree that the price for the oranges shall be $9 per bushel, payable in 30 days from this date.

| 2 | **Bill of Sale**

Know all men by these presents that I, _____, of _____, in consideration of One Hundred Dollars ($100.00) to me paid by _____ of _____, have bargained and sold to said _____ the following goods and chattels, to wit:

(Specify goods and chattels)

Witness by hand and seal this _____ day of _____, 20 _____.

(Signatures)

_____

In drafting any contract, always be sure to specify all consideration.

| 3 | **Guarantee**

In consideration of the mortgage entered into this _____ day of _____, 20 ____, between _____ of _____, and _____ bank, we, the undersigned, do hereby guarantee all payments due under said mortgage should said mortgagor be found in default.

(Signatures)

CHAPTER SUMMARY

Consideration is the third major element of every valid contract. It is the subject matter of the contract for which the parties have bargained.

Consideration is generally defined as a benefit conferred or a detriment incurred at the request of the other party. For the contract to be enforceable each party to the contract must give and receive consideration. This is known as mutuality of consideration.

The actual market value of the consideration is not important; it simply must be something legally sufficient to support the contract. The law is not concerned with the market value of the good, service, or forbearance described in the contract; it is only concerned with whether the consideration is actually bargained for and is not intended to mask a gift.

Past consideration, moral consideration, gifts, and illusory promises are never sufficient to support a contractual agreement. However, there are certain situations in which the law has determined that in the interests of public policy, a contract will be found even though consideration is lacking. These situations are accord and satisfaction agreements, charitable subscriptions, debtors' gratuitous promises to pay otherwise unenforceable debts, written guarantees, and statutorily defined formal contracts.

Closely associated with the concept of contractual consideration is the doctrine of promissory estoppel, which the court uses to enforce a promise for reasons other than lack of consideration, even though no contract exists. This occurs when the promises made are unsupported by consideration, but the promisee has materially changed his position in reasonable reliance on those promises. In this instance, the court will permit the promisee to recover what he has lost based on the promise.

For a contract to be enforceable, the consideration must always be definite, certain, and specifically described.

SYNOPSIS

Consideration
1. Benefit conferred
2. Detriment incurred
3. Each side must give and receive bargained-for consideration

What is not consideration
1.   Past consideration
2.   Moral obligations
3.   Gifts
4.   Illusory promises
5.   Legal duties
Sufficiency of consideration
Must be sufficient to support the contract
Promissory estoppel
Illusory promises enforced by the court if detrimentally relied on
Special agreements
1.   Accord and satisfaction
2.   Charitable subscription
3.   Debtor's promises
4.   Guarantees
5.   Formal contracts

Key Terms

Accord and satisfaction: a special agreement in which the parties to a disputed contract agree to new terms in exchange for forbearing to sue under the original contract

Caveat emptor: Latin phrase meaning "Let the buyer beware"

Caveat venditor: Latin phrase meaning "Let the seller beware"

Charitable subscription: pledge or promise to donate money to a charity; given the enforceability of a contract under law

Conditional promise: a promise dependent on the happening or non-happening of a future event

Consideration: a benefit conferred or a detriment incurred; a basic requirement of every valid contract

Co-signer: person who agrees to be equally liable with a promisor under a contract

Formal contract: written contract under seal specifically enforced by statute

Guarantee: an enforceable written promise to answer for the debts of another

Guarantor: person who agrees to be responsible to answer for the debts of another should the debtor default

Mutuality of consideration: the bargain element of a contract that requires each side to give and receive something of legal value

Nominal consideration: consideration of insufficient legal value to support a contract

Preexisting duty rule: promises to do what one is already bound to do is not consideration

Promissory estoppel: doctrine in which promises not supported by consideration are given enforceability if the promisee had detrimentally relied on the promises

Quid pro quo: Latin phrase meaning "this for that"; the mutuality of consideration

Sham consideration: legally insufficient consideration used to mask a gift in words of contract

Sufficiency of the consideration: doctrine that each party to a contract must contribute something of legal value for which he has bargained

EXERCISES

1. Give two examples of consideration as a detriment incurred not discussed in the chapter.
2. Discuss mutuality of consideration with respect to your contract with your school.
3. Under what circumstances would a person argue the doctrine of promissory estoppel?
4. Find out what contracts are considered formal contracts in your jurisdiction.
5. Find and analyze a contract that requires a co-signer.

Cases for Analysis

The concept of consideration is generally one of the most confusing in contract law. To expand the previous discussion, the cases of Stark v. Soteria Imaging Services, Inc., and Nebraska Health Imaging, and Davis v. McCurry are included.

Stark v. Soteria Imaging Services, Inc., and Nebraska Health Imaging
276 F. Supp. 2d 989 (D. Neb. 2003)

II. Factual Background

At the time of the events described in the complaint, the plaintiff, Dr. David Stark, was the chairperson of the Department of Radiology at the University of Nebraska Medical Center (UNMC). As a faculty member and physician at UNMC, Stark was also affiliated with University Medical Associates (UMA). Filing No. 1. In April 1999, Stark also began to engage in professional activities beyond his duties at UNMC. Id. One such activity involved business dealings with defendant Soteria Imaging Services, Inc. (Soteria). For example, Stark contracted with Soteria in March 2000 to operate an imaging facility in Massachusetts. Id.

On December 2, 1998, Stark and Soteria entered into a non-competition agreement (Non-Compete Agreement) in which Soteria agreed not to open an imaging center in or around Omaha, Nebraska, during the term of the agreement, set to expire on December 21, 2000. In exchange, Stark agreed to supply Soteria with the knowledge and expertise needed to operate, market, staff, and run an imaging center in Omaha. Id.

Before the Non-Compete Agreement expired, Stark began acting as an intermediary between UMA and UNMC on one side and Soteria on the other with the goal of establishing a medical imaging facility in Omaha to be known as Nebraska Health Imaging (NHI). Stark alleges that he offered to grant Soteria a limited waiver of the Non-Compete Agreement so that Soteria could negotiate with UMA. Id. Stark also alleges that UMA and Soteria were then to execute a License and Service Agreement (License Agreement), which would provide that Stark would be the managing director of NHI. In exchange for being named managing director, Stark would consult with and assist Soteria and UMA in getting NHI up and running. Id.

Stark and his attorney received preliminary drafts of the License Agreement and actively participated in its drafting. Stark claims that at all times while he was engaged in setting up NHI, the various drafts of the License Agreement all contained a clause obligating UMA to appoint him as NHI's managing director. Id. In February 2000, however, Stark claims that UMA asked Soteria to remove Stark's name from the draft License Agreement, allegedly assuring Soteria that UMA would issue a letter appointing Stark as NHI's managing director. Id.

Stark claims that Soteria and UMA thereafter signed the License Agreement without the clause appointing him managing director. UMA never issued a letter appointing Stark the NHI's managing director, even though Stark functioned in that capacity without pay until he left his employment with UNMC several months after the License Agreement was signed. Id. Stark states that Soteria refused to execute the limited waiver of the Non-Compete Agreement, but agreed to compensate him for his efforts in getting NHI set up, for his services as managing director, and for releasing Soteria from the Non-Compete Agreement. Id. According to the complaint, neither Soteria nor NHI has paid Stark any compensation to date. Id.

Stark alleges that Soteria estimates Stark's interest in NHI to be worth as much as $867,036. Id.

III.   Legal Standard

In reviewing a complaint on a Rule 12(b)(6) motion, the court must consider all of the facts alleged in the complaint as true, and construe the pleadings in a light most favorable to the plaintiff. See, e.g., Brotherhood of Maint. of Way Employees v. BNSF R.R., 270 F.3d 637, 638 (8th Cir. 2001). A dismissal is not lightly granted. "A complaint shall not be dismissed for its failure to state a claim upon which relief can be granted unless it appears beyond a reasonable doubt that plaintiff can prove no set of facts in support of a claim entitling him to relief." Young v. City of St. Charles, 244 F.3d 623, 627 (8th Cir. 2001). When accepting the facts of the complaint as true, a court will not, however, "blindly accept the legal conclusions drawn by the pleader from the facts." A dismissal under Rule 12(b)(6) is therefore granted "only in the unusual case in which a plaintiff includes allegations that show on the face of the complaint that there is some insuperable bar to relief," Schmedding v. Tnemec Co., 187 F.3d 862, 864 (8th Cir. 1999), such as a missing allegation about an element necessary to obtain relief or an affirmative defense or other bar, Doe v. Hartz, 134 F.3d 1339, 1341 (8th Cir. 1998). The court does not determine whether the plaintiff will ultimately prevail, but rather whether the plaintiff is entitled to present evidence in support of the claim.

IV.   Discussion

A.   Count I—Promissory Estoppel (Against Soteria and NHI)

Under Nebraska law, "a promise which the promisor should reasonably expect to induce action or forbearance on the part of the promisee or a third person and which does induce such action or forbearance is binding if injustice can be avoided only by enforcement of the promise." Hawkins Constr. Co. v. Reiman Corp., 245 Neb. 131, 511 N.W.2d 113, 117 (Neb. 1994) (quoting Rosnick v. Dinsmore, 235 Neb. 738, 457 N.W.2d 793, 799 (Neb. 1992)). The party asserting estoppel must have relied in good faith on the conduct or statements of the party to be estopped. Miller v. City of Omaha, 260 Neb. 507, 618 N.W.2d 628, 635 (Neb. 2000).

The complaint alleges that "through words and deeds," Soteria and NHI promised to appoint Stark the managing director, Filing No. 19, and that Stark reasonably relied on that promise, causing him to expend great time and effort in setting up NHI, id., PP 20-21. Soteria and NHI contend, however, that they did and said nothing to induce Stark's reliance. Any promise that Stark would be named the managing director came from UMA—which is not a party to this suit—rather than from Soteria or NHI. See id., PP 12-14.

This factual dispute about who, if anyone, promised Stark he would be the managing director of NHI should not be resolved in a Rule 12(b)(6) motion to dismiss. Accepting the allegations in the complaint as true, I conclude that Stark should be allowed to prove if Soteria's "words and deeds" constituted a promise that Soteria would name him NHI's managing director.

Soteria also argues, however, that even assuming Soteria made a promise to Stark, Stark could not have reasonably relied on it because he knew from his involvement in negotiations between UMA and Soteria that only UMA had the power to name NHI's managing director. Whatever the merits of this argument, the complaint alone does not establish how much or how little Stark knew about the organization's authority to make him the managing director. Stark is entitled to present evidence that he did reasonably rely to his detriment on statements made by Soteria.

If Stark presents sufficient evidence at trial that Soteria promised him the position and that he reasonably relied on that promise, the jury could find for Stark on his claim for promissory estoppel. Accordingly, the motion to dismiss Count I is denied.

B.   Count II — Unjust Enrichment (Against Soteria and NHI)

The doctrine of unjust enrichment is implicated only when the parties do not have an express contract. See Washa v. Miller, 249 Neb. 941, 546 N.W.2d 813, 819 (Neb. 1996) (noting that doctrine cannot "rescue a party from the consequences of a bad bargain."). To recover on a claim for unjust enrichment, a plaintiff must prove that the defendant "received and retained [benefits] under such circumstances that it would be inequitable and unconscionable to permit the party receiving them to avoid payment therefor." Hoffman v. Reinke Mfg. Co., 227 Neb. 66, 416 N.W.2d 216, 219 (Neb. 1987). Whether a defendant has been unjustly enriched is a question of fact. Sorenson v. Dager, 8 Neb. App. 729, 601 N.W.2d 564 (Neb. 1999).

The defendants' contention that the complaint fails to allege what benefits Stark conferred on them is somewhat disingenuous. The complaint clearly alleges that the defendants received the benefit of Stark's connections, knowledge, expertise, and effort in establishing NHI and getting it operating. Although the defendants characterize themselves as mere third party beneficiaries of an agreement between Stark and UMA with regard to NHI, the complaint plainly alleges that Stark provided the defendants with professional and consulting services.

Soteria and NHI further contend that the unjust enrichment claim must fall because the complaint fails to allege that they, as third party beneficiaries, engaged in fraud or misrepresentation.

The mere fact that a third person benefits from a contract between two other persons does not make such third person liable in quasi contract, unjust enrichment, or restitution. Moreover, where a third person benefits from a contract entered into between two other persons, in the absence of some misleading act by the third person, the mere failure of performance by one of the contracing parties does not give rise to a right of restitution against the third person. Haggard Drilling, Inc. v. Greene, 195 Neb. 136, 236 N.W.2d 841, 846 (Neb. 1975) (quoting 66 Am. Jur. 2d, Restitution and Implied Contracts §16 at 960). See also McIntosh v. Borchers, 201 Neb. 35, 266 N.W.2d 200, 203 (Neb. 1978) (finding no cause of action for unjust enrichment where the plaintiffs failed to allege or prove that third party defendants benefited from improvements placed on the plaintiffs' property or that they "committed or participated in any fraud, misrepresentation, or other wrongful conduct"); White v. State Farm Mut. Auto. Ins. Co., 1995 Neb. App. LEXIS 284, 1995 WL 521004 at *5 (Neb. Ct. App. 1995) (requiring plaintiff using unjust enrichment theory to allege and prove fraud, misrepresentation, or other wrongful conduct).

The most significant element of the doctrine of unjust enrichment is whether the enrichment of the defendant is unjust. Although unjust enrichment may arise from fraud or several other predicates, the element of fraud or tortious conduct on the part of a defendant is not necessary in an action for unjust enrichment. Kisicki v. Mid-America Fin. Inv. Corp., 2002 WL 31654490 at *6 (Neb. Ct. App. 2002) (quoting with approval 66 Am. Jur. 2d Restitution and Implied Contracts §12 at 609 (2000)).

The defendants' argument is valid, however, only if Soteria and NHI were in fact no more than third party beneficiaries of a contract between UMA and Stark, rather than parties to a contract or quasi-contract between themselves and Stark. Given Stark's allegations about his dealings with Soteria and NHI, such a legal conclusion would be premature. Moreover, even if Soteria and NHI are merely third party beneficiaries, the complaint can be construed to allege that Soteria's misrepresentations led Stark to believe that he would be named managing director in exchange for his professional efforts in setting up NHI.

I therefore find that Stark is entitled to present evidence on his claim of unjust enrichment. The defendants' motion to dismiss Count II is denied.

C. Count III — Implied Contract (Against Soteria Alone)

An implied contract is an "obligation[]" which arises from mutual agreement and intent to promise, when the agreement and promise have simply not been expressed in words. An implied contract arises where the intention of the parties is not expressed but where the circumstances are such as to show a mutual intent to contract. Turner v. Fehrs Neb. Tractor & Equip. Co., 259 Neb. 313, 609 N.W.2d 652, 659 (Neb. 2000) (citing Kaiser v. Millard Lumber, 255 Neb. 943, 587 N.W.2d 875, 882 (1999)). An implied contract cannot exist without evidence of mutual intent. Id. (citing Bloomfield v. Nebraska St. Bank, 237 Neb. 89, 465 N.W.2d 144 (Neb. 1991)). Whether the parties intended to contract is a question of fact. Kaiser v. Millard Lumber, 587 N.W.2d at 881 (citing 75A Am. Jur. 2d Trial §795 (1991)). Evidence of intent comes from "objective manifestations — the conduct of the parties, language used, or acts done by them, or other pertinent circumstances surrounding the transaction." Id. (citations omitted).

Soteria contends that Stark's implied contract claim must fail because the complaint fails to allege that Soteria intended to contract with Stark. Soteria is mistaken. Stark alleges that not only did he and Soteria intend to enter a contract with regard to Stark's establishment and management of NHI, but also that Stark's other business dealing with Soteria and its efforts to calculate Stark's compensation constitute circumstances that show a mutual intent to contract.

Taking all of the allegations in the complaint as true and construing them in Stark's favor, I therefore find that he is entitled to present the jury with evidence of the implied contract between himself and Soteria. Soteria's motion to dismiss Count III is denied.

D.   Count IV—Breach of Contract (Against Soteria Alone)

The complaint alleges that the Non-Compete Agreement between Stark and Soteria provided that Soteria would refrain from opening imaging centers in or around Omaha until December 2000 in exchange for Stark's agreement to share with Soteria certain confidential and proprietary information about radiology centers. Filing No. 1. Stark alleges that he offered to waive his rights under the Non-Compete Agreement in order to assist Soteria in reaching an agreement with UMA about opening NHI. In return for waiving his rights, Stark alleges that Soteria was to have appointed him the managing director of NHI. Soteria never executed the waiver of the Non-Compete Agreement. Consequently, Stark contends, Soteria breached the Non-Compete Agreement when it executed the License Agreement with UMA that failed to name him the managing director of NHI.

Soteria argues, however, that the claim for breach of contract must fail because Stark affirmatively alleges in the complaint that he waived his right to enforce the Non-Compete Agreement by permitting Soteria to work with UMA. Id. Waiver of an express contract, whether direct or inferential, may be "proved by express declarations manifesting the intent not to claim the advantage." Wheat Belt Pub. Power Dist. v. Batterman, 234 Neb. 589, 452 N.W.2d 49, 53 (Neb. 1990)). To establish a waiver, the evidence must show "clear, unequivocal, and decisive action of a party showing such a purpose, or acts amounting to estoppel on his part." Id. (citing Jelsma v. Scottsdale Ins. Co., 231 Neb. 657, 437 N.W.2d 778, 786 (Neb. 1989)).

Contrary to Soteria's assertion, the complaint nowhere states that Stark actually waived the Non-Compete Agreement. Instead, the complaint states that he 1) "was to grant a limited waiver" of the Agreement, Filing No. 1; 2) "was to waive his rights" under the Agreement, id.; and, 3) he "did not waive his rights," id. Further, the complaint states that Stark did not waive his rights under the Non-Compete agreement "because UMA and Soteria did not fulfill the promise to appoint Dr. Stark as Managing Director at NHI." Id. The complaint thus contains no allegation of an express waiver.

But Soteria also argues that by assisting Soteria in the development and operation of NHI, Stark demonstrated that he "waived any right he had to claim that [Soteria's] involvement with [NHI] violated the Non-Compete Agreement." Filing No. 15, Defendants' Brief, at 9. Such "waiver" is not apparent on the face of the complaint, however, since Stark alleges his conduct was induced by Soteria's promise to appoint him NHI's managing director. It is difficult to see why Stark would waive valuable protection under the Non-Compete Agreement if he did not expect a valuable promise or performance in return for his waiver.

The issue of waiver presents a factual dispute that, like the factual dispute in Count I, should not be resolved in a Rule 12(b)(6) motion to dismiss. Accepting the allegations in the complaint as true, I conclude that Stark should be allowed to prove to the jury whether Soteria breached the Non-Compete Agreement by executing the License Agreement with UMA. Accordingly,

IT IS ORDERED that the defendants' motion to dismiss is denied in its entirety.

Questions

1. How does the court define "promissory estoppel"?
2. According to the court, when would a claim for unjust enrichment be entertained? Discuss.
3. How would you reason that a non-competition agreement is supported by adequate consideration?

Davis v. McCurry
2000 Tex. App. LEXIS 2918

This is a suit on a note. Don Davis, appellant, signed a promissory note payable to Leah McCurry appellee, in the amount of $75,000.00 plus interest. The Note was payable in four yearly installments of $10,000.00, and one final payment of the balance. Davis never made any payments. He contends that the Note is unenforceable because it is not supported by consideration. We disagree.

McCurry filed suit on the Note, alleging breach of contract and seeking attorneys' fees. Davis asserted the affirmative defense of lack of consideration. McCurry moved for summary judgment, which the trial court granted on February 18, 1999. Davis appeals this judgment, contending that a genuine issue of material fact exists regarding whether he received consideration for making the Note. . . .

Affirmative Defense

We first address Davis' affirmative defense of "lack of consideration." Consideration is a present exchange bargained for in return for a promise. Roark v. Stallworth Oil and Gas, Inc., 813 S.W.2d 492, 496 (Tex. 1991); Connell v. Provident Life & Accident Ins. Co., 148 Tex. 311, 314-15, 224 S.W.2d 194, 196 (1949). It consists of either a benefit to the promisor or a detriment to the promisee. Roark, 813 S.W.2d at 496. The detriment must induce the making of the promise, and the promise must induce the incurring of the detriment. Id.; see Broadnax v. Ledbetter, 100 Tex. 375, 378, 99 S.W. 1111, 1112 (1907).

What constitutes consideration of a contract is a question of law. Brownwood Ross Co. v. Maverick County, 936 S.W.2d 42, 45 (Tex. App. — San Antonio 1996, no writ); Williams v. Hill, 396 S.W.2d 911, 913 (Tex. Civ. App. — Dallas 1965, no writ). Because this is a summary judgment proceeding, we assume Davis' version of the facts is accurate.

See *Sysco Food Services, Inc.*, 890 S.W.2d at 800. His rendition of the relevant facts is set forth as follows.

Davis has been a real estate developer since 1970. McCurry has been his personal friend since the 1980s. Golden Gate, Inc. ("GGI") is a Texas corporation through which Davis has conducted his real estate business. In December of 1991, Davis suggested to McCurry they form a limited partnership between GGI and herself. GGI would be the general partner and McCurry would be the limited partner, with each owning 50% of the limited partnership.

In early 1992, GGI and McCurry entered into the limited partnership, and named it Leah Ventures, Ltd. ("LVL"). McCurry paid an initial capital contribution of $152,500.00, and GGI made no initial capital contribution. The purpose of LVL was to invest the partnership's capital in various endeavors. The partnership agreement contained a clause stating that no partner believed that the partnership agreement amounted to any type of guarantee of "returns and profits," and that Don Davis was not personally liable for anything related to the partnership.

In early 1992, the limited partnership invested over one hundred thousand dollars in a division of GGI called the "GGI Development Fund" (GGIDF). GGIDF agreed to use its "best efforts" to provide LVL, an annual 10% return on its investment. In late 1996, a major GGIDF asset was sold, and LVL's return of investment was calculated. LVL's return from the investment of $112,675 was $35,046.

Davis contends that he has no personal liability for the loss sustained by LVL. We note, though, that the issue of whether or not Davis may have been personally liable in any way for the actions of either GGI, GGIDF, LVL, or 2100 Memorial, Ltd., is a legal question, and Davis' sworn statement to that effect is of no consequence. Nevertheless, Davis contends that despite the fact that he had no obligation to pay McCurry, he agreed to purchase McCurry's 50 percent interest in LVL. He paid her $55,000 for that interest.

After receiving the $55,000, McCurry still faced a loss of $57,675 from her initial capital contribution to LVL. Davis agreed to give her the $57,675 in lost capital, plus interest of $17,325, for a total of $75,000 in the form of a promissory note — the one at issue in this case.

To document this transaction, he entered into a bill of sale with McCurry purporting to purchase all of McCurry's interest in LVL. On the same date, he signed the $75,000 promissory note, and McCurry executed a release in favor of LVL, GGI, 2100 Memorial, Ltd., and Don Davis, personally. Davis concedes he never made a payment pursuant to the terms of that Note.

The release that McCurry executed contemporaneously with the Note states:

> For and in consideration of Ten and No/100 Dollars and other good and valuable consideration to Releasor paid, the receipt and sufficiency of which is hereby acknowledged and confessed, Releasor does hereby . . . release, acquit and forever discharge Releasees . . . from all claims, demand,

and causes of action of whatsoever nature, known or which through the exercise of reasonable diligence should be known to Releasor, whether in contract, tort, pursuant to statute, or otherwise, from personal injuries, property damages, punitive damages, trebled damages, or any other damages which have accrued or may ever accrue to Releasor . . . for or on account of any alleged actions or omissions or Releasees arising from or related to Releasor having been a limited partner in LEAH VENTURES, LTD.

We hold that the release is sufficient consideration to support the promissory note. *Accord* Copeland v. Alsobrook, 3 S.W.3d 598, 607 (Tex. App. — San Antonio 1999, *pet. denied*) (holding that release executed by former wife of decedent so that proceeds of policy on which she was still erroneously named as beneficiary could be paid out without court order constituted consideration); Trantham v. Roper, 308 S.W.2d 195, 197 (Tex. Civ. App. — Texarkana 1957, *writ ref'd n.r.e.*) (forbearance to sue is sufficient consideration to support a contract).

A valuable and sufficient consideration for a contract may consist of either a benefit to the promisor or a loss or detriment to the promisee. In other words, sufficient consideration for the agreement may consist of some right, interest, profit, or benefit that accrues to one party, or, alternatively, of some forbearance, loss, or responsibility that is undertaken or incurred by the other party. Accordingly, it is not necessary that the promisor receive a benefit under the agreement. On the contrary, if the promisee parts with some legal right or sustains some legal injury as the inducement for the agreement, this will be sufficient.

Specifically, it is well settled that a forbearance to institute legal proceedings constitutes valid consideration to support a contract. Leonard v. Texaco, Inc., 422 S.W.2d 160, 165 (Tex. 1967); Executives Condominiums, Inc. v. State, 764 S.W.2d 899, 903 (Tex. App. — Corpus Christi 1989, *writ denied*). Likewise, postponement of enforcement of a debt has been held to be sufficient consideration, Swofford v. Tri-State Chemicals, Inc., 764 S.W.2d 24, 26 (Tex. App. — El Paso 1989, *writ denied*), as has a mere agreement to continue doing business with a party. Gooch v. American Sling Co., Inc., 902 S.W.2d 181, 185 (Tex. App. — Fort Worth 1995, *no writ*). Even an extension of time in which to pay a debt is adequate consideration for a contract. Bonner Oil Co. v. Gaines, 108 Tex. 232, 191 S.W. 552 (Tex. 1917); Victoria Bank & Trust Co. v. Brady, 779 S.W.2d 893, 903 (Tex. App. —Corpus Christi 1989), *rev'd in part on other grounds*, 811 S.W.2d 931 (Tex. 1991).

Regardless of Davis' beliefs regarding his individual liability, he received a benefit from the release signed by McCurry. McCurry released Davis *individually*, along with all the other entities through which he was conducting his real estate business from any and all claims which might arise on her behalf resulting from her involvement in LVL. The merits of any such suit are indeterminable at this point, but that does not diminish the fact that the release constituted a detriment to McCurry and a benefit to Davis. By signing the release, McCurry gave up any possible chance of seeking legal recompense for her loss sustained during her involvement with LVL. Once he obtained the signed release, Davis was able to continue doing business free from potential liability or legal fees related to defending against a suit by McCurry related to LVL. We find that McCurry's forbearance from instituting legal proceedings, as evidenced by the release, constitutes valid consideration for the $75,000.00 promissory note as a matter of law.

Because we find the release constitutes valid consideration supporting the Note, we do not address the arguments regarding whether McCurry's initial capital contribution constituted valid consideration for the Note.

We AFFIRM the judgment of the trial court.

Questions

1. How does the court define "consideration"?
2. Is forbearance to institute legal proceedings valid consideration?
3. What was the benefit Davis received?

Suggested Case References

1. Does having a contract under seal negate the necessity of having consideration? Read what the Massachusetts court said in Thomas v. Kiendzior, 27 Mass. App. Ct. 370, 538 N.E.2d 66 (1989).

2. Can forbearance of right to assert a valid and mature claim be consideration for a promise? First Texas Sav. Ass'n v. Comprop Inv. Properties, Ltd., 752 F. Supp. 1568 (M.D. Fla. 1990).

3. For a definition of consideration by an Arkansas court, read Bass v. Service Supply Co., Inc., 25 Ark. App. 273, 757 S.W.2d 189 (1988).

4. For a detailed discussion of the preexisting duty rule, read Rosati Masonry Co. v. Jonna Constr. Co., 1998 Mich. App. LEXIS 2418.

5. Is a reporter's promise of anonymity contractual consideration? Read Cohen v. Cowles Media Co., 44 N.W.2d 248 (Minn. App. 1990).

5 Legality of Subject Matter and Contractual Capacity

Learning Objectives

After studying this chapter you will be able to:

- Discuss the concept of the legality of the subject matter
- Define *malum in se*
- Define *malum prohibitum*
- List the six types of contracts that come under the Statute of Frauds
- Discuss what is meant by "usury"
- Explain the concept of "contractual capacity"
- Differentiate between infants and minors
- Know which types of contracts a minor cannot avoid
- Discuss the effect of alcohol and drugs on a person's contractual capacity
- Apply the concepts of legality and capacity to your everyday life

CHAPTER OVERVIEW

The first three elements of a valid contract—offer, acceptance, and consideration—discussed in the preceding chapters focus on the actual terms of the agreement itself. The last three requisite elements of a valid contract are concerned with the circumstances surrounding the agreement—the legality of the subject matter, the ability of the parties to enter into enforceable contractual agreements, and the intent of the parties. This chapter examines the fourth and fifth requirements: legality and capacity.

For a contract to be valid and enforceable, the contract must be formed for a legal purpose. If the subject matter of the agreement violates statutory law or public policy the court would be unable and unwilling to permit its provisions to be carried out. Consequently, even though all the other elements of a valid contract may be present, if the subject matter of the contract is illegal, no enforceable agreement can exist.

In addition to the legality of the subject matter, the law is also concerned with the legal ability of the parties to create a valid contract. The law has decided that under certain circumstances and conditions a person is legally incapable of forming a valid contract. These standards of contractual capacity are based on the person's age and mental condition at the moment the contract is entered into.

Legality of the Subject Matter

Contracts that are entered into for an illegal purpose are not enforceable. The reason is obvious. How can a court, designated to uphold the law, enforce an agreement that purports to break the law?

However, not all laws involve heinous actions, and the law has divided "illegality" into two broad categories. The first category contains laws that support the very nature and fabric of society. Violation of these rules go against all public policy, and contracts violating them are completely void and unenforceable. The second category includes minor illegalities, those laws created by statute that bar actions which are not, in and of themselves, morally reprehensible. Contracts that violate this second category may still permit the injured party some form of **quasi-contractual** relief.

Malum in Se

The first category of illegality, those contracts that violate public policy, are deemed **malum in se** — bad in and of themselves. The actions prohibited by these laws are considered to be morally reprehensible, and contracts formed for purposes *malum in se* are entirely unenforceable. Typical examples of these types of laws are felonies, contracts in restraint of trade, contracts found to discriminate against a protected category of citizen (race, age, sex, national origin, and so forth), and contracts that are deemed unconscionable.

 EXAMPLES:

1. Wally enters into a contract with Eddie, promising Eddie $10,000 if Eddie can find a hit man to kill Wally's business partner.

Although all the other requisite elements of a valid contract may exist, in this instance the contract is still unenforceable because murder is considered *malum in se*.

2. Gamma, Inc. and Beta Corp. enter into a contract to fix their prices, thus driving all other competition out of their market. This contract is unenforceable because its purpose is to restrain trade, which is *malum in se*.

3. Violet needs a new secretary and hires an employment agency to find her a suitable employee. Violet makes it a condition of her agreement with the agency that they find her only white male secretaries. This contract is unenforceable. The provisions are meant to discriminate against persons based on race and sex, which is *malum in se*.

Malum Prohibitum

The second category of illegal subject matter encompasses actions that are not morally reprehensible or against public policy but are still minor violations of the law. This category is known as **malum prohibitum**—a prohibited wrong, or something prohibited by statutory regulation. Although contracts that are *malum prohibitum* are unenforceable, some quasi-contractual relief may be available if the aggrieved party can demonstrate that to deny recovery would unjustly enrich the other party to the agreement. The following is a sample list of contracts that are viewed as *malum prohibitum*. Every state code has its own statutory prohibitions, and you should review each state's laws independently.

Contracts that Violate the Statute of Frauds.   The **Statute of Frauds** is a law that requires certain types of contracts to be in writing in order to be enforceable. Typically, six types of contracts come within the provisions of the Statute of Frauds:

1. contracts for an interest in realty;
2. contracts that are not to be performed within one year;
3. contracts in consideration of marriage;
4. guarantees;
5. sale of goods valued at over $500; and
6. executors' promises to pay the decedent's debts.

A complete discussion of the Statute of Frauds appears in Chapter 7, Contract Provisions.

Although the statute requires these types of contracts to be in writing, if the parties actually perform under the oral agreement, their performances will take the contract out of the Statute of Frauds and make it enforceable.

EXAMPLES:

1. In consideration of her promise to marry him, Donald promises to give $5 million to Marla. For this contract to be enforceable in a court of law, Marla had better get the promise in writing. Otherwise it violates the Statute of Frauds and is *malum prohibitum*.

2. Cathy and LaWanda enter into an oral agreement whereby LaWanda agrees to buy Cathy's summer home for $25,000. Because the agreement is for the sale of an interest in real estate, the Statute of Frauds applies, and the parties can avoid the agreement because it is *malum prohibitum*.

3. Cathy and LaWanda enter into an oral agreement whereby LaWanda agrees to buy Cathy's summer home for $25,000. Two weeks after the agreement was reached, LaWanda gives Cathy a check for the purchase price. The next day Cathy changes her mind and tries to avoid the agreement by saying it violates the Statute of Frauds. Because LaWanda has already performed, the court would most probably decide that LaWanda's performance has taken the contract out of the category of *malum prohibitum*.

Usury.   Usury laws regulate the legal rate of interest that can be charged for extending credit. A contract for the loan of money that indicates a rate of interest above the legal limit is *malum prohibitum* because it is usurious and therefore unenforceable. If the lender has already performed, some courts will permit him to receive the legal rate of interest; to do otherwise would mean the borrower received the money interest-free, which would be unfair to the lender. (In some states, the usurer cannot even collect the principal. Each state statute must be specifically checked.)

EXAMPLE:

Rhonda agrees to lend Lennie $2000 at an annual rate of interest of 50 percent. The contract is unenforceable as being *malum prohibitum*. However, if Rhonda actually gave the money to Lenny, Lenny may be required to repay the loan at the legal rate of interest.

Gambling.   Gambling, except in certain locations and under certain prescribed situations, is illegal. Consequently, a contract entered into for the purpose of betting is *malum prohibitum*.

EXAMPLE:

Saul leases a building to operate a gambling casino in downtown St. Louis. Gambling is not permitted in Missouri, and so the contract is *malum prohibitum*. The lease may still be operative if the building can be used for a legal purpose.

Licensing Statutes. State and local communities have various licensing statutes, laws that require certain types of occupations or enterprises to receive a governmental permission to operate. Any contract that would violate the government licensing statute is *malum prohibitum*.

EXAMPLE:

Sherree and Latoya enter into an agreement to open and operate a beauty and hair salon. Beauticians and hairdressers are required to be licensed by the state. If neither Sherree nor Latoya is licensed, the contract is *malum prohibitum*.

Laws that impose licensing requirements are created either to protect the public or to provide the government with income from the licensing fees. If the agreement violates a licensing law designed to protect the public, no recovery at all is possible. If the purpose of the licensing statute is merely to raise revenue, some quasi-contractual remedy may be available.

EXAMPLES:

1. Ernie goes to Veronica for medical assistance. Although Veronica holds herself out to be a doctor, she, in fact, is not a doctor. Therefore, Veronica's agreement with Ernie for a fee is *malum prohibitum*. In this instance, Veronica cannot recover the value of her services to Ernie. To do so would potentially endanger the public.

2. La Dolce Vita, an Italian restaurant, serves alcohol and wine to its customers. The restaurant does not have a liquor license. In this instance, even though the contract for the sale of liquor is *malum prohibitum*, the restaurant may be allowed to recover the cost of the alcohol it sold. This statute is designed to raise revenue for the government.

As indicated above, contracts that are *malum prohibitum* are not considered as seriously wrong as those that are *malum in se*, although neither category creates a valid contract. But because the law generally favors contractual relationships, it does sometimes permit an agreement that has both legal and illegal provisions to be **severed**: that is, the legal portion of the contract, if possible, is separated from the illegal portion and upheld, whereas the illegal portion remains unenforceable. This concept was exemplified above in the examples where portions of the agreement were permitted to stand, such as the lease of the building in St. Louis and the loan of the money.

Contractual Capacity

Contractual capacity, the fifth requisite element of every valid contract, refers to the parties' legal ability to enter into a binding contractual relationship. In reality, the concept of contractual capacity is concerned more with defining contractual incapacity than it is with defining contractual capacity. There are four major areas of contractual capacity, which are discussed below.

Age

Age is the most common capacity issue to arise. The law divides a person's age into two major categories: *adulthood* (or **majority**) and **minority**.

An *adult* is anyone over the *age of consent*, which most states designate to begin at age 18. (Some statutes, however, may establish younger limits for the age of consent.) Adults are considered contractually capable with respect to age.

A minor is anyone under the age of consent pursuant to state statute. Minors are further subdivided into **natural infants** and **children of tender years**. A natural infant, a child younger than 7, is considered totally incapable of entering into any contract because of extreme youth. A child of tender years, a minor between the ages of 7 and 14, is usually considered too young to form a valid contract, but that decision is based on the particulars of the contract in question.

Those persons between puberty and the age of consent, the group inbetween the above-mentioned categories, are deemed to be minors. As mentioned in Chapter 1, minors are generally considered to lack contractual capacity. It is this age group that causes the most concern with respect to the capacity of a person to enter into a valid contract. Minors may avoid contracts they enter into at any point up to reaching their majority without being in breach of contract. The contracts entered into by minors are considered **voidable** at the option of the minor, which is why most people who contract with minors require that an adult, usually the minor's parent, guarantee the contract.

EXAMPLE:

Floyd, a 17-year-old, has just received several CDs as a holiday present. Floyd doesn't own a CD player, but he sees one advertised at a price he can afford. If he enters into a contract with the store owner to buy the CD player, Floyd can rescind his acceptance anytime prior to reaching age 18 without being in breach of contract. However, Floyd may be charged for the use of the CD player until his disavowal of the agreement.

There are certain categories of contracts that the law has determined that minors cannot avoid. These contracts are contracts to provide the minor with **necessaries**—items deemed essential to support life such as food, clothing, shelter, and medical aid. Be aware, though, that some states require only **emancipated** minors to be bound to contracts for necessaries. Emancipated minors are those no longer under the legal care of an adult; they are responsible for all their own actions. These situations are usually treated as quasi-contracts; that is, the reasonable value of the item, not necessarily the contract price, may be recovered.

In addition, many states prohibit a minor from avoiding contracts for education or marriage, and the federal government has determined that minors cannot avoid their voluntary military enlistment simply because of age.

 EXAMPLE:

Nick graduates high school at age 17 and decides to enlist in the army to fulfill a lifelong dream of becoming a soldier. After eight days of boot camp, Nick regrets his decision and tells his sergeant he wants out. Too late. A minor may not avoid his contract for enlistment with Uncle Sam.

Mental Capacity

A mentally deficient person lacks contractual capacity. If the person is in a mental institution, this lack of capacity exists until such time as he is adjudged mentally competent by an appropriate authority. If, on the other hand, the person merely suffers occasional mental lapses and is not confined, his mental capacity is determined by the nature of the contract, and whether or not he understands the nature of what he is undertaking. Any question dealing with a person's mental capacity is always determined on the facts and circumstances of each individual situation.

EXAMPLE:

Marvin hears voices that tell him what clothes to wear and what horses to bet on. After placing a bet with his bookie, Charlotte, Marvin gets hungry and goes to a fast food restaurant for a hamburger and fries. The contract with the restaurant is valid. Marvin's mental state has no affect or relationship to this particular contract.

Alcohol and Drugs

A person who is under the influence of alcohol or drugs is incapable of entering into a valid contract. The incapacity is only temporary, however. When the effect of the alcohol or drug wears off, provided no other problems exist, the person is considered to be contractually capable once again. Any contract entered into during the period of incapacity may be reaffirmed and made valid once the temporary incapacity is removed. As with mental incapacity, the determination as to the person's mental state at the moment of contract is determined on a case-by-case basis.

 EXAMPLE:

Bess is 80 years old and takes medication whenever she has a heart palpitation. As a side effect of the drug, Bess becomes dizzy and disoriented. During the period of disorientation, an encyclopedia salesperson rings Bess's doorbell and convinces her to buy a set of encyclopedias. The next day, when the effect of the medicine wears off, Bess realizes what she has signed but feels the books would be a good gift for her son. Bess can either avoid the contract, because of her drug-induced mental state at the time of the signing, or affirm the contract now that the medicine has worn off.

CHAPTER SUMMARY

Even if an agreement possesses the elements of a valid offer and acceptance and is supported by legally sufficient consideration, the contract will still fail if it is formed for a legally proscribed purpose or if one of the parties lacks contractual capacity.

A contract is considered formed for an illegal purpose if the subject matter is either *malum in se* or *malum prohibitum*. Agreements that are *malum in se* are those formed for purposes that go against the moral grain of society. Such contracts are unenforceable as a matter of public policy. Some examples of *malum in se* agreements are agreements to commit crimes, to discriminate, or to restrain trade.

By comparison, a contract is considered *malum prohibitum* if its subject matter violates some less serious prohibition. This type of illegality is not considered morally reprehensible, and, consequently if injury can be shown, the court will permit the injured party some remedy based on a quasi-contractual claim. Some examples of *malum prohibitum* agreements are those that violate the Statute of Frauds, usury or licensing laws, or gambling statutes.

Each state has determined the legal age of contractual consent for its citizens. If a contract is entered into by someone considered a minor under the appropriate state statute, that contract is voidable by the minor any time until the minor reaches majority. Although the contract is voidable, on reaching majority the minor may choose to affirm the contract, thereby making it enforceable. Note that exceptions to this rule are made for contracts entered into by minors for necessaries, marriage, and enlistment in the armed services.

In addition to the age of the party to a contract, the law also looks to the person's mental state at the time of contracting. Persons who are mentally incapable lack contractual capacity. Persons who are under the influence of drugs or alcohol are considered to be temporarily incapable, but they may affirm the contract once the temporary infirmity is removed.

In any instance, anytime a person has performed his contractual obligation, except for contracts *malum in se* or when the person is totally incapable, that performance will usually entitle him to some form of legal recovery so as to avoid injury and to prevent unjust enrichment.

SYNOPSIS

Legality of subject matter
1. *Malum in se*: Unenforceable
2. *Malum prohibitum*: Quasi-contractual recovery may be permitted

Contractual capacity
1. Age
2. Mental condition
3. Alcohol
4. Drugs

Contracts formed when a party is incapable may be affirmed once the incapacity is removed.

Key Terms

Children of tender years: children between the ages of seven and fourteen

Contractual capacity: the statutory ability of a person to enter into a valid contract

Emancipation: a minor no longer under the legal care of an adult

Majority: adulthood; above legal age of consent

Malum in se: bad in and of itself; against public morals

Malum prohibitum: regulatory wrong; violates statute
Minority: person under the legal age of consent
Natural infant: a child under the age of seven
Necessaries: food, clothing, shelter, medical aid
Quasi-contract: implied-in-law contract (see Chapter 1)
Severability: ability to separate a contract into its legal and illegal portions
Statute of Frauds: statute requiring certain types of contracts to be in writing
     (see Chapter 7)
Usury: rate of interest higher than the rate allowed by law
Voidable contract: a contract capable of being avoided without being in
     breach of contract (see Chapter 1)

EXERCISES

1. Check your own state statutes for the age of consent and contracts that are deemed to be *malum in se* and *malum prohibitum.*
2. Why can a person receive some remedy even if the contract is *malum prohibitum?*
3. What factors would determine a person's lack of mental capacity?
4. Are there circumstances in which a person's physical, not mental, state can cause her to lack contractual capacity? Why?
5. Dr. Doe firmly believes in the terminally ill's right to die. He has contracts to assist Richard Roe, an 80-year-old man dying of cancer, in committing suicide. The fee agreed on is $1000. After Mr. Roe's death, Dr. Doe requests the fee from the Roe estate, which refuses to pay him. Argue for and against the legality of the contract.

Cases for Analysis

It is often difficult for a court to determine whether a party to a contract has sufficient capacity to contract. In addition to the elements of capacity discussed in this chapter, sometimes by the nature of the relationship a person may not have capacity to be bound. Such was the issue for the court in Calloway v. E.H. Smith Electrical Contractors, Inc. Also, even if a contract may be *malum prohibitum*, the injured party may still be entitled to some form of relief, Bandal v. Baldwin.

Callaway d/b/a Callaway & Associates v. E.H. Smith Electrical Contractors, Inc. et al.
814 So. 2d 893 (Ct. App. Ala. 2001)

In November 1998, H.D. Callaway, doing business as Callaway & Associates (hereinafter "Callaway"), sued E.H. Smith Electrical Contractors,

Inc. ("Smith Electrical"), and its chief executive officer, Linda DiAnn Smith ("Smith"), in the Circuit Court of Mobile County. Callaway's complaint alleged that Smith Electrical and Smith had failed to make payments that Callaway contended were due under a professional-services contract; Callaway also sought relief in quasi-contract. After a bench trial, the trial court entered a judgment in favor of the defendants; that court later denied Callaway's postjudgment motion, and Callaway appeals.

In his brief to this court, Callaway contends that the trial court's judgment is erroneous because, among other things, it failed to enforce unambiguous terms of a written agreement.

The record reveals that Callaway is an engineer who works as a "construction-contract-claims consultant" assisting contractors in itemizing, preparing, and presenting claims for payment arising from construction work. His background includes a civil engineering degree from Auburn University, service as a "construction claims negotiator" for the United States Army Corps of Engineers, and service as a "supervisory civil engineer" with the Naval Facilities Engineering Command. Since 1978, Callaway has been in the business of assisting contractors in the accounting, presentation, and negotiation of claims. He has authored or co-authored two books regarding construction and doing business with the government.

As a construction-contract-claims consultant, Callaway works with contractors experiencing problems or disputes with parties with whom they have contracted. Part of his job is to analyze documents, contracts, and change orders; to talk to the people involved; to determine what the issues are; to distill the issues; to prepare a claim document; and to help the contractor negotiate settlement of those issues to the extent that they can be negotiated. When negotiations fail, Callaway assists in litigating the dispute as needed.

In April 1997, Callaway and Smith entered into negotiations concerning whether, and under what terms, Callaway would act on behalf of Smith Electrical in making various claims. On April 22, 1997, Callaway sent a letter to Smith, in her capacity as chief executive officer of Smith Electrical, referencing several numbered tasks, or "jobs," that had been undertaken by Smith Electrical in connection with the construction of an automobile plant near Vance, Alabama, but for which Smith Electrical had not been fully paid by the owner of the plant or its general contractor, Universal Construction Company ("Universal"). Callaway's letter incorporated several terms that had been proposed by Callaway in an earlier draft contract, along with a number of changes suggested by Smith; that letter, in pertinent part, stated:

"I have reviewed the information provided to me on the following Job Numbers at the Mercedes Benz plant at Vance, Alabama: 1135, 1139, 1140 and 1144.

"It is my understanding that the sum of these four contracts as modified to date is $2,802,255 and that you have been paid $2,505,182 to date, leaving a balance presently owed in the amount of $297,068 [sic]. I will assist you in the collection of this money for 5%.

"It is my understanding that there are outstanding contract modifications on Job Numbers 1135, 1139 and 1140 totaling $423,063. I will assist you in the collection of these funds for a commission of 12%.

"It is my understanding that the total direct cost to date on all four contracts is $3,386,650. There is some question in my mind if this number is inclusive of only Field Overhead and not Home Office G&A expenses. Depending on whether or not the Home Office G&A is included in the $3,386,650 or not, a total cost claim, if the issues support such, could yield a total cost claim in the range of [$500,000] to $1,150,000 above the proposed and outstanding unmodified change orders discussed above.

"This would require significant further review of the job cost records and financial statement with your CPA. In any event, I will assist you in the pursuit of these claims to the extent I consider them compensable for a commission of 15%.

"I will require a $2,000 retainer to be paid within 30 days. All commissions are due upon receipt of the funds from Universal or the Owner.

"You had asked that I give you my opinion as to whether you could sue Universal in the event the parties could not resolve their differences. After a careful review of the subcontract documents provided, I find them silent on the issue of disputes.

"To me this would mean that the parties could agree on whether to use arbitration, if mutually agreeable, or have access to the courts if one party dissented and wanted to go to court. Of course you should confirm this with a qualified legal opinion.

"Any travel and/or other necessary expenses would be in addition to the previously discussed rates. If you agree with this proposal and wish for me to proceed, please sign in the space below indicating your agreement to retain my services based upon the above percentages and your agreement to pay the $2,000 retainer within 30 days."

Smith signed the letter as chief executive officer of Smith Electrical, and a signed copy was sent via facsimile to Smith Electrical by Callaway on April 27, 1997.

After the contract was executed, Smith Electrical sent Callaway a $2,000 retainer, and Callaway began working on Smith Electrical's claims. Initially, Callaway reviewed between 8 and 12 file drawers' worth of documentation regarding Smith Electrical's potential claims. In May 1997, he traveled to Huntsville to attend a meeting with Universal and Smith Electrical representatives at which Smith Electrical's right to additional funds was discussed, although representatives of Universal would not allow Callaway to speak at the meeting. At that meeting, Universal offered to settle Smith Electrical's claims for $219,745. However, that offer was rejected by Smith Electrical as being too low, and Callaway continued to work on preparing a final, comprehensive claim for all outstanding monies allegedly owed to Smith Electrical on the automobile-plant project. Callaway prepared five formal claim booklets on behalf of Smith Electrical, containing narrative summaries and other claim documentation, that were presented to Universal in a subsequent meeting between representatives of those entities in August 1997. At the August 1997 meeting, which Callaway and one of his employees attended, Universal increased its offer to $400,000; however, that offer was also refused by Smith Electrical, which insisted on a payment of $750,000.

After Universal's second compromise offer had been rejected, Smith Electrical retained legal counsel to represent it in its dispute with Universal. Callaway rendered assistance to Smith Electrical's counsel, including providing explanations of various documents, and counsel reviewed the claim documents in their preparation of a complaint on behalf of Smith Electrical against Universal. Callaway met with Smith Electrical's counsel on several occasions, both in their Mobile office and in Montgomery, where counsel for Smith Electrical and Universal's Atlanta-based counsel were meeting. Although counsel for Smith Electrical filed suit against Universal, that action was settled in November 1998 upon Universal's payment of $487,500 to Smith Electrical.

After Universal had paid Smith Electrical, Callaway billed Smith Electrical $34,564, which represented five percent of the $297,068 stated as being owed in the parties' contract plus 12 percent of sums above that amount. However, Smith Electrical did not pay Callaway's bill. In the trial court, Smith testified that she did not "contemplate having to pay a contingent fee if [Callaway] did not recover the money without the assistance of a lawyer."

To prevail on his breach-of-contract claim against Smith Electrical, Callaway was required to prove "(1) the existence of a valid contract binding the parties in the action, (2) his own performance under the contract, (3) the [defendants'] nonperformance, and (4) damages." Southern Med. Health Sys. v. Vaughn, 669 So. 2d 98, 99 (Ala. 1995). The trial court, as we have stated, entered a judgment in favor of the defendants. Although that judgment contained no express factual findings, we "will assume that the trial judge made those findings necessary to support the judgment." TransAmerica Commercial Fin. Corp. v. AmSouth Bank, 608 So. 2d 375, 378 (Ala. 1992). Under the applicable standard of review, both "the trial court's judgment and all implicit findings necessary to support it carry a presumption of correctness and will not be reversed unless found to be plainly and palpably wrong." *TransAmerica*, 608 So. 2d at 378. Therefore, we infer that the trial court found Callaway's proof lacking as to at least one element of his breach-of-contract claim against the defendants, and we must address whether that determination was "plainly and palpably wrong."

We first consider the first element, the existence of a valid contract binding "the parties." The April 22, 1997, letter that forms the basis of Callaway's contract claim is addressed to "Ms. Linda DiAnn Smith, CEO[,] E.H. Smith Electrical Contractors, Inc." Thus, the contract proposal as last presented by Callaway names Smith as an agent for Smith Electrical. Under Alabama law, "an agent is presumed to intend to bind his principal only and to incur no personal liability and unless an intention to substitute or superadd his personal liability for or to that of his principal is clearly shown, he will not be bound in his individual capacity." Sealy v. McElroy, 288 Ala. 93, 104, 257 So. 2d 340, 350 (1972). In this case, Smith testified that there were no discussions with Callaway regarding personal responsibility on her part for the payment obligations under the contract, and Callaway admitted that Callaway had acted in a representative capacity for Smith Electrical. We conclude that the trial court could properly have concluded that Smith was not personally bound by the contract at issue, although Smith Electrical was bound thereby. As a result, we conclude that the trial court's judgment is due to be affirmed insofar as it was in Smith's favor on the breach-of-contract claim, but must proceed to review the other elements of Callaway's breach-of-contract claim against Smith Electrical.

Could the trial court properly have determined that Callaway did not perform according to the terms of the contract? This is the principal issue disputed by the parties on appeal. Smith Electrical intimates that this question is to be answered in the affirmative—that Callaway is asking for an award of "contingency fees" for services that he did not "successfully complete" because "the contract expressly stated that Callaway would only recover . . . if his services led to a settlement of claims." . . . Thus, Smith Electrical's premise is that the "performance" Callaway was due to render under the contract was the securing of a settlement from Universal solely through his own efforts.

However, the contract that Callaway prepared after having consulted with Smith and that Smith signed on behalf of Smith Electrical does not contain any language that supports the position taken by Smith Electrical. Instead, the parties agreed that Callaway, in exchange for five percent of the $297,068 that the parties agreed was then due from Universal on the four specified job numbers plus 12 percent of the $423,063 allegedly due from Universal on several contract modifications, would "assist . . . in the collection" of those moneys. Simply put, the contract requires Callaway's "assistance"—it does not require Callaway to himself collect the subject funds from Universal, nor does it require that Callaway be the efficient cause of Smith Electrical's collection of those funds. "Compensation may be due an agent who has accomplished a result leading to the final result, upon the happening of which the agent's compensation is conditional." 2 Restatement (Second) of Agency §448 comment b (1958). It is clear from the record that Callaway did perform services that amounted to "assistance" to Smith Electrical in its ongoing efforts to collect the disputed funds, including extensive document review, attendance at bilateral meetings, preparation of detailed claim statements that would later be used by Smith Electrical's counsel, and consultation with Smith's counsel before and after suit was filed against Universal seeking payment of the disputed moneys. Also, it is undisputed that Smith Electrical ultimately received funds from Universal that were contemplated in the parties' contract, which was the sole other contingency contemplated within the four corners of the contract. In the ordinary case, a principal "cannot make [an] agent's compensation dependent upon some contingency not contemplated by the agency contract." 3 C.J.S. Agency §330 (1973); cf. Long-Lewis Hardware Co. v. Ewing, 13 Ala. App. 435, 68 So. 794 (principal could not deny liability for commission due on sale of roofing material simply because specific material sold by agent was not then being manufactured), *cert. denied*, 193 Ala. 678, 69 So. 1018 (1915).

As we have noted, Smith testified that she did not "contemplate" having to pay a contingent fee if Callaway did not recover the money without the assistance of a lawyer, and the trial court's judgment may be predicated on that testimony of Smith's subjective intent. However, as the Alabama Supreme Court stated in Acstar Insurance Co. v. American Mechanical Contractors, Inc., 621 So. 2d 1227 (Ala. 1993), "the law of contracts is premised upon objective rather than subjective manifestations of intent," and "a subjective intent on the part of the actor will not alter the relationship or duties created by an otherwise objectively indicated intent." 621 So. 2d at 1232 (citations and internal quotations omitted). While the parties may have had differing views as to what actions on the part of Callaway would cause his right to compensation to mature, the objective language of the contract required Callaway to "assist" Smith Electrical in collection of the disputed moneys. Therefore, we conclude that an implicit finding in favor of Smith Electrical on the issue of Callaway's performance would be plainly and palpably wrong.

Similarly, there was no substantial evidence presented to contradict Callaway's proof as to the two remaining elements of his breach-of-contract claim. It was undisputed that Smith Electrical did not pay more than $2,000 to Callaway, although that amount was far less than even the five percent of the $297,068 stated for the amount that the parties agreed was due from Universal. Smith Electrical's failure to pay the sums due under the parties' contract constituted nonperformance of its contractual obligations, thereby causing Callaway to suffer damages. Thus, the record provides no basis to conclude that Callaway failed to prove either the defendant's nonperformance or damages resulting therefrom. Accordingly, the trial court erred in entering a judgment in favor of Smith Electrical on the breach-of-contract claim.

However, we affirm the judgment in favor of the defendants on Callaway's quasi-contract claim. "The existence of an express contract generally excludes an implied agreement relative to the same subject matter." Vardaman v. Florence City Bd. of Educ., 544 So. 2d 962, 965 (Ala. 1989). As we have discussed, Smith Electrical and Callaway entered into a valid, binding contract concerning Callaway's provision of assistance in securing payment of disputed sums from Universal, and Callaway's argument as to this claim expressly assumes the unenforceability of that contract. Moreover, Callaway testified to having provided services on behalf of Smith Electrical, as opposed to Smith individually, from which testimony the trial court could have concluded that Smith should not be individually responsible for paying for Callaway's services. As to that claim, we conclude that the trial court's judgment was not in error.

In light of the facts and authorities discussed above, we affirm the trial court's judgment except as to Callaway's breach-of-contract claim against Smith Electrical. In that single respect, the trial court's judgment is reversed, and the cause is remanded for further proceedings.

AFFIRMED IN PART; REVERSED IN PART; AND REMANDED.

Questions

1.   What did Callway's status have to do with his contractual capacity with respect to the contract in question?

2.   What did the court say about the validity of the contract binding the parties?

3.   What does this decision add to your understanding of contractual capacity? Discuss.

Bandal v. Baldwin

2000 Minn. App. LEXIS 1169

Appellant S. Kris Bandal sued respondent Marlo Baldwin on an alleged personal guarantee after respondent defaulted on a $70,000 business loan. Appellant's complaint alleged claims of breach of contract, promissory estoppel, and fraud. The district court dismissed the action, ruling that the statute of frauds barred the claims. We agree that the statute of frauds bars the contract claim, but because appellant's complaint also sets forth a valid promissory estoppel claim, which is an exception to application of the statute of frauds, we reverse and remand on that issue. Because appellant's complaint does not properly set forth a fraud claim, which would otherwise also be exempt from application of the statute of frauds, we affirm on that claim.

Decision

Minnesota's statute of frauds provides:

> No action shall be maintained, in either of the following cases, upon any agreement, unless such agreement, or some note or memorandum thereof, expressing the consideration, is in writing, and subscribed by the party charged therewith:
> (1)   Every agreement that by its terms is not to be performed within one year from the making thereof;
> (2)   Every special promise to answer for the debt, default or doings of another[.]

Minn. Stat. §513.01 (1998). The purpose of this statute is to "'defend against frauds and perjuries by denying force to oral contracts of certain types which are peculiarly adaptable to those purposes.'" Smith v. Woodwind Homes, Inc., 605 N.W.2d 418, 423 (Minn. App. 2000) (*quoting* In re Guardianship of Huesman, 354 N.W.2d 860, 863 (Minn. App. 1984)).

Contract Claim

Appellant orally agreed to lend respondent $70,000 for a business loan and released the funds to respondent before a written agreement was fully executed. The term of the loan was for 31 months, and the alleged guarantee covered this term. Courts have typically treated a promise to pay in monthly installments for a definite term of over one year to be within the statute of frauds. See John D. Calamari & Joseph M. Perillo, *The Law of Contracts* §19.18, at 744 (4th ed. 1998). Because the term of the alleged guarantee necessarily covered the term of the loan, it came within the statute of frauds. Thus, the district court properly dismissed the contract claim because, as a matter of law, any guarantee did not comply with the statute of frauds' writing requirement for contracts not to be performed within a year.

Promissory Estoppel

Appellant argues that his complaint set forth a valid promissory estoppel claim that would preclude respondent from claiming the statute of frauds as a defense. In Minnesota, promissory estoppel may be claimed in an attempt to circumvent a valid statute of frauds defense. See, e.g., Berg v. Carlstrom, 347 N.W.2d 809, 812 (Minn. 1984); Del Hayes & Sons, Inc. v. Mitchell, 304 Minn. 275, 284-85, 230 N.W.2d 588, 594 (1975); Norwest Bank Minn. v. Midwestern Mach. Co., 481 N.W.2d 875, 880 (Minn. App. 1992), *review denied* (Minn. May 15, 1992). Promissory estoppel exists if "a party makes a promise knowing another party reasonably relies and acts upon that promise, and the promise must be enforced to avoid injustice." *Norwest Bank Minn.*, 481 N.W.2d at 880 (citation omitted). However,

> the trier of fact is in the best position to judge whether oral promises were made, what the mutual understanding of the parties was, and whether the promisor's benefits were merely incidental.

Mill & Elevator Mut. Ins. Co. v. Barzen, 553 N.W.2d 446, 451 (Minn. App. 1996) (citation omitted), *review denied* (Minn. Nov. 20, 1996).

Here, a fact issue exists on whether respondent promised to personally guarantee the $70,000 loan to induce appellant to release the funds to him before the loan agreement was fully executed. The evidence before the district court also includes respondent's fax of his home address and social security number, as well as the $70,000 check, which was made payable both to respondent and his company. This evidence, in addition to the alleged promise, and appellant's reliance on that promise to his detriment, tends to support respondent's promissory estoppel claim. Because the alleged facts must be presumed true for the purposes of this appeal, we conclude that the district court erred in dismissing appellant's promissory estoppel claim. See In re Milk Indirect Purchaser Antitrust Litig., 588 N.W.2d 772, 775 (Minn. App. 1999) (allegations of complaint dismissed for failure to state a claim must be accepted as true and viewed in light most favorable to plaintiff on appeal).

Fraud

Appellant also claims that respondent's conduct constituted fraudulent misrepresentation. He alleges that respondent represented that "the loan documents would be executed, the loan would be secured . . . , and the loan would be paid in full at the interest rate" set forth in their agreement. He also alleges that the representations were false, that respondent knew the representations were false, and that respondent induced appellant to make the loan.

A claim of fraudulent misrepresentation includes the following conduct by the tortfeasor:

> ... a representation (2) that was false (3) having to do with a past or present fact (4) that is material (5) and susceptible of knowledge (6) that the representor knows to be false or is asserted without knowing whether the fact is true or false (7) with the intent to induce the other person to act (8) and the person in fact is induced to act (9) in reliance on the representation (10) that the plaintiff suffered damages (11) attributable to the misrepresentation.

Gorham v. Benson Optical, 539 N.W.2d 798, 802 (Minn. App. 1995) (*quoting* M.H. v. Caritas Family Servs., 488 N.W.2d 282, 289 (Minn. 1992)).

Minn. R. Civ. P. 9.02 requires fraud claims to be stated with particularity. Where the allegations of frauds are not specific, the record will not sustain an action for fraud. Westgor v. Grimm, 318 N.W.2d 56, 58 (Minn. 1982); Stubblefield v. Gruenberg, 426 N.W.2d 912, 914-15 (Minn. App. 1988). In fraudulent misrepresentation cases, this rule has been interpreted to require particular allegations of specific false or fraudulent representations. See Alho v. Sterling, 266 Minn. 71, 71-73, 122 N.W.2d 869, 870 (1963); Seafirst Commercial Corp. v. Speakman, 384 N.W.2d 895, 899 (Minn. App. 1986) ("all elements of a fraud cause of action must be pleaded") (citations omitted).

The facts alleged here do not satisfy rule 9.02. The representations alleged in the complaint are vague and lack content. See Juster Steel v. Carlson Cos., 366 N.W.2d 616, 619 (Minn. App. 1985) (affirming summary judgment for defendant where complaint alleging fraudulent misrepresentation "only vaguely referred to the content of the misrepresentations"). Also, the alleged facts do not include a representation that was false or known to be false at the time it was made. Because appellants failed to satisfy rule 9.02, the district court properly granted summary judgment dismissing their fraud claim.

Finally, appellant also claims that the district court erred in making findings that are contrary to the facts as alleged in his complaint. These findings, however, merely established a factual setting for the dispute. Thus, we conclude that the district court did not indulge in impermissible factfinding in this case.

Affirmed in part, reversed in part, and remanded.

Questions

1. Why did the district court dismiss the contract claim?
2. What are the factors that must appear in a claim for fraudulent misrepresentation?
3. On what facts was the promissory estoppel claim based?

Suggested Case References

1. May a person who is suffering from a progressive mental disease still be mentally competent to contract? Read Butler v. Harrison, 578 A.2d 1098 (D.C. App. 1990).

2. May an elderly person suffering from great mental lapses still have capacity to contract? Read Brown v. Resort Developments, 238 Va. 527, 385 S.E.2d 575 (1989).

3. Contracts for the sale of sexual favors are *malum in se*, at least in Oregon. State v. Grimes, 85 Or. App. 159, 735 P.2d 1277 (1987).

4. Does marital status affect contractual capacity? See what the court said in United States v. Yazell, 334 F.2d 454 (5th Cir. 1964).

5. May one spouse exert undue influence over the other? See Butler v. Harrison, 578 A.2d 1098 (D.C. App. 1990).

6 Contractual Intent

Learning Objectives

After studying this chapter you will be able to:

- Define what is meant by "contractual intent"
- Define "fraud"
- Differentiate fraud from misrepresentation
- Explain the concept of duress
- List the three types of duress that may be encountered in contract law
- Discuss what is meant by undue influence
- Define a contract of adhesion
- Discuss the effect of a mistake on contract formation
- Discuss the enforceability of contract entered into with a unilateral mistake
- Understand how the concept of contractual intent may be applied to void contracts

CHAPTER OVERVIEW

The sixth, and final, requisite element of every valid contract is the contractual intent of the parties. For the contract to be enforceable, the parties to the agreement must intend to enter into a binding contractual relationship. Even if all of the other requirements are satisfied, if the parties do not objectively intend to contract, there is no binding agreement.

The intent of the parties relates back to the concept of mutual assent. If a person does not freely and voluntarily agree to the terms of a contract, regardless of how clear and specific those terms appear, there is no valid consent. Generally, the genuineness of a person's assent to a contract may be suspect in three situations: one, if the person is induced to enter the relationship by fraud; two, if the person is coerced or forced into agreeing to the terms of the contract; or three, if the parties are in some way mistaken about the terms of the agreement.

A contract is fraudulently entered into if the innocent party is purposely misled or lied to in order to induce his contractual promise. The law will not enforce a contract that is induced by fraud.

If the person is forced to agree to a contractual relationship, by threats of physical, emotional, or economic duress, the person obviously lacks voluntary contractual intent.

Finally, if the parties to the contract are mistaken as to the subject matter of the contract, no contract exists because there is no meeting of the minds. This is true even though the mistake is an innocent one. As long as the parties to the agreement do not contemplate the same subject matter, no contract can be formed.

Just as with the requirements of contractual capacity and legality of subject matter, this final requirement of intent concerns the circumstances surrounding the agreement, not the terms of the agreement itself. On its face, an agreement may appear to meet all of the formalities of contract law, but if the parties do not truly intend to contract, the agreement will fail.

Contractual Intent Defined

As introduced in Chapter 1, there must be a meeting of the minds before an agreement can be deemed an enforceable contract. The parties to the contract must actually intend to enter into a contract for the same bargain at the same time. If it can be demonstrated that a contract was not intended by one, or both, of the parties, no contract can exist because there is no mutual assent.

 EXAMPLE:

Susan and Jon have been friends since childhood. Susan has to turn in a book report for school tomorrow, and asks Jon to come to her house to help her. To induce his promise, Susan offers him $10,000 for his help, and Jon laughingly accepts. There is no contract. The parties did not intend a contractual relationship; as friends they were merely agreeing to help one another.

The example given above is a situation in which the parties are joking with each other, based on a long-standing relationship. The intent to contract is obviously missing. As in most cases when contractual intent is called into question, it is the circumstances surrounding the transaction that determine intent.

Generally, when determining the contractual intent of an agreement, there are three areas of possible concern: fraud, duress, and mistake. Each of these situations will be discussed below.

Fraud and Misrepresentation

In **fraud**, one party to an agreement tricks a second party into entering the agreement. Only if all five of the elements of fraud are shown will a contract fail. The five elements of contractual fraud are

1. the misrepresentation
2. of a material fact
3. made with the intent to deceive and
4. relied on by the other party
5. to his or her detriment.

If an agreement is induced by fraud, the innocent party has the option either to avoid the contract, because she lacked the requisite intent, or to fulfill the contract.

What, however, would be the result if the deception is innocent — that is, the person making the statements does not intend to deceive the other party? In this instance, there is no fraud, but there is a **misrepresentation.** If a material fact (a fact that goes to the heart of the transaction) is misrepresented, the injured party is entitled to the same relief she would be granted if she had been defrauded.

 EXAMPLES:

1. Paul is walking down the street when he sees a man selling watches. The man tells Paul the watches are Cartiers and offers to sell one to Paul for $50. Paul buys the watch, but two days later it breaks down. He brings the watch to a licensed Cartier dealer for repairs and discovers the watch is not a Cartier, but a cheap imitation. If Paul can ever find that man on the street again, he can get his money back. The contract was induced by fraud. The man lied about the subject matter to Paul to induce Paul's assent to the contract, and Paul was economically injured.

2. Lola is in the market for a Van Gogh painting. Charles is an art dealer selling a painting said to be a Van Gogh, although he has not bothered to check its origins. Charles sells the painting to Lola, who discovers that the painting is a forgery. This is an example of misrepresentation. Charles was negligent in not establishing the genuineness of the painting, but he did not intend to deceive Lola. There is no mistake, because the genuineness of the painting could have been checked had Charles not been careless. Lola can get her money back.

3. In a recent trial decision, a man sued his ex-wife for fraud. After many years of marriage, the wife admitted to the husband that she never loved him. After the divorce, the former husband sued the wife for fraud in the marriage contract and won. The wife purposely misled the husband by saying that she loved him in order to induce the marriage. This constitutes a fraud, because marriage is a contract. The detriment the husband suffered was the property the wife acquired from him during the marriage.

A contract that is induced by fraud or misrepresentation is **voidable** by the innocent party. This means that even though the innocent party was misled into entering the contract, if he wishes to complete the agreement, he may do so. The innocent party may also avoid the obligation because of the other party's fraudulent actions. Fraud and misrepresentation are determined by the facts of each individual situation.

Duress

Duress connotes some form of force or coercion exercised over one party to the contract in order to induce that party's promise to contract. Because the innocent party is forced to enter into the agreement, there is no contract. The party did not freely intend to contract.

Duress can take several forms. The most obvious example of duress would be **physical duress**. Physical duress occurs when one party forces the other to enter into the contract by threatening physical harm.

 EXAMPLE:

Bill holds a gun to Morris' head and tells him to sign a contract deeding over Blackacre to Bill for a stated price. There is no contract. Morris was forced to sign the contract at gun point, and so he did not freely intend to contract. Note that on its face the contract itself would appear to be valid; it is the surrounding circumstances that invalidate the agreement.

Another form of duress is **economic duress**, wherein, a person is induced to contract for fear of losing some monetary benefit. At the turn of the century, before unionism, this concept was exemplified by the saying, "If you don't come in Sunday, don't come in Monday." Workers were forced to work a seven-day week or lose their jobs. They did not agree to work seven days of their own free will but were forced to come in for fear of losing their livelihoods entirely. Any form of economic force used to induce agreement to a contract is economic duress.

 EXAMPLE:

Iris receives a letter from her state tax department stating that she has underpaid her taxes and ordering an audit of her returns. Under the state law, the tax department can only audit returns for the previous three years. When Iris goes to the audit, the agent tells her that if she doesn't sign a waiver to permit an audit of all of her previous returns he will order all of her assets frozen until a final determination of her tax liability is made. Iris agrees to the waiver. This is an example of economic duress, and the waiver is invalid.

A third type of duress is **mental duress**, wherein a person is coerced to enter into a contract by psychological threats. As with all forms of duress, the ability of a particular threat to induce a party to contract is determined on a case-by-case basis. It is the impact on the particular party that is conclusive of the duress.

One important factor that goes into this determination is the relationship of the threatening party to the innocent party. The greater the degree of psychological control the threatening person exercises, the more likely it is to be found that the contract was induced by mental duress. When the mental duress is exercised by someone who is in a close relationship with the innocent party, it is known as **undue influence**.

 EXAMPLES:

1. Maxwell is 92 years old and lives in a nursing home. The owner of the home convinces Maxwell to sign over all of his property to the home in consideration of all of the loving care the home gives him. This contract is invalid because it was induced by the undue influence the owner of the home exercised over Maxwell.

2. Mary and David are getting divorced. David convinces Mary to sign a joint custody agreement for their three children by threatening to take the children out of the country if she refuses. The contract is unenforceable. Mary was coerced into signing the agreement because of the fear of never seeing her children again. This is mental duress.

3. Hilda is 80 years old and frail. A real estate developer convinces her to sell her house by telling her that, because of her frail health, the state is going to take her house away and put her in a home. There is no contract. This is an example of both mental duress and fraud.

A type of contract known as a **contract of adhesion** also falls under the category of duress. A contract of adhesion is a contract in which one side has an unfair bargaining position, a position that is so unequal that the other party's assent is suspect. Even though no actual duress exists, because of the inequality of the parties the contract is called into question. These types of contracts are voidable by the innocent party because of the unconscionable aspect of the other side's bargaining position.

Generally, if a contract of adhesion can be shown, the party with the weaker bargaining position can avoid his obligation. The unequal bargaining position can come about because of lack of competition in the area, forceful salesmanship, or because the innocent party perceives the other person as having special knowledge or expertise and is relying on that person's greater experience.

 EXAMPLES:

1. Leo lives in a small town, and there is only one car dealership within a 100-mile radius. When Leo is talked into buying a car for several thousand dollars more than he wanted to spend, the contract may be deemed a contract of adhesion because, if Leo wants a car, he really has no other choice. The dealer is in an unfair bargaining position.

2. Sylvio, having put on a few pounds over the last several years, walks into a health club to inquire about joining. The club salesman, a powerfully built young man, walks Sylvio around the facility, takes him into his office, and tells him about a "special deal" only available for that day. If he signs up right now, he saves $300; if he doesn't sign immediately, he loses the opportunity. The salesman also tells Sylvio that he is not getting any younger, and the longer he waits the harder it will be to take off the weight. Sylvio signs up for a three-year membership and immediately regrets it. This is a contract of adhesion. Because of aggressive salesmanship, Sylvio was put in a position of signing an

agreement without having a chance to consider the possibilities. He can avoid this contract. Be aware that many states have special consumer protection laws specifically dealing with health club memberships because of the clubs' sales techniques.

3. Wanda, the wistful widow of Winnetka, wants to put more fun in her life, and so she signs up for dance lessons. Her instructor is young and handsome Raoul. After the initial ten sessions are over, Raoul convinces Wanda to sign up for the advanced course because of her great dance potential. Halfway through the advanced course, Wanda attends a community dance where all of her partners comment on how badly she dances. Wanda sues to get her money back from the dance school. Wanda will prevail. Because of his perceived expertise, Raoul was able to convince Wanda to spend money on dance lessons. This is a contract of adhesion.

When dealing with any form of duress or with contracts of adhesion, it is the perception of the party involved that determines intent. If, under the circumstances, the innocent party reasonably believed that she was threatened, no contract will exist, even if the fear seems unfounded. Also, a contract of adhesion may be enforceable if the injured party wishes to fulfill the contract. It is voidable or enforceable at the election of the innocent party.

Mistake

The third situation that brings into question the parties' intent to contract is **mistake**. Mistake occurs when one (or both) of the parties is under a misconception as to the subject matter of the contract. Mistake is distinguishable from contractual fraud in that, with mistake, there is no intent to deceive or misrepresent; the mistake is due to the honest and innocent belief of the parties.

Contractual mistakes are divided into two broad categories: **mutual mistake** and **unilateral mistake.** A mutual mistake concerns the underlying consideration of the contract itself.

 EXAMPLES:

1. Sheila and Kathleen enter into a contract for the sale of Sheila's summer house, but unknown to both parties, the house is destroyed by a hurricane. There is no contract because the basic assumption of the contract, that the house exists, is mistaken.

2. Edward agrees to lease some property to Eve so that Eve can operate a retail store at that location. Unknown to both Edward and Eve, the town council passes a zoning ordinance restricting the use of the area in question to residential use only. There is no contract. Both parties are mistaken with respect to a basic assumption underlying the agreement, that is, that the property could be used for commercial purposes. This is an example of mutual mistake.

A mutual mistake is a defense to contract formation if the mistake goes to a basic assumption of the agreement, the mistake has a material adverse effect on the parties, and the mistake was of the type that could not be foreseen.

A unilateral mistake usually concerns a situation in which only one party to the contract is mistaken because of some typewritten or computation error. In this instance, the contract may still be enforceable by the innocent party, the one who neither caused nor knew that there was in fact a mistake.

 EXAMPLE:

Arnold submits a contracting bid to Ace, Inc., for the construction of a warehouse. Arnold makes a mistake in computing his expenses, and the bid is $2000 lower than it should be. Ace accepts. There is a contract. This is an example of a unilateral mistake in which Ace, the innocent party, has no way of knowing that Arnold has miscalculated his bid, and so a valid contract exists. Note, however, that if Arnold's bid had itemized all his expenses and only the total was incorrect, there would be no contract at the low bid because Ace could see the mistake simply by doing the totals itself. Also, if Arnold realized his error before Ace accepted and he notified Ace, Ace could not accept the low bid because it would then be aware of the error.

A similarity exists between the concept of mistake and the concept of the ambiguity of the terms discussed in Chapter 2, Offer. There are circumstances in which the ambiguity of the language used by the parties can create mistaken impressions. In those instances, the law will go with the most reasonable and most legally fair interpretation of the parties' intent. Generally, ambiguities are held against the party who drafted the contract.

Take careful note of the fact that the concept of mistake does not concern itself with the risk of contracting, that is, the risk that one or both of the parties may not get the bargain for which he or she had hoped. As discussed previously in Chapter 4, Consideration, the law is not the insurer of every contractual agreement. It cannot and will not guarantee that every contract will be as economically beneficial as the parties had hoped. However, the law will guarantee that the parties do receive the object or service for which they bargained.

 EXAMPLES:

1. Sophie offers to sell Lindsay a blue stone she has in her possession for $100. Sophie thinks the stone is a blue quartz; Lindsay thinks the stone is a sapphire. Lindsay agrees to the contract. Later, Lindsay discovers the stone is a blue quartz, and wants her money back, claiming she was mistaken as to the object of the contract. The contract is valid. Because the parties only contracted for the sale of a "blue stone," the fact that a party was mistaken as to its value is irrelevant. She received exactly what she bargained for. Let the buyer beware!

2. Sophie offers to sell Lindsay a blue stone designated as a blue quartz she has in her possession for $100. Sophie and Lindsay both think the stone is a blue quartz. Lindsay agrees to the contract for the sale of a blue quartz. Later, Lindsay finds out the stone is a sapphire worth $10,000. The contract is not valid. Sophie sold a blue quartz, but Lindsay received a sapphire. In these circumstances, since the contract specified the blue quartz, the contract is not enforceable.

As indicated above, when dealing with a contractual mistake it is important to differentiate between a mutual mistake and a unilateral mistake. With a mutual mistake, both parties are intending different subject matter, and so no contract exists because there is no meeting of the minds. With a unilateral mistake, only one party to the contract is mistaken, and the contract can be enforced by the innocent party (the one who did not cause the error).

CHAPTER SUMMARY

For a contract to be deemed enforceable, it must be shown that both parties actually intended to enter into a contractual relationship. If it can be demonstrated that this requisite element of contractual intent is missing, then no contract is formed.

Just as with the legality of the subject matter and contractual capacity, the contractual intent is concerned with the circumstances surrounding the formation of the agreement, not the provisions of the agreement itself. Even if the contract meets all of the other five requirements to create a valid contract, if the intent to contract is lacking, there is no contract.

Contractual intent is a concept that is always determined by the facts and circumstances of each individual situation. If it can be shown that the particular party lacked contractual intent, even though such a situation would seem unreasonable, there is no contract.

There are three major legal concepts associated with intent: fraud, duress, and mistake. If a party to an agreement is defrauded into entering the agreement, no contract exists. If the party is coerced into entering the agreement, no contract exists. And finally, if the parties are mistaken as to the subject matter of the contract, no contract exists.

SYNOPSIS

No contract exists if the contract is induced by fraud, duress, or mistake
Fraud
1. A misrepresentation
2. of a material fact,
3. made with the intent to deceive and
4. relied on by the other party
5. to his or her detriment

Duress
1. Physical
2. Economic
3. Mental (undue influence)
4. Contracts of adhesion: Unfair bargaining position

Mistake
1. Mutual mistake: No contract
2. Unilateral mistake: May be enforced

Key Terms

Contract of adhesion: contract entered into where one party has an unfair bargaining position; voidable

Duress: force or coercion used to induce agreement to contract

Economic duress: threatening loss of economic benefit to induce a person to contract

Fraud: a misrepresentation of a material fact made with the intent to deceive; relied on by the other party to his or her detriment

Mental duress: psychological threats used to induce a person to contract

Misrepresentation: misstatement of a material fact relied on by the other party to his or her detriment; no intent to defraud

Mistake: misconception of the subject matter of a contract

Mutual mistake: misconception of the subject matter of a contract by both
    parties; unenforceable
Physical duress: threatening physical harm to force a person to contract
Undue influence: mental duress by a person in a close and particular rela-
    tionship to the innocent party
Unilateral mistake: misconception of the subject matter of a contract by only
    one party to the contract; may be enforceable
Voidable contract: a contract that one party may void at his option without
    being in breach of contract

EXERCISES

1. A salesman tells you that the diamond ring you want to purchase
    is "the best quality diamond he has in the entire store and, in fact,
    is the best diamond he has ever seen." After you buy the diamond
    you discover that the diamond is a very low grade. Have you been
    defrauded? Why?
2. Give two examples of contracts of adhesion not discussed in the
    chapter.
3. Explain the difference between a mutual mistake and ambiguity.
4. Explain the difference between misrepresentation and fraud.
5. Give an example of a contract induced by economic duress not
    discussed in the chapter.

Cases for Analysis

To highlight the concepts of undue influence, fraud, and contracts
of adhesion, the following case summaries are presented for analysis.
Lancaster v. Lancaster concerns duress and undue influence with respect
to a property settlement agreement, and LaFournaise v. Montana Developmental Center involves a collective bargaining agreement as a contract of
adhesion.

Lancaster v. Lancaster
138 N.C. App. 459, 530 S.E.2d 82 (2000)

Robert Lee Lancaster and Patricia Price Lancaster married in 1970
and their two children are now emancipated. During the marriage,
Ms. Lancaster worked outside the home for the first three years, then
she stayed home for several years to raise the children. During the
last five years of their marriage, Ms. Lancaster once again worked outside
of the home, earning about $215 each week. Mr. Lancaster earned

approximately $1,700 each week at the end of the marriage. Mr. Lancaster handled most of the family's finances and made most of the family decisions. He paid most of the family's expenses out of his salary and he provided Ms. Lancaster with a generous monthly allowance to be spent however she wished. As time went on, the couple argued often. On 17 May 1996, Ms. Lancaster moved out of the family home.

Shortly before Ms. Lancaster moved out, she and Mr. Lancaster visited an attorney — Page Dolley Morgan — to discuss entering into a separation agreement. At first Ms. Lancaster thought that Ms. Morgan would represent both of them, but Ms. Morgan informed her that while she could answer Ms. Lancaster's questions seeking information, she could only give legal advice to Mr. Lancaster. On one of her visits, Ms. Morgan's paralegal suggested that Ms. Lancaster get her own attorney. Ms. Lancaster declined to seek the advice of another attorney. Mr. Lancaster and Ms. Lancaster signed the separation agreement on 14 June 1996. It dictated the terms of their property settlement, alimony, and settled the date of separation as 16 June 1995.

On 15 January 1997, Mr. Lancaster filed a complaint seeking a divorce based on one year separation and seeking the incorporation of the separation agreement. Ms. Lancaster filed an answer and counterclaim in which she denied the date of separation alleged by Mr. Lancaster, denied the validity of the separation agreement, and requested an equitable distribution of the marital property and alimony. The district court entered a divorce judgment on 30 July 1997, holding all other issues until a later date.

On 11 February 1998, Ms. Lancaster obtained an order requiring Mr. Lancaster to respond to her discovery requests. Mr. Lancaster's attorney provided Ms. Lancaster with the requested information. The date of the trial was pushed back a number of times, with the hearing finally set for 5 October 1998. On 1 October 1998, Ms. Lancaster obtained an order requiring Mr. Lancaster to produce certain documents at the hearing. The district court struck that order the next day after determining that Mr. Lancaster had already furnished the requested information to Ms. Lancaster. The hearing occurred on 5 October and the trial court entered judgment on 18 November 1998, finding that the separation agreement was valid. Ms. Lancaster appealed to this Court.

I.

Ms. Lancaster first argues that the trial court erred in declaring the separation agreement and property settlement valid because the evidence showed the existence of a fiduciary relationship by Mr. Lancaster to Ms. Lancaster and showed unconscionability regarding the alimony and distribution terms of the agreement. We disagree.

To be valid, "a separation agreement must be untainted by fraud, must be in all respects fair, reasonable, and just, and must have been entered into without coercion or the exercise of undue influence, and with full knowledge of all the circumstances, conditions, and rights of the contracting parties." Harroff v. Harroff, 100 N.C. App. 686, 689, 398 S.E.2d 340, 342 (1990), *review denied*, 328 N.C. 330, 402 S.E.2d 833 (1991) (citation omitted). We may hold a separation agreement invalid if it is manifestly unfair to one because of the other's overreaching. See Stegall v. Stegall, 100 N.C. App. 398, 401, 397 S.E.2d 306, 307 (1990), *review denied*, 328 N.C. 274, 400 S.E.2d 461 (1991).

During a marriage, a husband and wife are in a confidential relationship. In this relationship, the parties have a duty to disclose all material facts to one other, and the failure to do so constitutes fraud. See Daughtry v. Daughtry, 128 N.C. App. 737, 740, 497 S.E.2d 105, 107 (1998). Further, a presumption of fraud arises where the fiduciary in a confidential relationship benefits in any way from the relationship. See Curl by and Through Curl v. Key, 64 N.C. App. 139, 142, 306 S.E.2d 818, 821 (1983), *rev'd on other grounds*, 311 N.C. 259, 316 S.E.2d 272 (1984). In such a case, the burden shifts to the fiduciary to show that the transaction was a voluntary act of the alleged victim. See id. Finally, even spouses not in a confidential relationship may not engage in unconscionable behavior when entering into a separation agreement. See King v. King, 114 N.C. App. 454, 457, 442 S.E.2d 154, 157 (1994). Unconscionability is both procedural — consisting of fraud, coercion, undue influence, misrepresentation, inadequate disclosure, duress, and overreaching; and substantive — consisting of contracts that are harsh, oppressive, and one-sided. See id. at 458, 442 S.E.2d at 157.

Ms. Lancaster argues that she and Mr. Lancaster had a confidential relationship at the time they entered into the separation agreement. Ms. Lancaster asserts that Mr. Lancaster stood in a fiduciary relationship to her, and he must be held to the stringent rules set forth above. However, while a husband and wife generally share a confidential relationship, this relationship ends when the parties become adversaries. See Avriett v. Avriett, 88 N.C. App. 506, 508, 363 S.E.2d 875, 877, *aff'd*, 322 N.C. 468, 368 S.E.2d 377 (1988). It is well established that when one party to a marriage hires an attorney to begin divorce proceedings, the confidential relationship is usually over, see id., although the mere involvement of an attorney does not automatically end the confidential relationship. See *Harroff*, 100 N.C. App. at 690, 398 S.E.2d at 343; Sidden v. Mailman, 137 N.C. App. 669, 529 S.E.2d 266, 2000 N.C. App. LEXIS 493, 2000 WL 517914 (N.C. App. 2000). Further, when one party moves out of the marital home, this too is evidence that the confidential relationship is over, although it is not controlling. See *Harroff; Sidden*.

Ms. Lancaster asserts that, although she and Mr. Lancaster were proceeding with a divorce and she had moved out of the family home, their confidential relationship continued. She bases this argument on the fact that she and Mr. Lancaster tried to work out the terms of the separation themselves, see *Harroff*, and because they consulted the same attorney for advice. She further asserts that because she did not seek her own counsel or advice from her family, but instead trusted Mr. Lancaster to treat her fairly, the confidential relationship continued.

However, the trial court found, and we agree, that the confidential relationship between Mr. Lancaster and Ms. Lancaster did not exist when the parties signed the separation agreement. The record shows that Ms. Morgan was Mr. Lancaster's attorney only, despite Ms. Lancaster's assertion that she *thought* Ms. Morgan represented both of them. First, Ms. Lancaster visited Ms. Morgan's office only two or three times, as compared to the numerous visits made by Mr. Lancaster. Second, the separation agreement explicitly states that Ms. Morgan is Mr. Lancaster's lawyer. Third, at the Lancasters' initial consultation, Ms. Morgan stated that she could answer Ms. Lancaster's questions seeking information, but could only give legal advice to Mr. Lancaster. Finally, Ms. Morgan's paralegal advised Ms. Lancaster to seek her own counsel before signing the separation agreement. Ms. Lancaster's refusal to seek her own counsel may not now be used as a means of alleging unconscionability. Indeed, the facts before us are quite similar to those in *Avriette*, in which we held that the use of an attorney by one party but not the other ended the confidential relationship.

Further, although working out the terms of a separation agreement themselves indicates that a divorcing couple is not adversarial but still in a confidential relationship, the record shows that the Lancasters did not amicably agree to all of the agreement's terms, but rather argued over such things as the amount of alimony. Moreover, Ms. Lancaster moved out the family home shortly after first meeting Ms. Morgan, but before signing the separation agreement. Her contention that she moved out because she feared Mr. Lancaster also indicates that the couple did not share a trusted and confidential relationship.

We distinguish the factually similar case of Sidden v. Mailman, supra, in which we found a fiduciary duty between a separating husband and wife. The evidence in the case at bar shows the end of a fiduciary duty between Mr. Lancaster and Ms. Lancaster based on the fact that the parties here were more clearly adversaries. Mr. Lancaster's attorney did more than merely formalize the terms of an amicable separation, but rather advised and assisted Mr. Lancaster alone. Also, Ms. Lancaster had left the family home out of fear of her husband. As further comparison, the wife in *Sidden* alleged a breach of fiduciary duty based on her husband's failure to disclose the existence of a $158,100 retirement account. In this case, Ms. Lancaster does not allege such a material breach, but rather argues only that the separation agreement was unfair.

Since no confidential relationship existed between the Lancasters, we now review the agreement as we would any other bargained-for exchange between parties who are presumably on equal footing. See Knight v. Knight, 76 N.C. App. 395, 398, 333 S.E.2d 331, 333 (1985). In determining the validity of a separation agreement, we are not required to make an independent determination as to whether the agreement is fair. Absent a showing of any wrongdoing by a party to the agreement, "we must assume that this arrangement was satisfying to both spouses at the time it was entered into." Hagler v. Hagler, 319 N.C. 287, 293, 354 S.E.2d 228, 234 (1987).

In this case, the trial court found, and we agree, that there was no evidence of fraud, duress, or undue influence by Mr. Lancaster on Ms. Lancaster to sign the agreement. Further, we do not find that the agreement was so inequitable as to be unconscionable. A separation agreement is not invalid merely because one party later decides that what she bargained for is not as good as she would have liked.

II.

Ms. Lancaster next argues that the trial court erred by failing to address issues raised by the pleadings of reformation of the separation agreement to conform with uncontroverted evidence of both parties. We disagree.

Ms. Lancaster alleges four different areas of contention: (1) She and Mr. Lancaster agreed that $18,000 of their savings account would be used to pay for their daughters' education; however, no provision was made for these funds in the separation agreement; (2) both parties agreed that Mr. Lancaster's retirement plans would be divided equally by a qualified domestic relations order; however, the parties disagree as to which separation date should be used and therefore, the amount of benefits to be divided; (3) the balance of the parties' saving and checking accounts, after deducting $20,000 of Mr. Lancaster's separate property and $18,000 for the daughters' education, would be split evenly; but apparently, it was not split evenly; and (4) the parties intended to divide their furniture equally but did not do so. Ms. Lancaster alleges that these "mutual mistakes" should be rectified by this Court, since the separation agreement did not reflect the true intentions of the parties.

It is well established that the existence of a mutual mistake as to a material fact comprising the essence of the agreement will provide grounds to rescind a contract. See Mullinax v. Fieldcrest Cannon, Inc., 100 N.C. App. 248, 251, 395 S.E.2d 160, 162 (1990). "A mutual mistake of fact is a mistake 'common to both parties and by reason of it each has done what neither intended.'" Swain v. C & N Evans Trucking Co., Inc., 126 N.C. App. 332, 335, 484 S.E.2d 845, 848 (1997) (citation omitted). Although Ms. Lancaster argues that the separation agreement contains "mutual mistakes," Mr. Lancaster offers no such argument, thereby negating the contention that the alleged mistakes were "mutual." Moreover, Ms. Lancaster's attempts to rescind or alter the contract are barred by the parol evidence rule, which forbids the admittance of evidence used to alter the written terms of a contract. The parol evidence rule provides that when parties have formally and explicitly expressed their contract in writing, that contract shall not be contradicted or changed by prior or contemporaneous oral agreements. See Gaylord v. Gaylord, 150 N.C. 222, 230, 63 S.E. 1028, 1032 (1909). Ms. Lancaster attempts to add or change four terms of the separation agreement by arguing that she and Mr. Lancaster really agreed to terms other than those expressly written in the agreement. However, the parol evidence rule bars that evidence.

III.

Ms. Lancaster next argues that the trial court erred by failing to address the issue of [rescission] of the separation agreement based on Mr. Lancaster's material breach thereof. We disagree.

Ms. Lancaster alleges that Mr. Lancaster breached the separation agreement by not revealing the full extent of his property as required by the agreement. Specifically, Ms. Lancaster alleges that Mr. Lancaster failed to disclose the fact that he belonged to his current employer Weyerhauser's retirement plan and the value of that plan, despite a court order requiring that he provide that specific information. She also argues that he failed to disclose to her that using an earlier separation date in the agreement could affect the value of her share of his retirement plans.

Rescission of a separation agreement requires a material breach of the agreement — a substantial failure to perform. See Cator v. Cator, 70 N.C. App. 719, 722, 321 S.E.2d 36, 38 (1984). Small lapses or inconsequential breaches are not substantial breaches requiring rescission.

Mr. Lancaster provided information about his former employer West-vaco's retirement plan, in which he was enrolled until summer 1995. Mr. Lancaster's retirement plan at Weyerhauser began in December 1995. The parties agreed to use 16 June 1995 as their date of separation. They also agreed to equally divide Mr. Lancaster's retirement property from the date of marriage until the date of separation set forth in the agreement. Although Mr. Lancaster did not disclose his enrollment in the Weyerhauser retirement plan, this nondisclosure did not affect the terms of the agreement, nor did it affect Ms. Lancaster's share of the property since Mr. Lancaster did not join this program until after their agreed-upon date of separation. We, therefore, conclude that Mr. Lancaster did not commit a material breach of the separation agreement.

IV.

We have reviewed Ms. Lancaster's remaining arguments and finding no error, we affirm the decision of the trial court to uphold the validity of the separation agreement.

Affirmed.

Questions

1. How does the marital relationship affect the court's determination of undue influence?
2. How does the concept of mutual mistake factor into this lawsuit?
3. Did the court find the agreement unconscionable? Discuss.

LaFournaise v. Montana Developmental Center
77 P.3d 202 (Mont. 2003)

Margery LaFournaise (LaFournaise) brought the underlying wrongful discharge action against her former employer, the Montana Developmental Center (MDC). MDC moved for summary judgment and the Fifth Judicial District Court, Jefferson County, granted MDC's motion and entered judgment. LaFournaise appeals and we affirm.

In November of 2000, MDC terminated LaFournaise's employment as a licensed practical nurse. LaFournaise filed a sex discrimination complaint with the Human Rights Bureau of the Montana Department of Labor and Industry and also filed a grievance through her union, the American Federation of State, County and Municipal Employees Local 971. The Human Rights Bureau later dismissed LaFournaise's complaint on the basis she had not offered sufficient evidence to give rise to an inference that unlawful discrimination had occurred. According to LaFournaise, the grievance process proceeded through several steps, after which her union representative told her the union would not proceed further and, if she wanted to continue to pursue the matter, she should file a complaint in court.

In November of 2001, LaFournaise filed a complaint in the District Court alleging that she was terminated from her employment at MDC based upon her sex and in retaliation for whistle-blowing. MDC moved for summary judgment on the basis that LaFournaise was a union member covered by a written collective bargaining agreement (CBA). It pointed out that, in Montana, the Wrongful Discharge From Employment Act (WDEA) — codified at §§39-2-901 through -915, MCA — generally provides the exclusive remedy for wrongful discharge, and argued that §39-2-912(2), MCA, precludes an employee covered by a CBA from seeking relief under the WDEA. In response, LaFournaise asserted that genuine issues of material fact existed regarding whether her discharge was wrongful. She filed an affidavit stating she was told by the union that she could sue MDC, but must do it on her own. She also waived her claim of sex discrimination.

At oral argument in the District Court on MDC's motion for summary judgment, LaFournaise advanced a new argument. She argued that, if she is precluded from bringing an action for wrongful discharge solely because her employment was subject to a CBA, then the WDEA unconstitutionally deprives her of her right of access to the courts. The District Court ordered additional briefing on that issue, and LaFournaise argued in her supplemental brief that arbitration had become unavailable and impractical. She filed an affidavit stating she had never been given a copy of any agreement between the union and the state providing that her right to go forward with arbitration or to sue her employer is dependent upon the will of the union.

After reviewing the briefs, the court granted MDC's motion for summary judgment, stating LaFournaise had failed to adequately support her arguments and had not refuted the cases which MDC cited. The court further determined that no evidence supported LaFournaise's arguments that the CBA — which is not of record — requires arbitration but that arbitration is unavailable or impractical. LaFournaise appeals.

A contract of adhesion is a contract with terms dictated by one contracting party to another party who has no voice in the contract's formulation. Contracts of adhesion are unenforceable if not within the reasonable expectations of the weaker party or if they are unduly oppressive, unconscionable, or against public policy. Kloss v. Edward D. Jones & Co., 2002 MT 129, P24, 310 Mont. 123, P24, 54 P.3d 1, P24 (citations omitted).

LaFournaise compares this case to Iwen v. U.S. West Direct, 1999 MT 63, 293 Mont. 512, 977 P.2d 989. In *Iwen*, we held that a standardized form agreement which U.S. West used to market its yellow page advertising was a contract of adhesion because Iwen was unable to negotiate the terms of the agreement and his only choice was to accept or reject it. *Iwen*, P29. We further held that the contract provision requiring arbitration was unconscionable and oppressive because the rights of the contracting parties were one-sided and unreasonably favorable to the drafter. *Iwen*, P32.

LaFournaise also contends this case is analogous to *Kloss*. In *Kloss*, a 95-year-old brokerage firm customer sued the firm and her broker, alleging violations of state securities statutes, negligence, unfair and deceptive business practices, breach of fiduciary obligations and fraud. The firm and broker defended on the basis that the customer had signed two agreements to submit any disputes to arbitration. The district court agreed with the defendants and issued an order compelling arbitration. The customer appealed. *Kloss*, P1. This Court held the arbitration provision, on a standardized form prepared by the firm and presented to the customer with no opportunity for negotiation, rendered the agreements contracts of adhesion which were unenforceable because the arbitration clauses were not within the customer's reasonable expectations. *Kloss*, PP27-28.

LaFournaise posits that when, as in this case, a union member employee is powerless to move the grievance process forward to arbitration, the provision in the contract mandating arbitration defies public policy because it cuts off the employee without a remedy. She argues that here, as in *Iwen* and *Kloss*, the contract is one of adhesion and is invalid.

There are several problems with LaFournaise's arguments. First, because the CBA is not of record, we cannot even ascertain what provisions it contains.

Moreover, assuming *arguendo* that LaFournaise correctly represents the terms of the contract, her reliance on *Iwen* and *Kloss* totally ignores the fact that the contract involved in this case is a collective bargaining agreement between her union and MDC. In Montana, public employees have the right to organize and join a labor organization, and to bargain collectively through representatives of their own choosing on matters relating to wages and other conditions of employment. See §39-31-201, MCA. Here, as noted above, LaFournaise is a member of the American Federation of State, County and Municipal Employees Local 971, and the union has a

CBA—covering its members—with MDC. Such collective bargaining agreements arise only after the public employer and the exclusive representative of the union have met their legal duties to bargain collectively and in good faith. See §39-31-305, MCA. Thus, under basic Montana labor law applicable to public employees, and in the total absence of evidence from LaFournaise to the contrary, no standardized form of agreement exists in this case and neither contracting party dictated the terms of the CBA to the other. Consequently, the requirements for a contract of adhesion set forth in *Kloss* and *Iwen* have not been met.

In addition, a court's determination of whether a contract is unconscionable or not within a contracting party's reasonable expectations is made only after an initial determination that the contract is a contract of adhesion. See *Iwen*, PP28, 30; *Kloss*, P24. Because LaFournaise has not presented evidence that the contract between her union and MDC is a contract of adhesion, we need not address whether the contract was unconscionable or within the contracting parties' reasonable expectations.

In *Circuit City*, a former electronics store employee appealed from a federal district court's order compelling arbitration of disputes concerning the employee's termination. The Ninth Circuit Court of Appeals ruled that, because there was no meaningful opt-out opportunity for the employee when he signed his employment contract including an arbitration provision, the arbitration agreement was procedurally unconscionable. *Circuit City*, 335 F.3d at 1107. Unlike the present case, no bargaining unit or collective bargaining agreement was involved; the employment contract was between the individual employee and the employer. See Circuit City, 335 F.3d at 1104. Therefore, the discussion of—and rationale concerning—the lack of an opt-out opportunity is inapplicable to the facts of LaFournaise's case.

LaFournaise also cites Cape-France Enterprises v. Estate of Peed, 2001 MT 139, 305 Mont. 513, 29 P.3d 1011, as authority that a party may be relieved of the provisions of a contract when adhering to the contract is impracticable. In that case, a buyer of real estate for subdividing rescinded the sales contract on the property after subdivision became impractical because it was suspected the groundwater under the property was contaminated. This Court affirmed a district court ruling that the contract could be rescinded on the basis of impracticability. *Cape-France*, PP12, 38. LaFournaise argues the same reasoning applies here: her obligation to go forward with arbitration was impracticable and any obligation should be discharged because of that impracticability.

Cape-France is not a contract of adhesion case and, for that reason, it does not support LaFournaise's contract of adhesion argument. Further, the contract declared impracticable in *Cape-France* was not a collective bargaining agreement; it was a contract for sale of real property.

We conclude the District Court did not err in granting MDC summary judgment in spite of LaFournaise's claim that the CBA is a contract of adhesion. . . .

Affirmed.

Questions

1. How does the court define a "contract of adhesion"?
2. What are the problems the court finds with respect to the employee's arguments?
3. Which portion of the collective bargaining agreement forms the basis of the lawsuit?

Suggested Case References

1. Contracting for the sale of leases that the seller knows, or has reason to know, have expired is not a mistake, but fraud. Read what the federal court sitting in Texas said in Matter of Topco, 894 F.2d 727, *reh'g denied*, 902 F.2d 955 (5th Cir. 1990).

2. A manufacturer attempts to avoid its collective bargaining agreement with a union. Under the contract, the manufacturer agreed to offer its employees the same insurance plan the employees had with a separate manufacturer, a copy of which was shown to the company. The company now asserts it was mistaken with respect to the clauses of the insurance plan. Is this a mistake permitting avoidance of the contract? Read what the federal court sitting in California had to say in Libby, McNeil & Libby v. United Steelworkers, 809 F.2d 1432 (9th Cir. 1987).

3. Even if both parties to a contract are mistaken as to the value or usefulness of the goods sold, as long as the goods are properly identified, the mistake does not invalidate the contract because it only pertains to the value of the subject matter. Fernandez v. Western Ash Builders, Inc., 112 Idaho App. 907, 736 P.2d 1361 (1987).

4. If a party seeks to avoid a contract induced by duress, must he return the consideration he has received pursuant to that agreement? Read Solomon v. FloWARR Management, Inc., 777 S.W.2d 701 (Tenn. App. 1989).

5. To read what the Delaware court says about the effects of disclaimers see Alabi v. DHL Airways, Inc., 583 A.2d 1358 (Del. Super. 1990).

Contract Provisions

Learning Objectives

After studying this chapter you will be able to:

- Distinguish between a covenant and a condition
- List the most generally encountered contractual rules of construction
- Apply general contract rules of construction to analysis of contract provisions
- List the types of contracts that are governed by the Statute of Frauds
- Define an antenuptial agreement
- Categorize conditions by when they create or extinguish a contractual duty
- Categorize conditions by the method whereby they have been created
- Define a condition subsequent, a condition precedent, and a condition concurrent
- Explain the parol evidence rule
- Analyze contractual clauses to determine the parties' rights and obligations

CHAPTER OVERVIEW

The preceding six chapters have discussed the general law of contracts that must be kept in mind when analyzing the validity of a contractual agreement. The time has now come to look at the actual provisions of a contract itself.

As indicated in the first chapter, contracts may be valid whether or not they are in writing. However, there is a small group of contracts that the law mandates must be in writing to be enforceable. This requirement exists for agreements that are described in the Statute of Frauds. However, regardless of the form, written or oral, all contract terms are given similar weight and interpretation.

Contracts are composed of various clauses, or paragraphs, that indicate the promises each party has made to the other. These specific promises form the consideration of the contract and are the parties' contractual obligations. Once there has been a meeting of the minds over the subject matter, these promises form the basis of the parties' enforceable rights. Such provisions are known as **covenants**.

The mere promise to perform is not totally indicative of the moment that the promise becomes enforceable in a court of law. Incident to every covenant is an element of timing: at what point is the promisor obligated to perform, and at what point does the promisee have an enforceable right? Although many everyday contracts lack this timing element, since the promise and the performance occur simultaneously, many contractual situations exist in which the contractual obligation is conditioned on some event that is not a specific part of the contract itself. This timing element, which forms its own clause in the contract, is known as a **condition**. A condition specifies the moment at which the covenant becomes legally enforceable.

Consequently, when analyzing any contract, these two separate elements must be specifically determined: one, what has been promised in the contract; and two, at what point does that promise become enforceable in a court of law. If a disputed provision winds up in court, the court has adopted several rules or guidelines to interpret and prove contract provisions. These guidelines are called **rules of construction** and will be discussed below.

The Statute of Frauds

The law generally makes no distinction between contracts that are written and contracts that are oral; each is given legal validity. The primary distinction between them deals not with contract law, but with the law of evidence. It is simply easier to demonstrate a contractual promise if the trier of fact can read the contract itself. If the terms of the contract have to be proven by oral testimony, there can be a conflict between what the parties to the agreement remember about the terms, and so an extra burden is placed on the trier of fact. Before he can determine what the parties' contractual rights are, he must first determine what the contract says.

Despite the preceding, the overwhelming majority of contracts entered into on a daily basis are either oral or implied, not written. Buying a newspaper, taking a bus, buying a cup of coffee, or purchasing clothing are usually effectuated without any written agreement. At most, a person might receive a receipt, which merely memorializes the transaction without meeting any of the requirements of a written contract. However, for historical reasons that will be discussed below, there are six situations in which the law has determined that, to be enforceable, the agreement must be in writing.

The law that requires certain contracts to be in writing is known as the **Statute of Frauds**. Every state has adopted a version of the Statute of Frauds, either legislatively or judicially. The origin of the Statute of Frauds lies in feudal England and is worth some mention.

In feudal times, travel and communication were extremely difficult, and the life expectancy of most people was very short. The major contractual relationships of the day dealt with land ownership and land rights. Consequently, to protect persons over geographic and time spans, the Statute of Frauds was enacted. The Statute of Frauds provided some assurance that the contract in question did in fact exist. The "fraud" in the Statute of Frauds was not the contractual concept of fraud discussed previously, but concerned preventing perjury and fraud with respect to proving contractual clauses. The Statute of Frauds required that, to be enforceable, the following six types of contracts had to be in writing:

1. contracts for an interest in real estate;
2. contracts in consideration of marriage;
3. contracts that are not to be performed within one year;
4. guarantees;
5. contracts for the sale of goods valued over a specified amount; and
6. executor's promises to pay a decedent's debts.

Contracts for an Interest in Real Estate

Because the entire concept of a feudal society was based on land ownerships, the Statute of Frauds required that any contract for an interest in real estate be in writing. In medieval times, requiring that deeds be in writing assured persons that ownership could be specifically traced without recourse to faulty memories. Also, contractual terms could be proved even if persons involved in the agreement had died and therefore could not testify about the contract. Land rights were too important to be left to such vagaries, and consequently the statute was enacted.

This provision is still in force today. To be enforceable, every contract for an interest in real estate must be in writing. Contracts for the sale of land are also permanently recorded in governmental offices in the county where the property is located. This insures that the title to the property can be traced and determined.

EXAMPLE:

Joseph agrees to sell the house he inherited in Florida to Mindy. They enter into a written contract for the sale of the house. When each side has performed under the contract — Mindy paying for the house and Joseph conveying the deed — the sale is recorded in the county Recorder's Office in the county where the house is located so that title to the property will read from Joseph to Mindy by contract of sale.

This provision of the Statute of Frauds is only concerned with the land itself. Anything that may be considered the "fruits of the land" (crops, minerals, and so on) are not within the provisions of the statute. Contracts for the sale of crops may be enforceable even if they are oral.

EXAMPLES:

1. Gary agrees to buy all of the potatoes Bob grows on this farm this year for a set price per pound. The agreement between Gary and Bob is not in writing. The contract is enforceable because the subject matter of the agreement is crops, not the land itself. The Statute of Frauds does not apply.

2. The Greens have just bought a house next to the Richards. To get to the nearest shopping center, it is most convenient for the Greens to pass over a portion of the Richards' property. The Richards orally agree to assign this right over their property (called an *easement*) to the Greens for a nominal fee. This agreement may not be enforceable. An easement deals directly with an interest in the land and so comes within the Statute of Frauds. Generally, easements must be in writing.

The determining factor of whether the contract must be in writing is whether the agreement directly concerns the land itself or whether it concerns something that can be removed from the land. If the latter, it is not within the Statute of Frauds.

Contracts in Consideration of Marriage

In feudal times, marriage was more a matter of property transfer than of love and affection. The medieval husband was entitled to a dowry from his intended wife's family, and the law required this dowry to be written down. If the wife's family did not deliver the goods specified in the contract, the groom could sue to have the property transferred or, in certain countries, could return the wife.

Although nowadays dowries are exceedingly rare in the United States, the concept that any promise given in consideration of marriage must be in writing still exists. This usually takes the form of an **antenuptial**, or **prenuptial, agreement**. An antenuptial agreement is a contract between the intended bride and groom specifying each one's property rights in case of death or divorce. It is not unusual for wealthy, well-known persons to have prenuptial agreements, but even persons who are neither wealthy nor famous enter into such contracts.

 EXAMPLES:

1. Gussie and Izzy are about to be married. The bride and groom are each in their 70s, it is a second marriage for both of them, and they each have children and grandchildren. Gussie wants to make sure that the money she inherited from her late husband goes to her children on her death, and Izzy feels the same way about his money and family. Consequently, they draw up a written prenuptial agreement specifying that each relinquishes claims to the other's estate in case of death or divorce. The agreement is valid and enforceable. The consideration is the impending marriage.

2. Hedda has agreed to marry Osbert, the unattractive son of a wealthy industrialist. To induce Hedda's promise, Osbert's father has promised to give $100,000 to her after the ceremony. Hedda gets this promise in writing and, after the ceremony, places the written agreement before her father-in-law. This agreement is enforceable, and he must now give Hedda the cash.

Do not get confused between contracts in consideration of marriage and what has become known as **palimony**. Palimony is an invented term used to enforce promises made between persons who are not legally married at the time of their break-up. The theory of law used to enforce these agreements is a contractual one, but it is specifically not based on a promise in consideration of marriage.

Contracts Not to Be Performed Within One Year

In feudal times, human life expectancies were so short that it could not be guaranteed that parties to a contract, or people who knew of the contract, would live long enough to testify about its provisions should a problem arise. Therefore, if the contract in question contemplated that the performance would take more than one year, it was required that the contract be in writing so that its provisions could be analyzed should there be a breach.

Today, this provision of the Statute of Frauds still exists. However, be aware that even though the statute requires the contract to be in writing, if the parties actually perform or make a substantial beginning on the performance, those actions will make the contract enforceable under equitable concepts previously discussed. Also note that for determining the applicability of the statute, the period starts from the day of the agreement, not the date on which the performance is to start.

EXAMPLES:

1. Maud agrees to buy Stacey's mink coat, which she's always admired. However, Stacey is asking $1500, and Maud doesn't have that much cash on hand. Maud and Stacey enter into an agreement whereby Maud agrees to pay Stacey $100 per month until the coat is paid for. To be valid, the contract must be in writing because the performance will take more than one year.

2. Mark agrees to work as a paralegal on a temporary basis for the firm of Blacke & Blewe, P.C. on February 1. The job that Mark is assigned to do will take eight months and is to start on September 1. This contract does have to be in writing because performance will not be completed in less than one year or the date on which the agreement was made.

3. Kenny agrees to buy Jose's car for $1800. They orally agree on a payment schedule whereby Kenny pays Jose $100 per month until the car is paid for, at which point Jose will transfer the registration. After Kenny makes five payments, Jose changes his mind and tells Kenny the deal is off. Because they have no written agreement, Jose claims there is no contractual obligation. Kenny sues. In court, because Kenny has already made a substantial performance, the contract would most likely be upheld because to do otherwise would be unfair to Kenny.

This provision of the Statute of Frauds is concerned with situations in which it is impossible for the performance to be completed within just one year. If, under *any* conceivable circumstance, the performance could be completed within 12 months, the contract does not come within the statute.

Additionally, if the performance is conditioned on some future uncertain event (say, for example, a life expectancy), the contract does not fall within the statute. Because any uncertain event *may* occur in less than one year, the statute does not apply. The statute will apply if the performance of only one party to the contract will take more than one year.

EXAMPLE:

Arthur is terminally ill, and Danielle agrees to nurse him for a specified salary as long as he lives. This contract is not within the Statute of Frauds. Arthur could live one month or ten years. Because life expectancy is uncertain, performance of the contract could be performed within one year.

Guarantees

As discussed in an earlier chapter, a **guarantee** is a promise to answer for the debts of another. A guarantee is also a type of formal contract. The concept of a guarantee comes from the Statute of Frauds. Because there is, in fact, no consideration for this promise, it must be in writing to be enforceable. This provision of the statute is still in force today.

Contracts for the Sale of Goods

Historically, contracts for the sale of goods valued above a specified amount (the amount has increased over the years) had to be in writing to be enforceable. The concept evolved from the idea that personal property was not as valuable as real property until a certain value was reached. At that monetary point, the property became sufficiently important for the law to require a writing to protect parties.

Today, this provision of the Statute of Frauds has been absorbed by the **Uniform Commercial Code (UCC)** for most commercial contracts. The UCC, a version of which has been adopted in every jurisdiction, provides that any contract for the sale of goods valued at over $500 must be in writing to be enforceable. The UCC will be fully discussed in Chapter 8; for the moment simply realize that this type of contract is now governed by the UCC, not the Statute of Frauds.

Executor's Promise to Pay Decedent's Debts

Under the Statute of Frauds, an executor's agreement to pay the debts of the deceased out of the executor's own pocket must be in writing. This provision evolved in a manner similar to that of guarantees, and the same theories hold true for both.

This section of the Statute of Frauds concerns estate administration, not contracts, and is most appropriately discussed in a work dealing with that area of law. It is noted here only to complete our discussion of the Statute of Frauds.

What the Statute of Frauds Is Not

Bear in mind that the Statute of Frauds is concerned with the *enforceability* of a contractual agreement, not with the *validity of its terms*. The validity of any contract is determined by its meeting the six requirements mentioned in the earlier chapters. Enforceability is concerned with whether the contract can be given force in a court of competent jurisdiction.

Nor does the Statute of Frauds change the interpretation of the contract clauses. It merely places an additional requirement on the formation of those clauses for certain categories of contracts — the requirement that those contracts be in writing. Aside from that one point, the interpretation given to the clauses is identical, whether written or oral. The clauses will represent either the enforceable promises of the parties or the timing element with respect to when those promises must be performed.

Regardless of the statute, if the parties have performed or made a substantial beginning on the performance, the contract is taken out of the statute. Also, if the entire contract is not in writing but the parties have made a written memorandum that sufficiently details the provisions of their agreement, that memo will take the contract out of the statute. (Note that a memo will not be sufficient if the contract is for an interest in realty; that must still be a complete written contract.)

Covenants

A **covenant** is defined as an unconditional, absolute promise to perform. It is the contractual promise to which no conditions are attached. If a party fails to fulfill his contractual covenant, it is deemed to be a breach, or violation, of the entire contract per se (in and of itself).

What is an unconditional, absolute promise to perform? It is consideration that the party has promised to give to induce the other side's promise. It is the promise to convey the textbook in a contract for the sale of a book; it is the promise to perform paralegal duties in an employment contract; it is the promise to pay for a mink coat in a sales contract. If a person fails to perform on her covenant, the contract is breached, and she can be sued. Furthermore, the other party is relieved of all other performance promised under the contract.

 EXAMPLE:

Suzanne agrees to work as a paralegal for the firm of White & Lace, P.C. The agreed-on salary is $300 per week, payable every two weeks. At the end of her first two weeks, Suzanne expects a paycheck. When the firm's partner apologizes and says the firm cannot afford to pay her, the firm has breached the contract. Suzanne is no longer obligated to work for the firm, and she can sue them for back wages. In this contract, Suzanne's covenant is to perform paralegal services, and the firm's covenant is to pay Suzanne a salary of $300 per week.

Not every clause in a contract is considered to be a covenant. The covenants are only the specific contractual promises. Consequently, if there are any terms that a party wants to make determinative of contractual rights, they should be phrased as unconditional promises and thus as covenants. Any clause that would otherwise be a condition can be made a covenant by the intent and wording of the parties.

Conditions

The covenant is the specific promise made by the parties to the contract. It is the basis of the contractual agreement. However, as incident to every contractual covenant, the parties must come to some agreement with respect to when the promises are to be performed. This timing element for performance of the covenant is known as a condition.

A **condition** is a fact or event, the happening or nonhappening of which creates or extinguishes an absolute duty to perform. Simply stated, the covenant is what must be performed, and the condition indicates when it is to be performed. In the example given above, with the paralegal Suzanne and the law firm, the covenants were the promises to perform paralegal duties and to pay a salary; the condition was Suzanne's performing for two weeks *before* the firm was to pay her. In other words, Suzanne's performance created the timing element of the contract. If she didn't perform, the law firm would not be obligated to pay her. Conversely, once she had performed for two weeks, the condition or timing element of the contract had been met, and the firm was obligated to pay. Any words modifying a provision contingent on an uncertain event create a condition.

How do you know that a particular contract contains conditions as well as covenants? The answer lies in what the parties themselves have either specifically agreed to, what can be inferred from their actions, or what has been imposed by the law.

Conditions are categorized by *when* they create, or extinguish, the duty to perform the covenant. There are three such categories of conditions:

1. conditions precedent;
2. conditions subsequent; and
3. conditions concurrent.

Conditions are categorized not only by their timing element, as indicated above, but also by *how* the parties have arrived at them.

Once again, there are three categories to indicate how the conditions were created:

1. express conditions;
2. implied-in-fact conditions; and
3. implied-in-law conditions.

Each of the six categories of covenants is examined more carefully below.

Conditions Precedent

A **condition precedent** is a condition that must occur before the contractual promise becomes operative and enforceable. The example above, of Suzanne and the law firm, is an example of a condition precedent: Suzanne must perform for two weeks *before* the firm becomes obligated. If Suzanne decides not to work for the firm, the firm is under no contractual obligation.

 EXAMPLE:

Karen and Bertram enter into a contract for the sale of Bertram's house. Bertram promises to sell, and Karen promises to buy, the house for $95,000. However, Karen inserts a clause in the contract conditioning the sale on her ability to arrange financing within 30 days of the date of signing the agreement. This is a condition precedent. For the parties to be contractually obligated, Karen must arrange financing. The financing is an external event that gives rise to her enforceable promise to purchase. Should she not be able to arrange financing, the contract for the sale of the house would not come into existence.

Conditions Subsequent

A **condition subsequent** is a condition that extinguishes a previous absolute duty to perform. This type of condition relieves the parties of their contractual obligations without being in breach of contract.

 EXAMPLES:

1. Helen buys a blouse on credit at Macy's. When she gets home she decides she doesn't like the blouse, and the next day she goes back to Macy's to return it. Macy's has a return policy that says if an item is returned within seven days of the purchase, with all tags

and receipts attached, Macy's will accept the return. Helen has met all of the store's conditions, and the store credits her charge account. This is an example of a condition subsequent. At the time of purchase Macy's was obligated to give Helen the blouse, and Helen was obligated to pay for it. Because of Macy's return policy, Helen has the option of returning the blouse for a full refund; in other words, her returning the item extinguishes her previous duty to pay for the blouse.

2. Dorothy and Jack are getting divorced. As part of the divorce settlement, they agree to alimony payments for Dorothy. The alimony payments are to be paid monthly until Dorothy or Jack dies, or Dorothy remarries. Dorothy's remarriage is an example of a condition subsequent. Jack is obligated to make these payments until the condition (Dorothy's remarriage) extinguishes his absolute duty to perform.

Conditions Concurrent

A **condition concurrent** is the most typical type of condition encountered in everyday contracts. A condition concurrent occurs when the mutual performances of the parties are capable of simultaneous execution, and the parties expect the promise and the performance to occur at the same time. Most contracts are formed and executed at the same time.

 EXAMPLES:

1. Hazel agrees to sell, and Olivia agrees to buy, Hazel's textbook for $10. When Olivia gives the money she expects to receive the book; when Hazel gives the book she expects to receive the money. This is an example of a condition concurrent.

2. Raymond goes to his neighborhood grocery store to buy his weekly food supplies. At the checkout counter, Raymond pays for the goods as the checker bags and gives him the items. Once again, the promise and the performance occur simultaneously.

Express Conditions

An **express condition** is a condition that has been specifically manifested in so many words by the parties themselves. This manifestation can either be written or oral, depending on the nature of the contractual agreement.

EXAMPLE:

Leah agrees to purchase Phyllis' used car for $900; however, Phyllis still has $200 outstanding on the loan she took out when she first bought the car. The parties condition the sale on Phyllis' paying off the loan before the sale goes through so that Leah won't have to worry about a problem of title to the automobile. This is an example of an express condition, specifically agreed to by the parties. It is also a condition precedent, because the contract for the sale will not obligate the parties until and unless the prior loan is paid off.

Implied-in-Fact Conditions

An **implied-in-fact condition** comes about out of necessity; it is what the parties would, in good faith, expect from each other. As contrasted with an express condition, in which the parties have specifically manifested some timing element, an implied-in-fact condition comes about because of what the parties could reasonably expect under the circumstances; no words are used at all.

 EXAMPLE:

Felix agrees in writing to buy Oscar's house for a certain sum of money. Although nothing is specifically stated, it is reasonable that Felix would assume that Oscar has a transferable title to the house. Although this is not specifically stated by the parties, it is implied in the transaction and, consequently, is deemed an implied-in-fact condition. If Oscar does not have a transferable interest, there is no contractual obligation on Felix's part to buy the house.

Implied-in-Law Conditions

An **implied-in-law condition**, also known as a **constructive condition**, is a condition that the law imposes in the interest of fairness. This category of conditions arises in situations where the parties have not specifically agreed to any definite time element. Its purpose is to give each party to the agreement the same amount of time in which to perform. There are three general rules with respect to constructive conditions.

1. When one party's performance requires time to complete, the other side may take the same amount of time.
2. When a date is set for one party's performance, the other party is expected to perform on that date as well.

3. When the performances can be simultaneous, they will be simultaneous.

As can be seen, implied-in-law conditions impose an element of fairness with respect to the timing of the performances. Of course, the parties themselves are totally free to establish any particular conditions they wish, but if none are expressed or implied in fact, the law gives each side an equivalent amount of time to perform.

Court Doctrines: Rules of Construction and the Parol Evidence Rule

The courts have fashioned several principles to assist them in interpreting and enforcing contract provisions. These rules should always be kept in mind when drafting contracts. Knowing how the court will interpret clauses and what kind of evidence will be permitted to prove clauses is critical for the practitioner in drafting these provisions.

Rules of construction are the guidelines that the courts use to interpret all contractual provisions. The rules of construction attempt, if possible, to uphold contracts as valid and to give proper interpretation to the presumptive intent of the contracting parties. There are four primary rules of construction with respect to analyzing the validity of contractual provisions.

1. *Lengthy communications are viewed as a whole, and any inconsistent words are discarded.* Many contracts form only after a lengthy negotiation process. In the course of this extended negotiation period, the parties may create inconsistent clauses. Because the prime objective of the court is to salvage the contract, the court will examine the entire negotiation and discard any provisions that are inconsistent with the existence of a valid contract.

2. *Contracts are to be interpreted according to business custom and usage.* People in business or business situations contract with certain expectations based on the nature, history, and customs of a particular industry. The court refers to industrywide standards, as well as to the history between the parties, in interpreting the meanings of a contract's provisions.

3. *Words are to be construed according to their ordinary meaning.* Unless the parties stipulate otherwise, the words used in an offer or completed contract are given their ordinary dictionary interpretation. However, the parties are always free to define any words they wish to in the contract itself, and the parties' specific definition will prevail. Consequently, in drafting a contract, it is essential to define specifically any words to which the parties want to give a specialized meaning or that may create definitional problems at a later time.

4. *If there is an inconsistency with words that are printed, typed, or handwritten, handwriting prevails over typing, and typing prevails over mechanical*

printing. The purpose behind this rule of construction is to ascertain the exact intent of the parties at the moment of signing the contract. Handwriting presumably would be done at the last moment, and therefore it most clearly reflects the intent at the time of contracting. Typing may be inserted on a preprinted form to make changes or insertions and so, again, indicates intent close to the moment of contracting.

All of these rules exist to help uphold existing contracts, but be careful not to convolute the rules and argue for the existence of a contract where one does not legally exist. These rules are intended to facilitate interpretation, not creation, of contractual clauses.

Another principle adopted by the courts deals with written contracts and how disputes over the terms of those contracts are to be handled. The **parol evidence rule** was created to prevent parties from attempting to change the provisions of a written agreement by offering oral evidence to dispute the terms of a contract. The basic rule states that once a contract is reduced to writing, the writing itself prevails. Oral testimony will not be admitted to vary the terms of a written instrument. It is assumed that the writing will speak for itself.

There are four exceptions to the parol evidence rule that permit a court to accept oral testimony in interpreting a written contract. Although these four instances are called "exceptions" to the Rule, in fact they are not. Exceptions would indicate instances in which oral testimony is permitted to vary the written terms. In the following instances, the oral evidence is not being used to vary the terms of the writing but to show something outside the writing that changes the meaning of the contract.

The first exception involves showing a failure of consideration. Here the contract provision is not being questioned, but the fact that the consideration was not what was promised in the writing.

EXAMPLE:

A contract says that the buyer paid for the object of the sale by check. Oral testimony shows that the check bounced. Note that the written contract provision isn't being changed at all. It is the failed consideration that the oral testimony addresses.

The second exception permits a party to show that the contract was induced by fraud, duress, or mistake, and therefore the party to the contract lacked the requisite intent to enter into the contractual relationship. If the intent is there, the contract as written will still stand unquestioned.

EXAMPLE:

Lee holds a gun to Ingrid's head and tells her to sign a contract for the sale of her house. Ingrid's testimony is not used to change the written provision, but to show that she was forced to sign the contract and lacked the intent to contract.

The third exception permits oral testimony to prove the existence of a collateral oral agreement. Again, the written contract isn't being questioned, but the existence of a second, oral contract is being proved. The purpose of this exception is to permit *both* contracts to be considered.

 EXAMPLE:

Connie has a written contract with Bill to sell him her gold bracelet for $100. After the contract is signed, Connie agrees to sell Bill her gold ring as well for a price of $150 for both pieces of jewelry. Oral testimony may be used to show the existence of both these contracts.

Finally, the fourth exception to the parol evidence rule permits oral testimony to explain ambiguities in a written contract. A writing on its face may appear unambiguous, but there may in fact be ambiguities. Consider the offer mentioned about the sale of a house in Los Angeles. On the face of the writing it would appear to indicate only one house, but in fact two could fit the description given. Oral testimony can be used to show this ambiguity.

The preceding rules are rules of the court. They are used when problems arise between the parties to a questionable contract, but they should always be kept in mind when drafting offers and contracts. Knowing how the court will most probably interpret clauses and prove their intent suggests how these clauses should be created.

SAMPLE CLAUSES

$\boxed{1}$

In an antenuptial agreement:

All monies or property hereinafter acquired by the above-mentioned parties, or either of them, shall be held in joint or equal ownership.

In the case of the death of one of the above-mentioned parties, all of said property shall, subject to the claims of creditors, vest absolutely in the survivor.

The above two clauses are examples of covenants. Each of the parties has specifically promised that all property acquired during the marriage shall be owned equally and shall go to the survivor upon the death of the other. In this case, the consequence of death is not a condition but is made part of the covenant to which the parties have agreed.

$\boxed{2}$

In a construction contract:

Said building shall be completed according to all of the above-mentioned specification by _____, 20 _____, time is of the essence.

In this instance, the date of completion of performance has been made a specific covenant of the contract. It is not merely a condition. How? By the insertion of the term **time is of the essence**. The term "time is of the essence" makes a covenant of a timing element. Whenever there is a specific need that performance be completed by a certain date, these words should be inserted so as to give the parties greater protection. See Chapters 10 and 11.

$\boxed{3}$

In a promissory note:

Thirty (30) days after the date of this instrument I hereby promise to pay to the order of _____ the sum of Five Hundred Dollars ($500), in consideration of value received.

This **promissory note** is an example of both a covenant and a condition. The covenant is to repay the loan of $500. The condition is the timing element: 30 days after the date of the note. The promise to perform is only absolute at the end of the 30-day period.

CHAPTER SUMMARY

Contracts are deemed to be valid regardless of whether they are in writing or come about by the oral representations of the parties, provided that they meet the six requirements of all contractual agreements. The only exception to this general statement comes under the Statute of Frauds. The Statute of Frauds states that certain types of contracts, to be enforceable, must be in writing. However, even if the contract should be in writing because of the statute, if the parties actually perform their oral agreement, that performance may make the contract enforceable in a court of law. In other words, the Statute of Frauds generally makes contracts voidable, not necessarily void.

Regardless of how the contract comes into existence, all contractual provisions are classified either as covenants or conditions. A covenant is an absolute, unconditional promise to perform. It is the basis of the contractual agreement, and a party's failure to perform a covenant is deemed to be a breach of contract.

On the other hand, a condition is the timing element of the contract. A condition specifies when, if ever, the parties must perform. With conditions precedent, if the condition does not happen, no covenant comes into existence. With conditions subsequent, when the conditional event occurs, the parties are no longer obligated to perform. With conditions concurrent, the promise and the performance of the contract occur simultaneously.

Conditions are created either by the express words of the parties, by implication of what would be reasonable under the particular circumstances, or are imposed by law in the interest of fairness.

If possible, the court attempts to uphold contracts. To this end the court has established certain guidelines, referred to as rules of construction. It uses these rules to interpret contractual clauses. The four main rules of construction with respect to contracts state: (1) lengthy communications are viewed as a whole, and inconsistent words are discarded; (2) contracts are to be interpreted according to business use and custom; (3) words are construed according to their ordinary meanings; and (4) handwritten words prevail over typewritten ones, and typewritten words prevail over printed ones in construing the final terms of a contract.

In addition to the rules of construction, the court has adopted the parol evidence rule, which states that oral testimony cannot be used to vary the terms of a writing. The written offer, or contract, must stand or fall on its own.

SYNOPSIS

Statute of Frauds: Requires certain types of contracts to be in writing
1. Contracts for an interest in realty
2. Contracts in consideration of marriage
3. Contracts not to be performed within one year
4. Guarantees
5. Contracts for the sale of goods over $500 (UCC)
6. Executor's promise to pay a decedent's debts

Contractual clauses
1. Covenant: Unconditional promise to perform
2. Condition
    a. Timing element
        i. Precedent
        ii. Subsequent
        iii. Concurrent
    b. Created
        i. Express
        ii. Implied in fact
        iii. Implied in law

Court doctrines
   1. Rules of construction
   2. Parol evidence rule

Key Terms

Antenuptial agreement: contract entered into prior to marriage determining
      parties' rights on dissolution of the marriage; must be in writing
Condition: fact or event, the happening or nonhappening of which creates or
      extinguishes an absolute duty to perform
Condition concurrent: promise to perform and performance occur simul-
      taneously
Condition precedent: fact or event that must occur before an absolute duty
      to perform is created
Condition subsequent: fact or event that extinguishes an absolute duty to
      perform; no breach of contract
Constructive condition: same as implied-in-fact condition
Covenant: an absolute, unconditional promise to perform
Express condition: condition created by words of the parties
Guarantee: promise to answer for the debts of another; must be in writing
Implied-in-fact condition: condition created by the reasonable expectations
      of the parties
Implied-in-law condition: condition imposed by law in the interest of
      fairness
Palimony: payment made to a person under certain circumstances pursuant
      to the break-up of a nonmarital relationship
Parol evidence rule: oral testimony may not be used to vary the terms of a
      contract writing
Prenuptial agreement: same as antenuptial agreement
Promissory note: written promise to pay money in repayment of a loan
Rules of construction: court guidelines used to interpret contractual
      provisions
Statute of Frauds: law requiring certain types of contracts to be in writing to
      be enforceable
Time of the essence clause: contractual clause that makes a covenant of a
      timing element
Uniform Commercial Code: statutory enactment that covers the sale of
      goods valued at over $500, among other things (see Chapter 8)

EXERCISES

   1. Find and analyze your own state's Statute of Frauds.
   2. How can a condition precedent become a condition subsequent?
       Draft an example.

3. Must a lease for an apartment be in writing to be enforceable? Why?
4. Give two examples of implied-in-fact conditions not discussed in the chapter.
5. How can a condition become a covenant? Draft an example.

Cases for Analysis

One of the most typically encountered provisions in a contract is a restrictive covenant. To show how the court enforces such provisions, Maintenance Technologies International, LLC v. Vega is included. In addition, the importance of a condition precedent to contract formation is highlighted in The Catholic Charities of the Archdiocese of Chicago v. Thorpe.

Maintenance Technologies International, LLC v. Vega
2006 Conn. Super. LEXIS 136

Presently before the court is the plaintiff's application for a temporary injunction and order to show cause, as authorized by General Statutes §52-471 *et seq.* The plaintiff, Maintenance Technologies International, LLC, has instituted this action against a former employee, Daniel Vega (Vega) and the present employer of Vega, Schultz Electric Co. (Schultz), to enforce a contractual covenant not to compete.

Based on the evidence presented at an evidentiary hearing held on December 19, 2005, the court finds the following facts. The plaintiff is a company located in Milford, Connecticut, that performs highly specialized engineering maintenance services. The defendant Vega, an engineer, commenced employment with the plaintiff on February 25, 2002, after having previously worked for the plaintiff in 1990. As a field service specialist, the defendant performed highly technical services such as vibration analysis, infra-red thermography, motor testing and laser alignment.

On February 25, 2002, the plaintiff and the defendant signed an employment agreement. Section 2.4, entitled "Noncompetition," of the agreement states in relevant part: "The Employee agrees that all times during the term of his employment hereunder and for a period of two (2) years after the termination of his employment hereunder, howsoever brought about, whether voluntary or involuntary, he will not, within 150 miles of the current principal place of business of the Employer, engage in any business engaged in by the Employer and shall not be the owner of any of the outstanding capital stock of any Corporation other than Employer or an Officer, Director or employee of any Corporation (other than Employer or a Corporation affiliated with Employer), or a partner or employee of any Partnership or member, manager or employee of any limited liability company or an owner or employee of any other business, which conducts a similar business within 150 miles of the current principal place of business of the Employer. In the event that the provisions of this Section should ever be deemed to exceed the time, geographic or occupational limitations permitted by the applicable laws, then such provisions shall be reformed to the maximum time, geographic or occupational limitations permitted by the applicable laws."

By letter dated October 7, 2005, the defendant gave written notice that "due to family related issues and a personal ambition to finish [his] master's degree in theology," he was resigning from his position with the plaintiff. On October 30, 2005, the defendant began working for Schultz, a competitor of the plaintiff with major locations in Connecticut, Maine, Massachusetts and New Jersey.

On November 28, 2005, the plaintiff filed the present application for a temporary injunction and order to show cause seeking a temporary and permanent injunction enjoining: (1) the defendant from continued employment with Schultz; and (2) Schultz from continuing to employ the defendant. An evidentiary hearing was held on December 19, 2005, at which time the defendant and Robert Davis, president of Schultz, appeared pro se.

"The principal purpose of a temporary injunction is to preserve the status quo until the rights of the parties can be finally determined after a hearing on the merits." (Internal quotation marks omitted.) Clinton v. Middlesex Mutual Assurance Co., 37 Conn. App. 269, 270, 655 A.2d 814 (1995). The standard for granting a temporary injunction in Connecticut is well settled. "In general, a court may, in its discretion, exercise its equitable power to order a temporary injunction pending final determination of the order, upon a proper showing by the movant that if the injunction is not wanted he or she will suffer irreparable harm for which there is no adequate remedy at law. . . . In exercising its discretion, the court, in a proper case, may consider and balance the injury complained of with that which will result from interference by injunction." (Citations omitted; internal quotation marks omitted.) Moore v. Ganim, 233 Conn. 557, 569, n.25, 660 A.2d 742 (1995). There is a four-part test for the issuance of a temporary injunction: "(1) the plaintiff [has] no adequate legal remedy; (2) the plaintiff would suffer irreparable injury absent [the injunction]; (3) the plaintiff [is] likely to prevail . . . and (4) the balance of the equities [favors the issuance of the injunction]." Waterbury Teachers Ass'n v. Freedom of Information Commission, 230 Conn. 441, 446, 645 A.2d 978 (1994).

The standard for granting a temporary injunction to enforce a covenant not to compete, however, is somewhat different in that the plaintiff does not need to prove irreparable harm. "While ordinarily proof of imminent harm is essential, in this type of case there is no such requirement. It has long been recognized in this state that a restrictive covenant is a valuable business asset which is entitled to protection. . . . Irreparable harm would invariably result from a violation of the defendant's promises. . . . The reason for this is that such a plaintiff's actual injury is not susceptible of determination to its entire extent but is estimable largely by conjecture and prediction." (Citations omitted; internal quotation marks omitted.)

The standard is also different in that the plaintiff does not have to demonstrate that there is no adequate remedy at law. "While the plaintiff could maintain a claim for damages as to each violation that causes injury the difficulty of proof and the inefficiency of repetitive suits render inadequate the use of successive remedies at law, and injunctive relief is therefore warranted to protect the plaintiff from harm which the restrictive covenant was intended to prevent." (Internal quotation marks omitted.) Thus, the present application only requires this court to determine that the plaintiff is likely to prevail and that the balance of the equities favors the issuance of the injunction.

"A covenant that restricts the activities of an employee following the termination of his employment is valid and enforceable if the restraint is reasonable." New Haven Tobacco Co. v. Perrelli, 18 Conn. App. 531, 533, 559 A.2d 715, *cert. denied*, 212 Conn. 809, 564 A.2d 1071 (1989). In determining whether a covenant is reasonable, "the five factors to be considered . . . are: (1) the length of time the restriction operates; (2) the geographical area covered; (3) the fairness of the protection accorded to the employer; (4) the extent of the restraint on the employee's opportunity to pursue his occupation; and (5) the extent of interference with the public's interests." Robert S. Weiss & Associates, Inc. v. Wiederlight, 208 Conn. 525, 529 n.2, 546 A.2d 216 (1988).

The court first begins with an analysis of the geographical area covered. The court finds that the 150 mile geographical area is reasonable given the nature of the plaintiff's business. At the hearing, Ronald Hemming (Hemming), president and owner of Maintenance Technologies International, LLC, testified that the plaintiff's clients are located, among other places, in Boston, Massachusetts, northern Philadelphia, Albany, New York, and southern New Hampshire. "[A] restrictive covenant must be confined to a geographic area that is reasonable in view of the particular situation." New Haven Tobacco Co. v. Perrelli, *supra*, 18 Conn. App. 534. As explained by Hemming, the nature of the specialized services offered by the plaintiff is such that the plaintiff cannot limit itself to customers only in Connecticut but must also extend its services to customers in other states. The nature of the plaintiff's services, coupled with the fact that the plaintiff must travel to customers in other geographical areas to provide on-site services and training, make the 150 mile geographical area restriction reasonable.

With regard to the fairness of protection accorded to the plaintiff, the court finds that the covenant not to compete is a reasonable protection of the plaintiff's business. "If . . . a restriction is to be upheld and enforced it must be reasonably necessary for the fair protection of the employer's business, good will or rights. . . ." May v. Young, 125 Conn. 1, 5, 2 A.2d 385 (1938). "Restrictions are valid when they appear to be reasonably necessary for the fair protection of the employer's business or rights . . . due regard being had to the subject-matter of the contract and the circumstances and conditions under which it is to be performed. Especially if the employment involves the imparting of trade secrets, methods or systems and contacts and associations with clients or customers it is appropriate to restrain the use, when the service is ended, of the knowledge and acquaintance, so acquired, to injure or appropriate the business which the party was employed to maintain and enlarge." Id., 6-7.

The evidence before the court establishes that the plaintiff invests a great deal of time and money in training its employees. For instance, Hemming testified that it generally takes three to five years to fully train an employee. He also testified that the plaintiff's employees are its "assets." The evidence further establishes that the plaintiff's employees have direct access to customer information, pricing, databases, electronic and printed forms, and other confidential information used in the business. The plaintiff understandably seeks to protect this information from such competitors as Schultz. Because the plaintiff's employees and its customer relationships are the plaintiff's most valuable assets, it is important to protect that interest by enforcing the covenant not to compete. The restrictive covenant, therefore, provides a fair and reasonable degree of protection to the plaintiff.

Next, the court considers the extent of the restraint on the defendant's opportunity to pursue his occupation. The Connecticut Supreme Court has recognized that "the interests of the employee himself must . . . be protected, and a restrictive covenant is unenforceable if by its terms the employee is precluded from pursuing his occupation and thus prevented from supporting himself and his family." Scott v. General Iron & Welding Co., 171 Conn. 132, 137, 368 A.2d 111 (1976). Here, the covenant allows the defendant to work outside the restricted area. Further, the covenant does not prohibit him from engaging in any business not engaged in by the plaintiff. Thus, the court finds that the covenant does not unfairly restrain the defendant from pursuing his occupation.

The court now determines the extent of the covenant's interference with the public's interests. "In order for such interference [with the public interest] to be reasonable, it first must be determined that the employer is seeking to protect a legally recognized interest, and then, that the means used to achieve this end do not unreasonably deprive the public of essential goods and services." New Haven Tobacco Co. v. Perrelli, supra, 18 Conn. App. 536. "In determining whether a restrictive covenant unreasonably deprives the public of essential goods and services, the reasonableness of the scope and severity of the covenant's effect on the public and the probability of the restriction's creating a monopoly in the area of trade must be examined." Id.

"An employer can protect its business in the area where it does business." Daniel V. Keane Agency, Inc. v. Butterworth, Superior Court, judicial district of Fairfield, Docket No. 313181 (February 22, 1995, Levin, J.); see also Robert S. Weiss & Associates v. Wiederlight, supra, 208 Conn. 533; May v. Young, supra, 125 Conn. 7. Here, the plaintiff's interest in protecting itself against the defendant's use of confidential and customer information by a competitor of the plaintiff is a legally protected interest. See May v. Young, supra, 125 Conn. 7 (employment which involves acquisition of confidential knowledge involved in business and acquaintance with employer's clientele is appropriate to restrictions against use of such knowledge in competition with employer). Furthermore, this restriction does not create a monopoly or interfere with the public's ability to procure engineering maintenance services.

After hearing the testimony of the parties and examining the documentary evidence, the court finds that the plaintiff has met its burden of demonstrating the probability that it will succeed on the merits. Moreover, the nature of the employment demonstrates a reasonable basis for including the covenant not to compete in the agreement signed by the parties. Furthermore, there is no evidence that the defendant did not fully understand his obligations under the written agreement.

The defendant had informed Hemming that he was resigning in order to help his father part-time in the ministry and to pursue a master's degree. However, a week after his resignation with the plaintiff, he commenced work with Schultz. Moreover, the defendant testified that he had been using a headhunter to locate a new job since August of 2005. Hemming, on the other hand, tried to find ways to accommodate the defendant so that he could continue to work for the plaintiff. The court notes that the defendant was less than candid with his former employer regarding his future.

Lastly, while the agreement calls for a two-year restriction on future employment, the court is concerned that this time period may be somewhat inequitable. Because of this concern, the court will at this time grant the injunction for one year and invite the parties to submit further argument *prior* to the expiration of the one year as to a potential extension of the injunction until October 28, 2007.

Accordingly, the application for a temporary injunction is granted without bond. It is hereby ordered that the defendant is enjoined from employment with Schultz for a period of one year from the date of his termination with the plaintiff, which was October 28, 2005.

Questions

1. How does the court reason that the covenant not to compete is appropriate in this instance?

2. How did the court decide which of the covenant's provisions was unreasonable?

3. How does the concept of "irreparable harm" enter into the decision?

The Catholic Charities of the Archdiocese of Chicago v. Thorpe
318 Ill. App. 3d 304, 741 N.E.2d 651 (2000)

Defendants George Thorpe and Terry Pearson (collectively "Buyer") appeal from the summary judgement of the circuit court of Cook County granted in favor of plaintiff the Catholic Charities of the Archdiocese of Chicago ("Seller") for the earnest money as liquidated damages on a contract to purchase real estate. On appeal, Buyer argues that no contract was formed because the payment of earnest money was a condition precedent to formation of the contract and was never performed; that the liquidated damages clause is unenforceable because the seller retained the option of recovering actual damages; that the liquidated damages clause is not enforceable if the seller (Catholic Charities) sustained no actual damages; and that the circuit court erred by refusing to permit Buyer to obtain discovery regarding the amount of Seller's actual damages. For the reasons discussed below, we reverse.

The essential facts of this case, as stated in Buyer's complaint, follow. On or about April 29, 1996, Buyer entered into a purported contract (the "contract") with Seller to purchase a parcel of real estate (the "property") located at 1300 South Wabash Avenue in the City of Chicago. The contract stated that Buyer "has paid $10,000 as earnest money to be increased to $25,000 upon acceptance" of the contract by Seller. Buyer paid the initial deposit of earnest money in the sum of $10,000 with a personal check, which was returned for insufficient funds and thereafter remained unpaid. The closing of the transaction was scheduled for June 6, 1996, and was extended to June 25, 1996, at Buyer's request. Seller appeared at the appointed time and place on June 25 for the closing; however, Buyer did not appear. Seller subsequently sold the property to a third party and the trial court refused to allow Buyer to discover the price at the sale. Seller subsequently filed suit for the earnest money as liquidated damages and the trial court granted summary judgement in its favor. This appeal followed.

We first note that we are reviewing an order granting summary judgement. "It is well settled that summary judgment should be granted only when the pleadings, depositions, affidavits and admissions show that there is no genuine issue of material fact and that the moving party is entitled to judgment as a matter of law." Largosa v. Ford Motor Co., 303 Ill. App. 3d 751, 753, 708 N.E.2d 1219, 1221, 237 Ill. Dec. 179 (1999). "On a motion for summary judgment, the court must consider all the evidence before it strictly against the movant for summary judgment and liberally in favor of the nonmovant." Largosa, 303 Ill. App. 3d at 753, 708 N.E.2d at 1221. "When reviewing a trial court's order granting a motion for summary judgment, the standard of review is de novo." Largosa, 303 Ill. App. 3d at 753, 708 N.E.2d at 1221.

Buyer first argues that Seller is not entitled to a judgement for the earnest money because no contract was ever formed between Buyer and Seller. In support, Buyer contends that the payment of the earnest money was a condition precedent to the formation of the contract and that the earnest money was never paid. In response, Seller argues that the payment of the earnest money was not a condition precedent to the formation of the contract, but was a condition precedent to Seller's performance. We find that the payment of the earnest money is not a condition precedent to the formation of the contract.

A "condition precedent is one that must be met before a contract becomes effective or that is to be performed by one party to an existing contract before the other party is obligated to perform." McAnelly v. Graves, 126 Ill. App. 3d 528, 532, 467 N.E.2d 377, 379, 81 Ill. Dec. 677 (1984). "Whether an act is necessary to formation of the contract or to the performance of an obligation under the contract depends on the facts of the case." *McAnelly*, 126 Ill. App. 3d at 532, 467 N.E.2d at 379. If "a condition goes solely to the obligation of the parties to perform, existence of such a condition does not prevent the formation of a valid contract." *McAnelly*, 126 Ill. App. 3d at 532, 467 N.E.2d at 379.

Thus, whether a contract exists herein turns on whether the payment of the earnest money is a condition precedent to the formation of the contract. As the District of Columbia Court of Appeals has observed, the resolution of this question turns on the intent of the parties.

> "The issue really is not whether a 'condition' must occur before a contract comes into existence but whether the parties have mutually assented or agreed to make it a binding contract. If there is such mutual assent, agreed on conditions clearly affect only the duty to perform. If no mutual agreement is reached, there is no contract. The 'condition precedent' to the formation or existence of a contract is thus the mutual assent or agreement of the parties." Edmund J. Flynn Co. v. Schlosser, 265 A.2d 599, 601 (1970).

The intent of the parties to create a condition precedent to the formation of a contract is a question of law where the language in the instrument is unambiguous. IK Corp. v. One Financial Place Partnership, 200 Ill. App. 3d 802, 810, 558 N.E.2d 161, 166-67, 146 Ill. Dec. 198 (1990).

The language in the instrument at issue is unambiguous and does not express an intent by the parties to make payment of the earnest money a condition precedent to the formation of a contract. Hudson v. Wakefield, 645 S.W.2d 427, 430 (Tx. 1983) (payment of earnest money not a condition precedent to the formation of the contract). The instrument states that "purchaser has paid $10,000 (to be increased to $25,000 upon acceptance of contract by seller) as earnest money to be applied on the purchase price." The additional $15,000 in earnest money (which brings the total to $25,000) is clearly a promise which must be performed once the contract is agreed to. Nor does this language specifically require that the initial $10,000 earnest money be paid as a condition to the contract being formed, but merely purports to recite a history of what has already taken place.

All the Illinois cases which our research has disclosed which found a condition precedent to the formation of a contract contain express language on the face of the contract to support that construction. For example, in McAnelly v. Graves, 126 Ill. App. 3d 528, 531, 467 N.E.2d 377, 378, 81 Ill. Dec. 677 (1984), the court found that a provision in a lease stating that "it was 'subject to' the lessee's obtaining all necessary mining permits and stated that, if such permits were not issued, the lease was to be of no force and effect and the entire advance royalty payment was to be refunded to the lessee" was not a condition precedent to the formation of the contract. The court reasoned that "the language and circumstances of the lease in question belie the . . . contention that formation of the contract was dependent on the plaintiff's obtaining the . . . permits" because the "lease itself did not require the permits to be issued before it became effective." *McAnelly*, 126 Ill. App. 3d at 533, 467 N.E.2d at 379. Rather, the language indicated that the parties intended the issuance of the permits to be a condition precedent to performance. The court then distinguished the case of Albrecht v. North American Life Assurance Co., 27 Ill. App. 3d 839, 840, 327 N.E.2d 317, 318 (1975), where a contract provision stating that employee "shall be insured" under an insurance policy after completing an application for insurance created condition precedent to formation of a contract. *McAnelly*, 126 Ill. App. 3d at 533, 467 N.E.2d at 379.

We concur with the analysis in *McAnelly* and find *Albrecht* to be similarly distinguishable. In *Albrecht* the instrument in question stated on its face that an "employee shall become insured hereunder . . . on the date of completion of a written application for insurance." This language clearly states that no contract of insurance covers the employee until after an application is completed. The completion of the application is thus clearly a condition precedent to the formation of a contract of insurance covering the employee. (*Cf.* IK Corp., 200 Ill. App. 3d at 810-11, 558 N.E.2d at 167, which indicates that the term "subject to" may denote a condition precedent depending on the surrounding context, but agrees with the underlying principle that to be construed as a condition precedent the intent to do so must be clear from the fact of the document).

Thus as is manifest from each of the forgoing cases a condition precedent to the formation of a contract will not be found unless the intent to create such a condition is apparent from the face of the agreement. In the case at bar, the language of the contract does not purport to formulate the payment of earnest money as a condition precedent to the formation of the contract and therefore no such intent should be read into it.

Nor need we determine whether the language in this contract renders the payment of the earnest money a condition precedent to performance as opposed to being an independent promise (see generally 3A *Corbin on Contracts* §633 (1960)), since neither of these constructions would be of any aid to Buyer. If indeed the provision is a condition precedent to performance, the contract would have been formed in any event and would require the Buyer to deposit the earnest money, which he did not do. 3A *Corbin on Contracts* §633 at 27-8 (1960) ("a contract can be so made as to create a duty that the fact operative as a condition shall come into existence . . . such a condition might be described as a promissory condition").

Moreover, even assuming that the payment of the earnest money is a condition precedent to the formation of the contract, performance of that condition by Buyer was waived by Seller. A party to a contract may waive performance of a condition precedent by the other party where the condition precedent is intended for the benefit of the waving party. Quake Construction, Inc. v. American Airlines, Inc., 181 Ill. App. 3d 908, 915, 537 N.E.2d 863, 868, 130 Ill. Dec. 534 (1989) ("a party may waive a condition precedent to the formation of a contract"); Bartels v. Denler, 30 Ill. App. 3d 499, 501, 333 N.E.2d 640, 642 (1975) ("It is well established that a party to a contract may waive provisions contained in the contract for his benefit"); 13 R. Lord, *Williston on Contracts* §39:24, at 599 (4th ed. 2000) ("a contracting party may unilaterally waive a provision of the contract, including, as a general rule, any condition precedent, which has been placed in the contract for his or her benefit").

There can be no question that the earnest money provision in the contract is for the benefit of Seller. This provision, along with its liquidated damages component, is manifestly designed to protect Seller in the event that Buyer were to refuse to perform the contract. Seller waived this condition by suing to enforce the contract. C.P.D. Chemical Co. v. National Car Rental Systems, Inc., 148 Ga. App. 756, 757, 252 S.E.2d 665, 667 (1979) (party may waive contract condition through its actions). Thus if payment of the earnest money were a condition precedent to the formation of the contract, the seller would have waived that condition. C.P.D. Chemical, 148 Ga. App. at 758, 252 S.E.2d at 667 (waiver may be determined as a matter of law); Liberty Mutual Insurance Co. v. Westfield Insurance Co., 301 Ill. App. 3d 49, 53, 703 N.E.2d 439, 441, 234 Ill. Dec. 578 (1998) ("When there is no dispute as to the material facts and only one reasonable inference can be drawn therefrom, it is a question of law whether facts proved constitute waiver").

Moreover, the same result would also apply without a general waiver analysis since in this particular instance it is the promisor who is attempting to take advantage of his failure to perform as the basis of his own avoidance of any further liability under the agreement. Grill v. Adams, 123 Ill. App. 3d 913, 918, 463 N.E.2d 896, 900, 79 Ill. Dec. 342 (1984) ("[a] party cannot take advantage of his own conduct and claim that failure of the fulfillment of a condition therefore defeats his liability"); accord Eggan v. Simonds, 34 Ill. App. 2d 316, 321, 181 N.E.2d 354, 356 (1962).

Buyer next argues that the liquidated damages clause in the contract is optional and a penalty and therefore not enforceable pursuant to our decision in Grossinger Motorcorp, Inc. v. American National Bank & Trust Co., 240 Ill. App. 3d 737, 607 N.E.2d 1337, 180 Ill. Dec. 824 (1992) (holding optional liquidated damages clause unenforceable). Seller argues in response that Buyer has waived this argument by his failure to raise this issue below. Seller also contends that the liquidated damages clause is not optional. Seller attempts to argue that the word "option" does not denote that Seller may alternatively pursue a remedy of liquidated damages or actual damages at its option. Rather Seller insists that the word "option" should merely be construed to mean that it is under no obligation to sue for liquidated damages but may forebear seeking any remedy. Seller therefore contends that *Grossinger* is not controlling, because unlike in *Grossinger*, the clause at issue here does not specify that Seller has the option of seeking "actual damages."

In response to Seller's contention that Buyer's argument from *Grossinger* was waived by defendant's failure to raise this issue below, Buyer contends that the issue was raised, albeit obliquely and briefly. Buyer contends that the issue was sufficiently raised by him in response to a motion to strike affirmative defenses where he argued that "to be valid a provision for liquidated damages must be for a certain sum," apparently contending that there is uncertainty insofar as Seller attempted to preserve his right to affirmative damages alternatively to his right to liquidated damages. He further contends that he cited *Grossinger* below, albeit not on this issue. We do not, however, feel constrained to examine the sufficiency of Buyer's contention, since in any event any waiver on his part is only binding on the parties and not binding on this court. Ward v. Community Unit School District 220, 243 Ill. App. 3d 968, 974, 614 N.E.2d 102, 107, 184 Ill. Dec. 901 (1993) ("the waiver rule is a limitation only on the parties, and this court has the power to decide any issue as long as the record contains facts sufficient for resolution of that issue"). This issue raises a clear question of law and the factual record is sufficient to permit its resolution without further input from the trial court below. Furthermore, we find that resolution of this issue is necessary to maintain a uniform body of precedent on this point. American Federation of State County & Municipal Employees, Council 31 v. County of Cook, 145 Ill. 2d 475, 480, 584 N.E.2d 116, 118-19, 164 Ill. Dec. 904 (1991) ("the responsibility of a reviewing court for a just result and for the maintenance of a sound and uniform body of precedent may sometimes override the considerations of waiver that stem from the adversarial nature of our system").

Turning to the merits of this argument, which has been fully briefed by the parties on appeal, we cannot accept the construction which Seller seeks to impose on the option language in the contract. The clause in the contract provides as follows:

> 5. If this contract is terminated without Purchaser's fault, the earnest money shall be returned to the Purchaser, but if the termination is caused by the Purchaser's fault, then at the option of the Seller and upon notice to the Purchaser, the earnest money shall be forfeited to the Seller and applied first to the payment of Seller's expenses and then to payment of broker's commission; the balance, if any, to be retained by the Seller as liquidated damages.

Seller's construction makes little sense as no one would ever consider that the Seller was under any duty to pursue any remedy provided to him under the agreement whether he deployed the term "at his option" or not. Thus, the addition of the clause "at the option of the seller" would be totally redundant unless we assign to it an intent to preserve his alternate remedy of actual damages in addition to his right to liquidated damages.

The construction which we urge here was expressly followed in Gryb v. Benson, 84 Ill. App. 3d 710, 712, 406 N.E.2d 124, 126, 40 Ill. Dec. 423 (1980), which interpreted a similar clause giving the seller the "option" of receiving liquidated damages without explicitly providing for the preservation of the seller's right to actual damages. There the court construed a liquidated damages clause identical to the one in the case sub judice as providing the seller with the option of suing for either liquidated damages or actual damages. Courts in other jurisdictions have similarly interpreted clauses such as the one at bar which provides the seller the option of liquidated damages, without specifying any alternative remedies to that option, as nevertheless being designed to give the seller the choice of suing for actual damages as an alternative to liquidated damages.

Since we have determined that a clause providing for the recovery of liquidated damages at the option of the seller in effect preserves the promisee's right to alternatively seek compensatory damages, the right to liquidated damages is rendered unenforceable. Our decision in Grossinger Motorcorp, Inc. v. American National Bank & Trust Co., 240 Ill. App. 3d 737, 607 N.E.2d 1337, 180 Ill. Dec. 824 (1992), controls this issue.

In *Grossinger* we held that an optional liquidated damages provision "which allows defendant to seek actual damages or alternatively to retain the earnest money as liquidated damages is unenforceable." *Grossinger*, 240 Ill. App. 3d at 752, 607 N.E.2d at 1347. We reasoned that this scheme distorts the very essence of liquidated damages, which in effect is to provide the parties with a pre-ordained settlement of a damage sum when actual damages would otherwise be difficult to determine. Hickox v. Bell, 195 Ill. App. 3d 976, 987-88, 552 N.E.2d 1133, 1140-41, 142 Ill. Dec. 392 (1990) ("a liquidated damages clause will be given effect if it is diffi-cult to determine the actual damages which would result in event of breach"). The preservation of an option to alternatively seek the recovery of actual damages reflects that the parties did not have the mutual intention to stipulate to a fixed amount as their liquidated damages, but rather to a minimum amount subject to increase if actual damages prove to exceed the amount provided as liquidated damages. In effect, the manifest purpose of the liquidated damages provision under such circumstances is to give the seller the option of penalizing the buyer by recovering an amount in excess of his actual damages where the actual damages are less than the liquidated sum. *Grossinger*, 240 Ill. App. 3d at 751, 607 N.E.2d at 1346 ("existence of the option reflects that the parties did not have the mutual intention to stipulate to a fixed amount as their liquidated damages in the event of a breach and indicates an intent to penalize the defaulting buyer"); *accord* Lefemine v. Baron, 573 So. 2d 326, 329 (Fla. 1991). Such a clause "is no settlement at all" as it "permits the seller to have his cake and ear it too." *Grossinger*, 240 Ill. App. 3d at 751, 607 N.E.2d at 1347.

Accordingly, in the instant case, once we have concluded that the option clause allows Seller to pursue either liquidated or actual damages at his option, the same result must follow as in *Grossinger*. As in *Grossinger*, this scheme does not purport to provide an anticipatory settlement of any damage claim between the parties since Seller is at all times free to pursue the recovery of actual damages if he believes that they would exceed the amount provided in liquidated damages. It is therefore not a settlement but an attempt to penalize the breaching buyer and is thus unenforceable.

Because we find that the liquidated damages clause is unenforceable due to its optional nature, we need not address Buyer's remaining arguments that the liquidated damages clause is unenforceable if Seller sustained no actual damages and that the trial court erred in not permitting Buyer to discover the extent of Seller's actual damages.

For the reasons discussed above, the judgement of the circuit court of Cook County is reversed and the cause is remanded to the circuit court for further proceedings not inconsistent with this opinion.

Reversed; cause remanded.

Questions

1. What is meant by "earnest money"?
2. Why does the court discuss the element of intent?
3. What does the court say about the liquidated damages provision?

Suggested Case References

1. A man is home recuperating from an illness when he is approached by a contractor about installing aluminum siding. The salesperson is very persuasive, but because of his health, the customer is able to insert a clause stating that the contract for the siding will be null and void if he cannot obtain disability insurance. The contractor starts the work, but the customer cannot get the insurance because his health is so poor. The customer tells the contractor that he could not get the insurance. The customer shortly thereafter dies. Is his estate liable for the siding? If not, why not? Read Cambria Savings & Loan Association v. Estate of Gross, 294 Pa. Super. 351 (1982).

2. For a discussion of time of the essence clauses, read Carter v. Sherburne Corp., 132 Vt. 88 (1974).

3. If a person fails to meet a condition of her contract, does she thereby lose all rights due to her under the agreement? Read Brauer v. Freccia, 159 Conn. 289 (1970).

4. For a discussion of restrictive covenants in an employment contract, see Nestle Food Co. v. Miller, 836 F. Supp. 69 (D. R.I. 1993).

5. In Loyal Erectors, Inc. v. Hamilton & Son, Inc., 312 A.2d 748 (Me. 1973), the court discusses the difference between a condition and a covenant.

The Uniform Commercial Code

Learning Objectives

After studying this chapter you will be able to:

- Explain the background of the Uniform Commercial Code
- Discuss the basic guidelines to be used when applying the UCC
- Indicate the obligations imposed by Article I of the UCC
- Discuss the concept of "custom and usage" as it applies to contracts
- Distinguish between contracts for goods and contracts for services
- Define the UCC concept of "merchant"
- Discuss the UCC express and implied warranties
- List and discuss conditional sales contracts
- List and discuss shipment contracts
- Discuss the various remedies afforded parties under the UCC
- Define a "secured transaction"
- Indicate the requirements to create a security interest
- Define a "financing statement"

CHAPTER OVERVIEW

The Uniform Commercial Code (UCC) is the major statutory basis of several important areas of contract law. Although it is not a universally applied federal statute, every state, plus the District of Columbia, has enacted some version of all or part of the Code. To fully understand American contract law, it is necessary to discuss several sections of the UCC.

Three of the Code's articles are directly concerned with contract law: Article I, General Provisions; Article II, Sales; and Article IX, Secured Transactions.

Article I establishes the general outline, purpose, and objectives of the Code. Primarily, the UCC was created to promote commerce and to establish certain basic guidelines for those parties involved in commercial transactions. The UCC requires every party whose actions it governs to act in good faith, to perform in a timely manner, and to heed the dictates of the custom and usage prevalent in the industry.

Article II forms the primary modern statutory basis for contracts involving the sale of goods. This article regulates the sale of goods valued at over $500 and sales between merchants. It imposes certain warranties, or guarantees, that are passed by the manufacturer and/or seller of the goods to the ultimate consumer of those products. Additionally, this article provides certain remedies that differ from the general contractual remedies usually available to injured parties in a contractual dispute. (See Chapter 11, Remedies.)

Article IX creates the basis for creditors to secure their debtors' obligations with specific items of property that may be attached by the creditors in case the debtors default. Article IX sets out the specific procedures that a creditor must follow to create and establish a security interest against all other creditors of the debtor.

Before detailing each of the specifics of the articles, it would be helpful to understand some of the history and general background of the Code.

General Background

In 1952, after many years of work, The American Law Institute and the National Conference of Commissioners on Uniform State Laws promulgated a model act known as the Uniform Commercial Code (UCC). The objective of the codification was to clarify and modernize laws governing commercial transactions and to attempt to make mercantile law uniform among all of the states. This model statute represented the first major attempt to codify general contract law; unlike many other areas of law, contract law still rested firmly on its common law base.

Being a model (or proposed) act, the UCC had to be adopted by each state individually; it is not a federal law. Eventually, every jurisdiction adopted some version of the UCC, either in whole or in part (some states have only adopted a few of the provisions of the Code). It is necessary to research each jurisdiction specifically to determine whether its version differs from that of any other state that is involved in the transaction.

The UCC is important to all mercantile practices and transactions. The purpose of the Code is to promote interstate commerce and to facilitate the furthering of business interests. Consequently, the UCC forms a basic part of almost all business law and operations. However, it is important to bear in mind that, except where specifically noted, the Code generally only codifies the common law of contracts. The UCC was not intended or designed to create a radically new concept of contractual arrangements. Rather, it was intended to unify conflicting common law doctrines and to regularize existing commercial practices.

The Code is divided into thirteen articles, the articles are subdivided into parts, and the parts are further divided into sections and subsections. The UCC covers a wide spectrum of law, from sales to banking, to letters of credit and bulk transfers. For the purpose of contract law, three of the articles assume primary importance: Article I, General Provisions; Article II, Sales; and Article IX, Secured Transactions. Each of these articles will be discussed individually, emphasizing concepts not otherwise covered in previous and succeeding chapters.

Article I, General Provisions

Article I of the UCC establishes the form and operation of the entire statute. Not only does it affirmatively state the purpose and intent of the conference members in promulgating the Code, but it also establishes several basic guidelines for applying and interpreting the provisions of the Code. It imposes certain obligations on all parties to transactions that fall within the Code's province.

Basic Guidelines

Article I establishes three basic guidelines to be used in applying the provisions of the Code:

1. The law of the state applies unless otherwise superseded by the UCC.
2. The parties to a contract may, by their agreement, vary the provisions of the Code.
3. The UCC is to be liberally construed.

Law of the State Applies

Unless expressly superseded by the state's adopted version of the UCC, under §1-103 the general law of the site where the transaction occurs applies.

When the states' legislatures adopted their own versions of the Code, if they intended the UCC to be the prevailing law in a given subject, that intent was specifically stated in the statute. For example, in New York, when the UCC Article on Commercial Paper was adopted, it was affirmatively stated that this article was to revise the preexisting New York Negotiable

Instrument Law, thereby superseding preexisting state law. Hence, when drafting a commercial agreement, you must determine exactly what the law of a given state is and whether the UCC supersedes it. You cannot assume that a UCC provision of one state is applicable in another state.

Parties May Agree to Vary UCC Provisions

The UCC was intended to help facilitate commerce; its rules were not intended, by their application, to hinder business. Therefore, §1-102 permits parties whose transaction comes within the UCC to vary the UCC terms by their own agreement in order to further their commercial interests. However, there must be evidence of the parties' agreement on the matter; if the parties are silent on a particular subject, the UCC provisions will prevail. Article I permits and encourages freedom of contract between the parties but supplies the legal standard should the parties be silent with respect to a given provision.

 EXAMPLE:

Delta, Inc., a Michigan corporation, is contracting with TGI, Inc., a New York corporation, for the purchase of cement, bricks, and other building materials for the construction of a Delta warehouse in New Jersey. Although the contract is signed in New York, and delivery is to be made in New Jersey, Delta wants the law of Michigan to apply because it is a Michigan corporation and is more familiar with that state's law. Although this would be contrary to general UCC provisions, Article I §1-105 permits the parties to agree that the law of Michigan determines the interpretation of the contract.

UCC Provisions Are to Be Liberally Construed

Most importantly, §1-102 of the UCC states that its provisions are to be liberally construed. It may seem a simple statement, but it is fairly unique for statutory law. Most statutes and codes are created as regulatory devices to be strictly complied with. The UCC is different. Because it is meant to promote, not hinder, commerce, the UCC is to be applied in a manner that helps business along, which may mean a liberal interpretation. Of course, this liberal construction must be reasonably formed; the interpretation must still be consistent with the Code as a whole.

Obligations Imposed by Article I

Article I §1-102 imposes three obligations on all parties who come within the purview of its provisions. These obligations are

1. to perform in "good faith" — honesty in fact;

2. to perform in a "reasonable time," "reasonableness" to be determined by the facts and circumstances of each situation; and
3. to perform according to past business dealings and practices (custom and usage).

 EXAMPLES:

1. Hiram agrees to sell 10,000 cardboard boxes to the Bon Ton Department Store, delivery to be within two weeks. Hiram knows that he cannot possibly meet that time limit but is willing to pay some damages for delays in delivery. Hiram is violating the UCC by not acting in good faith. He is contracting for promises he *knows* he cannot meet. Even though he may be willing to pay for the delay, he is knowingly injuring Bon Ton, which violates the intent of the Code to promote commerce.

2. Sylvester agrees to sell and deliver 10,000 nuts and bolts to the Mitchell Construction Company for a specific building project. Delivery is delayed, and Mitchell Construction must find a substitute supplier. Mitchell claims that Sylvester has failed to make delivery in a reasonable time. Sylvester's promise to deliver was conditioned, however, upon receipt of Mitchell's check, which was delayed in the mail. Under these facts, Sylvester's delivery was made within a reasonable time, and he is not in breach of contract or in violation of the UCC.

The most intriguing of these obligations is the codification of the concept of custom and usage. By establishing as law the past practices of the parties, the Code, in effect, is customizing the law to each particular industry and businessperson. In contracting under the UCC, it is necessary to determine the practices and terms peculiar to each industry and between the particular merchants, and make these customs a part of the contract itself. Consequently, contracts will vary with respect to the definitions of particular terms, dependent upon how each industry and the parties define those terms. There will be no one standard contract that can be used for all categories of business situations. Questions of proof also arise, i.e., what is the custom between these parties?

 EXAMPLES:

1. Azar manufactures men's topcoats and regularly buys fabric from Maria. For the past five years, Maria has billed Azar for payment 90 days after delivery. Suddenly, without any prior arrangement, Maria bills Azar for payment within 10 days of delivery. Azar still has 90 days in which to pay. Because the parties have not specifically agreed to payment within 10 days of delivery, they are still bound by their past practices and dealings. If Maria wants to change the payment date, she must make that a specific part of her agreement with Azar.

2. Hazel orders "standard" copper piping from Daniel. Hazel and Daniel have dealt with each other for years, and Daniel always sells Hazel piping 3½ inches wide; the standard pipe in the industry is 4 inches. If Daniel sends Hazel 4-inch piping for this order, Hazel can complain of breach of contract. Because of the past practices of the parties, "standard" for them means 3½-inch piping, not the industry "standard" of 4 inches.

The general provisions of Article I of the Code discussed above permeate all of the other provisions of the statute.

Article II, Sales

General Background

Article II §2-102 of the UCC states that contracts for the sale of goods must be in writing. This provision restates the Statute of Frauds (see Chapter 7) with respect to the sale of goods. In addition, this article reiterates the parol evidence rule and the rules of construction (see Chapter 7).

For the purposes of this chapter, Article II emphasizes three broad areas:

1. the type of contracts that are governed by the UCC;
2. specific contractual provisions regulated by the Code covering warranties and risk of loss; and
3. certain remedies that the contracting parties may be entitled to that differ from the general contractual remedies discussed in Chapter 11, Remedies.

The UCC both codifies the existing common law of contracts already discussed as well as makes some significant changes; all of those contract law concepts still apply unless otherwise stated.

Types of Contracts Covered by Article II

Generally, three types of contracts are regulated by UCC Article II:

1. contracts for the sale of goods;

2. contracts for the lease of goods; and
3. contracts between merchants.

Goods

As indicated above, Article II takes the place of the Statute of Frauds with respect to contracts for the sale of goods valued at over $500. **Goods** are defined by §2-105 as things that are existing and moveable. They may include such items as electricity, food or drink, or anything that can be removed from the land, such as minerals, oil, or crops.

In contracts for the sale of goods, the UCC holds the parties to a standard of **strict liability** with respect to the subject goods. Strict liability means that, regardless of how careful the manufacturer/seller may have been with respect to the making of the product, if the product proves defective, the seller is automatically liable to the injured party. Care, quality control, and like safeguards do not relieve the seller of its liability.

EXAMPLE:

Piedmont Pipes, Inc., sells 50,000 feet of copper pipes to Carl's Construction Company for the purpose of building several condominium units. After installation, the pipes disintegrate with the first use. Piedmont is automatically liable to Carl's because the contract, under the UCC, imposes strict liability on the manufacturer. It doesn't matter how careful Piedmont was in making the pipes; because the pipes failed to function properly, the maker is liable.

It is important to keep in mind that the UCC only covers transactions in goods; any contract for the sale of services is not governed by Article II (unless the provisions are specifically extended to contracts for mixed goods and services, which is addressed below).

EXAMPLE:

The law firm of Black & White, P.C., enters into an agreement with Elsie to represent her in pending litigation against her former employer. This contract is not covered by the UCC because the contract concerns services (legal representation), not goods.

If the contract is for the provision of services, the provider of the services will only be liable for injury to the other contracting party if the injured party can prove negligence, that is, that the provider failed to meet the standard of due care that exists for the particular service in question.

EXAMPLE:

Return to the example with Elsie and the law firm. After Elsie contracts with Black & White, the firm procrastinates and only files Elsie's suit after the Statute of Limitations has run. The case is thrown out, and Elsie sues the firm for negligence. In maintaining her action, Elsie must show that the firm failed to meet its standard of care.

What if the contract in question involves both goods and services? Is the standard one of strict liability or of negligence? According to Article II, if the contract cannot be determined to be one either strictly of goods or strictly of services, the court will determine the predominant category of the contract. Whatever the predominant category is determined to be will control the standard for the entire contract.

EXAMPLES:

1. Faye contracts with Ilona to have Ilona make Faye's wedding dress for $750. As Faye walks down the aisle, the dress starts coming apart at the seams and the embroidery falls off. Ilona is strictly liable. Why? Because, although services are involved in the contract (the sewing of the gown), the predominant object of the contract was to provide Faye with a wedding dress (a good). Consequently, the contract is deemed to be a contract for the sale of goods carrying strict liability.

2. Arnold is in a car accident and is rushed to City General Hospital, where he receives a nutrient solution intravenously. Later it is discovered that the solution was tainted, and Arnold develops hepatitis. Arnold sues the hospital. In this instance, the contract is for the providing of services (medical care), and the standard is one of negligence. If Arnold could sue the person who sold the solution to the hospital, that would be a suit for the sale of goods.

Article II of the UCC concerns itself with contracts for the sale of goods, not with contracts for the providing of services. Contracts for the sale of goods impose strict liability for the seller, and, as will be discussed below, the seller's liability can extend not only to the purchaser of the good, but to the ultimate user of the good as well. Contracts for the providing of services carry a standard of due care, and in order to be found liable, the service provider must be shown to have failed to meet the standard of care that exists for the particular service in question. Obviously, for the injured party, it is an easier burden to have the contract considered to be one for the sale of goods.

Leases

Several jurisdictions have added a new section to the UCC concerning the long-term lease of goods. Because this provision is fairly new and has not been universally adopted, each jurisdiction's version must be checked to determine whether the lease of goods is covered by the UCC or is found under general contract principles. See below. For an example of a contract for the lease of goods, see Chapter 12.

Contracts for the Sale of Goods Between Merchants

As discussed in Chapter 2, Offer, Article II makes several modifications to the general contract requirements if the contract is between merchants. The modifications exist so as to advance the Code's purpose to promote commerce, and it is assumed that merchants are the best judges of their own contractual needs. However, two problems may arise in these types of contracts.

The first problem arises from Article II's definition of **merchant** (§204). Because the UCC is to be liberally construed (Article I), Article II of the Code defines merchant as any person who regularly deals in the kind of goods covered by the contract, *or*, any person who, by his occupation, holds himself out as having knowledge or skill peculiar to the practice of dealing with the goods in question. What this means is that not only will a businessperson be deemed a merchant, but a hobbyist is considered a merchant for the purpose of Article II as well.

 EXAMPLE:

Lola has been collecting stamps as a hobby for the past 12 years. When she contracts with Aldo, a vendor of rare stamps, it is a contract for the sale of goods between merchants.

The second problem regarding merchants arises as an exception to the mirror image rule of contract formation (see Chapter 2). Merchants may meet the requirements of a writing by using purchase order forms, billing receipts, and the like. However, because businesses usually use preprinted forms, and each form is designed to protect the interests of the preparer, the writings that act as the memoranda of the verbal agreement may conflict. This is known as the **battle of the forms.** In this instance, the UCC indicates that the contract will be enforced according to the most reasonable expectations of the parties based on their past practices and their actual actions. Furthermore, as discussed in Chapter 3, merchant traders may vary the terms of the offer without that variance being deemed a rejection or counter-offer, unless the offer is "iron clad." Under the common law such negotiation would cause a significantly different result.

EXAMPLE:

Helen operates a business selling seeds to nurseries throughout the country. Helen sends her catalog to Randy, who sends Helen his printed purchase order form mandating a specific method of delivery. Helen acknowledges the order with her own preprinted form indicating a different method of delivery. Whose form created the contract? Under the common law, the catalog is an invitation to bid, the purchase order is an offer, and the acknowledgment would be a counteroffer (see Chapter 3, Acceptance); therefore, there is no contract. However, under the UCC, the parties would have a contract because a commercial understanding has been achieved. It would be necessary to determine whether the difference in method of delivery is a material change. If the difference is material, involving greater expense or time, it will not be considered part of the contract, and the parties' past practices and actions will determine the delivery provision.

Therefore, when the contract in question is between merchants, the UCC is particularly liberal and provides many exceptions to general contract principles in order to facilitate commercial transactions.

Contractual Provisions

Warranties

As stated above, when the contact involves a sale of goods, the manufacturer/seller may not only be liable to the buyer. He may also be strictly liable to the ultimate consumer of the good as well because goods, unlike services, have UCC **warranties** that attach to them.

A warranty is a guaranty with respect to the goods covered by the sale. The manufacturer of the goods warrants, or guarantees, that the product is exactly what has been ordered, that it is fit as sold for its intended use, and that the seller has title sufficient to pass the goods to the buyer. A warranty can be created either by the express representations of the seller or be implied by the operation of law.

Express Warranties.   Under §2-213, **express warranties** are created by the words or conduct of the seller. They can be created in three different ways:

1.   An express warranty can be created by the specific promise or affirmation appearing in the contract itself. Many contracts contain special warranty clauses, and the parties are specifically held to the words of the warranty to which they have agreed.

EXAMPLE:

In a sales contract, a clause states that the "Seller warrants that all items furnished hereunder will be in full conformity with Buyer's specification." In this manner, the seller is guaranteeing that she will provide goods exactly meeting the buyer's expressed description.

2.   An express warranty can be created by a description that the seller uses in a catalog.

EXAMPLE:

Dora's Dress Company sends out a catalog describing one of its dresses as having a 48-inch sweep. When Smart Shops orders 100 of the dresses, each one must have a 48-inch sweep, or the contract is breached.

3.   Finally, an express warranty can be created by a sample or model used by the seller to induce the sale.

EXAMPLE:

A Fuller Brush salesperson comes to Myra's house to demonstrate a vacuum cleaner. Delighted with the results, Myra buys one; however, when the vacuum cleaner arrives it contains modifications that did not appear on the sample the salesperson used to demonstrate the product. The company has breached its express warranty.

Implied Warranties.   Implied warranties, §2-314, come about by operation of law. There are two types of implied warranties: a **warranty of merchantability,** and a **warranty of fitness for a particular use.**

Warranty of Merchantability. This warranty guarantees the buyer that the goods as sold are in a fit condition for the ordinary purpose for which they were intended. In other words, if a retailer buys 500 pairs of shoes from a shoe manufacturer, the manufacturer implicitly guarantees that the shoes can be used as they are without defect. A warranty of merchantability applies only to goods sold by merchants.

Warranty of Fitness for a Particular Use. This warranty goes beyond that of a warranty of merchantability in that not only must the goods be capable of being used for their ordinary purposes, but the goods must be capable of performing any particular function the buyer has indicated. A warranty of fitness for a particular use applies both to merchants and nonmerchants.

EXAMPLE:

Hikers, Unlimited, is a chain of retail stores that sells hiking equipment. In a contract, Hikers buys 500 pairs of shoes from Seth Shoes after having indicated that the shoes are meant for mountain hikers. The shoes sold, although perfectly good shoes, do not have soles appropriate to mountain hiking. Seth Shoes has breached an implied warranty. Even though the shoes meet the description in Seth's catalog and are capable of being used, they do not meet the hiker's specific needs, of which Seth Shoes had been informed.

For there to be a warranty of fitness for a particular use, the particular use must be made known to the seller, and the buyer must be relying on the seller's expertise in purchasing the appropriate goods. The specific use could be made an express warranty if the parties include it as a part of the contract itself.

Warranty of Title.   Finally, §2-312 states that the seller must have **warranty of title:** title sufficient to sell the object to the buyer. The law does not intend buyers to purchase lawsuits along with the goods. The warranty of title means that the seller must own and have the right to pass ownership of the goods to the buyer free and clear of the interests of any other party to the goods, such as secured creditors. (Secured transactions are discussed later in this chapter.)

An important aspect of all warranties is that they extend not only to the contracting buyer, but to all subsequent purchasers as well, down to the ultimate consumer of the product. For example, any woman who purchased a dress from Smart Shops hoping for a 48-inch sweep could sue Doris, and any hiker who had her shoes fall apart while on a hike could sue Seth. These situations are most usually encountered in suits for defects in children's clothing, products, and toys. Parents, on behalf of the child, sue the manufacturer for breach of warranty, even though no direct contract exists between them. As the ultimate consumer, the child can maintain a suit against the manufacturer.

Risk of Loss

Another important provision of Article II of the UCC concerns the question of who bears the risk of the goods being destroyed after the contract has been signed. As a general rule, the risk of loss of the goods falls on the person who has control over the goods; however, the parties may specifically contract to determine at what point the risk passes from the seller to the buyer. Note that the risk of loss is a different concept than title.

It is imperative to understand the liabilities involved. Whoever bears the risk of loss has the right to maintain an action for the damages caused by the goods' destruction and has the responsibility to insure the goods. If the goods are destroyed when the seller bears the risk, the seller must replace the goods at his own expense. If the goods are destroyed when the buyer bears the risk, the buyer is still obligated to pay the seller for the goods. Careful drafting is always needed in these types of contracts.

In a general mercantile agreement, many of these contractual provisions are indicated merely by abbreviations of the terms. These abbreviations appear in the contracts without any words of explanation, because they are generally known. These provisions are extremely important in determining which party should insure the goods and who may maintain a suit should the goods be destroyed. A brief discussion of the most important of these clauses is in order and is given below.

Conditional Contracts. With conditional contracts, the sale is predicated upon certain conditions being met at the time of transferring the goods. There are four types of conditional contracts under Article II.

1. *Cost on Delivery (§2-310)*. A **cost on delivery,** or **COD,** provision indicates that the risk of loss of the goods remains with the seller until the goods have been delivered to *and paid for* by the buyer. The contract itself will indicate the place of delivery (for example, COD Buyer's Warehouse, 1000 Main Street, Garden City), and the buyer has no right of inspection unless specifically agreed to by the parties.

2. *Sale on approval (§2-326)*. In a **sale on approval** contract, the seller retains the risk of loss until the goods have been delivered to the buyer and the buyer has indicated his approval of the goods. Even if the goods meet the specifications, the buyer may choose to return the goods. In this type of arrangement, the buyer, who must be the ultimate consumer, has a right to inspect the goods, so the risk is retained by the seller for a longer period than with a COD contract.

3. *Sale or return (§2-326)*. With a **sale or return** provision, the risk passes to the buyer on delivery. If the buyer does not approve of the goods or chooses to return them, it is he who bears the risk and cost of returning the goods to the seller.

4. *Consignment (§2-326)*. In a **consignment** contract, the risk of loss remains with the seller until the buyer resells the goods; in other words, the buyer never has a risk of loss. Many small retail stores carry goods on consignment, in which the manufacturer leaves goods with the retailer/buyer in the hopes that the buyer can resell the items. If the goods are not sold by the buyer within a stated period of time, they are returned to the seller, who has born all the risk of loss.

Note that with all of the preceding types of contracts, the buyer may return the goods even if they conform to the contract specifications. These arrangements are only concerned with the risk of loss of the goods, not with other contractual rights of the parties.

Shipment Contracts. If the goods are transferred to the buyer by means of an independent carrier (the U.S. Postal Service, Federal Express, UPS, and so forth), a new element is added to the relationship: the third party. In a general **shipment contract,** the contract merely requires the seller to send the goods to the buyer. Therefore, once the goods are shipped, the risk passes to the buyer. However, the parties may make special contractual arrangements whereby the seller retains the risk for a slightly longer period, but still not to the point of delivery. There are three types of these special shipment arrangements.

  1.   *FOB (place of shipment) (§2-314).* FOB stands for *free on board,* and the risk stays with the seller until he places the goods in the hands of the carrier — for example, FOB Kennedy Airport, Air Express. In this instance, the seller bears the risk until the goods are given to the Air Express office at Kennedy Airport.

  2.   *FAS (vessel) (§2-319). FAS stands for free alongside,* and the vessel is the actual name of the mode of transportation — for example, FAS American Airlines Flight #100, Air Express, Kennedy Airport. In this instance, the seller retains the risk until the goods are actually taken alongside the plane ready for loading, at which point the risk of loss passes to the buyer. FAS (vessel) keeps the risk of loss with the seller for a longer period than with FOB (place of shipment).

  3.   *FOB (carrier) (§2-319).* With *FOB (carrier),* the seller bears the risk of loss until the goods are actually loaded onto the means of transportation. This arrangement keeps the risk of loss with the seller for a longer period than any of the preceding types of shipment contracts.

  Regardless of the type of shipment arrangement employed, the seller may agree to pay for insuring the goods during transportation, even though the risk of loss has passed to the buyer who would normally pay to insure the goods. This arrangement is indicated as **CIF** *(cost of insurance and freight).* Even though the seller has paid for the insurance, if the goods are lost, it is the buyer who bears the risk and who receives the insurance proceeds.

  Shipment contracts are most commonly used when the seller is in a better bargaining position than the buyer; the seller has desirable goods that are in limited supply. As can be seen, with these arrangements it is the buyer who has the greater risk. However, most commonly the buyer has the better bargaining position — all sellers need customers — and so instead of shipment contracts the parties use destination contracts.

  Destination Contracts.   With destination contracts, the seller retains the risk of loss of the goods until the goods arrive at a specified destination point. There are three types of destination contracts.

  1.   *FOB (place of destination) (§2-319).* As with *FOB* (place of shipment), in *FOB (place of destination)* the risk passes when the carrier delivers the goods to a general destination point — FOB Port of San Diego.

  2.   *Ex (ship) (§2-322).* With **Ex (ship),** the risk only passes to the buyer when the goods are off-loaded from the mode of transportation. In the example above, if the contract read Ex American Airlines Flight #100, the risk would only pass to the buyer once the goods were unloaded from the plane.

  3.   *No Arrival, No Sale (§2-324).* With **no arrival, no sale,** the risk only transfers to the buyer when the goods have arrived at the destination point and have been tendered to the buyer by the seller.

In each of these destination contracts, the risk remains with the seller for a slightly longer period of time than with a shipping contract.

These provisions are important in the drafting and interpreting of contracts for the sale of goods when transportation of the goods is involved. Typically, shipment provisions are simply indicated by the abbreviations given above and are not spelled out in further detail.

Remedies

For the most part, the remedies specified in Article II for the buyer and seller in a sales contract are the same remedies, both legal and equitable, permitted for all injured parties under general contract law. Chapter 11, Remedies, discusses these general remedies in detail.

Article II of the UCC grants certain additional remedies that are unique to the Code, which deserve some mention at this point.

Remedies Available to Seller

If the seller is the injured party to the contract, Article II, Part 7, permits three additional methods of rectifying the situation.

1. *Withhold delivery.* The seller may withhold delivery of the goods to the buyer if any one of the following circumstances arises:

   a. The buyer wrongfully rejects the goods.
   b. The buyer fails to pay for the goods as required by the contract.
   c. The buyer does not cooperate with the seller.
   d. The buyer repudiates the contract.
   e. The buyer becomes insolvent before delivery.

 EXAMPLE:

Under their contractual agreement, Rosie is obligated to send goods by a carrier that John is to name. John is prevaricating and won't specify a carrier. Rosie does not have to ship the goods because John is failing to cooperate according to the terms of the contract. Rosie has the right to resell the goods to another buyer.

2. *Stop delivery.* The seller may stop delivery of the goods in transit and resell them if one of the following circumstances arises:

   a. The buyer does not pay for the goods as required by the contract.
   b. The buyer repudiates the contract.
   c. The buyer becomes insolvent before delivery.

EXAMPLE:

John finally specifies a carrier to Rosie, who then ships the goods. Shipment will take two weeks. After one week elapses, John files for protection under the bankruptcy law. Under Article II, Rosie is permitted to stop delivery of the goods, provided John has not yet paid for them. The UCC does not require sellers to become creditors in the bankruptcy of insolvent buyers. Note, however, that if John had already paid for the goods, Rosie would be required to deliver them. If the goods are nonconforming, John still has the right to reject them.

3. *Reclaim goods from insolvent buyer.* The seller has the right to reclaim the goods from the buyer after delivery, but only if the goods are sold on credit, the buyer is insolvent, and the seller makes her demand within ten days of the buyer's receipt of the goods.

EXAMPLE:

Assume that Rosie sells the goods to John on credit but is unaware that John has filed for bankruptcy. Ten days after John receives the goods, Rosie discovers that John is insolvent; she immediately demands that John return the goods. Under the UCC, Rosie can reclaim the goods and thus avoid becoming one of John's creditors.

Remedies Available to Buyer

If the buyer is the injured party, in addition to general contractual remedies, UCC Article II offers him four specific remedies. Note that under the UCC a buyer is entitled to perfect performance and may reject nonconforming goods. The concept of substantial performance does not apply to merchant buyers unless the merchant buyer so wishes. This concept is known as **perfect tender.**

1. *Cover.* The buyer is entitled to **cover** if the seller breaches the contract. Cover is the purchase of goods that substitute for those that are the subject of the breached contract. The buyer can sue the seller for damages if the substituted goods cost more than what the buyer expected to pay under the original sales contract.

EXAMPLE:

Buymore Supermarkets has a contract to buy 1000 bushels of plums from Farmer Jones. When the plums arrive, they do not meet Buymore's specifications, and so it rejects the plums. Buymore purchases plums from Farmer Hicks as cover. The contract with Hicks costs Buymore $1000 more than the contract with Farmer Jones; Buymore can sue Jones for the extra $1000.

2. *Replevin.* If cover is not available, the buyer may *replevy* the goods he had previously rejected from the seller. **Replevin** is an equitable remedy that means retaking, or recovering, the goods identified in the contract. The buyer may believe that nonconforming goods are better than none.

EXAMPLE:

If in the above situation, Buymore could not find plums anywhere else, it could replevy the plums it has already rejected from Farmer Jones.

3. *Revocation.* If the goods do not conform to the contract specifications, the buyer can **revoke** his acceptance. This means that no contract exists.

EXAMPLE:

Assume the above situation. Because the plums did not conform to Buymore's specifications, Buymore could revoke its acceptance. No contract is ever formed.

4. *Claim goods from insolvent seller.* If the seller becomes insolvent, the buyer can claim the goods from him, provided that the goods have been paid for. Just as the UCC will not require a seller to become a creditor of an insolvent buyer, neither will it require a buyer who has paid for goods to become a creditor of an insolvent seller. At this point, the goods are in fact the property of the buyer; the seller's creditors have the purchase price the buyer has already given to divide up among themselves.

Written Assurances

In addition to the foregoing, both parties to a contract under Article II have the right to demand assurances in writing that performance will occur. This can arise if either party becomes concerned about the other party's ability to perform. Note that this is different from a situation in which one party affirmatively states that she will not perform (see Chapter 10). Written assurances also have no applicability to situations in which a party has been judicially deemed bankrupt. If the assurances are not given within 30 days of the request, the requesting party can act as if the other party has breached the contract.

Summary

Article II is one of the most important provisions of the Uniform Commercial Code with respect to contract law. This article covers three main categories of contracts: contracts for the sale of goods valued at over $500; contracts between merchants; and contracts for the lease of property. Article II imposes warranties, or guarantees, with respect to the quality and usefulness of the subject goods. Additionally, it indicates special types of arrangements apportioning the risk of having the goods lost or destroyed while in transit between the seller and the buyer. Lastly, Article II details certain remedies for the injured party in a breach of one of the aforementioned contracts unique to the UCC.

Article II-A, Leases

Several years ago many jurisdictions added a new subsection to Article II to deal with the lease of goods. There were several reasons for codifying the law with respect to such leases:

1. It was necessary to define the term "lease" so as to distinguish between a true lease and a hidden security agreement. A "true lease" is one in which, at the termination of the lease period, the item returns to the lessor. Conversely, with a hidden security agreement, the document reads like a lease but at its termination the lessee has the right to purchase the item at a nominal fee because its useful life has been exhausted during the leasehold. If the agreement is deemed to be a hidden security agreement, the provisions of Article IX must be complied with (see below).

2. If a lease exists, it must be analyzed to determine whether the lessor has made warranties to the lessee. If the contract is a sale, the regular warranties discussed above apply. However, without the codification of this article, the law was unclear as to whether lessors make any non-explicit warranties to lessees. Under the provisions of Article II-A, the UCC imposes express and implied warranties, as well as warranties against infringement and interference of the lessee's right to the use and possession of the good, as well as the methods to be employed to exclude or modify warranties. The provisions of each state's version of this article must be analyzed to ascertain the extent of such provision in a given jurisdiction.

3. It was necessary to determine whether the remedies available under Article II are available under Article II-A. Once again, the extent to which such remedies would be applicable in a given instance is determined by the UCC version adopted by the jurisdiction in question.

In drafting the model version of UCC II-A, the Commissioners took the view that there was no need to include security interests disguised as leases, so "leases" were defined specifically to exclude such security devices. However, to avoid any conflict with specific state of federal laws, Article II-A makes its provisions subject to title and consumer protection laws.

The codification of this section was greatly influenced by the basic common law tenets of contract interpretation that have been discussed throughout this text. In other words, except where specifically noted, all common law rules and principles still apply to lease arrangements. Basically, the sales provisions of Article II have simply been extended to commercial leases of goods because of the current practice in the business community of leasing equipment rather than making an outright purchase, even if the lease in question provides for an option to purchase at the conclusion of the leasehold.

Article IX, Secured Transactions

Secured Transaction Defined

Article IX of the UCC defines a **secured transaction** as any transaction, regardless of form, that is intended to create a security interest in personal property or fixtures, including *tangible goods, intangibles,* and *documents.* A *tangible good* (§9-105) is any good that can be touched and moved and whose value is incorporated into the item itself. Examples of tangible goods are furniture, clothing, and automobiles. An intangible (§9-106) is a right to property, rather than a physical object. Examples of intangibles are stock certificates, bank savings account books, bonds, patents, and copyrights. Documents are such items as bills of lading and dock receipts.

A **security interest** represents the right of the holder of the interest to attach specific property in case of a default. In terms of contract law, this means that if the promissor defaults on his contractual obligation, and the promissee has a security interest, the promissee can attach the promissor's property that is subject to that interest to satisfy the default. It affords the innocent party greater protection in case of breach of contract because she knows that there will at least be the value of the secured property to lessen her injury.

 EXAMPLE:

Heather goes to the state bank to take out a personal loan. Before the bank loans Heather the money, it asks her to put up some property as security. Heather gives the bank a pearl ring she owns. The bank retains this ring as **collateral** (property to secure payment of the debt) until Heather repays the loan. Should Heather default, the bank can sell the ring to satisfy Heather's debt. Physical possession is one method of creating a security interest.

Nearly all security interests in personal property and fixtures are covered under Article IX of the UCC. There are only six categories of property that are not subject to this article — enumerated in §9-104.

1.   *Real estate.* As indicated by the definition of a secured transaction in Article IX, real property is automatically excluded from this UCC provision, except for *fixtures.* A fixture is property that has been attached to real property but is capable of being removed without destroying or disturbing the real estate. Examples of fixtures would be door knobs, chandeliers, and light switches.

2.   *Interests perfected under federal statutes.* Certain types of property, such as patents and copyrights, are created by federal statutes that also provide methods for establishing security interests in that property.

3.   *Wage assignments. Wage assignments,* or *garnishments,* are covered by separate laws that protect the wage earner from having all of her wages taken from her to satisfy debts.

4.   *Mechanic's liens.* A **mechanic's lien** is the right of any person who works on a piece of property to attach that property if the owner does not pay for the work performed. Mechanic's liens have been in existence for hundreds of years, are part of the common law, and automatically afford protection to workers.

5.   *Claims arising out of judicial proceedings.* If a court of competent jurisdiction grants the specific right to a piece of property, the court's authority supersedes that of the UCC, and these claims are excluded from Article IX.

6.   *Consumer sales agreements regulated by state laws.* Many states have enacted laws to protect consumers from having property reclaimed by stores if the consumer fails to make a payment years after the purchase, and these sales are exempted from Article IX where such statutes exist.

A security interest gives the holder of the interest the right to attach specific property subject to the interest in the case of default. This type of creditor has greater rights to the specific property of the debtor than other creditors. Whenever payment for merchandise is not concurrent with delivery of the goods, contacts usually specify that the party who conveys the goods shall have a security interest in the goods until payment. This protects the person who has already given his consideration in case the other party defaults. However, merely having a clause in the contract may be insufficient to create a valid and enforceable security interest pursuant to Article IX.

Requirements to Create a Security Interest

To create a valid and enforceable security interest, the parties must intend to create a security interest and evidence such interest by meeting three requirements under Part Two of Article IX:

1.   There must be a security agreement.
2.   There must be attachment.
3.   There must be perfection.

1.   *Security agreement.* A **security agreement** is a writing signed by both parties. It describes the property that is subject to the security interest

and states that a security interest is being created in that property. The property is generally referred to as the collateral. Usually, the contract between the parties for the sale of the goods satisfies this requirement, provided that it contains a statement creating the security interest. For an example of such a statement, see the sample clauses given below.

2. *Attachment.* **Attachment** is the timing element of the security interest; it indicates the moment when the creditor gives consideration for the security interest. Typically, this occurs when the agreement is signed, or the security holder conveys his consideration to the other party, or the debtor takes possession of the collateral. At this moment the security holder has an inchoate right to the collateral.

What happens if the contract is for a loan, and the debtor is using the borrowed money to purchase the property that will become the collateral? The creditor's rights may not attach for several weeks. The reason that the attachment is delayed is because the property that is the subject of the security interest is not yet owned by the debtor. The debtor is using the borrowed money to purchase the collateral. During this time the debtor may default. Under these circumstances, the creditor has a **purchase money security interest** in the property the debtor buys with the creditor's funds. This interest is implied by law, and the debtor holds the property in trust for the creditor.

 EXAMPLE:

Leonard loans his brother-in-law Zack $50,000 to start a bottling company, and the loan states that Leonard will have a security interest in the bottling equipment. Zack orders the bottling equipment on credit and uses Leonard's money to buy office furniture and supplies. If Zack defaults prior to the equipment being delivered, Leonard has a purchase money security interest in the furniture and supplies because it was his money that paid for the items.

Another problem that can arise with respect to attachment occurs if the collateral is the inventory of the debtor. Many times, if money is loaned to a manufacturer, the creditor will take a security interest in the debtor's inventory. However, inventory is always being sold, so the specific items included in inventory one week are not the same items the following week. In this situation, the creditor is deemed to have a **floating lien,** giving her the right to attach any item that is included in inventory at the moment of default. The actual collateral is always being changed.

 EXAMPLE:

Assume that in the above example, instead of taking a security interest in Zack's equipment, Leonard takes a security interest in Zack's inventory. On the day the loan agreement is signed,

Zack has 100,000 bottles in inventory; on the day Zack defaults, his inventory contains 200,000 bottles. Leonard has a right to claim the 200,000 bottles, even though these specific bottles were acquired by Zack after the agreement. The floating lien gives Leonard the right to all existing inventory on the day of default up to the value of the debt.

3. *Perfection.* The third requirement to create a valid and enforceable security interest is **perfection.** Perfection is the process of protecting a creditor's rights to the collateral from all other claimants and can be effectuated in three ways:

First, in certain circumstances, the attachment itself is sufficient to perfect the interest, as in the case of a purchase money security interest.

Second, perfection can come about by the creditor having physical possession of the collateral. An example would be the state bank in the earlier instance with Heather and the loan. Because the bank is actually holding Heather's pearl ring, no one else can get control of it.

Third, and most typically, perfection can be accomplished by filing a **financing statement.** A financing statement is a document, signed by the parties, that contains their names and addresses and describes the collateral. (See sample financing statement on the next page.) A security agreement can be used as a financing statement, but the reverse is not true. The financing statement does not create the security interest. However, it is very rare that anyone uses the security agreement as the financing statement, because once the document is filed, it becomes publicly available. Most people do not want all the terms of their contractual arrangements to be public knowledge. Usually creditors file financing statements. These forms can be purchased from legal stationery stores and only indicate the minimum information required by Article IX.

Filing is mandatory for perfecting security interests in intangibles, inventory goods, and equipment, but is permissive for all other property. Filing is effective for a period of five years. If the debt is not satisfied within this period, the financing statement must be refiled. Where the financing statements are filed depends on the nature of the collateral: either the County Filing Office where the property is located, the County Recorder's Office (typically for timber, minerals, and crops), or the Secretary of State's Office. Part 4 of Article IX specifies the appropriate office, and therefore the version of the Code adopted by the state in question must be checked.

Not only does filing afford the creditor some protection against other claimants, but because filing is public, prior to agreeing to accept a security interest in a particular piece of property, a potential creditor must check the appropriate office to make sure that no one else already has a security interest in the collateral. This is crucial for the formation of an enforceable security interest.

But what happens if there are conflicting claims to the same property? Which creditor prevails? Part 3 of Article IX has established an order of priorities in such situations to determine which creditor has superior rights to the collateral.

FORM UCC-1

STATE OF MICHIGAN
UNIFORM COMMERCIAL CODE FINANCING STATEMENT
(Approved by the Secretary of State and Michigan Association of Registers of Deeds)

INSTRUCTIONS:
1. TYPE OR PRINT All information required on this Form.
2. If filing is made with the Secretary of State, send the WHITE copies to the Secretary of State, Lansing, Michigan. If filing is made with the Register of Deeds, send the YELLOW copies to the Local Register of Deeds. Retain the PINK copies for files of secured party and debtor.
3. Enclose filing fee.
4. IF ADDITIONAL SPACE IS NEEDED for any items on this Form, continue the items on separate sheets of paper (5" x 8"). One copy of these additional sheets should accompany the WHITE Forms, and one copy should accompany the YELLOW Forms. USE PAPER CLIPS to attach these sheets to the Forms (DO NOT USE STAPLES, GLUE, TAPE, ETC.) and indicate in Item 1 the number of additional sheets attached.
5. At the time of filing, the filing officer will return acknowledgement. At a later time, the secured party may date and sign the termination legend and use acknowledgement copy as a termination statement.
6. Both the WHITE and YELLOW Filing Officer copies must have original signatures. Only the debtor must sign the financing statement, and the signature of the secured party is not necessary, except that the secured party alone may sign the financing statement in the following 4 instances: Please specify action in Item 7 below.
   (1) Where the collateral which is subject to the security interest in another state is brought into Michigan or the location of the debtor is changed to Michigan.
   (2) "For proceeds if the security interest in the original collateral was perfected."
   (3) The previous filing has lapsed.
   (4) For collateral acquired after a change of debtor name etc., and a filing is required under MCLA 440.9402 (2) and (7);MSA 19.9402 (2) and (7).

1. No. of additional sheets	Liber	Page	For Filing Officer (Date, Time, Number, and Filing Office)
2. Debtor(s) (Last Name First) and address(es)	3. Secured Party(ies) and address(es)		
4. Name and address(es) of assignee(s) (if any)	CHECK ☒ if applicable		
	5. ☐ Products of collateral are also covered.		
	6. ☐ Collateral was brought into this state subject to a security interest in another jurisdiction.		

7. This financing statement covers the following types (or items) of property:

_____   by: _____
Signature(s) of Debtor(s)   (Signature of Secured Party or Assignee of Record)

SECRETARY OF STATE COPY

Order by Form 8411 Rev. 1/80 From Doubleday Bros. & Co., Kalamazoo, Mich. 49002 FINANCIAL PRINTERS

Priorities

Article IX has established an order of priorities for creditors in case of the debtor's default. Should there be conflicting claims for the same property, the claimant with the highest priority will prevail. The general rule is that secured creditors have greater priorities than unsecured creditors. Among secured creditors, priorities date from the time of filing *or* perfection of the security interest. The order of the priorities is:

1. creditors with a purchase money security interest;
2. creditors with a floating lien;

3. among creditors who perfect on the same day: creditors who filed first (this is the actual date of filing the financing statement, not the date the agreement was signed), then creditors with interests perfected other than by filing (attachment or possession); and

4. creditors whose interests attached first among nonperfected creditors.

EXAMPLE:

Julia loans $10,000 to Ariel, taking a security interest in Ariel's receivables. The loan agreement is signed and the money given on Monday. On Friday, Julia files her financing statement. In the interim, Ariel borrows $5000 from Mark, signing a security agreement for the receivables on Wednesday. Mark also files his financing statement on Wednesday. When Ariel defaults, Mark prevails because he filed before Julia (Wednesday versus Friday).

If the debtor defaults, the creditor with a valid security interest may either retain the collateral in satisfaction of the debt, sell the collateral to satisfy the debt (any amount above the debt acquired by the sale of the collateral belongs to the debtor), or may simply sue the debtor in an action for debt.

Generally, paralegals who work with contracts subject to Article IX of the UCC have very specific functions to perform. First, they must draft a legally accurate description of the property that will be subject to the security interest. If the property is inaccurately or incompletely described, the client will not have an effective security interest. Second, the legal assistant must check the appropriate government office to determine that no other security interest is attached to the subject property. Finally, the paralegal must file the financing statement in a timely manner in the appropriate office.

SAMPLE CLAUSES

1

MANUFACTURER HEREBY WARRANTS THAT THE MERCHANDISE WILL NOT FADE OR SHRINK.

This is an example of an express warranty made by a manufacturer. Any person who purchases these goods or who is the ultimate consumer (user) of these goods may sue the manufacturer if the goods do in fact fade or shrink. The warranty is a covenant of the seller.

| 2 |

We hereby grant to you a security interest in all receivables, as defined above, all present and future instruments, documents, chattel paper, and general intangibles (as defined by the Uniform Commercial Code), and all reserves, balances and deposits, and property at any time to our credit. All of the foregoing shall secure payment and performance of all of our obligations at any time owing to you, fixed or contingent, whether arising out of this or any other agreement, or by operation of law or otherwise.

The above is a contract clause intended to create a security agreement in documents and intangibles. Taken in conjunction with the entire agreement, which would indicate the parties' names, addresses, and signatures, this would constitute a valid security agreement, the first requirement to create an enforceable security interest under Article IX of the UCC.

| 3 |

You want waterproof? Breathable? Look at our clothing on page 20, all 100% waterproof and windproof, yet so breathable that overheating is a thing of the past.

The above catalog description constitutes an express warranty by the seller. Even though the word "warranty" is not used, because the description of the clothing appears in its sales literature, the manufacturer is held to guarantee that the clothes are 100 percent waterproof and breathable so that the customer will not get wet or overheated.

CHAPTER SUMMARY

The Uniform Commercial Code was created to promote and facilitate commerce among the states and to provide some uniformity in state laws with respect to commercial transactions. The UCC is a state law, and versions of the model UCC have been adopted in every jurisdiction including the District of Columbia. Three UCC articles have a direct impact on the law of contracts.

Article I, General Provisions, establishes the general guidelines for interpretation of the entire Code. This article restates the purpose of the Code and indicates that the Code is to be liberally, not literally, construed, within the bounds of reasonable interpretation. Additionally, the state law will always prevail unless specifically superseded by the Code.

Article I also establishes three obligations for all persons whose transactions are covered by the UCC: (1) they are obligated to act in good faith; (2) they are obligated to perform within a reasonable time; and (3) they are expected to perform according to the custom, usage, and past practices of the parties and industry involved.

Article II, Sales, concerns itself with contracts for the sale of goods. It is the modern interpretation of the Statute of Frauds with respect to these types of contracts. The UCC does not cover contracts for the performance of services.

The UCC provisions on sales regulate the concept of warranties, or guarantees, with respect to contracts for the sale of goods. In this manner, Article II makes the manufacturer/seller of goods contractually bound not only to his direct purchaser, but to anyone who ultimately uses or consumes the goods. These warranties may be either express (created by words or conduct) or implied (created by operation of law).

Article II further establishes contractual methods of determining when the risk of loss of the goods transfers from the seller to the buyer. The Code specifies several different clauses or agreements that the parties may insert in their contract to make this determination.

Additionally, the article on sales provides specific remedies in case of breach of contract for both the seller and the buyer. These Article II remedies go beyond those generally afforded under contract law.

Finally, Article IX, Secured Transactions, indicates how a creditor may contractually provide for a security interest in specific property, property that he may then attach and sell to satisfy the debt in the case of the debtor's default. By meeting the UCC requirements for creating a security agreement and for attachment and perfection, a creditor is given greater protection for recovery in the case of breach of contract. Commerce is thus promoted by making credit and loans less risky for the creditor.

SYNOPSIS

UCC purpose: Modernizing, clarifying, and unifying state commercial law
Article I, General provisions
    Obligations
    1. Good faith
    2. Reasonable time
    3. Custom and usage
Article II, Sales
    1. Contracts covered
        a. Sale of goods (not services)
        b. Lease of goods
        c. Contracts between merchants
    2. Contract provisions
        a. Warranties
            i. Express

               (1) Affirmation or promise
               (2) Description
               (3) Sample or model
          ii. Implied
               (1) Merchantability
               (2) Fitness for a particular use
         iii. Title
      b. Risk of loss
         i. Conditional
         ii. Shipment
         iii. Destination
   3. Remedies
      a. Seller
         i. Withhold delivery
         ii. Stop delivery in transit
         iii. Redeem goods from insolvent buyer
      b. Buyer
         i. Cover
         ii. Replevin
         iii. Revoke acceptance
         iv. Reclaim goods from insolvent seller

Article IX, Secured Transactions
   1. Exceptions
   2. Requirements
      a. Security agreement
      b. Attachment
      c. Perfection (filing)
   3. Priorities

Key Terms

Attachment: time at which security interest becomes an inchoate right

Battle of the forms: difference in forms used by merchants for sales agreements

CIF: cost of insurance and freight paid for by seller, even though risk of loss has passed to the buyer

COD: cost on delivery; conditional contract in which the risk of loss passes to buyer only after goods have been delivered and paid for

Collateral: property pledged to secure a security interest

Consignment contract: conditional contract in which risk of loss remains with seller until buyer resells the goods

Cover: remedy whereby buyer can purchase goods in substitution for breached contract

Express warranty: guarantee created by words or conduct of the seller

Ex ship: destination contract in which risk of loss passes to buyer when goods are off-loaded from the mode of transportation

FAS: free alongside; a shipping contract in which risk of loss passes to buyer when goods are placed alongside vessel used for transportation

Financing statement: document filed in government office to protect a security interest

Floating lien: security interest in after-acquired property

FOB (carrier):   shipment contract in which risk of loss passes when goods are loaded onto third-party carrier

FOB (place of shipment):   free on board; shipment contract in which risk of loss passes when goods are given to third-party carrier

Implied warranty: guarantee created by operation of law

Mechanic's lien: security interest given under common law to persons who repair property

Merchant: person who regularly trades in goods or who holds himself out as having knowledge peculiar to a specific good

No arrival, no sale: destination contract in which risk of loss passes to buyer when goods are tendered to the buyer

Perfect tender: buyers right to complete performance

Perfection: method of creating and protecting a security interest under Article IX of the UCC

Purchase money security interest: security interest created in the creditor whose money is used to buy the collateral

Replevin: equitable remedy in which buyer reclaims property previously rejected

Revocation: to recall an offer

Sale on approval: conditional contract in which risk of loss passes to buyer when buyer receives and approves goods

Sale or return: conditional contract in which risk of loss passes when buyer receives goods; buyer bears the cost of returning goods of which he does not approve

Secured transaction: any transaction, regardless of form, that creates a security interest in personal property or fixtures

Security agreement: document signed by debtor and creditor, that names the collateral, and creates a security interest in said collateral

Security interest: right acquired by a creditor to attach collateral in case of default by the debtor

Shipment contract: agreement whereby risk passes from seller to buyer when goods are transported by a third person

Strict liability: no standard of care; automatic liability if properly used goods do not meet the warranty

Warranty: guarantee made by manufacturer or seller with respect to quality, quantity, and type of good being sold

Warranty of fitness for a particular use: guarantee that goods can be used for a specified purpose

Warranty of merchantability: guarantee that goods can be used in their current condition

Warranty of title: guarantee that seller has a title sufficient to transfer goods to buyer

EXERCISES

1. Find two advertisements in your local newspaper that indicate warranties.
2. Discuss several methods of protecting a person's security interest.
3. Does the UCC in fact promote commerce? Explain.
4. Obtain and analyze a mortgage and chattel mortgage agreement.
5. Obtain the addresses of the appropriate government offices in your state for filing financing statements.
6. Check your own state statute for its version of the UCC.

Cases for Analysis

In re Hoskins highlights the concept of leases versus hidden security agreements, one of the most frequently litigated aspects of UCC II-A. The method of perfecting security agreements is addressed in Hergert v. Bank of the West.

In re Hoskins
266 B.R. 154 (W.D. Mo. 2001)

Factual Background

On May 24, 2001, Charles Henry Hoskins, Jr. and Sylvia Kaye Hoskins filed a voluntary petition for rehabilitation under Chapter 13 of the Bankruptcy Code. At that time, a lawsuit was pending in the Associate Judge Division of the Circuit Court of Jackson County, Missouri that had been filed by Ford Motor Credit Company ("Ford") against the Hoskins seeking to recover a deficiency balance in the amount of $3653.81, plus interest and attorney's fees, remaining due following the sale of an automobile that the Hoskins ha[ve] voluntarily surrendered to Ford after defaulting in making payments. The Hoskins filed an answer and a counterclaim in the action asserting that Ford was not entitled to recover the deficiency balance and that they were entitled to damages under Article 9 of the Missouri Uniform Commercial Code based upon Ford's failure to properly notify both of them of the pending sale of the automobile. Subsequent to the bankruptcy filing, Ford filed a Notice of Removal of the Jackson County, Missouri action to the United States District Court for the Western District of Missouri. By Order dated June 18, 2001, the Honorable Howard F. Sachs referred this matter to the United States Bankruptcy Court for the Western District of Missouri, and the adversary proceeding was assigned to the undersigned. On August 2, 2001, a hearing was held at which time the parties agreed that the Court could decide the matter based on the pleadings, including Ford's motion for summary judgment and the Hoskins' opposition thereto, that had been filed in the Jackson County, Missouri action, copies of which have been filed in this adversary proceeding.

The documents supplied by the parties provide the following pertinent information. On November 8, 1997, Charles and Sylvia Hoskins
entered into a written contract with Southtown Ford, Inc. entitled
"Motor Vehicle Lease Agreement" to "lease" a new 1998 Ford Windstar
for a period of 24 months. Charles and Sylvia Hoskins were designated as
"Lessee" and "Co-Lessee" in the contract, and Southtown Ford, Inc. was
designated as "Lessor." After execution, Southtown Ford, Inc. assigned this
contract to Ford. The contract stated that " 'Ford Credit' is Ford Motor
Credit Company. The 'Holder' is FMCC and its assigns. By signing
'You' (Lessee and Co-Lessee) agree to lease this Vehicle according to the
terms on the front and back of this lease."

The contract obligated the Hoskins to make payments in the amount
of $596.58 per month for 24 months. A portion of each monthly payment
was designated as "rent charge" in the total amount of $4010.48 for the
24-month term. Over the 24-month period the Hoskins were obligated to
pay Ford the total amount of $9420.00, which was designated as depreci-
ation for the vehicle's decline in value through normal use. The agreed
upon value of the vehicle on the date of execution of the contract was
$26,434.48. After payment of all amounts due under the contract, the
residual value of the vehicle would be $15,013.60 at the end of the
24-month term. The contract provided that at the end of the "Lease
Term" the Hoskins had the option to purchase the vehicle for $15,263.60,
plus official fees and taxes, as long as they had not defaulted or terminated
the lease early.

The contract further provided that the vehicle was covered by a
standard new vehicle warranty; placed the responsibility for maintenance
of the vehicle and repairing damage to the vehicle upon the Hoskins;
required the Hoskins to pay all license, title and registration costs; and
obligated the Hoskins to insure the vehicle during the lease term. The
contract provided for early termination of the lease term, however, in
the event of early termination the Hoskins still would be required to pay
the remaining sums due under the lease (the amount due depended upon
several factors), plus a $200.00 early termination fee. The contract provided
that, among other things, the Hoskins would be in default if they failed to
make any of the payments when due. Pursuant to the terms of the contract,
if the Hoskins defaulted, Ford could cancel the lease, repossess the vehicle
and sell it at a public or private sale. The contract was silent regarding
Ford's obligation to notify the Hoskins of any proposed sale of the vehicle
following default and repossession. Upon default, the Hoskins would also
be liable to pay the remaining sums due under the lease (once again the
amount due depended upon several factors), plus other expenses incurred
by Ford and reasonable attorney's fees. Finally, the contract provided that
the vehicle would be titled in the name of Ford.

The Hoskins ceased making payments after March 18, 1999, and on
May 28, 1999, they voluntarily surrendered the vehicle to Southtown Ford,
Inc. On June 3, 1999, Sylvia Hoskins signed a Voluntary Surrender form in
which she acknowledged that she was voluntarily surrendering possession
of the 98 Ford Windstar to Ford and that she understood that Ford would

sell the vehicle. The Voluntary Surrender form also provided that Sylvia Hoskins agreed to pay Ford for any deficiency resulting from the sale. On or about June 1, 1999, Ford sent Sylvia Hoskins a Red Carpet Lease Notice of Private Sale informing her that the vehicle would be sold by Ford at a private sale. This Notice of Private Sale again informed Sylvia Hoskins that she might be held liable if a deficiency resulted from the sale. Ford did not notify Charles Hoskins of the pending sale. On June 23, 1999, Ford sold the vehicle through a private sale. After crediting the Hoskins' account with the proceeds of the sale, a deficiency balance remained due in the amount of $3653.81. On August 24, 2000, Ford filed a lawsuit in the Jackson County, Missouri Circuit Court against the Hoskins seeking to recover this deficiency. The Hoskins filed an answer in which they contended, in relevant part, that Ford was not entitled to recover the deficiency balance remaining after the sale of the vehicle alleging that Ford had violated section 400.9-504 of the Missouri Uniform Commercial Code by failing to properly notify Charles Hoskins of the pending sale of the vehicle. The Hoskins also filed a counterclaim in which they asserted that because Ford had failed to properly notify Charles Hoskins of the pending sale of the vehicle, they were entitled to recover damages from Ford in the amount of $4952.48 pursuant to section 400.9-507 of the Missouri Uniform Commercial Code. In their response to Ford's motion for summary judgment, the Hoskins conceded that Ford had properly notified Sylvia Hoskins of the pending sale of the vehicle, but asserted that any recovery against her was subject to discharge under the Chapter 13 proceedings.

Discussion

The Hoskins do not dispute that a deficiency balance in the amount of $3653.81 remained after Ford sold the 1998 Ford Windstar. The determinative question is whether the written agreement between the Hoskins and Ford, as assignee, is a true lease or security for a conditional sales contract. If the agreement constitutes a true lease then Article 2A of the Missouri Uniform Commercial Code governs, and Article 2A does not require that notice of a pending sale of leased property be sent by the lessor to the lessee upon the lessee's default. See Mo. Rev. Stat. §400.2A-501 and §400.2A-502 (1994). Further the parties' contract does not provide for notice of sale to the Hoskins in the event of default. Accordingly, Ford would be entitled to a judgment against the Hoskins for the deficiency balance, and allowed to pursue recovery of same from the Hoskins to the extent permitted by the Bankruptcy Code, 11 U.S.C. §§101-1330. If, on the other hand, the agreement constitutes security for a conditional sales contract then Article 9 of the Missouri Uniform Commercial Code governs, and Ford was required to follow the procedures set forth in Mo. Rev. Stat. §400.9-504 (1994) following the Hoskins' default, or face the consequences of its noncompliance, including an award of damages in favor of the Hoskins, see Mo. Rev. Stat. §400.9-507 (1994), and denial of recovery of the deficiency balance, see In re Huffman, 204 B.R. 562, 563-64 (Bankr.

W.D. Mo. 1997); McKesson Corp. v. Colman's Grant Village, Inc., 938 S.W.2d 631, 633 (Mo. App. 1997).

"To determine a debtor's property rights, such as an interest in a lease, the bankruptcy court is required to look to state law." Brown v. Kempker (In re Kempker), 104 B.R. 196, 202 (Bankr. W.D. Mo. 1989) (*quoting* Johnson v. First Nat. Bank of Montevideo, Minn., 719 F.2d 270, 273 (8th Cir. 1983)). Section 400.2A-103(1)(j) of the Missouri Uniform Commercial Code defines "lease" to mean "a transfer of the right to possession and use of goods for a term in return for consideration, but a . . . retention or creation of a security interest is not a lease." Mo. Rev. Stat. §400.2A-103(1)(j) (1994). Section 400.9-102(2) of the Missouri Uniform Commercial Code states in relevant part that Article 9 "applies to security interests created by contract including . . . [a] lease . . . intended as security." Mo. Rev. Stat. §400.9-102(2) (1994). The term "security interest" is defined in section 400.1-201(37) of the Missouri Uniform Commercial Code, and in 1992 was amended to provide in pertinent part that:

> (37) **"Security Interest"** means an interest in personal property or fixtures which secures payment or performance of an obligation. . . .
>
> Whether a transaction creates a lease or security interest is determined by the facts of each case; however, a transaction creates a security interest if the consideration the lessee is to pay the lessor for the right to possession and use of the goods is an obligation for the term of the lease not subject to termination by the lessee, and
>
> (a) the original term of the lease is equal to or greater than the remaining economic life of the goods,
>
> (b) the lessee is bound to renew the lease for the remaining economic life of the goods or is bound to become the owner of the goods,
>
> (c) the lessee has an option to renew the lease for the remaining economic life of the goods for no additional consideration or nominal additional consideration upon compliance with the lease agreement, or
>
> (d) the lessee has an option to become the owner of the goods for no additional consideration or nominal additional consideration upon compliance with the lease agreement.
>
> A transaction does not create a security interest merely because it provides that
>
> (a) the present value of the consideration the lessee is obligated to pay the lessor for the right to possession and use of the goods is substantially equal to or is greater than the fair market value of the goods at the time the lease is entered into,
>
> (b) the lessee assumes risk of loss of the goods, or agrees to pay taxes, insurance, filing, recording, or registration fees, or service or maintenance costs with respect to the goods,
>
> (c) the lessee has an option to renew the lease or to become the owner of the goods,
>
> (d) the lessee has an option to renew the lease for a fixed rent that is equal to or greater than the reasonably predictable fair market rent for the use of the goods for the term of the renewal at the time the option is to be performed, or

(e) the lessee has an option to become the owner of the goods for a fixed price that is equal to or greater than the reasonably predictable fair market value of the goods at the time the option is to be performed. For purposes of subsection (37):

(x) Additional consideration is not nominal if (i) when the option to renew the lease is granted to the lessee the rent is stated to be the fair market rent for the use of the goods for the term of the renewal determined at the time the option is to be performed, or (ii) when the option to become the owner of the goods is granted to the lessee the price is stated to be the fair market value of the goods determined at the time the option is to be performed. Additional consideration is nominal if it is less than the lessee's reasonably predictable cost of performing under the lease agreement if the option is not exercised;

(y) **"Reasonably predictable"** and **"remaining economic life of the goods"** are to be determined with reference to the facts and circumstances at the time the transaction is entered into; and

(z) **"Present value"** means the amount as of a date certain of one or more sums payable in the future, discounted to the date certain. The discount is determined by the interest rate specified by the parties if the rate is not manifestly unreasonable at the time the transaction is entered into; otherwise, the discount is determined by a commercially reasonable rate that takes into account the facts and circumstances of each case at the time the transaction was entered into.

Mo. Rev. Stat. §400.1-201(37) (1994).

The comment to section 400.1-201(37) explains that the amendment was adopted because:

> Prior to this amendment, Section 1-201(37) provided that whether a lease was intended as security (i.e., a security interest disguised as a lease) was to be determined from the facts of each case; however, (a) the inclusion of an option to purchase did not itself make the lease one intended for security, and (b) an agreement that upon compliance with the terms of the lease the lessee would become, or had the option to become, the owner of the property for no additional consideration, or for a nominal consideration, did make the lease one intended for security.
>
> Reference to the intent of the parties to create a lease or security interest has led to unfortunate results. In discovering intent, courts have relied upon factors that were thought to be more consistent with sales or loans than leases. Most of these criteria, however, are as applicable to true leases as to security interests. Examples include the typical net lease provisions, a purported lessor's lack of storage facilities or its character as a financing party rather than a dealer in goods. Accordingly, amended Section 1-201(37) deletes all reference to the parties' intent.

Mo. Rev. Stat. §400.1-201(37) (1994), Uniform Commercial Code Comment.

This Court was unable to locate any Missouri appellate court case, Missouri bankruptcy court case or Eighth Circuit Court of Appeals case that has addressed the issue of true lease versus security interest in the context of section 400.1-201(37) of the Missouri Uniform Commercial Code as amended in 1992. However, there are several cases on point from bankruptcy courts applying the law of states that have adopted the same amendment to section 1-201(37) as did Missouri which provide guidance to this Court in construing Missouri's amended statute.

In Banterra Bank v. Subway Equip. Leasing Corp. (In re Taylor), 209 B.R. 482 (Bankr. S.D. Ill. 1997), a dispute arose over whether an equipment lease was a true lease or a disguised security agreement. In ruling that the contract at issue was a security agreement, the bankruptcy court applied Illinois law and opined:

> In any analysis under §1-201(37), the intent of the parties is no longer the primary consideration. Rather, the focus is on the "economic realities" of the transaction. . . . Under this approach, the lease will be construed as a security interest as a matter of law if the debtor cannot terminate the lease *and* one of the enumerated requirements is satisfied. . . . If the Court determines that the transaction is not a disguised security agreement *per se*, it must then look at the specific facts of the case to determine whether the "economics of the transaction" suggest such a result. . . .

Id. at 484-85 (citations omitted; emphasis in original). See also In re Macklin, 236 B.R. 403, 406 (Bankr. E.D. Ark. 1999) (applying Arkansas law) ("If the lease is not subject to termination by the lessee and one of [the] four additional conditions [enumerated in section 1-201(37)] also exist, the transaction is a sale with a security interest as a matter of law."); In re Kim, 232 B.R. 324, 329, 330 (Bankr. E.D. Pa. 1999) (applying Pennsylvania law) ("The revised [section 1-201(37)] seeks to correct the shortcomings of its predecessor by focusing the inquiry of the lease/security interest analysis on the economics of the transaction rather than on the intent of the parties. . . . For leases which satisfy the . . . test [in section 1-201(37)] the . . . inquiry comes to an end — such leases constitute security agreements as a matter of law."); In re Yarbrough, 211 B.R. 654, 657 (Bankr. W.D. Tenn. 1997) (applying Mississippi law) ("While subjective intent used to be the standard by which courts determined whether a transaction was a lease or security interest, under the new definition [of section 1-201(37)] courts look only to the economic realities of the transaction.").

In In re Owen, 221 B.R. 56, 60-61 (Bankr. N.D.N.Y. 1998), the bankruptcy court applying New York law explained that the first paragraph of section 1-201(37):

> set[s] out a bright line test whereby, as a matter of law, a transaction creates a security interest. Thus, if the Debtors do not have a right to terminate the purported lease prior to the expiration of its term, then the Court is to examine whether any of the four other enumerated conditions have been met which would establish that the parties entered into a security agreement. . . .

The court further interpreted section 1-201(37) to mean that if the debtor can terminate the lease, then the court need not consider the four factors in order to find that as a matter of law the parties' agreement does not create a security interest, however, the four factors are relevant in the court's continuing examination of the facts of the particular case to determine whether the contract constitutes a security agreement. Id. at 61.

Applying the foregoing analysis to this case, this Court first must determine whether the Hoskins had a right to terminate the agreement with Ford. The Court finds that although the contract provides a means by which the Hoskins could terminate the lease early, the Hoskins could not simply return the vehicle to Ford and then walk away from the transaction with no further future financial responsibility. Upon early termination and return of the vehicle, the Hoskins were still liable to Ford for the balance of the remaining payments that were due under the lease; the final amount due and owing depended on variable factors. The Court concludes that a termination provision in a contract which provides that a lessee remains financially liable to the lessor after termination of the lease for payments that become due after the date the lease is terminated does not constitute "termination" within the meaning of section 1-201(37). The Court finds that the Hoskins could not terminate the agreement with Ford, which satisfies the first criteria for finding a security agreement as a matter of law.

Next, the Court must determine whether any of the four enumerated conditions set forth in section 400.1-201(37) have been satisfied. Relevant here is whether the option price required to purchase the 1998 Ford Windstar at the expiration of the lease term constituted nominal consideration. In Banterra Bank v. Subway Equip. Leasing Corp. (In re Taylor), the bankruptcy court opined:

> Section 1-201(37)(x) of the Illinois Uniform Commercial Code provides, in pertinent part, that additional consideration is nominal if "it is less than the lessee's reasonably predictable cost of performing under the lease agreement if the option is not exercised." . . . This codification of what has traditionally been referred to as the "economic realities" test focuses on whether the lessee has, in light of all of the facts and circumstances, no sensible alternative but to exercise the purchase option. . . . Under this test, if only a fool would fail to exercise the purchase option, the option price is generally considered nominal and the transaction characterized as a disguised security agreement.

Banterra Bank, 209 B.R. at 486 (citations omitted). See also In re Copeland, 238 B.R. 801, 804 (Bankr. E.D. Ark. 1999) (applying Arkansas law) ("If a lessor cannot reasonably expect to receive back anything of value at the end of the lease term, then there is no residual value in the lessor and the transaction may be a sale and security interest."); In re Super Feeders, Inc., 236 B.R. 267, 270 (Bankr. D. Neb. 1999) (applying Nebraska law) ("Under the 'economic realities' test, courts consider the relationship of the purchase option price to the original purchase or list price."); *Kempker*, 104 B.R. at 203 (This case was decided prior to the 1992 amendment to section 400.1-201(37) of the Missouri Uniform Commercial Code, however, this Court acknowledged that "the 'economic realities test' . . . examines whether the terms of the lease and purchase option are such that the only sensible economical course for the lessee at the end of the lease term is to exercise the option and become the owner of the goods. If this is the case, the lease is actually a secured installment sale.").

In this case, the contract provided that the agreed upon value of the vehicle on the date of execution of the contract was $26,434.48. The agreement further provided that at the expiration of the 24-month term of the contract, the Hoskins had the option to purchase the vehicle for $15,263.60. The Court finds that the purchase option price of $15,263.60 does not constitute nominal consideration. Because neither of the four factors is satisfied, the document at issue herein is not a security agreement as a matter of law.

However, the Court's inquiry does not end. Although the contract does not constitute a security agreement as a matter of law, the Court must examine the specific facts of this case to determine whether the "economics of the transaction" suggest such a result. Guiding this Court's decision are a consideration of the four factors enumerated in section 400.1-201(37) along with the additional guidelines set out in the statute. Further, although the cases cited by the parties and unearthed by this Court's research were decided in the context of a version of section 400.1-201(37) of the Missouri Uniform Commercial Code that preceded the 1992 amendment, the factors relied upon by the courts in those cases when deciding whether a document was a true lease or a security agreement are still relevant, to the extent they are consistent with amended section 400.1-201(37), to a determination of whether under the facts of a particular case the transaction is a lease or security for a conditional sales contract.

In Commercial Credit Equip. Corp. v. Parsons, 820 S.W.2d 315, 319 (Mo. App. 1991), the Missouri Court of Appeals opined that "the true character and intention of the agreement is determined not from random phrases or formal designations — such as 'lease,' 'lessor,' 'lessee,' but from the economic reality of the agreement, whatever the disguise of the terminology." Under Missouri law, the pivotal factor in determining whether an instrument is a true lease or a security agreement is whether or not the lessee has an absolute obligation to purchase the rental property. See Carlson v. Tandy Computer Leasing, 803 F.2d 391, 396 (8th Cir. 1986) (quoting RCA Corp. v. State Tax Commission, 513 S.W.2d 313, 316 (Mo. 1974)) ("An agreement in which a purchase option existed was only a lease because 'there is no absolute obligation on the [lessee] to purchase, pay for, or assume title to the equipment." . . .) (emphasis in original). See also National Can Servs. Corp. v. Gateway Aluminum Co., Inc., 683 F. Supp. 719, 727 (E.D. Mo. 1988) ("Of significance is the character of the parties' rights to purchase or retain the equipment either at expiration or at termination prior to expiration of the lease."); In re Morris, 150 B.R. 446, 448 (Bankr. E.D. Mo. 1992) ("The existence of an *absolute obligation* by the lessee to purchase rental property is the touchstone in determining whether a security interest was intended.") (emphasis in original).

Here, the Hoskins did have an option to purchase the 1998 Ford Windstar at the expiration of the lease term provided they were not in default and had not terminated the lease early. However, they did not have an absolute obligation to purchase the vehicle. If the Hoskins had fulfilled their contractual obligations under the agreement, whether they purchased the vehicle at the end of the lease term was entirely up to them. Further, as discussed above, the purchase option price of $15,263.60 was not nominal consideration. Accordingly, based on the facts of this case, the Court finds that the agreement in question constitutes a true lease and not a disguised security agreement. In accordance with the guidelines established in amended section 400.1-201(37), the Court determines that the Hoskins' obligation to insure the vehicle during the lease term, maintain and repair the vehicle and pay all license, title and registration costs does not transform the lease into security for a conditional sales contract. In sum, the Court finds that the agreement in question constitutes a true lease.

Conclusion

Based on the above discussion, the Court determines that the Motor Vehicle Lease Agreement entered into between Charles and Sylvia Hoskins and Ford Motor Credit Company, as assignee, is a true lease and is not security for a conditional sales contract. Accordingly, Ford Motor Credit Company is entitled to a judgment against Charles and Sylvia Hoskins in the amount of $3653.81 for the deficiency balance remaining after the sale of the 1998 Ford Windstar. Ford Motor Credit Company may pursue recovery of same to the extent permitted by the Bankruptcy Code, 11 U.S.C. §§101-1330.

Questions

1.   What are the factors enumerated by the court that determine whether a transaction creates a lease or a security agreement?
2.   What is the effect of an absolute obligation on the part of the lessee to purchase the rental property on the determination of the character of the contract in question?
3.   What was the factual basis of the court's conclusion?

Hergert v. Bank of the West
275 B.R. 58 (D. Idaho 2002)

Relevant Facts

The Debtors' farming business was originally financed through Pacific One Bank ("Pacific"). As part of a merger in 1998, all of the assets of Pacific were acquired by the Bank.

These assets included three secured loans of the Debtors: (i) a commercial loan with an outstanding amount of principal, interest and late fees as of trial on January 8, 2002 of $182,051.68; (ii) a commercial loan with an outstanding amount of principal, interest and late fees as of January 8, 2002 of $51,595.44; and (iii) a consumer loan with an outstanding balance of $45,395.12 as of the Petition Date, August 9, 2001.

The two commercial loans are secured under an Agricultural Security Agreement and two Commercial Security Agreements. By their terms, these security agreements cross-collateralize the commercial loan obligations. The consumer loan is secured by an interest in the Debtors' manufactured home.

In connection with the Agricultural Security Agreement, and to perfect the security interest granted thereunder, Pacific filed a UCC-1F (farm products) financing statement. See Exhibit H. In connection with the Commercial Security Agreements, and to perfect the security interests described therein, Pacific filed a UCC-1 financing statement, Exhibit G, and obtained notation of its lien on certificates of title to several vehicles. In regard to the consumer loan, Pacific is shown as a lien-holder on the certificate of title ("Title") to the Debtors' manufactured home.

Both the UCC-1 and the Title identify the secured party as "Pacific One Bank" with a mailing address of P.O. Box 40108, Portland, Oregon, 97240 (the "Portland Address"). The UCC-1 lists an additional address of P.O. Box 9344, Nampa, Idaho 83652-9344 (the "Nampa Address") as the address to which the Secretary of State should return its "acknowledgment" copy of the filing.

The UCC-1F also identifies "Pacific One Bank" as the secured party, with the Nampa Address shown as the address of the secured party. The Debtors do not dispute that the names and addresses on the UCC-1 and UCC-1F were accurate when the documents were created and filed. See Pre-trial Stipulation, at p.2, P 6.

After origination of the Debtors' loans, and before the chapter 12 filing, Pacific was merged into the Bank. The Bank has never amended the secured party's name address(es) in any of the above-described documents.

The Bank has maintained and continues to use the Portland Address. The Bank has been receiving mail there since the merger, and today still is, even if the mail is addressed to Pacific.

At some point subsequent to the merger, the Nampa Address expired and the Bank no longer received mail there. This was the situation at the time of Debtors' chapter 12 petition on August 9, 2001. See Pre-Trial Stipulation, at p.3, P 9.

Ann Ybarguen, a special credits representative of the Bank, testified regarding this situation. The Nampa Address was for a post office box within the main building of the Karcher Mall, a retail shopping facility in Nampa, Idaho. Mail sent there after the Nampa Address had expired would be marked as undeliverable. Pacific's old physical address inside the Karcher Mall was also an invalid address. However, at times the local postman would take mail improperly addressed to Pacific's old physical address to the Bank's new physical location, which happened to be on a retail pad in the parking lot of the Karcher Mall. This method of delivery was inconsistent and unpredictable.

Analysis and Disposition

A. The Consumer Loan (Manufactured Home)

As explained by this Court in Agricultural Services, Inc. v. Fitzgerald (In re Field), 263 B.R. 323, 329-30, 01.2 I.B.C.R. 69, 71-2 (Bankr. D. Idaho 2001), a security interest in vehicles is perfected under Idaho Code §49-510(1) by notation of the interest by the Department of Transportation on the title certificate. Chapter 5 of Title 49 of the Idaho Code is silent concerning the effect on perfection when a party acquires the original lien-holder's interest through either succession or assignment. This Court held in *Field* that, so long as a new lien is not being created, once a creditor is perfected under I.C. §49-510(1) it is not necessary for an assignee to reper-fect by amending or obtaining a new certificate of title showing its interest. 263 B.R. at 329-30. The court has not been persuaded that acquiring an interest in a titled vehicle by succession rather than by assignment should yield a different result. The Court concludes that the holding in *Field*, as applied to assignees of a lien, also applies to the Bank as a successor in interest by reason of merger.

The Title, issued on November 17, 1997, lists Pacific as the first (and only) lienholder. The Bank acquired and succeeded to all of Pacific's interest. Thus, the Bank holds a perfected security interest in the Debtors' manufactured home.

B. The Commercial Loans

Idaho has repealed Idaho Code Title 28, Chapter 9 ("Old Article 9") and enacted a revised Chapter 9 of that Title ("New Article 9"). New Article 9 became effective on July 1, 2001 (the "Effective Date"). See revised I.C. §28-9-702, compiler's notes.

The parties disagree as to whether Old Article 9 or New Article 9 applies here, and as to the import of each on the questions presented. The Court must first determine whether Old Article 9 or New Article 9 controls.

1. Transition from Old Article 9 to New Article 9

The transition from Old Article 9 to New Article 9 is addressed in several sections of the new enactment. The starting point is set out in revised I.C. §28-9-702(a), which states:

> (a) Except as otherwise provided in this part, this act applies to a trans-action or lien within its scope, even if the transaction or lien was entered into or created before this act takes effect.

New Article 9 therefore applies to the security interests at issue here. The next question is how it applies.

Under revised I.C. §28-9-703(a), security interests which are perfected as of the Effective Date (July 1, 2001) remain perfected so long as no further action is required under New Article 9. That provision states:

(a) A security interest that is enforceable immediately before this act takes effect and would have priority over the rights of a person that becomes a lien creditor at that time is a perfected security interest under this act if, when this act takes effect, the applicable requirements for enforceability and perfection under this act are satisfied without further action.

Id.; see also, revised I.C. §28-9-703, Official Comment 1.

According to revised I.C. §28-9-704(3)(A), security interests which are unperfected under Old Article 9 will become automatically perfected if, on the Effective Date, the security agreement and financing statement satisfy the requirements for perfection of the interest under New Article 9. That provision states:

A security interest that is enforceable immediately before this act takes effect but which would be subordinate to the rights of a person that becomes a lien creditor at that time: . . .
(3) Becomes perfected:
(A) Without further action, when this act takes effect if the applicable requirements for perfection under this act are satisfied before or at that time[.]

Id.; see also, revised I.C. §28-9-704, Official Comment, which explains:

This section [§28-9-704] deals with security interests that are enforceable but unperfected (i.e., subordinate to the rights of a person who becomes a lien creditor) under former Article 9 or other applicable law immediately before this Article takes effect. These security interests remain enforceable for one year after the effective date, and thereafter if the appropriate steps for attachment under this Article are taken before the one-year period expires. (This section's treatment of enforceability is the same as that of Section 9-703.) The security interest becomes a perfected security interest on the effective date if, at that time, the security interest satisfies the requirements for perfection under this Article.

Id.

2.   The UCC-1

Former I.C. §28-9-402(1) established the basis requirements for an effective financing statement under Old Article 9, providing in part that:

[A] financing statement is sufficient if it gives the names of the debtor and the secured party, is signed by the debtor, gives an address of the secured party from which information concerning the security interest may be obtained, gives a mailing address of the debtor and contains a statement indicating the types, or describing the items, of collateral.

As stated in former I.C. §28-9-402(8):

(8) A financing statement substantially complying with the requirements of this section [§28-9-402] is effective even though it contains minor errors which are not seriously misleading.

The first alleged defect involves the change in the secured party's name from "Pacific One Bank" to "Bank of the West." The parties have not cited, nor has the Court been able to locate, any Idaho cases finding a name error of the sort involved here to be seriously misleading. However, the Ninth Circuit's interpretation of Montana's UCC Article 9 in In re Copper King Inn, Inc., 918 F.2d 1404 (9th Cir. 1990), is helpful. There, the Ninth Circuit held that the accuracy of a secured party's name is relevant only if a hypothetical creditor could somehow be materially led astray by an error in, or omission of, the secured party's name.

Facts or circumstances equivalent to those addressed in *Copper King* were not shown to exist here. Additionally, the Portland Address shown on the UCC-1 remained effective at all material times. The Court concludes that the UCC-1 did not contain any seriously misleading information, whether in regard to the name or the address of the secured party, and it was effective to perfect the security interest in the collateral described therein under Old Article 9.

Under revised I.C. §28-9-703(a), this perfected status will continue so long as no further action is required under New Article 9. It does not appear that further action is needed in order for the UCC-1 to be effective. See, e.g., revised I.C. §§28-9-502(a), 28-9-506(a), discussed below.[7] The UCC-1 of record as of the Effective Date meets these requirements of New Article 9 and remains effective. The interests therein identified remain perfected without additional action. This was still the situation as of the Petition Date.

3. The UCC-1F

a. Old Article 9

Under Old Article 9, additional requirements applied to financing statements for farm products. These were set forth in former I.C. §28-9-402(9):

(9) A financing statement for farm products is sufficient if it contains the following information:

(a) The name and address of the debtor;

(b) The debtor's signature;

(c) The name, address, and signature of the secured party;

(d) The social security number of the debtor, or in the case of a debtor doing business other than as an individual, the debtor's Internal Revenue Service taxpayer identification number;

(e) A description by category of the farm products subject to the security interest and the amount of such products (where applicable);

(f) A reasonable description of the real estate where the farm products are produced or located. This provision may be satisfied by a description of the county(ies), and a legal description is not required.

This provision was still subject to former I.C. §28-9-402(8), set out above, which excused errors which were not seriously misleading.

---

7. See also, revised I.C. §§28-9-507(b), 28-9-520(c), discussed below.

The UCC-1F was, by the parties' stipulation, fully adequate to perfect the security interest in farm products as of the date of its filing. At that time, there were no errors or deficiencies. However, the UCC-1F later became erroneous in that the Nampa Address at some point was no longer effective. When combined with the change in the secured party's name, the errors became seriously misleading.

Unlike the situation in *Wood*, discussed supra at n.6, a third party here could not have obtained further information concerning the Bank's security interest in the crops referenced in the UCC-1F by attempting to contact the Bank by mail addressed to the Nampa Address. See Pretrial Stipulation, at p.3, P 9. Further, if an inquiring party decided to physically search Nampa after 1998, whether at or near Karcher Mall or otherwise, it apparently would not find "Pacific One Bank" due to the merger with the Bank.

Thus the situation with the UCC-1F is unlike that involving the UCC-1. The name change combined with the defunct Nampa Address could stymie a reasonably diligent inquiring third party.

The Court will assume, without deciding, that at some point prior to the Effective Date the Bank's perfected status regarding farm products was questionable. However, the conclusions reached above regarding transition from Old Article 9 to New Article 9 eliminate the need for greater analysis or further scrutiny of the UCC-1F financing statement under Old Article 9. Rather, the Court can simply assume that the interest was unperfected as of the Effective Date. The pertinent question is whether, from and after the Effective Date, the UCC-1F of record was sufficient to perfect the interest under New Article 9. See revised I.C. §28-9-704(3)(A).

b.   New Article 9

To evaluate the effectiveness of the UCC-1F on the Effective Date, reference is first made to revised I.C. §28-9-502, which establishes the prerequisites for effective financing statements. In pertinent part, it provides:

> (a) Subject to subsection (b) of this section, a financing statement is sufficient only if it:
> (1) Provides the name of the debtor;
> (2) Provides the name of the secured party or a representative of the secured party; and
> (3) Indicates the collateral covered by the financing statement.
> (b) Except as otherwise provided in section 28-9-501(b), to be sufficient, a financing statement that covers as-extracted collateral or timber to be cut, or which is filed as a fixture filing and covers goods that are or are to become fixtures, must satisfy subsection (a) of this section and also:
> (1) Indicate that it covers this type of collateral;
> (2) Indicate that it is to be filed in the real property records;
> Provide a description of the real property to which the collateral is related sufficient to give constructive notice of a mortgage under the law of this state if the description were contained in a record of the mortgage of the real property; and
> (4) If the debtor does not have an interest of record in the real property, provide the name of a record owner. . . .

(e) A financing statement covering farm products is sufficient if it contains the following information:
(1) The name and address of the debtor;
(2) The debtor's signature;
(3) The name, address and signature of the secured party;
(4) The social security number of the debtor, or in the case of a debtor doing business other than as an individual, the debtor's internal revenue service taxpayer identification number;
(5) A description by category of the farm products subject to the security interest and the amount of such products, where applicable;
(6) A reasonable description of the real estate where the farm products are produced or located. This provision may be satisfied by a designation of the county or counties, and a legal description is not required.

Under revised I.C. §28-9-520(a), a filing officer shall refuse to accept a financing statement if it is not in compliance with revised I.C. §28-9-516(b). Revised I.C. §28-9-516(b)(4) indicates that a filing officer is entitled to reject a financing statement if it lacks a name or mailing address for the secured party. Revised I.C. §28-9-516(b)(8) indicates that the filing officer may reject a farm products financing statement if it does not contain all the information specified in revised I.C. §28-9-502(e) or conform to the official form of the Idaho secretary of state.

However, revised I.C. §28-9-520(c) protects improper statements so long as they are in fact filed and contain certain essential information. That section states:

A filed financing statement satisfying section 28-9-502(a) and (b) is effective, even if the filing office is required to refuse to accept it for filing under subsection (a) of this section.

Id.; see also, revised I.C. §28-9-516, Official Comment 9 (Effectiveness of Rejectable but Unrejected Record); revised I.C. §28-9-520, Official Comment 3 (Consequences of Accepting Rejectable Record).

Note that under revised I.C. §28-9-520(c), the filed statement need only meet the requirements of subsections (a) and (b) of revised I.C. §28-9-502 in order to benefit from the protection which actual filing affords. Unlike revised I.C. §28-9-502(e), those two subsections do not contain a requirement for the secured party's address or signature, only its name. See revised I.C. §28-9-502(a)(2).

i. Name
The name of the secured party shown on the UCC-1F on the Effective Date was Pacific, not the Bank. To determine whether this is sufficient identification of the secured party, the Court looks to several provisions of New Article 9.

First, revised I.C. §28-9-506 provides in part:

(a) A financing statement substantially satisfying the requirements of this part is effective, even if it has minor errors or omissions, unless the errors or omissions make the financing statement seriously misleading.

(b) Except as otherwise provided in subsection (c) of this section, a financing statement that fails to sufficiently provide the name of the debtor in accordance with section 28-9-503(a) is seriously misleading.

Subsection (b) makes a failure to sufficiently provide the name of the debtor a seriously misleading error. Negative inference would indicate that an error in the name of the secured party is not of the same magnitude. At a minimum, it is not automatically or *per se* seriously misleading.

Second, Official Comment 2 to revised I.C. §28-9-506 states, in part:

In addition to requiring the debtor's name and an indication of the collateral, Section 9-502(a) requires a financing statement to provide the name of the secured party or a representative of the secured party. Inasmuch as searches are not conducted under the secured party's name, and no filing is needed to continue the perfected status of a security interest after it is assigned, an error in the name of the secured party or its representative will not be seriously misleading. However, in an appropriate case, an error of this kind may give rise to an estoppel in favor of a particular holder of a conflicting claim to the collateral. See Section 1-103.

Third, revised I.C. §28-9-511 indicates that the secured party identified in the financing statement is the "secured party of record" and will remain such until the situation is altered by amendment. Official Comment 3 to revised I.C. §28-9-511 recognizes:

Application of other law may result in a person succeeding to the powers of a secured party of record. For example, if the secured party of record (A) merges into another corporation (B) and the other corporation (B) survives, other law may provide that B has all of A's powers. In that case, B is authorized to take all actions under this Part that A would have been authorized to take. Similarly, acts taken by a person who is authorized under generally applicable principles of agency to act on behalf of the secured party of record are effective under this Part.

While amendments of financing statements can be made, see revised I.C. §§28-9-511, 28-9-512, nothing in those sections appears to indicate that they must be made. It is particularly relevant here that revised I.C. §28-9-511 does not require an amendment of the financing statement to reflect a succession in interest such as by merger, but instead addresses the question as one of the actor's authority.

ii. Address
Closely related to questions under New Article 9 regarding the name of the secured party are questions of that party's address. New Article 9 recognizes that a limited function is served by the inclusion on the financing statement of the secured party's address; it only indicates a place to which others can send any required notifications. See revised I.C. §28-9-516, Official Comment 5:

5. Address for Secured Party of Record. Under subsection (b)(4) and Section 9-520(a), the lack of a mailing address for the secured party of

record requires the filing office to reject an initial financing statement. The failure to include an address for the secured party of record no longer renders a financing statement ineffective. See Section 502(a). The function of the address is not to identify the secured party of record but rather to provide an address to which others can send required notifications, e.g., of a purchase money security interest in inventory or of the disposition of collateral. Inasmuch as the address shown on a filed financing statement is "an address that is reasonable under the circumstances," a person required to send a notification to the secured party may satisfy the requirement by sending a notification to that address, even if the address is or becomes incorrect. See Section 9-102 (definition of "send"). Similarly, because the address is "held out by [the secured party] as the place for receipt of such communications [i.e., communications relating to security interests]," the secured party is deemed to have received a notification delivered to that address. See Section 1-201(26).

For all these reasons, the errors in name or address on the UCC-1F cannot be viewed as rendering the filing of that statement ineffective to perfect the security interest in farm products as of the Effective Date. The structure of New Article 9 makes the absence of a name or address grounds for the filing officer to reject the statement, but if accepted for filing it will be effective. Errors in the secured party's name or address as shown are, by virtue of the structure of New Article 9, not seriously misleading, and do not vitiate the effectiveness of the filing.

Lastly, in order to move from the status of the UCC-1F as of the Effective Date to its status as of the Petition Date, the Court must address revised I.C. §28-9-502(f). This section provides:

> (f) A financing statement described in subsection (e) of this section must be amended in writing within three (3) months, and similarly signed and filed, to reflect any material changes. In the event such form is not incorporated within the financing statement, the effectiveness and continuation of that form is to be treated as if it were a part of the financing statement with which it is filed.

This continues the approach taken in former I.C. §28-9-402(10).

Because this is a provision not found in the model revised Article 9, there is no explanation in the Comments as to its anticipated operation, nor any cross-reference to the other provisions of New Article 9. For example, as the Court has set out above, revised I.C. §§28-9-502, 28-9-507, 28-9-516, and 28-9-520 all speak to the consequences of errors in financing statements, either at inception or arising later as once correct information has turned incorrect. Errors in name and address of the sort at issue here are not fatal to perfection.

Notwithstanding the operation of these several provisions, should the merger of Pacific into Bank and the resultant change of name, and the loss of use of the Nampa Address, be viewed as "material changes" requiring amendment? If so, what is the consequence of a failure to amend?

The Court need not resolve these questions in this case. Here the effect of the recorded UCC-1F is measured, pursuant to revised §28-9-704(3)(A), on the Effective Date of July 1, 2001. That financing statement was sufficient to perfect the farm products security interest on that date. If revised I.C. §28-9-502(f) required amendment due to "material change" which arguably impacted the effectiveness of the statement after July 1, 2001, the Bank had 3 months from that date to do so. The bankruptcy petition was filed on August 9, 2001. The 3-month period of §28-9-502(f) had yet to run. Therefore, when evaluating whether the Bank was perfected on the Petition Date — the precise question posed by the litigants — the answer is still yes.

The Court therefore concludes that the UCC-1F financing statement was effective as of the petition date under New Article 9 to perfect Bank's security interest in farm products as described therein.

IV.   Conclusion

The Effective Date of New Article 9 was July 1, 2001. This preceded the filing of the Debtors' chapter 12 petition on August 9, 2001. On the date this bankruptcy case commenced, both the UCC-1 and UCC-1F financing statements of record were sufficient to perfect the security interests granted the Bank.

Based upon the foregoing, the Court finds and concludes that the Bank has a valid, perfected security interest in the property described in the UCC-1 and in the UCC-1F, and in the manufactured home shown on the Title. These are the sole questions posed by the parties' pleadings and stipulations. Counsel for the Bank shall prepare a form of Judgment consistent with this Decision.

Questions

1.   What is the importance of distinguishing the former act from the current act?

2.   What is required of the registrant with respect to its name and address?

3.   How was the security interest in this case attempted to be perfected?

Suggested Case References

1.   For a discussion of the difference between an implied warranty of merchantability and an implied warranty of fitness for a particular use, read Crysco Oilfield Services Inc. v. Hutchison-Hayes International Inc., 913 F.2d 850 (10th Cir. 1990).

2.   A security agreement specified that the debtor's collateral could be his inventory of hogs, but it did not specifically state that it would include after-acquired property. Does this failure to specify after-acquired property destroy the creditor's ability to have a floating lien? Coats State Bank v. Grey, 902 F.2d 1479 (10th Cir. 1990).

3.   To see how courts grappled with the concept of a lease versus a sale prior to the enactment of UCC II-A, read Matka v. Tolland County Times, 1993 Conn. Super. LEXIS 671 (1993).

4.   If equipment is leased only for one day, do the provisions of the UCC still apply? See what the court said in Kebish v. Thomas Equip., 541 Pa. 20, 660 A.2d 38 (1995).

5.   To distinguish between honesty in fact and reasonable commercial standards, read Sherrock v. Commercial Credit Corp., 290 A.2d 648 (Del. 1972).

Third Party Contracts

Learning Objectives

After studying this chapter you will be able to:

- List the different types of third party contracts
- Discuss third party creditor beneficiary contracts
- Discuss third party donee beneficiary contracts
- Distinguish between an intended and an incidental beneficiary
- Define a contractual assignment
- Discuss the effect of an assignment on the original contracting parties
- Indicate how a gratuitous assignment may become irrevocable
- Differentiate between an assignment and a novation
- Distinguish a delegation from an assignment
- Explain the effect of the UCC on third party contracts

CHAPTER OVERVIEW

Typically, when a person enters into a contractual agreement, she expects to perform or deliver the consideration she has promised and to receive the consideration the other contracting party has promised her. Although this is the most usual contractual arrangement, there are situations in which the person who actually entered into the contract does not receive the promised consideration or does not perform her contractual promises herself.

One form of contract in which the promisee does not receive or expect to receive the bargained-for consideration is known as a third party beneficiary contract. In this contractual arrangement, the parties do not intend to contract to benefit themselves but intend to benefit some outside third person. All of the general contract rules and provisions still apply. The only difference between this and what would be considered the more usual contractual situation is that one of the parties to the contract agrees to convey the consideration not to the other contracting party, but to someone the other contracting party has designated when the contract was formed. In other words, the promisor conveys the consideration not to the promisee, but to a third party who, as a consequence, is benefiting from the contractual agreement.

If, in a similar situation, one party to the contract wishes, after the contract was formed, to have the consideration given not to her but to some third person, she may do so under certain circumstances. In this situation, known as an *assignment*, the promisor agrees, after formation of the contract, to convey the consideration not to the promisee but to the promisee's designee. Because this changes the promisor's contractual obligations, this type of arrangement may only be effectuated if the promisor agrees.

Finally, there are times when the promisor needs or desires assistance in fulfilling his contractual promise. Although a person may not relinquish his contractual obligation without being in default, in most instances a promisor may have some third person assist him in completing his promise. This situation is known as a *delegation*. Unlike the first two situations indicated above, this third person, the promisor's helper, receives no benefit from the contract itself.

When drafting and interpreting contract provisions, it is important to keep the above in mind. There are special contractual clauses that create or permit these arrangements, and these clauses become determinative of the contracting parties' rights and obligations under the contract. In each type of situation, the outside party may be entitled to some equitable relief for enforcement of the contract, even though he is not a contracting party himself.

Third Party Beneficiary Contracts: Generally

Third party beneficiary contracts are agreements in which the original intent of one of the contracting parties, when entering into the contractual arrangement, is to have the promised-for consideration pass not to her, but to some outside person. Generally, there are two reasons why a contracting party would desire this type of arrangement, and consequently, third party beneficiary contracts are divided into two categories.

The first category is a **third party creditor beneficiary** contract. In this type of third party contract, the purpose of the promisee's agreement is to extinguish a debt or obligation owed to some third person. In other words, the promisee was already obligated to the third person, his creditor, and the purpose for which he entered into the contract was to receive some consideration that would terminate his debt to the creditor.

EXAMPLE:

Last month Peter had extraordinary expenses and didn't have enough money to pay his rent. Wendy loaned Peter $500 to help him meet his expenses, and he promised to repay the loan this month with interest. Now, Peter has met all his regular expenses but doesn't have the money to repay the loan. To repay Wendy, Peter agrees to sell his CD player to Ralph, and Peter asks Ralph to give the money for the CD player to Wendy. Wendy agrees. This is a third party creditor beneficiary contract. The reason Peter entered into the sales contract with Ralph was to repay his debt to Wendy. Wendy was the person Peter intended to benefit from his contract with Ralph.

The second category of third party beneficiary contracts is a **third party donee beneficiary** contract. As the name might indicate, the purpose of this contract is to confer a gift on a third person. The promisee of the contract is under no preexisting obligation to the third person but wishes to give the third person a present. Under current legal terminology both the creditor and donee beneficiaries are called **intended beneficiaries**.

EXAMPLE:

Peter suddenly comes into some money. He is still grateful to Wendy for helping him out when he had financial difficulties. Even though his debt to Wendy is now extinguished, he feels that he would like to do something nice for her. While watching a shopping channel on television, Peter sees a bracelet he thinks Wendy would like. He calls the station and orders the bracelet, telling the vendor that the bracelet is a gift. He directs the vendor to send the bracelet to Wendy and to bill him. This is a third party donee beneficiary contract. The reason Peter entered into the contract with the television vendor was to convey a gift to Wendy. He owed no debt, and he never intended the bracelet for himself.

The most important aspect of a third party beneficiary contract is the intent of the parties when the contract is formed. For the contract to be considered a third party beneficiary contract, it must be evidenced that the purpose of the contract is to benefit a person not a party to the contractual agreement. If the desire to benefit some outside person comes about after the contract already exists, it is not a third party beneficiary contract (but an assignment, which will be discussed later).

Bear in mind the specific terminology that is being used in a third party beneficiary contract. In every contractual situation, there must be a mutuality of consideration; in all bilateral contracts each party to the contract is both a promisor and a promisee. He is a promisor for the consideration he promises to convey, and a promisee for the consideration the other party promises to give him. When describing third party beneficiary contracts, the term **promisee** designates the person who entered the contract intending to benefit the third person. He is expecting to have the consideration he was promised conveyed to the outsider. **Promisor** describes the party conveying the consideration to the third person, because of the promisee's wishes and intent when contracting. This transfer to the third person is part of the promise the promisor makes when entering into the contract.

 EXAMPLE:

In the examples discussed above with Peter, Wendy, Ralph, and the shopping channel, in both instances the contract was between Peter and either Ralph or the vendor. In the first instance, Peter promised to convey his CD player to Ralph, and Ralph promised to convey the purchase price of the CD player to Wendy. Peter is the promisee for the receipt of the money, and Ralph is the promisor who has agreed to convey the cash to Wendy as part of his contractual promise to Peter. In the second instance, Peter promised to pay for the bracelet that the vendor promised to convey to Wendy. Peter is the promisor for payment, and the promisee for the receipt of the merchandise. The shopping channel is the promisee of Peter's payment, and the promisor for sending the jewelry. In each instance, Wendy, the third party, is receiving the consideration from Peter's promisors.

In a third party beneficiary contract, the third party, although not a contracting party, is given certain rights with respect to the contract. Legally, the beneficiary may be able to bring the contracting parties into court to have the contract enforced in his favor. This is true even though the beneficiary is neither a party to the agreement nor has any enforceable obligation with respect to the agreement. To understand the rights and obligations that attach to the two categories of third party beneficiary contracts, each will be discussed separately.

When analyzing the enforceable rights of a third party beneficiary, it is important to note that enforceable rights attach only to third persons intended primarily to benefit from the contract. Should a third person benefit secondarily from the contract, i.e., his benefit was not the intent of the contract, that person is known as an **incidental beneficiary** and has no enforceable rights. For example, in the situation given above, the shipper the shopping channel uses to send its merchandise benefits from the channel's sales contract, but this benefit is totally incidental to the contract itself.

Third Party Creditor Beneficiary Contracts

The starting point for any discussion of a third party creditor beneficiary contract is the determination that the promisee owes some debt to a third person. The debt must be in existence prior to the third party contract being formed. Remember, the purpose of a third party creditor beneficiary contract is to extinguish a debt owed to a third person, so that debt must in fact exist.

Because the contract is formed to benefit this creditor, the creditor is considered to be a **real party in interest.** He becomes the focal point of the central contract between the debtor and the promisor. As a real party in interest, he may be entitled to enforce the contract if the promisor does not fulfill his contractual obligation.

To have enforceable rights, it must first be demonstrated that those rights exist. This means that the creditor must show that his rights have **vested** (become enforceable in a court of law). For a third party creditor beneficiary, the rights in the contract vest as soon as he detrimentally relies on the contract's existence.

What constitutes "detrimental reliance"? As discussed previously, detrimental reliance usually means some economic loss suffered in reliance on the promise. For creditor beneficiaries, this detrimental reliance is simply assumed to be his willingness to accept payment from the promisor. Because the debt must exist as a prerequisite to the formation of a third party creditor beneficiary contract, the creditor can always go to court to enforce the debt against the debtor/promisee. Because the creditor is forestalling taking that action in reliance on the contract between the debtor and the promisor, just as with an accord and satisfaction, it is deemed sufficient to vest his rights in the third party contract. Also, as soon as the intended beneficiary is aware of the contract, or institutes a suit to enforce it, the beneficiary's rights are deemed vested.

 EXAMPLE:

Pedro enrolls in his city's Paralegal Institute. Pedro doesn't have the money for the tuition but arranges for a student loan from a local bank at the school's suggestion. The loan contract is a third party creditor beneficiary contract, entered into between Pedro and the bank for the purpose of paying Pedro's debt to the Institute. The Institute's willingness to take payment from the bank on Pedro's behalf constitutes its reliance on the contract, and its rights have vested.

Once the third party creditor beneficiary's rights have vested, she has enforceable rights. This means that she may sue the promisor of the contract if the promisor fails to convey the consideration. Because the creditor is the real party in interest, and the promisor has agreed to convey the consideration to her, failure to fulfill this promise is a breach of contract that the real party in interest can sue to have remedied.

EXAMPLE:

In the example given above with Peter, Wendy, and Ralph, if Ralph does not give Wendy the money he promised in his contract with Peter, Wendy can take Ralph to court. Because Ralph's promise is to convey the money to Wendy, his failure to do so is a breach. As the real party in interest, Wendy is the one whom the breach injures. Consequently, she has the right to enforce the contract against Ralph.

Should, for whatever reason, the creditor fail to get satisfaction from the promisor, he can always sue the promisee. Why? Because the promisee is still the debtor of the third party, and until that debt is extinguished he remains liable on the original obligation.

EXAMPLE:

Wendy discovers that Ralph is insolvent. Because Peter still owes her $500 plus interest, she can enforce her claim directly against Peter because the third party contract has not extinguished his debt.

Of course, the creditor is limited to just one recovery. She cannot sue both the debtor and the promisor and recover from both. Recovery from one excuses the other.

If the creditor attempts to enforce his rights under the contract, the promisor can defend himself by asserting any defense he might have against the debtor/promisee. Because it is the contract between the debtor/promisee and the promisor that is in question, any defense that would render the contract unenforceable relieves the promisor of any obligation to the creditor.

EXAMPLES:

1. When Wendy sues Ralph for the purchase price of the CD player, Ralph can defend by asserting that Peter never gave him the CD player, or that the CD player delivered was not the one promised. In each instance, Ralph is claiming that Peter is in default, and

Peter's default relieves Ralph of his contractual obligations to Peter. Because this obligation was to convey money to Wendy, if Ralph prevails, he is under no obligation to Wendy.

2. Pedro starts classes, but the Institute has not received the tuition from the bank. The Institute attempts to enforce the loan contract between Pedro and the bank. The bank defends by proving that its obligation was conditioned on Pedro's submitting proof of attendance, which he has failed to do. Consequently, the bank is not obligated under its loan agreement, and the Institute must look to Pedro directly for the tuition.

In addition to the third party creditor beneficiary having enforceable rights, the contracting parties themselves always have enforceable rights against each other. The promisee and the promisor of the contract can sue each other to have the contract enforced.

 EXAMPLE:

When Wendy attempts to collect from Peter, Peter discovers that Ralph has not lived up to his obligation. Provided that Peter did in fact convey to Ralph the CD player he promised, Peter can sue Ralph to have the contract enforced because he, Peter, is a contracting party.

To summarize, in a third party creditor beneficiary contract, the third party creditor beneficiary has vested, enforceable rights in the contract once he has detrimentally relied on the contract. This detrimental reliance can simply take the form of agreeing to accept payment from the promisor rather than suing the debtor for payment. Once these rights have vested, the creditor beneficiary can sue the promisor of the contract to have these rights enforced. The promisor can defend by asserting any claim he may have against the promisee. The creditor may also sue the debtor on the original obligation if he receives no satisfaction from the promisor. Finally, the promisor and promisee of the contract can sue each other to have the contract provisions enforced.

Third Party Donee Beneficiary Contracts

The major difference between third party creditor beneficiary and third party donee beneficiary contracts is the element of the underlying debt. To have a creditor beneficiary contract, it must be shown that a debt exists between the promisee and the creditor. To have a donee beneficiary contract, it must be shown that the promisee intended to confer a gift on the donee (she is not repaying a debt).

Because the purpose of the contract is to convey a gift to the donee, the donee beneficiary is considered to be the real party in interest to the contract. As the real party in interest, she may have enforceable rights with respect to the contract once it is established that those rights have vested. For a third party donee beneficiary, the rights in the contract vest once she learns of the existence of the contract. No detrimental reliance is necessary.

 EXAMPLE:

In the example given above with Wendy, Peter, and the shopping channel, when Peter calls Wendy to tell her that she should expect a bracelet that he has bought for her, her rights have vested. When two weeks pass without the bracelet arriving, Wendy can call the vendor to complain and to find out when the bracelet will arrive.

Once the donee beneficiary's rights have vested, she can sue the promisor of the contract to have the promise enforced. Just as with third party creditor beneficiary contracts, the promisor can defend against claims of the third party donee by asserting any defenses he would have against the promise of the contract.

 EXAMPLES:

1. Several weeks pass, and Wendy still hasn't received the bracelet. She sues the shopping channel to have the contract enforced. The vendor can defend by proving that Peter attempted to pay for the bracelet with a check that bounced. Because Peter breached his promise to the shopping channel, the vendor is relieved of its contractual obligations.

2. Babs takes out a life insurance policy on her life with Connecticut Life, Inc., and names her best friend, Abdul, as the beneficiary. Babs is lost at sea, and Abdul claims the insurance. The company can defend by saying that Babs failed to make the premium payments, or that there is no proof that Babs is actually dead.

Unlike a third party creditor beneficiary, because there is no obligation between the donee and the promisee, the donee beneficiary, under contract law, cannot sue the donor/promisee for enforcement of the contract. A promise to give a gift, unless a charitable donation, is not enforceable under contract law. However, if the donee can show that she detrimentally relied on the promised gift, under property law concepts, she may be able to recover against the donor.

EXAMPLE:

When Peter tells Wendy about the bracelet, Wendy, in expectation of its arrival, buys a dress especially designed to show off the jewelry. When the bracelet doesn't arrive, Wendy may be able to recover the cost of the dress from Peter if she can prove that she only purchased it in expectation of the bracelet, and without the bracelet she has no use for the dress. Remember, the claim is based on property law concepts, and recovery may be permitted under the court's equitable jurisdiction to prevent injustice. It is not a contract case.

Of course, just as with creditor beneficiary contracts, the promisor and promisee of the contract can always sue each other for enforcement of the contract provisions.

EXAMPLE:

When Peter finds out the shopping channel failed to send the bracelet to Wendy, he can sue the vendor directly. If Peter can show a cancelled check for payment, the vendor's original defense would fail, and it would have to ship out the bracelet.

In summary, a third party donee beneficiary contract is created for the purpose of conveying a gift to the third party. The donee has vested rights in the contract once she learns of its existence. Once the rights have vested, the donee can sue the promisor to have the contract enforced. Under contract law, the donee has no enforceable rights against the promisee (there is no consideration for a gift). The promisor and promisee of the contract can sue each other to have the contract enforced.

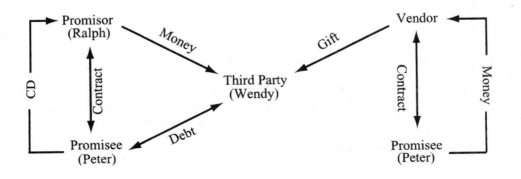

Third Party Beneficiary Contracts

Creditor Beneficiary	*Donee Beneficiary*
Created to extinguish debt	Created to confer gift
Rights vest with detrimental reliance*	Rights vest on knowledge*
Can sue promisor or promisee	Can sue promisor only
Promisor/promisee can defend by asserting any claim he has against the other contracting party	Promisor can defend by asserting any claim he has against promise

*With respect to the vesting of third party beneficiary rights, some courts have adopted the approach that a third party beneficiary's rights vest, regardless of whether he is a creditor or donee beneficiary, only if he assents to the contract, sues to have it enforced or shows detrimental reliance. The standard followed by each jurisdiction should be specifically checked.

Assignment

An **assignment** is the transfer of a promisee's rights under an existing contract. At first blush, it appears to be very similar to third party beneficiary contracts. Although they are similar, there are two important differences between assignments and third party beneficiary contracts:

1. Assignments come into existence *after* the original contract is created. The benefit to the third party is not the reason the contract was formed; it is an afterthought.
2. Because assignments are created *after* the original contract, a promisee may not assign his rights without the consent, express or implied, of the promisor.

Creating the Assignment

An assignment may be oral or written, subject to requirements of the Statute of Frauds. If the basic contract must be in writing, so must the assignment.

 EXAMPLE:

Sharona and Vince enter into a written contract for the sale of Vince's house. After the contract is signed, Vince wants to transfer his right to receive the purchase price to his son. The contract permits assignments. Because the contract concerns an interest in real estate, both the contract and the assignment must be in writing.

A person may assign her rights to a contract either gratuitously or for consideration. In other words, the promisee may use the assignment to confer a gift or to fulfill an obligation under a separate contract.

EXAMPLES:

1. In the example given above, Sharona decides to give the house as an anniversary gift to her parents. In writing, she assigns her right to receive the house's title to her parents. This is a gratuitous assignment.

2. Sharona decides that she really doesn't want Vince's house, but her friend Wilma thinks that the house is "perfect." In writing, Sharona agrees to assign to Wilma her right to the title to Vince's house in consideration of Wilma giving Sharona $1000. This is an example of an assignment for consideration. Sharona is transferring her rights under her contract with Vince to fulfill her promise under her contract with Wilma.

The **assignor,** the person who is transferring the contract right, may also make a partial assignment of rights to the **assignee** (the transferee of the rights). An assignment need not be an all-or-nothing situation.

EXAMPLE:

Fabio sold his tape deck to Tom for $30. Before he receives payment, Fabio assigns $15 to Leon to extinguish a debt he owes to Leon. The assignment is valid, even though it transferred only part of Fabio's rights.

However, not all contracts are capable of being assigned. There can be no assignment if the rights assigned consist of personal services or are dependent on the personal confidence or circumstances of the recipient.

EXAMPLES:

1. Pavarotti has signed a contract with the New York Metropolitan Opera to perform *Pagliacci*. The Met cannot transfer its rights to the Omaha Civic Opera Company to have Pavarotti sing. Although Pavarotti may want to sing for the Met, he may not want to travel to Omaha. A person cannot be forced to perform for someone for whom he does not want to perform.

2. Sid purchases a health insurance policy from Connecticut Insurance, Inc. He cannot assign his contract's rights to Paul. The insurance company sold Sid the policy based on Sid's health and personal history; the same policy and premiums may not apply to someone with Paul's health and history. Because the insurance company's performance is dependent on the confidence it has in Sid's health, Sid cannot assign.

As with third party beneficiary contracts, if the assignment is valid, the assignee becomes the real party in interest and has enforceable rights against the promisor.

 EXAMPLE:

In the situation given above, when Wilma gives Sharona $1000 for Sharona's rights to receive title to Vince's house, should Vince fail to transfer the title after payment of the purchase price, Wilma can take Vince to court to have the right enforced. Wilma is the real party in interest, the person who is entitled to receive the property.

Consent of the Promisor

Because the assignment comes into existence after the contract is formed, it is usually necessary to get the consent of the promisor because conveying the consideration to a third person was not what he agreed to under the contract. The assignment has the effect of changing the promisor's contractual obligation, and this can only be done with his consent.

Under the law, most contracts are assignable, subject to the exceptions noted above. However, if the effect of the assignment would be to *materially* change the promisor's obligation or duty, the promisor's consent must be specifically given. The consent may take the form of a clause in the contract in which the promisor agrees to an assignment. This clause can also specify the terms on which the promisor's consent is given.

 EXAMPLE:

Rhoda leases an apartment from Brenda. In the lease, Brenda agrees that Rhoda may assign her rights to occupy the apartment, provided that written notice be given to Brenda at least 30 days prior to the assignee taking occupancy, and further provided that Brenda meets the assignee prior to the assignment taking effect. This clause gives

Brenda's consent prospectively, provided certain conditions precedent are met. (See Chapter 7.)

What is considered a "material" change in the promisor's duty? The term is not specifically defined but is determined on a case-by-case basis. As long as the assignment does not create an unnecessary burden on the promisor, it most probably will not be considered material.

EXAMPLE:

In the earlier example, when Peter purchased a bracelet from a television shopping channel as a gift for Wendy, suppose Peter and Wendy have a falling out before the bracelet is mailed and before Wendy is told about the gift. Peter calls the vendor and tells the vendor to send the bracelet to Peter's mother instead of to Wendy. This is an assignment of Peter's right to receive the bracelet. Because the cost of shipping was already paid for, it makes no difference to the vendor who the recipient is, and so this would not materially affect its obligations. However, if Peter's mother lived in a foreign country that had stringent requirements regarding importing jewelry, and in order to ship the bracelet the vendor would have to fill out many custom forms, shipping documents, and pay extra mailing fees, Peter could not make the assignment without the vendor's consent. This assignment to Mom creates a wholly different obligation on the part of the seller.

Under general contract law principles, most contracts are assignable if they are silent on the point. However, the contract may state affirmatively that its rights may not be assigned. Such a "nonassignment clause" is a common provision in many contracts. This clause is usually inserted to protect the contracting parties. With this clause, each party to the contract knows exactly to whom he must perform his promise. There are no late surprises.

Effect of Assignment

The effect of an assignment is to transfer the assignor's rights to the assignee. The assignee thereby becomes a real party in interest with enforceable rights against the promisor.

If the assignor makes the assignment for consideration, as in the example of Sharona assigning her rights to Vince's house to Wilma for $1000, the assignment is irrevocable. When the promisor conveys the consideration to the assignee, he is relieved of all his obligations under the original contract. However, if he conveys the consideration to anyone other than the assignee, he does so at his own risk.

EXAMPLE:

After Sharona assigns her rights to Wilma, she informs Vince of the assignment. When Vince transfers the title to Wilma, he has fulfilled his contractual obligation to Sharona. Should Vince, however, transfer title to Sharona instead of Wilma, Wilma can take him into court. His obligation, after the assignment to which he has agreed, is to convey title to Wilma and to no one else.

On the other hand, if the assignment is gratuitous, the assignor may revoke, thereby cancelling the assignee's rights. Nevertheless, there are five situations in which a gratuitous assignment may become irrevocable:

1. delivery of a token chose;
2. writing;
3. estoppel;
4. performance; and
5. novation.

1.   Delivery of a Token Chose.   A **token chose** is merely some thing symbolic of the assignment. Although it may not have much monetary value, its existence is considered sufficient to make a gratuitous assignment irrevocable.

EXAMPLE:

When Peter's mother hears about the bracelet Peter is having sent to her, she sends him a rose to commemorate the occasion. The rose is a token chose, and the assignment is irrevocable.

2.   Writing.   Simply putting the assignment in writing, for historical legal reasons, makes the gratuitous assignment irrevocable.

EXAMPLE:

Peter writes to his mother telling her of the bracelet. The writing makes the assignment irrevocable.

3.   Estoppel.   If the assignee is attempting to assert a claim of **estoppel** because the assignment is a gift, the donee/assignee must show detrimental reliance on the promise to make it irrevocable.

EXAMPLE:

When Peter's mother hears about the bracelet, she buys a dress to show off the jewelry. This may create detrimental reliance that would bar, or estop, Peter from changing his mind.

4. Performance. If should be obvious that if the promisor has already performed and conveyed the consideration to the assignee before the assignor revokes, the assignment becomes irrevocable.

5. Novation. A **novation** is a substitution of parties in a contract; it is an interesting subset of assignments. Generally, assignments only transfer rights; they never transfer contractual obligations. In a novation, the original party to the contract is substituted by a third person, and the third person not only receives the benefits of the transferor but also assumes all of the transferor's obligations. The contract, after the novation, reads as though the original contracting party never existed.

EXAMPLE:

When Sharona decides that she does not want to purchase Vince's house, she asks to novate her contract to Wilma. Vince agrees, and now the contract reads as though it always was a contract for the sale of Vince's house to Wilma. Sharona's rights and obligations are totally transferred to Wilma.

Novations are very rare because the other party to the contract must agree to the novation. Whereas a person may be willing to contract with one person, she may not have the same reliance with someone else. With few exceptions, a person cannot be forced to enter into a contractual agreement with someone with whom she does not want to contract. Therefore, there must be a clause in the contract specifying the novation. Typically, these clauses indicate specific conditions that must be met before the other contracting party's assent to the substitution will be given.

Multiple Assignees

If an assignor assigns his rights to more than one assignee, a problem arises with respect to which assignee is entitled to the transferred rights. The general rule is that, with successive assignees, the first in time prevails, unless a later assignee has stronger equities (a greater equitable claim to the consideration).

EXAMPLE:

Lynn sells her car to Edward for $900. On Monday, Lynn assigns her right to receive the money to her mother as a birthday gift. The next day, Lynn buys Joan's pearl necklace and, instead of giving Joan a check, Lynn assigns to Joan her right to receive the $900 from Edward. When Mom and Joan both claim the money, the money will go to Joan. Even though Joan is a later assignee, because she gave consideration for the assignment she has the greater equity. Also, because the first assignment is gratuitous it may be revoked. Making the second assignment acts as a revocation of the first, revocable, assignment.

Take note that under the Uniform Commercial Code (UCC), assignees of certain types of contracts, specifically those involving a security interest, are required to file a notice of their claims with various county and state offices. This filing constitutes notice to all subsequent assignees that the property in question has been previously assigned and cuts off the rights of later assignees. For a complete discussion of UCC filing requirements, see Chapter 8, The Uniform Commercial Code, and Chapter 12, Drafting Simple Contracts.

An assignment is only a transference of the assignor's contractual rights. The assignor is still liable for her performance as promised under the contract. A person cannot assign obligations; she may only assign rights.

Delegation

Unlike third party beneficiary contracts and assignments, a **delegation** does not involve a transfer of rights. In a delegation, the promisor of a contract authorizes another person to perform some duty owed by the promisor under the contract. In other words, the promisor delegates someone to assist him in fulfilling his contractual obligations. The delegated person has absolutely no rights under the contract, unlike third party beneficiaries or assignees, nor does she have any obligations under the contract. The delegate's only obligation is to the promisor, and the promisor remains totally liable under the contract.

EXAMPLE:

Rosario is a paralegal working for attorney Janet. Janet's firm has accepted a case from a client, and to assist her Janet has given Rosario several tasks to perform. The firm is the promisor under the contract with the client, and Rosario and Janet are delegates. The firm remains liable to the client, and Rosario is responsible to Janet.

Generally, all nonpersonal duties owed under a contract may be delegated. If the duty does not involve the personal services of the promisor, unless otherwise denied under the contract, the promisor may delegate. However, it is important to remember that the promisor *always* remains liable under the contract if the delegate fails to perform.

 EXAMPLES:

1. Mel has a contract with Warner Brothers to play a leading role in a new film. After the contract is signed, Mel realizes that he has another commitment. He delegates his responsibilities to Paul. This is invalid. The contract between Mel and Warner Brothers involves personal services and consequently may not be delegated.

2. In the situation with Rosario and Janet, Janet tells Rosario to complete a summons and complaint and to file them with the appropriate court. Rosario forgets, and the statute of limitations runs, barring the action. The firm is the one responsible to the client, and it may be charged with malfeasance. As the promisor, the firm remains personally liable for the promised performance under the contract. (This is not a contract for personal services because these types of agreements assume the firm will act by delegation, unless otherwise specified in the contract.)

In summary, only rights can be assigned, and only duties can be delegated. The only obligations under a contract that may be assigned are those that do not involve personal services or confidence, and the promisor always remains liable under the contract. The delegate has no rights or obligations under the contract. Finally, a delegation may be gratuitous, as in asking a friend for assistance, or may be contractual, as with a lawyer and a paralegal.

SAMPLE CLAUSES

1

Notwithstanding anything to the contrary contained herein, X may not assign any right, or delegate any duty hereunder without the prior written consent of Y. Y may assign any right, or delegate any duty hereunder to any person or entity controlled, directly or indirectly, by it or any of its shareholders.

The above clause is an example of a contractual provision in which both parties have some rights to assign or delegate, but the contractual provision to do so is unequal. X must first obtain written approval from Y, and should X not obtain such approval, the contract with respect to X is nonassignable and nondelegable. On the other hand, Y, in the clause itself, has the automatic right to assign or delegate, but the assignee and/or delegate is limited to certain described persons or entities. Therefore, as long as the assignee or delegate meets the definitional requirements of this provision, Y may assign or delegate without reference to X, and X must accept such action.

2   Proxy

The undersigned hereby constitutes and appoints X as his, her, or their proxy to cast the votes of the undersigned at all general, special, and adjourned meetings of the shareholders of Acme, Inc., from time to time and from year to year, when the undersigned is not present at any such meeting. This proxy shall be effective for one (1) year from the date hereof unless sooner revoked by written notice to the Secretary of the corporation.

Dated: /ss/ _____

The above is an example of a general proxy used by a corporation shareholder. The contract in question is the contract the shareholder has with the corporation for the purchase of the shares; voting is a right incident to the stock ownership. The shareholder is assigning his right to vote to the proxy holder. Although not specified above, the proxy may be gratuitous or may be subject to its own contractual relation between the shareholder and the proxy holder (the proxy holder paying the shareholder for the right to cast the vote). Remember, an assignment indicates a legal effect and is not necessarily determined by the words used. A proxy is an assignment, not a delegation, because it is a right of a shareholder, not a duty.

3   Life Insurance Policy

The _____ Life Insurance Company agrees, subject to the terms and conditions of this policy, to pay the Amount shown on page _____ to the beneficiary upon receipt at its home office of proof of the death of the insured.

The above is a clause from a whole-life insurance policy. A life insurance policy is an example of the third party donee beneficiary contract. The insured contracts with the insurance company (the promisor); the insured promises to pay the stated premiums; and the insurer, conditioned upon proof of the insured's death, promises to pay the policy amount to the beneficiary. After the insured's death, the beneficiary has enforceable rights against the insurer should the insurer fail to pay. The insurer can always defend by proving the insured failed to meet the premiums or lied about his age or physical condition, by showing that proof of death was not given, or by using any other defense against the insured's meeting the contract provisions.

CHAPTER SUMMARY

Not every party to a contract is the person who will receive the contract rights or who will perform the contractual obligations. There are several situations in which some outside individual will either reap the benefit of the contract or will perform the obligation imposed by the agreement.

A third party beneficiary contract is formed for the express purpose of benefiting some noncontracting party. This noncontracting party is intended to receive the contract right as the repayment of a debt owed to him by the promisee or as a gift to him from the promisee. In the first instance, this noncontracting party is known as a third party creditor beneficiary; in the second instance, the noncontracting party is a third party donee beneficiary. Once the contract right vests in this third person, he becomes the real party in interest and has enforceable rights against the promisor. The promisor can defend against suits instituted by the third party by asserting any defense he may have against the promisee. If the underlying contract is unenforceable, the third party beneficiary's rights are likewise incapable of enforcement. The creditor beneficiary may proceed against the promisee to enforce the original debt the promisee owed to him. Donee beneficiaries may proceed against the promisee only if the donee can prove detrimental reliance based on the third party beneficiary contract.

If the contract is already in existence when one of the parties wishes to transfer rights under the agreement, such transference of rights is known as an assignment. In an assignment, the assignee becomes the recipient of rights to a contract to which she was not an original party. Assignments can be distinguished from third party beneficiary contracts by determining the underlying purpose behind the contract's formation. If the contract was formed to benefit a third person, it is a third party beneficiary contract; if the intent to benefit a third person arose after the contract existed, it is an assignment.

Just as with a third party beneficiary, an assignee becomes a real party in interest and has enforceable rights against the promisor of the original contract. The promisor can defend by asserting any claim he may have against the assignor. The assignee's ability to proceed against the assignor is dependent on the nature of the assignment itself, gratuitous or for consideration.

If instead of assigning rights, the promisor is attempting to have a third person assist him in fulfilling his contractual obligations, then he is making a delegation. Rights may be assigned; duties may be delegated. However, unlike third party beneficiaries and assignees, the delegate never becomes a real party in interest to the contract, and the promisor remains fully liable for her own performance under the contract.

SYNOPSIS

Third party beneficiary contracts
    1. Third party creditor beneficiary contracts
       a. To extinguish existing debt
       b. Rights vest on detrimental reliance
       c. Creditor can sue promisor or promisee
       d. Promisor can defend by asserting any defense he has against promisee
    2. Third party donee beneficiary contracts
       a. To confer a gift
       b. Rights vest on knowledge of contract
       c. Donee can sue promisor
       d. Promisor can defend by asserting any defense she has against promisee
Assignment
    1. Transfer of contract right
    2. Assignee becomes real party in interest
    3. Can be gratuitous or for consideration
    4. Gratuitous assignments can be revoked unless certain situations exist
    5. Assignments for consideration are irrevocable
    6. UCC filing requirements
Delegation
    1. Having a third party assist in fulfilling contractual obligation
    2. Cannot delegate contracts based on personal services or confidence
    3. Promisor remains liable for contractual obligations

Key Terms

Assignee: transferee of contractual right
Assignment: transference of contractual right by the promisee to a third person
Assignor: transferor of contractual right

Delegation: promisor having assistance in fulfilling contractual duties
Estoppel: equitable term; barring certain actions in the interest of fairness
Incidental beneficiary: person who benefits tangentially from a contract
Intended beneficiary: third party donee or creditor beneficiary
Novation: substitution of a party to a contract; novated person takes over all rights and obligations under the contract
Promisee: one who receives consideration in a bilateral contract
Promisor: one who gives consideration in a bilateral contract
Real party in interest: person with enforceable contractual rights
Third party beneficiary contract: contract entered into for the purpose of benefiting someone not a party to the contract
Third party creditor beneficiary: person who receives the benefit of a contract in order to extinguish a debt owed him by the promisee
Third party donee beneficiary: person who receives the benefit of a contract in order to receive a gift from the promisee
Token chose: item of symbolic, rather than monetary, significance that makes a gratuitous assignment irrevocable
Vested: having a legally enforceable right

EXERCISES

1. How does an assignment differ from a delegation?
2. Give two examples of students being third party beneficiaries. Draft the clauses.
3. What factors would influence a third party beneficiary to sue the promisee rather than the promisor? Give examples.
4. How can you distinguish between a third party beneficiary and an incidental beneficiary?
5. Can a unilateral contract be a third party beneficiary contract? Explain.

Cases for Analysis

To exemplify the problems of interpreting third party contracts and arrangements, the following case summaries are presented. Burks v. Federal Insurance Co. discusses the requirements to be a third party beneficiary under a contract. Imperial Hotels Corp. v. Dore et al. highlights the difference between an assumption and a novation.

Burks v. Federal Insurance Company
2005 Pa. Super. 297, 883 A.2d 1086 (2005)

Appellant initially brought an action against PNC for personal injuries she sustained to her wrist and lower back when she fell in one of PNC's branches. During the trial, Appellant sought compensation for the injuries and damages, which included medical expenses that resulted from the fall. The jury found that Appellant sustained $30,000 in damages as a result of the accident. The jury also found Appellant to be contributorily negligent, and particularly, that 40% of the causal negligence was attributable to her. Thus, the verdict was molded to $18,000. This award was paid in full on PNC's behalf by its insurer, the defendant, and the appellee in the instant action, Federal.

After Appellant received the $18,000 for the damages that she sustained in her accident, she then sought to collect payment of her medical bills under the insurance policy between Federal and PNC. The provision under which she sought to recover states:

> Subject to the Applicable Limits of Insurance, we will pay each person who sustains *bodily injury* caused by an accident all *medical expenses* incurred and reported to us within three years from the date of the accident.
> The accident must take place during the policy period and the *bodily injury* must arise out of premises or operations for which you are afforded *bodily injury* liability coverage under this contract. The injured person must submit to examination, at our expense, by physicians of our choice as often as we reasonably require.

Reproduced Record (R.) at 88a-89a. In her Complaint, Appellant averred that an unidentified individual from PNC instructed Appellant to deliver her medical bills to the PNC branch office for payment. Complaint, 12/23/03, at 6a. It was further averred on "information and belief" that PNC submitted these bills to Federal, and Federal refused to pay for them. *Id.*; R. at 6a.

Appellant then filed this action against Federal. Federal filed preliminary objections in the form of a demurrer claiming that Appellant was not a third party beneficiary to the insurance contract between Federal and PNC. The trial court agreed, and therefore, it sustained the preliminary objections and dismissed Appellant's complaint. Appellant then filed this appeal.

Although Appellant has framed three questions for our review, their resolution hinges on one issue: whether the trial court abused its discretion in determining that Appellant was not a third party beneficiary to the contract between Federal and PNC. In considering this issue, we are mindful that when we review a trial court's order granting preliminary objections in the nature of a demurrer, we apply "the same standard employed by the trial court: all material facts set forth in the complaint as well as all inferences reasonably deducible therefrom are admitted as true for the purposes of review." Vosk v. Encompass Ins. Co., 2004 Pa. Super. 168, 851 A.2d 162, 164 (Pa. Super. 2004).

As stated above, the crux of this appeal is whether Appellant is a third party beneficiary to the insurance policy between PNC and Federal. If she is not, then she certainly cannot assert a claim against Federal under the contract. In Scarpitti v. Weborg, 530 Pa. 366, 609 A.2d 147 (Pa. 1992), our Supreme Court set forth the current standard for determining whether someone is a third party beneficiary to a contract: "In order for a third party beneficiary to have standing to recover on a contract, both contracting parties must have expressed an intention that the third party be a beneficiary, and that intention must have affirmatively appeared in the contract itself." Id. at 149. Furthermore, to be a third party beneficiary entitled to recover on a contract it is not enough that it be intended by *one* of the parties to the contract and the *third person* that the latter should be a beneficiary, but *both parties to the contract* must so intend and must indicate that intention in the contract; in other words, a promisor cannot be held liable to an alleged beneficiary of a contract unless the latter was within his contemplation at the time the contract was entered into and such liability was intentionally assumed by him in his undertaking. Spires v. Hanover Fire Ins. Co., 364 Pa. 52, 70 A.2d 828, 830-31 (Pa. 1950). While *Spires* was overruled in Guy v. Liederbach, 501 Pa. 47, 459 A.2d 744 (Pa. 1983), it was only overruled "to the extent that it states the exclusive test for third party beneficiaries." Id. at 751.

In *Guy*, our Supreme Court established a "narrow class of third party beneficiaries." *Scarpitti,* 609 A.2d at 151. This narrow exception established a "restricted cause of action" for third party beneficiaries by adopting Section 302 of the Restatement (Second) of Contracts (1979), which states:
Intended and Incidental Beneficiaries

> (1) Unless otherwise agreed between promisor and promisee, a beneficiary of a promise is an intended beneficiary if recognition of a right to performance in the beneficiary is appropriate to effectuate the intention of the parties *and either*
> 　　(a) the performance of the promise will satisfy an obligation of the promisee to pay money to the beneficiary; or
> 　　(b) the circumstances indicate that the promisee intends to give the beneficiary the benefit of the promised performance.
> 　　(2) An incidental beneficiary is a beneficiary who is not an intended beneficiary.

Guy, 459 A.2d at 751 (quoting Restatement (Second) of Contracts §302 (1979)). The court explained that Section 302 involves a two-part test to determine whether one is a third party beneficiary to a contract, which requires that: (1) the recognition of the beneficiary's right must be appropriate to effectuate the intention of the parties, and (2) the performance must satisfy an obligation of the promisee to pay money to the beneficiary or the circumstances indicate that the promisee intends to give the beneficiary the benefit of the promised performance.

Therefore, even when the contract does not expressly state that the third party is intended to be a beneficiary, as in the instant case, the party may still be a third party beneficiary under the foregoing test. But *Guy* did not alter the requirement that in order for one to achieve third party beneficiary status, that party must show that *both* parties to the contract so intended, and that such intent was within the parties' contemplation at the time the contract was formed.

The exception annunciated in *Guy* was applied in *Scarpitti*, where the court held that the plaintiffs, who had purchased real estate lots in a residential subdivision, were third party beneficiaries to the contract between the subdivision developer and the architect even though the contract did not state that the lot owners were third party beneficiaries. See *Scarpitti*, 609 A.2d at 151. In *Scarpitti*, the plaintiffs had submitted building plans to the architect who, pursuant to the contract between himself and the subdivision developer, was to enforce building restrictions within the subdivision. The plaintiffs' building plans included three-car garages for the homes. The architect disapproved these plans because they were in violation of a building restriction that required each home to have either a two or two and one-half-car garage. The plaintiffs then built their homes accordingly with either two or two and one-half-car garages. Subsequently, the architect approved building plans for homes with three-car garages for other lot owners.

The plaintiffs then brought an action against the architect for breach of contract under the theory that they were third party beneficiaries to the contract between the subdivision developer and the architect. The court began its analysis by expounding upon the meaning of the two-part test set forth in *Guy* as follows:

The first part of the test sets forth a standing requirement which leaves discretion with the court to determine whether recognition of third party beneficiary status would be appropriate. The second part defines the two types of claimants who may be intended as third party beneficiaries. If a party satisfies both parts of the test, a claim may be asserted under the contract.

The *Scarpitti* court reasoned that because in the underlying contract the architect promised to review all building plans and enforce restrictions within the subdivision, "the purpose of this agreement was to make the lots more attractive to prospective purchasers by assuring that other home-owners in the subdivision would be required to abide by the recorded subdivision restrictions." Id. at 151. Accordingly, "*at the time of contracting,*" *both* parties contemplated that the subdivision lot owners would be third party beneficiaries to the contract because the future home owners would have the greatest interest in uniform enforcement of the building restrictions, and they would be the ones primarily "benefited by the establishment of a vehicle to enforce the restrictions." Id. (emphasis added). The court held that although the contract did not expressly state that the parties intended to benefit the future home owners, the circumstances were "so compelling" that "recognition of a right to uniform enforcement of the deed restrictions in [the plaintiffs] is appropriate to effectuate the intention of the parties." Id. at 150-51.

Guided by the foregoing precedent, we find the central issue in this case to be whether the trial court abused its discretion in determining that Appellant did not meet the first part of this test because granting her standing would not be appropriate to effectuate the intention of Federal and PNC. The Honorable R. Stanton Wettick, Jr., presided over this matter in the trial court, and he sustained Federal's preliminary objections on the basis of a previous opinion issued in the case of Newman v. CAN Commercial Ins. Co., No. AR99-1170 (Allegheny 1999), wherein he stated:

> Plaintiff argues that Coffee Cafe "being a restaurant that strives to accommodate its patrons" intended that its patrons be third party beneficiaries of the policy. Plaintiff states that it makes no sense for the insurance company to charge a premium for a benefit that it will pay only if it chooses to do so.
>
> My difficulty with this argument is that it assumes that Coffee Cafe and its insurance company both intended that no decisions about paying medical benefits regardless of fault could be made by either party. The insurance policy is not posted on the walls of Coffee Cafe. Consequently, the patron is not going to know that there is insurance providing for payment of medical benefits unless Coffee Cafe chooses to trigger the provisions providing for payment of medical expenses regardless of fault by paying the customer's medical expenses and looking to the insurance company for reimbursement or by advising the customer and the insurance company that payment of the medical expenses should be made.
>
> The purpose of the provision providing for payment of medical expenses regardless of fault is to further Coffee Cafe's business interests. Payment is not necessarily consistent with these business interests. There will be situations in which Coffee Cafe wishes the insurance company to pay the medical expenses of a customer injured on the premises regardless of fault in order to maintain goodwill. However, there may be other situations where Coffee Cafe may not want the payments to be made unless the injured party agrees not to bring suit for other damages, where Coffee Cafe does not want payments to be made because of the fear of increased insurance premiums, or where Coffee Cafe does not want to accommodate the injured party.
>
> Consider, for example, the situation in which a patron was injured on the premises when he attacked, while intoxicated, two employees of Coffee Cafe who had asked him to leave the premises. Coffee Cafe never intended for its insurance policy to be construed to require payment of medical expenses in this situation. Coffee Cafe, instead, intended to retain the option to decide when to provide these benefits because retention of the option is most consistent with its business interests.

On appeal, Appellant argues that "having submitted the medical expense payment to the Manager of PNC for payment as she was instructed, the bank intended to give [Appellant] the benefit of the promised performance of her medical expenses therefore making [Appellant] an intended third party beneficiary of the contract as set forth under Pennsylvania law." Brief for Appellant at 9. There are two problems with this argument. First, even if we were to assume that PNC's actions somehow demonstrated an intent to benefit Appellant, it is not only PNC's intent with which we are here concerned. In addition, Appellant must show that Federal also intended to benefit Appellant, as one party to a contract may not unilaterally designate a third party as a beneficiary without the other party to the contract also intending the same. Second, PNC's actions occurred well after PNC and Federal entered into their contract, and in order to determine whether someone is a third party beneficiary, we must attempt to discern the parties' intent at the time of contracting. See *Scarpitti*, 609 A.2d at 151.

And when we consider PNC's intent at the time of contracting, it seems clear that its intention was to procure medical payment coverage that would permit PNC to compensate an individual for bodily injury sustained on its premises *if it chose to*, and independent of its actual legal liability to compensate the individual. In a similar case, the Illinois Appellate Court set forth some reasons why an insured would want such coverage:

> We do not find that the insurance contract between Sears and Allstate contemplates a direct action against the insurer for an injured party's medical expenses whenever any person is injured on the insured premises of a Sears store. The medical payments coverage may be viewed as a salutary attempt to *allow*, but not require, Sears to pay relatively small, easily ascertainable medical reimbursements, without a formal determination of fault. This would allow Sears, as insured, to facilitate settlement of some claims by paying actual medical costs without admitting or contesting liability. . . . Moreover, absent such a provision allowing the insured to pay medical expenses, the insured would risk waiving its claim for indemnity against the insurer if the insured went ahead and voluntarily assumed payment for the injured party's medical expenses.

Thus, the coverage which PNC purchased from Federal would serve many of its own interests. At its discretion, it could choose when to trigger the medical payments coverage, and in so doing it could consider several factors that serve its best interests. For instance, whether the injured person was an important customer, whether PNC was entirely at fault, or whether the injury was relatively minor. Conversely, it may decide not to trigger the coverage because the individual injured was entirely to blame for the accident as a result of his or her own negligence. Furthermore, the amount of money that Federal would pay out under the medical payment coverage would certainly affect PNC's premiums. Consequently, PNC would undoubtedly seek to exercise control over when such a claim could be made.

To hold otherwise would be to confer a blanket accidental medical insurance policy to all individuals that sustain bodily injury that arises out of PNC's operation of its premises for which it has bodily injury liability coverage. Such medical payment coverage would exist regardless of the identity of the individual injured or whether that person was entirely at fault for the injury. Most importantly, PNC, the contracting party that pays the premiums for the coverage, would have absolutely no control over when to trigger the coverage. We cannot agree that this was the intention of PNC at the time that it contracted for this coverage.

Likewise, there is nothing in the insurance policy or the circumstances surrounding this case that would indicate that Federal intended to permit a direct claim against itself for medical payment coverage. In fact, the insurance policy contains a provision that sets forth the circumstances under which a party may bring legal action against Federal. Reproduced Record at 99a. It *does not state* that an individual may directly sue Federal for payment of medical bills under the medical coverage provision, which demonstrates that the legal action provision was written with the intent of insulating Federal from direct causes of action, intending instead to divert these claims to proceed directly against PNC, for which Federal may then be liable under its policy with PNC.

Thus, we conclude that the trial court did not abuse its discretion in holding that recognizing Appellant as a third party beneficiary would not be appropriate to effectuate the intent of PNC and Federal at the time that they entered into the insurance contract. While persons injured on PNC's premises would benefit from PNC's triggering of its medical payment coverage, unlike in *Scarpitti*, the benefit of the contract is not meant to primarily protect these individuals' interests.

In conclusion, we also note that Appellant has wholly ignored the fact that she filed a previous action against PNC sounding in negligence in which she sought to recover damages for the injuries that she sustained as a result of the accident. Reproduced Record (R.) at 7a. The certified record contains Federal's Brief in Support of Preliminary Objections, in which it states that in Appellant's suit against PNC, she sought payment for the medical expenses that she incurred as a result of the accident. Indeed, this is certainly a reasonable inference from the fact alleged in Appellant's Complaint that her suit against PNC was to collect damages for the injuries that she sustained as a result of PNC's negligence. See Vosk v. Encompass Ins. Co., 2004 Pa. Super. 168, 851 A.2d 162, 164 (Pa. Super. 2004) (stating that when reviewing a court's order granting preliminary objections in the nature of a demurrer, "an appellate court applies the same standard employed by the trial court: all material facts set forth in the complaint as well as all inferences reasonably deducible therefrom are admitted as true for the purposes of review"). We cannot imagine a situation in which an attorney would not seek to recover medical expenses in a personal injury action. Nor can we discern a reason why a jury would not award medical expenses to a plaintiff when the jury has found that the defendant's negligence is the proximate cause of the plaintiff's injuries.

Thus, we conclude that a jury has already compensated Appellant for the payment of her medical expenses. And in doing so, the jury determined that due to Appellant's contributory negligence, she was responsible for 40% of these damages. Appellant should not now be permitted to seek payment for $10,000 of her medical expenses when a jury has already determined that she was partially to blame for the accident. Furthermore, to permit a plaintiff to file two actions, one sounding in negligence against the insured, and a second for breach of contract against insurer, would unsalutarily encourage the multiplicity of lawsuits. See Trouten v. Heritage Mut. Ins. Co., 2001 S.D. 106, 632 N.W.2d 856, 862 (S.D. 2001).

Order AFFIRMED.

Questions

1.   How does the court distinguish between a third party beneficiary and an incidental beneficiary?
2.   What is the import of the *Scarpitti* ruling on this court's reasoning?
3.   What is your opinion of this decision?

Imperial Hotels Corp. v. Dore et al.
257 F.3d 615 (6th Cir. 2001)

Imperial Hotels Corp. sued three corporations and one individual to collect on a note originally executed by another party. On Mainstream Capital Corp.'s motion for summary judgment, the district court held that Imperial was an intended third-party beneficiary of Mainstream Capital Corp.'s agreement with Jay Ambe Corp. to assume responsibility for payments on the original note. The court further held that a subsequent assumption agreement between Dore Development Co. and Jay Ambe Corp., to which Imperial expressed consent, constituted a novation relieving Mainstream of its liability to Imperial. Because Michigan law on novations looks to the subjective intent of all the parties and because in this case there is a genuine issue of material fact as to intent, the court erred in entering summary judgment for Mainstream. We therefore reverse and remand for further proceedings.

I

This diversity case arises out of a dispute concerning the financing of a motel in Bay City, Michigan, known as the Gateway Regency Motel. In 1983, Nick Khatiwala purchased from a division of Imperial '400' National, Inc., the furniture, fixtures, furnishings, and equipment of a motel located at 50 Sixth Street in Bay City, along with the leasehold interest in and improvements upon that property. Khatiwala executed a security agreement and a promissory note in favor of Imperial in the amount of $160,000, payable over 25 years with 10% annual interest on the unpaid balance. A 1984 amendment to the note raised the interest rate to 10.5% and re-amortized the payment schedule. Neither the original note nor the amendment (collectively, the "Khatiwala Note") contained an acceleration clause, although the final note automatically raised the interest rate to 11% should Khatiwala transfer his interest in the property.

In the ensuing years, apparently, Khatiwala transferred his rights in the motel and obligations under the Khatiwala Note to Jay Ambe Corp. ("Ambe"). In September 1987, Mainstream Capital Corp. ("Mainstream") purchased the motel from Ambe, at which time it executed a note in favor of Ambe in the amount of $318,000. This "Mainstream Note," which gave Ambe the right to accelerate Mainstream's debt in the event of default, provided that Mainstream assumed Ambe's debt payable to Imperial based on the Khatiwala Note, on which $153,095.81 in principal remained outstanding. Mainstream agreed to make its payments to Ambe, with Ambe to remit payments to Imperial in accordance with the terms of the Khatiwala Note. This sort of arrangement is known in the trade as "wrap-around" financing because, as here, a promissory note encompasses a promise to pay an amount equal to a prior existing debt plus additional funds advanced by a second lender. See Mitchell v. Trustees of United States Real Estate Inv. Trust, 144 Mich. App. 302, 375 N.W.2d 424, 428 (Mich. Ct. App. 1985).

In 1989, Mainstream defaulted on its obligation to Ambe under the Mainstream Note, but Ambe did not accelerate the indebtedness. On September 9, 1990, Mainstream and Arthur P. Dore, then acting "only as agent for a corporation then in existence or to be formed" (presumably Dore Development Co.), entered into a "Purchase Agreement" whereby Dore promised to purchase the motel from Mainstream for a total of $550,000. This purchase price included a cash component, a promise concerning services to be rendered, and the assumption of five separate debts. With respect to two of these debts, the Purchase Agreement provided: "F) The assumption of the principal balance of the outstanding obligation as is evidenced by a Note and Mortgage due to [Imperial]," a copy of which was attached, and "G) The assumption of the principal balance of the outstanding obligation as is evidenced by a Note as amended and extended due to Jay Ambe Corp.," a copy of which was attached. Thus, the parties planned to have Dore Development Co.'s obligation wrap around both the Khatiwala Note and the Mainstream Note. The Purchase Agreement required Dore Development Co. to ascertain from Imperial the amount of debt due and outstanding under the Khatiwala Note.

Ambe and Dore Development Co. closed their transaction on November 20, 1990. As part of the consideration called for by the Purchase Agreement, Ambe and Dore Development Co. executed a "Debt Assumption Agreement," effective November 20, 1990, by which Dore Development assumed Mainstream's obligations. Mainstream was not a party to this agreement, nor was Imperial. Jay Ambe Corp. and Dore Development Co. executed the Debt Assumption Agreement, as did Arthur P. Dore as guarantor. As of November 20, 1990, $146,240.48 in outstanding principal remained due on the Khatiwala Note, with interest accruing at 11%. Under the Mainstream Note, Mainstream owed Jay Ambe Corp. $30,000 in principal, plus interest and a late fee, for a total indebtedness of $38,798.18. By the Debt Assumption Agreement, Ambe amended the Mainstream Note, and Dore Development Co. assumed it as amended. The provisions "relating to payments to [Imperial] . . . remained unchanged." Dore Development Co. promised to repay the full $38,798.18 that Mainstream owed to Ambe by paying $10,000 immediately and the remainder in installments over time. Arthur P. Dore personally guaranteed performance of Dore Development Co.'s obligation.

As Dore Development and Ambe prepared for their November 20th closing, Imperial sent a fax to Dore Development Co.'s attorney, Kenneth Schmidt, on November 9, 1990. Signed by Imperial's Controller and

Assistant Secretary, the transmission stated, "Ken, included are the numbers required to bring the note current. [Imperial] would consent to assumption of this note by Dore Development Co. provided the note is brought current per the attached worksheet." The worksheet indicated $146,240.48 in total principal outstanding, with a regular $3,060.48 principal payment and $10,723.62 in unpaid interest due as of October 31, 1990. These figures obviously correspond to the obligations under the Khatiwala Note. With interest continuing to accrue until November 20, 1990, the amount required to bring the Khatiwala Note debt current as of that day was $14,144.06. On November 20th, Schmidt sent a check in that amount to Imperial and explained that the check represented the total principal and interest then due on the note "assumed by Mainstream Capital Corporation and now assumed by my client Dore Development Co." Schmidt's letter and the payment to Imperial purported to "confirm[ ] your consent to the assumption of the Note by Dore Development Co. provided the Note is brought current."

Dore Development Co. continued to make payments pursuant to the Debt Assumption Agreement until August 1996. The record does not disclose why Dore Development Co. stopped making payments at that time, nor does it indicate whether Jay Ambe Corp. is making payments to Imperial under the terms of the Khatiwala Note that Ambe assumed prior to 1987.

Imperial sued Arthur P. Dore, claiming a right to recovery based on the personal guarantee he made in the Debt Assumption Agreement. Dore filed a motion to dismiss, and the district court ultimately granted Imperial leave to amend its complaint. The amended complaint added Jay Ambe Corp., Dore Development Co., and Mainstream Capital Corp. as defendants, asserting against all defendants claims of breach of contract, breach of duty to a third-party beneficiary of a contract, and promissory estoppel. Jay Ambe Corp. was never served, so it never became a party to this litigation. Imperial eventually consented to dismissing Dore Development Co. and Arthur P. Dore from the case, with prejudice. Mainstream filed a motion to dismiss and a motion for summary judgment. Imperial conceded that it had no claims against Mainstream based on breach of contract and promissory estoppel, leaving only its third-party-beneficiary claim. Imperial did not file a cross-motion for summary judgment.

The district court held that, in the Mainstream Note, Mainstream explicitly assumed the remaining debt on the Khatiwala Note owed to Imperial, thereby intentionally undertaking to perform an act directly for Imperial's benefit. Although Mainstream sent payments to Jay Ambe Corp., it did so for the express purpose of having them remitted to Imperial. Thus, the court held Mainstream liable to Imperial on a third-party-beneficiary theory. Yet the court further held that Imperial released Mainstream from its third-party obligation under the Mainstream Note when Imperial consented to the assumption of this obligation by Dore Development Co., while Dore Development Co. supplied consideration to Imperial by bringing the Mainstream Note current. Imperial's consent to the Debt Assumption Agreement and Dore's bringing the Mainstream Note current constituted a novation that released Mainstream from its obligation, the court held.

The district court entered judgment in favor of Mainstream, and Imperial timely appealed. Mainstream has not cross-appealed, so the question of whether Imperial was a third-party beneficiary of the Mainstream Note is not before this court. The only matter presented for our consideration is whether Imperial's "consent" to Dore Development Co. assuming the Mainstream Note's Khatiwala Note component and the circumstances surrounding the assumption constitute, as a matter of law, a novation releasing Mainstream of its third-party-beneficiary liability to Imperial.

II

Jurisdiction over this matter derives solely from 28 U.S.C. §1332. Accordingly, this court follows federal procedural law but must apply the substantive law of Michigan "in accordance with the then-controlling decision of the highest court of the state." Pedigo v. UNUM Life Ins. Co., 145 F.3d 804, 808 (6th Cir. 1998). "To the extent that the state supreme court has not yet addressed the issue presented, it is [the federal courts'] duty to anticipate how that court would rule." Bailey Farms, Inc. v. NOR-AM Chem. Co., 27 F.3d 188, 191 (6th Cir. 1994) (*citing* Mahne v. Ford Motor Co., 900 F.2d 83, 87 (6th Cir. 1990)).

For more than ninety years, Michigan law has set forth four elements of a novation: "(1) parties capable of contracting; (2) a valid obligation to be displaced; (3) the consent of all parties to the substitution based upon sufficient consideration; (4) the extinction of the old obligation and the creation of a valid new one." Macklin v. Brown, 111 Mich. App. 110, 314 N.W.2d 538, 540 (Mich. Ct. App. 1981) (*citing* In re Dunneback's Estate, 302 Mich. 73, 4 N.W.2d 472, 474 (Mich. 1942), and others). "All of these elements must be established by the evidence; not necessarily by direct evidence, but by evidence of such facts and circumstances [surrounding the transactions] as logically leads one to the conclusion that a new contract has been made." Harrington-Wiard Co. v. Blomstrom Mfg. Co., 166 Mich. 276, 131 N.W. 559, 561 (Mich. 1911). Imperial argues that the evidence before the district court did not establish, as a matter of law, the third and fourth elements.

"Assumption of liability is not novation, unless there concur the consent of the one party to accept the substitute in lieu of the other party to the original contract, and a discharge of the latter. There must be consent by the creditor to take the new debtor as his sole security and to extinguish the claim against the former. Such consent is not to be implied merely from the performance of the contract by the substitute, for that might well consist with the continued liability of the original. . . ."

Harrington-Wiard Co., 131 N.W. at 564-65 (*quoting* Illinois Car & Equip. Co. v. Linstroth Wagon Co., 112 F. 737, 740 (7th Cir. 1902) (*citing* Butterfield v. Hartshorn, 7 N.H. 345 (1834))); see also Fender v. Feighner, 265 Mich. 536, 538, 251 N.W. 536 (Mich. 1933) (*quoting* same cases). The circumstances surrounding a series of transactions may be considered, in addition to the text of any written instruments, in determining whether the parties reached a novation that extinguished the liability of one debtor and substituted for it the liability of another. However, a third party's payment accepted by a creditor does not, without more, establish a novation. See Hutchings v. Securities Exch. Corp., 287 Mich. 701, 284 N.W. 614, 617 (Mich. 1939); Gorman v. Butzel, 272 Mich. 525, 262 N.W. 302, 304 (Mich. 1935).

The Purchase Agreement and the Debt Assumption Agreement are contracts between Jay Ambe Corp. and Dore Development, to which neither Imperial nor Mainstream became parties. Mainstream relies on the written "consent" Imperial supposedly gave to Dore Development's proposal to pay off the overdue debt owed to Imperial under the Mainstream Note, i.e., the fax from Imperial's controller to Dore Development's attorney. In that fax, Imperial stated that it "would consent to assumption of this note," provided Dore brought it current. Mainstream argues that this transmission constituted an offer of novation that Dore Development accepted when it brought the Khatiwala portion of the Mainstream Note current as of the November 20th closing. To further support its contention, Mainstream points to language in the Debt Assumption Agreement, "Creditor [Ambe] consents to Debtor's [Dore Development's] assumption of said [Mainstream] Note," from which it *infers* Ambe's and *Imperial*'s consent to release Mainstream. Mainstream also notes that, for six years following the Debt Assumption Agreement, Dore Development directly paid and Imperial accepted installments on the Khatiwala portion of the Mainstream Note. Finally, Imperial took no actions between November 20, 1990, and the filing of the instant lawsuit that recognized or asserted a continuing obligation by Mainstream.

Imperial stresses that nothing in the fax (or anything else, for that matter) indicated any intention on Imperial's part to *release* Mainstream from its obligation under the Mainstream Note, and it does not appear that Mainstream ever asked to be released. Moreover, Imperial points out that nothing in the record even remotely suggests that Mainstream consented *at the time* to Imperial's supposed release of Mainstream and substitution of Dore Development. See Keppen v. Rice, 257 Mich. 299, 241 N.W. 156, 157 (Mich. 1932) ("Consent of all the parties to the novation is necessary, but need not be expressed in writing. It is sufficient if it appears from the facts and circumstances surrounding the transaction.").

From these two versions of the facts, Imperial argues that nothing supports the district court's conclusion that it released Mainstream. Of course, this is a position Mainstream describes as "clearly incorrect," insofar as Imperial consented to Dore Development's assumption of the Khatiwala Note obligation. At this stage of litigation, both parties draw extravagant conclusions from an ambiguous record. Although one side may be drawing inferences consistent with the actual intent of the parties, a trier of fact must ultimately decide that question. Because the district court did not draw all inferences from the undisputed facts in favor of the non-moving party, it effectively made findings of fact on a question Michigan law generally reserves to factfinders. Accordingly, the court erred in holding that a novation releasing Mainstream occurred when Imperial offered to consent to Dore Development's assumption of the Khatiwala Note obligation.

As Imperial points out, nothing in the fax transmission indicated any intention to release Mainstream. The word "assumption," directed to Dore Development, does not by itself indicate an intention by Imperial to release Mainstream from its third-party-beneficiary obligation under the Mainstream Note. Although Imperial may have intended to release Mainstream, its consent might just as well have meant only that it was pleased another party would become obligated to pay amounts owing under the Khatiwala Note. Imperial's having accepted payments directly from Dore Development is as consistent with this view of the facts as it is with the inference that Imperial intended to release Mainstream.

Moreover, assumption and substitution do not mean the same thing. Although the latter term may strongly imply intent to release the old debtor upon the new debtor's involvement, the former term carries no such implication. Substitution connotes assumption plus release, but assumption does not necessarily imply release. Michigan law recognizes that a creditor may consent to a new debtor's assuming an obligation without releasing the old debtor from its liability. See Harrington-Wiard Co., 131 N.W. at 563 (holding that assumption of liability is not novation). The elements of a novation require the creditor's intention both that the new debtor assume the obligation and that the old debtor be released. See id. at 563-64; Devitt v. Quirk, 105 Mich. App. 94, 306 N.W.2d 405, 407 (Mich. Ct. App. 1981) (creditor's consent to a transaction between old debtor and third party did not necessarily indicate release of old debtor). The record proves *at most* that Imperial intended Dore Development to assume the Khatiwala Note obligation. Nothing in the record directly speaks to an intention by Imperial to release Mainstream; any such intention must be inferred from the surrounding circumstances. Such inferences cannot be drawn against a non-moving party at the summary judgment stage.

Additionally, nothing in the record suggests that Mainstream sought to be released. Even if Imperial intended its contacts with Dore Development to release Mainstream, Mainstream was not, evidently, a party to this supposed "novation." That is, the record does not contain evidence of the "consent of all parties to the substitution. . . ." Macklin v. Brown, 314 N.W.2d at 540; cf. Keppen, 241 N.W. at 157 (enforcing an agreement among three parties to release the original debtor and substitute the assignee in its place). Of course, Mainstream would seem to have no reason to want to remain liable, i.e., no reason to withhold consent to its release, but on this record Mainstream never expressed such consent. Indeed, an affidavit by Mainstream's vice president indicates that Mainstream and Imperial had engaged in "no communication . . . concerning any matter" after March 1989. Without communication, reaching an agreement to do anything seems rather difficult, if not impossible. But see Gorman, 262 N.W. at 305 (recognizing a novation where, without involving old debtor, creditor and new debtors executed a new agreement patently inconsistent with an intent to keep old debtor liable).

The district court erred in failing to draw all reasonable inferences in favor of the non-moving party, Imperial. It committed a related error in making, at the summary judgment stage, findings of fact on a question Michigan law reserves for triers of fact. Michigan cases on the subject reveal a variety of circumstances in which novations have been found, but the factual backgrounds and procedural histories of these cases confirm that Michigan law generally deems improper a grant of summary judgment on the question of novation.

In Ceabuske v. Smolarz, 229 Mich. 100, 200 N.W. 945, 945-46 (Mich. 1924), the court, reviewing conflicting evidence of intent, affirmed a jury's verdict that the plaintiff had not intended to release the defendant from obligations on a note. Plaintiff had sold a business to defendant, who in turn sold it to a third party with plaintiff's consent. Plaintiff, who had never surrendered defendant's note, obtained a note from the third party but also testified that he warned defendant that he would be responsible in the event the third party failed to pay.

In Fender v. Feighner, plaintiffs sold real estate to defendant, who assigned to Barker, who in turn assigned to McVay, with both assignments sent to plaintiffs. Even though plaintiffs gave McVay receipts for payment in his name, dealt directly with him when payments fell behind, and made no demand on the defendant until after default — 10 years after the assignment — the court rejected the defendant's claim of novation because the lower court did not err in finding that nothing indicated plaintiffs' intent to release defendants. "Had defendant desired to be relieved from his obligation, he should have secured a release in writing so providing," the court commented. Fender, 251 N.W. at 539.

In Devitt v. Quirk, the court affirmed a trial court's finding that no novation occurred because: the defendants retained property of the original sale subject to the prior security interest of the plaintiffs; the defendants, by written document executed shortly after the transfer to the third-party, acknowledged the continuance of their obligation to the plaintiffs; the consent executed by the plaintiffs to the defendant-third party transaction contained no words of release of the defendants; and the plaintiffs testified that no release or substitution was intended. See Devitt, 306 N.W.2d at 407.

In Matter of Yeager Bridge & Culvert Co., the court reversed as clear error a finding of no novation because the record contained "evidence that all parties consented to the substitution." There, the parties reached a "mutual agreement to discharge [the original supplier] from its obligation to perform and to substitute [a new supplier] in order to provide [the promisee] with a fixed delivery date" for materials it needed to profitably fulfill its contract with the state. The trial court erred in finding the substitution of a new supplier an attempt to mitigate the promisee's damages because all parties clearly agreed to release the original supplier and substitute the new one in its place. See Matter of Yeager Bridge & Culvert Co., 150 Mich. App. 386, 389 N.W.2d 99, 109-11 (Mich. Ct. App. 1986).

Finally, in Gorman v. Butzel, plaintiff sold land on a contract to defendant, and defendant assigned the property and note to Freud, which assignment plaintiff also signed, though without explanation. Freud later sold to Fry, who sold part of her interest to the Eddys, who sold theirs to the Aldriches. An agreement was executed by plaintiffs, Freud, Fry, and the Aldriches, in which the Aldriches agreed to make payments on their contract with Fry directly to plaintiff, whereupon plaintiff would credit Freud, Freud credit Fry, and Fry credit the Aldriches on their respective contracts. If the Aldriches made all payments, plaintiff promised to deed the property to Freud, who would deed it to Fry, who would deed it to the Aldriches. Defendant was not a party to this four-party contract; his name was not mentioned in it, nor did he have notice of its execution. The court explained: plaintiff's "execution of the assignment, being unexplained, may have been meant either as an indorsed acknowledgment of receipt of the assignment; or it may have been intended to create privity of contract between [plaintiff] and Freud on the latter's promise to pay the contract balance, without releasing [defendant]; or as a complete novation of Freud for [defendant] as contract vendee. If the latter was intended, a legal novation occurred even without express agreement with [defendant]." Gorman, 262 N.W at 304. The court examined the surrounding circumstances, particularly the four-party agreement, and affirmed the lower court's finding of novation because "it would be difficult, in the absence of a most explicit and direct contract, to imagine circumstances more clearly indicating an intention by vendor and assignee to expel the vendee from the transaction and continue it as between themselves." Id. at 305.

As Mainstream observes, Ceabuske involved a direct warning of defendant's liability despite plaintiff's consent to the assignment to a third party. The Fender court went no further than holding that payments alone do not prove a novation. And Devitt relied in part upon the defendants' acknowledgment of continuing obligation. But these nuanced factual distinctions between the cases demonstrate that Michigan law considers the question of novation extremely fact-intensive. Each of the cases that give any procedural history reached an appellate court after a trier of fact made findings, not after summary judgment on the question of novation. Read together, these cases point toward a rule that, unless a writing conclusively shows a creditor's intent to permit assumption and grant release, summary judgment is inappropriate because a trier of fact must determine from all the facts and circumstances whether the creditor intended to release the original debtor. A survey of jurisdictions across the county indicates adherence to just this sort of rule. Therefore, we hold that a Michigan court would deny summary judgment on the question of novation when the party urging novation relies on a written statement of bare consent to an assumption and on the surrounding circumstances.

Michigan law requires intent to release, and Mainstream's contention that "there is no legitimate dispute that [Imperial] expressly consented to the substitution of Dore Development for Mainstream as obligee of the monies then owed to [Imperial]" is simply wrong. Nothing in the record reveals express consent to anything more than Dore Development's assumption, although a factfinder might conclude, after hearing the conflicting evidence and the arguments of both parties, that Imperial concomitantly intended to release Mainstream and thereby effect a substitution. But that question is properly posed to a trier of fact.

III

Because the evidence before the district court contained unresolved genuine issues of material fact, and the court failed to draw all reasonable inferences in favor of the non-movant, the court erred in granting summary judgment. Accordingly, we REVERSE and REMAND for proceedings consistent with this opinion.

Questions

1. What are the elements of a novation under Michigan law?
2. How does the court say an assumption differs from a novation?
3. What does the court say about payments being proof of a novation? Explain.

Suggested Case References

1. A municipality enters into a contract with a private company to construct sewers and make street repairs. The company agrees to be liable for any property damage resulting from its work. Are the citizens third party beneficiaries of this contract with enforceable rights against the company? Read Lundt v. Parsons Construction Co., 181 Neb. 609 (1967), and Anderson v. Rexroad, 182 Kan. 676 (1954).

2. To be a third party beneficiary to a contract, must a person be specifically named in the contract? Read what the New Mexico court said in Stotlar v. Hester, 582 P.2d 403 (N.M. App. 1978).

3. Is any particular form needed to create a valid assignment? Stoller v. Exchange National Bank of Chicago, 199 Ill. App. 2d 674, 557 N.E.2d 438 (1990).

4. Is an insurer's right of subrogation the same as an assignment of rights by the insured to the insurer? The Missouri court discusses this question in Farmer's Insurance Co., Inc. v. Effertz, 795 S.W.2d 424 (Mo. App. 1990).

5. Are union members third party beneficiaries in a reorganization agreement between a corporation and its creditors? Read what the Iowa court said in Bailey v. Iowa Beef Processors, Inc., 213 N.W.2d 642 (Iowa 1973).

10

Discharge of Obligations

Learning Objectives

After studying this chapter you will be able to:

- List the methods whereby a contractual obligation may be discharged
- Define "voluntary disablement"
- Discuss the concept of "anticipatory breach"
- Understand what is meant by tendering performance
- Differentiate between a material breach and a minor breach
- Define "mutual rescission"
- Explain the concept of impossibility of performance
- Exemplify frustration of purpose
- Understand which contracts are divisible contracts
- Discuss the effect of discharge on the parties to the agreement

CHAPTER OVERVIEW

The contract is now complete. Every clause has been analyzed and discussed, and the contract meets all of the legal requirements to be an enforceable agreement. Does this mean that the parties to the contract are required to fulfill their promised performances? The answer is a resounding "Not necessarily."

In several situations a contracting party's performance is discharged, or excused, without his actually having fulfilled his contractual obligations.

The circumstances that create these situations generally involve occasions when either the other party or external situations negate the necessity of performance.

Suppose that one of the conditions specified or implied in the contract fails to occur. Because the condition is a timing element for performance, if the condition giving rise to that performance does not come to pass, no performance is expected under the terms of the contract.

A contracting party's performance is excused if the other contracting party breaches. Because a valid contract requires mutuality of consideration, when one side fails to deliver the promised-for consideration, the other side is excused from performance as well.

The parties to the contract, for one reason or another, may agree that the contract is not worth completing. In these circumstances the parties are perfectly free to rescind or modify their existing obligations. As a consequence of this new "meeting of the minds," the obligations imposed under the original contract are no longer applicable. The parties agree to be bound to a new contractual arrangement instead.

Finally, situations that occur through no fault of either side may discharge the parties' contractual obligations. These are cases where outside forces have made fulfillment of the contract impossible, such as a change in the law or the unforeseen destruction of the subject matter of the contract. The law does not require the parties to perform the impossible or the illegal simply because a contract is in existence. Changed circumstances can change contractual obligations.

In summary, once the contract itself is determined to be valid and enforceable, it is necessary to see what happens after the agreement has been entered into. Dependent upon what the parties themselves, or what external factors, do, a party to a contract may not be legally bound to fulfill his contractual promises. The specifics of these methods of discharging contractual obligations are discussed below.

Methods of Discharge

A party to a contract may be discharged, or excused, from her contractual obligation in the following eight circumstances:

1. excuse of conditions;
2. performance;
3. breach of contract;
4. agreement of the parties;
5. impossibility of performance;
6. supervening illegality;
7. death or destruction of the subject matter or parties; and
8. frustration of purpose.

Each of these eight methods of discharge will be discussed individually.

Excuse of Conditions

As discussed in a previous chapter, a **condition** is a timing element of a contractual agreement. The condition either creates or extinguishes a party's duty to perform. Consequently, if the condition fails to occur, the performance does not come into play; conversely, a condition subsequent can terminate the obligation to perform.

EXAMPLES:

1. Abdul contracts to purchase Mamet's house. The contract is conditioned on Abdul finding financing for the purchase within 30 days. If Abdul is unable to find a mortgage within the 30 days, the contractual promises are excused. The condition precedent has not taken place, and so Abdul does not have to purchase Mamet's house. Mamet is free to sell the house to someone else.

2. Under their divorce settlement, Max has agreed to pay Fanny a set amount of alimony each month until one of them dies or Fanny remarries. When Fanny does remarry, Max is excused from his contractual obligation. The condition subsequent, Fanny's remarriage, discharges Max from his alimony obligations.

In each of the two examples above, the condition itself discharged the contractual obligation. In addition, because contractual conditions usually involve some element of time (either short, long, or indefinite), there exists the possibility that during the contractual time frame one of the parties will do something that will prevent or excuse the other side's performance. While such circumstances occur during the *time period* of the condition they are not situations in which *the condition itself* discharges the contractual obligation, as in the examples given above. Generally, there are four circumstances that fall into this category.

1. Performance Prevented. In this situation, one side, during the period of the condition, engages in some act that makes it impossible for the promisor to fulfill her obligation. The promisor will be excused from performing. The person who prevents the performance only excuses the counter performance of the other side; the wrongdoer is still contractually bound.

EXAMPLE:

Jessie agrees to paint Fred's house on Thursday. When Jessie arrives at Fred's, Fred has bolted and locked the gate, making entrance to the house impossible. Fred's conduct excuses Jessie's performance, but Fred will still be liable for Jessie's costs and expenses.

If the party who must perform *after* the condition occurs is the one who prevents the condition happening, he will not be excused and must perform. A person cannot benefit from his own wrongdoing.

 EXAMPLE:

Ted hires Irene to remodel his house for a set sum and requires that after completion Irene give Ted an architect's certificate stating the remodeling meets all current standards. Ted prevents the architect from giving the certificate. Ted must pay Irene. Because Ted is the one who prevented the condition from occurring, it does not excuse his contractual obligation.

2. Voluntary Disablement. Voluntary disablement means that one party to a contract voluntarily engages in some conduct that makes it virtually impossible for him to fulfill his obligation. It is not absolutely impossible, but the circumstances are such that it would be more than extremely unlikely that he will be able to perform. In these circumstances, the other side is excused from her obligations. The law will not force one side to perform if it is unlikely or impossible for the other side to perform. For contracts covered by the Uniform Commercial Code (UCC), voluntary disablement would give rise to the other party's right to seek written assurances of performance. (See Chapter 8). If such assurances were not given within 30 days, the party seeking such assurances could consider the voluntary disablement a breach of contract.

 EXAMPLE:

Becky agrees to purchase Patti's antique vase. Payment and delivery are to take place in two weeks. One week after their contract is entered into, Patti sells the vase to Rose. Because there still is one week left until Patti has to convey the vase to Becky, it is conceivable that she could repurchase the vase from Rose so as to be able to give it to Becky, but the likelihood is negligible. This is an example of voluntary disablement. Patti has voluntarily engaged in an action that makes it unlikely that she will be able to fulfill her contractual obligation to Becky. Consequently, Becky's obligation to Patti is discharged.

The majority of states considers that voluntary disablement constitutes a full breach of contract, entitling the injured party to sue immediately for contractual relief in the courts. In those jurisdictions where it is not considered a breach of contract, the promisee must wait until the time element has passed to ascertain whether the other party will perform before being able to seek judicial relief.

3. Insolvency. If one party to the contract becomes judicially insolvent, the other side is excused from performing. The law does not require that a person become a judicial creditor of a bankrupt, nor will it permit someone to attempt to fulfill a contract with a bankrupt resulting in increased debts for the insolvent party.

EXAMPLE:

Farmer White has a contract to deliver 1000 bushels of sweet potatoes to Eatwell Supermarkets, Inc., at the end of the month. Three weeks prior to delivery, Eatwell files for protection under the bankruptcy laws. Neither Eatwell nor Farmer White is required to fulfill their contractual obligations to each other.

4. Anticipatory Breach. Anticipatory breach occurs when one party to the contract, during the time of the condition, states that she has decided not to fulfill her contractual obligations. In other words, one party tells the other that she has no intention of conveying the promised-for consideration. In this situation, the innocent party does not have to perform.

For the contracting party's conduct to be considered anticipatory breach, the words indicating her intentions must be positive, unconditional, and unequivocal. A person cannot merely suggest that her performance will not be forthcoming; she must state that in no uncertain terms. In anticipatory breach, both sides must have executory duties to perform. If the innocent party has already performed, with no other duty to fulfill, there is no "anticipatory" breach; the other side is in total breach.

EXAMPLES:

1. Maura agrees to sell her used Property book to Wallace. Before payment and delivery, Maura tells Wallace that she has changed her mind, and that she is going to keep the book rather than sell it. This is anticipatory breach.

2. Maura agrees to sell her used Property book to Wallace. Wallace pays her and agrees to pick up the book the following week. Before the book is picked up, Maura tells Wallace that she has changed her mind, and that she is going to keep the book. This is not anticipatory breach; it is a breach of contract because Wallace has already performed, and his duties are executed.

In all of the situations discussed above, the injured, innocent party to the contract cannot simply sit back and sue the other person. The law imposes a duty on the injured party to a failed contract to attempt to minimize her injury. This is known as **mitigation of damages.** The injured party must make a reasonable attempt to find a replacement for the failed party's contractual performance. For example, in the situations given above, Jessie would have to find someone else's house to paint on Thursday, Farmer White would have to look for a new sweet potato purchaser, and Wallace would have to seek someone else's used book. In this fashion, the injured party will minimize the damages the injuring party will have to pay.

The injured party only need make "reasonable" attempts to mitigate. Extremely hard or expensive measures are not called for. What is "reasonable" is determined on a case-by-case basis. Also, should the innocent party make a better deal in attempting to mitigate what he originally had, the breaching party is totally excused from the contract.

One word about the antique vase and mitigation of damages. Because an antique vase is a unique piece of property, it is unlikely that the innocent party would be able to mitigate. This does not mean that she is not required to try, but the likelihood of success is reduced in these circumstances.

Performance

The simplest method of being excused from contractual obligations is to perform these obligations. Once performed, the duties are executed, and there is nothing more for the promisor to do. Fortunately, most contractual obligations are fulfilled in this fashion. The overwhelming majority of contractual duties are satisfied by the parties' actual performances.

Must a party perform completely to be excused from his obligations under the contract? The answer is no. Obviously, once a party has fully and completely performed nothing else could reasonably be expected. However, a party may be ready, willing, and able to perform, and the other side refuses the performance. The promisor in this instance is said to have **tendered complete performance,** which is legally sufficient to discharge him from his obligations. Remember the example above when Jessie arrived to paint Fred's house, only to find the entrance barred. In this instance, Jessie tendered complete performance. He arrived, ready, willing, and able to perform. His actual performance was forestalled by Fred's actions, and so Jessie was relieved of further obligations.

What happens if, instead of completely performing or tendering complete performance, a party only partially performs? Will she still be relieved of her contractual obligations? The answer depends on the nature of the promised performance and the extent of the performance actually given. Recall the case of Jimmy the Human Fly. In that instance, the court held that Jimmy climbing almost to the very top of the Washington Monument constituted "substantial" performance, satisfying his contractual obligation. If the performance is substantial, the performing party will be discharged, although she may have to compensate the promisee for the difference between the full performance and the substantial performance given.

EXAMPLE:

Lonnie agrees to sell 25 CDs to Bruce for $100. In fact, Lonnie only delivers 23 CDs. Lonnie did not breach her obligation; her performance is substantial. However, she is not entitled to the full $100. Bruce may deduct the price of two CDs from the total payment to Lonnie.

If, on the other hand, the performance delivered is insubstantial, the promisor is not relieved of his contractual obligation. Insubstantial performance never discharges a promisor's contractual obligation *unless* the promisee accepts that performance. Regardless of the performance actually given, if the promisee accepts the performance in complete satisfaction of the promisor's contractual obligation—be that performance complete, substantial, or insubstantial—that acceptance relieves the promisor of any further contractual responsibility.

As discussed in Chapter 8, part performance for merchant traders is unacceptable. A merchant buyer is entitled to perfect tender, and if the goods delivered do not completely conform to the contract specifications, the merchant buyer may reject the entire shipment or accept only conforming goods. The option is with the buyer. However, the UCC demands that the buyer give the seller the opportunity to remedy the defect within a reasonable time.

EXAMPLE:

Sally is a collector of old books. Bruce agrees to sell to Sally a 1902 edition of the Book of Knowledge, a set containing 20 volumes, for a certain price. On delivery day Bruce conveys only 3 volumes, all he actually has. Sally still thinks the sale is a good buy, and accepts the 3 volumes. Even though the performance is rather insubstantial, Sally's acceptance discharges Bruce from further performance.

Breach of Contract

To **breach** a contract means to break one's obligation made under the agreement. If a party to a contract breaches, the other side, the innocent party, has an immediate cause of action. A breach means the promisor has not lived up to what he has promised, and the injured party may sue to recover what she expected to receive under the contractual agreement.

EXAMPLE:

Harry agrees to buy Minnie's pearl necklace as a gift for his wife. Harry pays Minnie, but Minnie fails to deliver the necklace. Minnie has breached her promise, and Harry can sue her, either to get his money back or to have her convey the necklace.

Not all breaches give rise to an immediate cause of action. A **material breach** of contract always gives rise to an immediate cause of action for breach of the entire contract because it goes to the heart of the contract itself. A **minor breach** of contract, on the other hand, only gives rise to a cause of action for that minor, or insignificant, breach; the contract itself is still in force and effect.

 EXAMPLES:

1. Corrinne agrees to sell Gary her car for $1500. When Gary takes possession, he discovers that the car is totally broken down and does not meet the contract specifications. This is a breach of the entire contract, giving Gary an immediate cause of action for the full purchase price.

2. When Gary takes possession of the car, he discovers that the spark plugs are worn out. Although the contract specified that the car was in perfect working order, this is only a minor breach, because replacing spark plugs is basically insignificant. Gary has a cause of action against Corrinne for the cost of replacing the spark plugs, but the contract is still valid and enforceable.

What factors determine whether a breach is material or minor? There is no set standard, but generally the courts look at the intent of the parties, the words used in the contract, the degree of hardship the breach imposes, and the extent to which the injured party can be compensated. As a general rule, if any portion of a contract is deemed to be of special importance to one of the parties, it should be identified in the contract as a "material" clause. One such example would be a time of the essence clause discussed in Chapter 2.

The distinction between material and minor breaches gives rise to another legal concept, that of the **divisible contract.** As discussed in Chapter 7, one of the contractual rules of construction used by the courts is to attempt to uphold contracts if at all possible. As a consequence of this doctrine, the courts have created the concept of divisible contracts. A divisible contract is one that can be divided into several separate, but equal, portions. The contract can either expressly state that it is divisible (or that it is not divisible, if the parties so wish), or its divisibility can be implied from the contract terms themselves. If the contract is deemed divisible, then a breach would only affect that one small divided contract; the rest of the contract relationships would remain intact. In this method, even if the breach were material, the materiality may only go to one portion of the contract, and the remaining portions would still be in effect.

EXAMPLE:

Mitzi rents an apartment from Louise for a 2-year period, with a monthly rent of $300. Mitzi pays her rent for the first 6 months, but in the seventh month her rent check bounces. Although Mitzi is in breach, the contract can be considered a divisible contract. The lease is for 24 months, with a monthly rent of $300, which could be looked at as 24 separate leases. In this context, Mitzi's breach is only a breach of one of those 24 contracts; all the remaining contracts are still deemed in effect.

The court will find a contract to be divisible only if it can be evenly and easily divided, and the parties themselves have not specified that the contract is nondivisible. Under the UCC, all contracts in which delivery is to be made in installments are deemed divisible unless such assumption would cause an undue hardship on the buyer merchant.

Agreement of the Parties

The parties to a contract are always free to rearrange their contractual agreements by mutual assent. As long as *both* parties agree to a change in the performances, the parties may be discharged from their original obligation without any negative consequences.

This mutual reagreement of the parties can come about in two ways. First, the original contract may contain a provision providing for the dissolution of the agreement. An example would be a lease providing for a tenancy at will where either party is free to terminate the relationship by providing notice to the other party. Or, a contract could contain a time period escape clause, meaning that during a specified period of time the parties could dissolve the contract without damage. An example of this type of arrangement would be a contract for schooling. From registration until the beginning of class, any student can change her mind and get a full tuition refund. Each contract must be individually analyzed to determine whether it contains some provision for the parties' termination of the contract without damage.

The second situation in which the parties can change their mutual obligations comes about not by the original contract, but by the parties forming a new contractual arrangement. There are six types of new agreements that have the effect of discharging the parties from their former contractual obligations.

1. Mutual Rescission. A **mutual rescission** occurs when both parties to the contract agree that they do not want to proceed any further under the agreement. Both sides agree to rescind, or take back, the original obligation. The consideration supporting this agreement is the detriment incurred by each party of not receiving the promised-for consideration of the original contract. For rescission to be applicable the contract must be executory.

EXAMPLE:

Barry and Lynette agree to be partners in a retail store. The partnership is evidenced by a written partnership agreement. Prior to establishing the business they have a falling out and decide to rescind the contract. Because the provisions are executory, this is valid.

2.   Release.   A **release** is a contract in which one side relieves the other of any obligation existing under a previous contract. Many times people hear the term "release" in the context of tort claims, but the concept is contractual as well. Usually, the releasing party receives some consideration for her agreement to release the other side from his original obligation.

EXAMPLE:

Tina has a contract with Melinda in which Melinda has agreed to supply Tina with 20 dresses each week for Tina's clothing store for a 2-year period. After several problems arise, Tina agrees to release Melinda from the contract in consideration of a certain sum of money. The release is very much like a private settlement between parties to a contractual dispute.

3.   Accord and Satisfaction.   An **accord and satisfaction** is a special contractual situation in which the parties to a disputed contract agree to settle their dispute by changing the obligations of the contract itself with the new agreement. Accord and satisfactions are discussed in Chapter 4, Consideration, and can be reviewed in that section.

4.   Substituted Agreement.   A **substituted agreement** is a new contract that incorporates the original contract in the new provisions. Because the original obligations are now absorbed by the new agreement, the original contractual duties are deemed discharged.

EXAMPLE:

Judy is having a yard sale. Rise sees a shawl she likes, and the two women agree on a price. Before paying for the shawl, Rise spots a hat and a serving tray she would like to purchase. After some haggling, Judy agrees on one price for all three items. The original contract for the sale of the shawl is now absorbed into this substituted agreement, which covers three items instead of just one.

 5. **Novation.** As discussed in Chapter 9, Third Party Contracts, a **novation** is a substitution of parties into an existing contractual agreement. When the novation is effectuated, the original party no longer has any rights or obligations under the contract. That person's contractual duties are discharged; they are now the responsibility of the novated party.

 6. **Modification.** As discussed previously, if the contract is for the sale of goods between merchants, the merchants may make good faith modifications to their contractual obligations.

Impossibility of Performance

Under certain circumstances a contracting party's performance may become impossible to fulfill through no fault of his own. The law feels it would be unfair and unjust to hold the person responsible to a contractual obligation that could not possibly be met.

What constitutes **impossibility of performance** depends on the facts and circumstances of each individual case. It also must be ascertained whether the performance is totally incapable of being performed or whether the impossibility is of a temporary nature. If the impossibility is only temporary, the promisor is not discharged from her obligation, but her performance is temporarily suspended until the situation rectifies itself; at that point the promisor must fulfill her original obligation. Take careful note that circumstances that merely make the performances more difficult or expensive than originally believed, but not impossible to perform, do not relieve the promisor of her obligations. This is the risk of contract. However, for contracts covered by the UCC, if performance becomes unduly expensive due to events that could not be foreseen or assumed when the contract was formed, the party *may* be discharged.

 EXAMPLES:

 1. Buycheap Markets has a contract with Australian Produce, Ltd. to purchase various food products from the latter. One contract concerns the purchase of 5000 bushels of Tasmanian oranges that Australian Produce has agreed to ship to the port of San Diego. As the ship pulls into the harbor, the longshoremen go on a national strike, and the oranges cannot be off-loaded anywhere in the United States. The oranges begin to perish. Australian Produce is relieved of its obligation by the impossibility of performance.

 2. In a second contract, Buycheap has agreed to buy tinned lamb from Australian Produce, shipment to be to the port of Los Angeles.

This ship arrives the same day as the one in the previous example, and the goods cannot be off-loaded. Australian Produce is not permanently relieved of its obligation. Because canned goods have an indefinite life, and time is not of the essence, Australian Produce's obligation is merely suspended until the strike is over.

Supervening Illegality

A **supervening illegality** will discharge contractual obligations because, since the inception of the contractual arrangement, the purpose for which the contract was created has become illegal. The law will not permit persons to engage in illegal activities, and therefore the parties are deemed discharged from their contractual duties.

 EXAMPLE:

Jan and Dean enter into a contract to open and manage a gambling casino in Atlantic City, New Jersey. Six months after the casino opens, the town officials of Atlantic City rescind the ordinance permitting gambling in the town. Jan and Dean are now discharged from their contractual promises by a supervening illegality. The law will not allow them to break the law just to fulfill a contract.

Death of the Parties or Destruction of the Subject Matter

If the subject matter of the contract is destroyed, obviously the contract cannot be fulfilled. This is true provided that the object in question is unique and is not destroyed by an act of one of the parties. If the object is capable of near exact replacement, the promisor is expected to find a substitute product and fulfill his obligation. The fact that it might be more expensive for him is of no concern to the law. That is a risk of contract.

Death is self-evident; a person cannot be expected to perform from the grave. Note that a person's estate may be liable for contracts entered into by the deceased prior to death. If the decedent merely had to convey property she had sold or pay for property she had purchased, the estate is capable and expected to fulfill these obligations.

 EXAMPLES:

1. Ian has agreed to buy Peg's house. Before closing, the house is destroyed by fire. Ian is discharged from his obligation by the destruction of the subject matter of the contract.

2. Willie has agreed to let his prize race horse stud with Liz's fillie for a fee. Before consummation of the contract, Willie's horse dies. Willie and Liz are relieved of their contractual obligations.

Frustration of Purpose

Probably the least common method of discharge, but the most interesting, is **frustration of purpose.** Frustration of purpose occurs when the contract, on its face, is both valid and apparently capable of performance, but the underlying reason for the agreement no longer exists. This reason is not specified in the contract itself but is discernible by the circumstances surrounding the contract's creation.

 EXAMPLE:

The most famous of the cases regarding frustration of purpose are known as the Coronation Cases, dealing with the coronation of Edward VII of England. At the turn of the century, after Queen Victoria's death, her son and heir, Edward, was to be crowned king after a 60-year wait. The procession route was announced months in advance, and people with homes and offices overlooking the route found themselves in possession of desirable real estate. One-day leases were entered into for the day of the coronation, so that the "tenants" could have a view of the parade. Two days before the ceremony Edward developed appendicitis, and the coronation was postponed for several months. The one-day landlords brought the tenants into court for rent when the tenants refused to pay. The court held that, while the contracts, on their faces, were valid and enforceable, the purpose of the contracts — to view the coronation procession — no longer existed. Consequently, the tenants were discharged from their rental obligations because of frustration of purpose.

SAMPLE CLAUSES

1

If, during the term of the lease, the described premises shall be destroyed by fire, the elements, or any other cause, or if they be so injured that they cannot be repaired with reasonable diligence within six (6) months, then this lease shall cease and become null and void from the date of such damage or destruction, and the lessee shall immediately surrender the premises to the lessor and shall pay rent only to the time of such surrender.

Here, the parties to the contract indicate a discharge caused by the loss or destruction of the subject matter. By having this clause in the original instrument specifying the grounds for discharge, the parties have hopefully avoided a lawsuit to have their obligations excused.

2

In the event bankruptcy or state proceedings should be filed against the lessee, his heirs or assigns, in any federal or state court, it shall give the right to said lessee, his heirs or assigns, immediately to declare this contract null and void.

This provision, as the preceding one, would appear in the original contract and specifies insolvency as a ground for discharging the contractual obligation.

3

If Subscriber within five (5) days after the execution of the Agreement notifies Seller in writing that Subscriber wishes to withdraw from the Agreement, the amount theretofore paid by him under the Agreement will be returned to him and thereafter all rights and liabilities of Subscriber hereunder shall cease and terminate.

This clause in the original sales contract provides a conditional time period during which the subscriber can withdraw from the contract without any negative effect. In this manner, the parties have agreed to a method of discharge in the original agreement.

4

If any obstacle or difficulty shall arise in respect to the title, the completion of the purchase, or otherwise, the vendor shall be at full liberty, at any time, to abandon this contract on returning the deposit money to the purchaser.

In this instance the parties in a contract for the sale of real estate have specified an excuse of conditions in the original contract. Of course, the specific obstacle or difficulty has not been definitely defined or described, which could create questions of interpretation later on. In drafting contracts, it is always a matter of judgment with respect to specificity.

The more precise the clauses, the less leeway later on; the less precise the clauses, the more potential for a lawsuit.

CHAPTER SUMMARY

A party to a contract does not necessarily have to perform what he has promised under the agreement itself. There are several situations and circumstances that act to discharge a promisor from his duties without any negative consequences to the party himself. Generally, there are eight situations that have the effect of discharging the promisor's obligations. They are:

1. having the performance excused by a contractual condition not being met;
2. performing, either fully or partially, and having that performance accepted by the promisee;
3. by the other side's breach of contract;
4. by having the parties mutually agree to a new or different performance;
5. by impossibility of performance;
6. by having the law change so as to make the contract illegal;
7. by the death or destruction of the subject matter or parties; or
8. by frustration of purpose.

When any of these preceding situations occur, the promisor is excused from any further obligation under the contract.

SYNOPSIS

Methods of discharging excusing performance
1. Excuse of conditions
   a. Condition fails to create or extinguishes duties
   b. Other side prevents performance during time of condition
      i. Prevention
      ii. Voluntary disablement
      iii. Insolvency
      iv. Anticipatory breach
2. Performance
   a. Full
   b. Tendered full performance
   c. Substantial v. insubstantial
3. Breach
   a. Material or minor

    b. Divisible contracts
  4. Agreement
      a. In original contract
      b. New agreement
          i.   Mutual rescission
          ii. Release
          iii. Accord and satisfaction
          iv. Substituted agreement
          v.   Novation
  5. Impossibility of performance
      a. Permanent
      b. Temporary
  6. Supervening illegality
  7. Death or destruction
  8. Frustration of purpose: Coronation cases

Key Terms

Accord and satisfaction: new contract based on parties' agreement to settle
    dispute existing under a contract
Anticipatory breach: positive, unconditional, and unequivocal words that a
    party intends to breach his contractual obligations
Breach: breaking one's contractual promise
Conditions: a fact or event, the happening or nonhappening of which creates
    or extinguishes an absolute duty to perform
Divisible contract: contract capable of being broken down into several equal
    agreements
Frustration of purpose: purpose for which the contract was formed no
    longer exists
Impossibility of performance: promisor's performance is incapable of being
    fulfilled due to outside forces
Material breach: breach of contract that goes to the heart of the agreement
Minor breach: breach of contract that goes to an insignificant aspect of the
    contract
Mitigation of damages: duty imposed on injured party to lessen, by reason-
    able means, the breaching party's liability
Mutual rescission: agreement by both contracting parties to do away with
    the contract
Novation: substitution of contracting parties
Release: contract relieving promisor from an obligation under an existing
    contract
Substituted agreement: a new contract that incorporates the original con-
    tract in the new provisions.
Supervening illegality: change in law that makes the performance of the
    contract illegal

Tender complete performance: being ready, willing, and able to perform
Voluntary disablement: volitional act by a promisor that makes her obligation virtually incapable of being performed

EXERCISES

1. Give two examples of impossibility of performance.
2. What factors determine whether a contract is divisible? Draft a divisible contract.
3. What would be the result of an injured party failing to mitigate damages? Why?
4. Give an example of frustration of purpose other than the Coronation Cases?
5. What factors determine whether performance is substantial or insubstantial? Draft a contract clause that would help in this determination.

Cases for Analysis

The following case summaries are included to demonstrate how contracts may or may not be discharged by the contracting parties. In OWBR LLC v. Clear Channel Communications, Inc., the court discusses the events of 9/11 as the basis of a frustration of purpose claim, and in Werner v. Ashcraft Bloomquist, Inc., the court is called upon to determine whether commercial frustration may be the basis for discharging contractual obligations.

OWBR LLC, d/b/a Outrigger Wailea Resort v. Clear Channel Communications, Inc.
266 F. Supp. 2d 1214 (D. Haw. 2003)

Background

This lawsuit arises from a contract dispute between Plaintiff OWBR, d.b.a. Outrigger Wailea Resort ("Outrigger") and Defendants Clear Channel Communications ("Clear Channel") and SFX Multimedia Group ("SFX"). On November 19, 2000, Plaintiff entered into an agreement with "Urban Network—SFX Multimedia Group" (the "Agreement"). The Agreement, written by Plaintiff and executed by Plaintiff's Director of Sales and Marketing, Gary Collins, and Miller London, the "Executive Vice-President/President" of "Urban Network—SFX Multimedia Group," provided that Plaintiff would host (at the Outrigger Wailea Resort) Power Jam 2002, a music industry event/conference produced by Defendants and scheduled for February 13-17, 2002.

Pursuant to the contract, the Outrigger held 2,270 sleeping room nights for the convention's attendees. (Pl.'s Concise Statement of Facts ("CSF") Supp. Mot. Summ. J., Ex. A, at 1.) These room nights are broken down by six guest room categories, and the Agreement lists the individual room night rates for each room category, ranging from $235 to $900 per night. (Pl.'s CSF Supp. Mot. Summ. J., Ex. A, at 2.) The Agreement also contains a liquidated damages clause governing any cancellation of the Agreement. This provision provides that should cancellation of the event occur zero to thirty days prior to the group's scheduled arrival, liquidated damages in the amount of one-hundred percent of the "Total Guest Room Revenue," plus applicable taxes, would be due. (Pl.'s CSF Supp. Mot. Summ. J., Ex. A at 4.)

In addition, the Agreement contains a Force Majeure clause, which states the following:

> The parties' performance under this Agreement is subject to acts of God, war, government regulation, terrorism, disaster, strikes (except those involving the Hotel's employees or agents), civil disorder, curtailment of transportation facilities, or any other emergency beyond the parties' control, making it inadvisable, illegal, or impossible to perform their obligations under this Agreement. Either party may cancel this Agreement for any one or more of such reasons upon written notice to the other.

(Pl.'s CSF Supp. Mot. Summ. J., Ex. A, at 9.)

On January 16, 2002, less than thirty days prior to the Power Jam 2002 event, Miller London sent a letter to Mr. Cordeiro cancelling the event. The letter, in pertinent part, states:

> The Urban Network will not be able to move forward with its conference scheduled for February 2002. The events of September 11th coupled with the fragile condition of the U.S. and international consumer economies have resulted in the withdrawal of commitments to this event from many of our sponsors and participants.

(Pl.'s CSF Supp. Mot. Summ. J., Ex. C, at 4.) The letter was signed by Miller London, whose title was listed as:

> Executive Vice President, Urban Entertainment Clear Channel Entertainment, Multimedia The Urban Network

(Id.) Defendants assert that the statements in the letter are based on the fact that by December 2001, of the five hundred rooms SFX reserved for Power Jam 2002, only 150 had been booked and only three were secured by a credit card. (Def. SFX's CSF Supp. Mot. Summ. J. P 15.) Additionally, only thirty-eight companies were planning to attend, as opposed to the 102 companies that had participated in the same event the previous year. (Id.)

Following the letter, on March 4, 2002, Plaintiff filed this breach of contract action against Clear Channel Communications, Inc. and SFX Multimedia Group, LLC seeking, inter alia, $625,912.65 in liquidated damages.

Plaintiff claims that the amount was derived from the amount of Total Guest Room Revenue to be produced under the terms of the contract, plus applicable state and local taxes, minus a previous $10,000 deposit.

Plaintiff and Defendant SFX and Defendant Clear Channel filed separate Motions for Summary Judgment on November 13, 2002. In Plaintiff's Motion for Summary Judgment, Plaintiff seeks summary judgment on three main issues. First, Plaintiff argues that the Agreement was entered into by a division of Clear Channel Communications, Inc. doing business as "Urban Network — SFX Multimedia Group," and thus Clear Channel Communications is liable under the Agreement. Second, Plaintiff argues that Defendants' performance under the Agreement was not excused by the Agreement's Force Majeure provision in that holding the February 2002 Power Jam event was not "inadvisable." Third, Plaintiff argues that the Agreement's liquidated damages clause is enforceable and thus they should be awarded the damages dictated under this clause.

Defendants, on January 3, 2003, filed a joint Opposition to Plaintiff's Motion for Summary Judgment. In the Opposition, Defendants argue that the Agreement was solely between Plaintiff and SFX, not Clear Channel, as SFX is a subsidiary, not a division, of Clear Channel. Accordingly, they argue, because SFX did not have either actual or apparent authority to act on its behalf, Clear Channel is not liable under the Agreement. Defendants also respond to Plaintiff's motion by arguing that SFX's performance under the agreement was rendered "inadvisable" because of the events of September 11, other acts of terrorism, and their after effects. Furthermore, Defendants contend that the liquidated damages provision in the Agreement is an unenforceable penalty provision and thus Plaintiff is not entitled to damages even if Defendants are found to have breached the Agreement. Plaintiff's Reply to Defendant's Opposition was filed on January 13, 2003.

In Defendants Motions for Summary Judgment, the issues are essentially the same as those addressed in the Plaintiff's Motion for Summary Judgment and the Oppositions thereto. Defendant Clear Channel's Motion for Summary Judgment deals solely with the issue of whether it was a party to the Agreement. Plaintiff's Opposition to this Motion was filed on December 31, 2002, and Clear Channel's Reply was filed on January 10, 2003. SFX's Motion for Summary Judgment argues that SFX's performance under the Agreement was "inadvisable" under the Force Majeure clause and that the liquidated damages clause is an unenforceable penalty provision, and thus Plaintiff is not entitled to any damages if SFX is found to have breached the Agreement. Plaintiff's Opposition to this Motion was filed on December 31, 2002, and SFX's Reply was filed on January 10, 2003. In addition, Defendant Clear Channel, on November 13, 2002, filed a Substantive Joinder in SFX's Motion for Summary Judgment.

Following the filings of the Motions for Summary Judgment, Plaintiff, on December 24, 2002, filed a Motion to Strike SFX's Summary Judgment Evidence. Specifically, Plaintiff seeks to strike portions of the reports of two of SFX's experts, Dr. Lawrence Boyd and Douglas Wheeler, as well as portions of the declarations of Miller London and Carole Carper, as inadmissible opinion evidence and hearsay. Defendant SFX filed its Opposition on January 3, 2003, and Plaintiff filed its Reply on January 13, 2003.

A hearing on these matters was held on January 22, 2003.

Standard of Review [Omitted]

Discussion

I.   Plaintiff's Motion for Summary Judgment

A.   Clear Channel's Liability Under the Agreement [Omitted]
Force Majeure Clause
Defendants in this matter argue that SFX's performance under the Agreement was excused by the Force Majeure provision, which states, in pertinent part:

> The parties' performance under this Agreement is subject to acts of God, war, government regulation, terrorism, disaster, strikes (except those involving the Hotel's employees or agents), civil disorder, curtailment of transportation facilities, or any other emergency beyond the parties' control, making it inadvisable, illegal, or impossible to perform their obligations under this Agreement.

Defendants claim that the September 11, 2001 terrorist acts "severely disrupted travel, decimated the tourism industry, and created a pervasive sense of fear that gripped the country." Based on this effect around the country, Defendants argue, performance under the Agreement — holding the Power Jam 2002 event — was "inadvisable" as referenced in the Force Majeure clause.

Plaintiff counters that the events of September 11, 2001, did not make it "inadvisable" to travel to or to hold events in Hawaii five months after the terrorist attacks. Plaintiff argues that the actual reason that Defendant SFX cancelled the event was because of the economic downturn, which although due in part to September 11, is too attenuated from the events of September 11 to excuse performance under the Agreement's Force Majeure clause.

Under Hawaii law, contract interpretation is a matter of law. Reed & Martin v. City and County of Honolulu, 50 Haw. 347, 440 P.2d 526, 527 (Haw. 1968). It is well settled that contractual terms should be interpreted according to their plain, ordinary meaning and accepted use in common speech, unless the contract indicates a different meaning. State Farm Fire and Cas. Co. v. Pacific Rent-All, Inc., 90 Haw. 315, 978 P.2d 753, 762 (Haw. 1999). In interpreting undefined or disputed contract language, courts should apply an objective standard, which insures predictability in contracting. See N.A.P.P. Realty Trust v. CC Enters., 147 N.H. 137, 784 A.2d 1166, 1169 (N.H. 2001) (reasoning that applying a subjective standard of contract interpretation would accomplish nothing more than the restatement of the parties' conflicting positions); see also Dan Nelson Constr. v. Nodland and Dickson, 2000 ND 61, 608 N.W.2d 267, 275 (N.D. 2000) ("Courts construing changed conditions clauses apply an objective, reasonable person standard, in which a court places itself into the shoes of a 'reasonable and prudent' contractor [to] decide how such a contractor would act in appellant's situation.").

According to Defendants, essential in determining whether Defendant SFX can rely on the Force Majeure clause to excuse its performance is the issue of whether holding the Power Jam 2002 event in February 2002 was "inadvisable" as used in the Agreement's Force Majeure clause. Although there are no common law definitions of "inadvisable" in the context of force majeure clauses, the parties agree that the plain, ordinary meaning of "inadvisable" is: not advisable, inexpedient, or unwise. Webster's Unabridged Dictionary 964 (2001). "Advisable" is defined as "proper to be advised or recommended; desirable or wise, as a course of action." Id. "Unwise" is defined as "not wise; foolish; imprudent; lacking in good sense or judgment." Id.

While the Court agrees that the specific language used in the Force Majeure provision is significant, the term "inadvisable" may not be divorced from the remainder of the clause. Blacks Law Dictionary defines a force majeure clause as a "contractual provision allocating the risk if performance becomes impossible or impracticable as a result of an event or effect that the parties could not have anticipated or controlled." Black's Law Dictionary 657 (7th ed. 1999). The clause "defines the scope of unforeseeable events that might excuse nonperformance by a party." Stand Energy Corp. v. Cinergy Servs., Inc., 144 Ohio App. 3d 410, 760 N.E.2d 453, 457 (Ohio Ct. App. 2001). The party who relies on a force majeure clause to excuse performance bears the burden of proving that the event was beyond the party's control and without its fault or negligence. *Stand Energy*, 760 N.E.2d at 457 (*citing* Gulf Oil Corp. v. Fed. Energy Regulatory Comm'n, 706 F.2d 444 (3rd Cir. 1983)).

In the absence of statute or case law on the subject, Hawaii courts often look to the Restatement (Second) of Contracts. See, e.g., Zanakis-Pico v. Cutter Dodge, Inc., 98 Haw. 309, 47 P.3d 1222, 1237 (Haw. 2002), Hough v. Pac. Ins. Co., 83 Haw. 457, 927 P.2d 858, 869 n.15 (Haw. 1996). Although the Restatement of Contracts does not specifically address force majeure clauses, §261 does provide for discharge of contractual duties by reason of supervening impracticability. See B.F. Goodrich Co. v. Vinyltech Corp., 711 F. Supp. 1513, 1519 (D. Ariz. 1989) (looking to the Restatement of Contracts §261 to interpret a force majeure provision, and finding that an unexpected drop in market prices was not in the contemplation of the agreement's force majeure provision). Section 261 states:

> Where, after a contract is made, a party's performance is made impracticable without his fault by the occurrence of an event the non-occurrence of which was a basic assumption on which the contract was made, his duty to render that performance is discharged, unless the language or the circumstances indicate the contrary.

Comment b to §261 states that "mere market shifts or financial inability do not usually effect discharge under the rule stated in this Section."

In defining the impracticability defense, courts have held that a contract becomes impracticable when its performance becomes excessively and unreasonably difficult or expensive. See CIT Group/Equipment Financing, Inc. v. Taylor, 1991 U.S. Dist. LEXIS 18171, at 9 (N.D. Cal.) ("The impracticability defense largely pertains to the performance of a physical act."), Publicker Indus. v. Union Carbide Corp., 1975 U.S. Dist. LEXIS 14305, 17 UCC Rep. Serv. 989 (E.D. Pa. 1975) (finding that a loss of $5.8 million did not render contract impracticable or excuse performance under the force majeure clause) ("Increased cost alone does not excuse performance unless the rise in cost is due to some unforeseen contingency which alters the essential nature of the performance."). In fact, "the unforeseen cost increase that would excuse performance 'must be more than merely onerous or expensive. It must be positively unjust to hold the parties bound.'" La. Power & Light Co. v. Allegheny Ludlum Indus., 517 F. Supp. 1319, 1325 (E.D. La. 1981); see also Iowa Elec. Light & Power Co. v. Atlas Corp., 467 F. Supp. 129 (N.D. Iowa 1978) (holding that an increase in seller's costs by 52.2%, resulting in the seller's loss of approximately $2.67 million, failed to constitute commercial impracticability), rev'd on other grounds, 603 F.2d 1301 (8th Cir. 1979).

Similarly, courts interpreting force majeure provisions have held that nonperformance dictated by economic hardship is not enough to fall within a force majeure provision. See, e.g., Stand Energy, 760 N.E.2d at 458 (finding that unseasonably hot temperatures resulting in record demand for power and unprecedented high hourly prices for electric power did not excuse, under the force majeure clause, defendant's inability to deliver the power required under the contract). "Mere increase in expense does not excuse performance [under a force majeure provision] unless there exists extreme and unreasonable difficulty, expense, [or] injury." Butler v. Nepple, 54 Cal. 2d 589, 354 P.2d 239, 244-45, 6 Cal. Rptr. 767 (Cal. 1960) (emphasis added) (holding that the fact that compliance with the contract would involve greater expense than anticipated, due to a steel strike, did not excuse performance).

Defendants, in their Opposition, focus on how September 11 economically impacted Power Jam 2002. They contend that by December 2001, of the five hundred rooms reserved for Power Jam 2002, only 150 had been booked and only three were secured by credit cards. (Declaration of Carole I. Carper, filed November 19, 2002, P 19.) In addition, they assert that only thirty-eight companies were planning to attend the event as compared to the 102 companies that participated in Power Jam the year before. (Id.) Based on these figures, Defendants argue that "good business sense and judgment pointed squarely to cancelling the event where SFX could have had to pay out-of-pocket the full non-discounted rates for, at least, 350 rooms." (Defs.' Opp., at 17.) Therefore, they contend, "it was undoubtedly inadvisable for SFX to proceed with Power Jam 2002." (Id.) To bolster their claim, Defendants cite claims from their economic experts that performing under the Agreement was "inadvisable." (See Expert Reports of Lawrence W. Boyd, Ph.D., and Douglas H. Wheeler, SFX's Mem. Supp. Mot. Summ. J., Exs. K, L.)

From an economic standpoint, it was certainly unwise, or *economically* inadvisable, for Defendants to continue with the Power Jam 2002 event. Nonetheless, a force majeure clause does not excuse performance for economic inadvisability, even when the economic conditions are the product of a force majeure event. See *Butler*, 54 Cal. 2d 589, 354 P.2d 239, 6 Cal. Rptr. 767; see also *Stand Energy*, 760 N.E.2d at 458. The Force Majeure clause does not contain language that excuses performance on the basis of poor economic conditions, lower than expected attendance, or withdrawal of commitments from sponsors and participants.

In addition, the Court notes the significance of Defendant waiting to cancel the Power Jam 2002 event until less than one month before the event was scheduled, and a full four months after September 11. Had cancelling the event been about the security or safety of holding the event due to terrorism and not the economics of doing so, it is likely that Defendant SFX would not have waited until January to do so.

Moreover, SFX contends that as late as December 2001 it agreed, at Plaintiff's request, to release one hundred rooms per night for Power Jam 2002 — evidencing the feeling that no force majeure event had occurred as of that date and that there was no need to seek release of the remaining rooms. See 7200 Scottsdale Road Gen. Partners v. Kuhn Farm Machinery, Inc., 184 Ariz. 341, 909 P.2d 408, 417 (Ariz. Ct. App. 1995) ("In late January, after the United States attacked Iraq and when the threat of terrorism was at its highest level, Kuhn implicitly confirmed the convention date by reducing the reserved room block from 190 to 140.").

Even if economics were not a significant factor in SFX cancelling the Agreement, the Court would still find that SFX could not properly invoke the Force Majeure clause based on the events of September 11. To excuse a party's performance under a force majeure clause ad infinitum when an act of terrorism affects the American populace would render contracts meaningless in the present age, where terrorism could conceivably threaten our nation for the foreseeable future. Certainly had the Power Jam 2002 event been scheduled for the weeks immediately following September 11, Defendants' argument that holding the convention was "inadvisable" would be much stronger. However, five months following September 11, when there was no specific terrorist threat to air travel to Maui or to Maui itself, Defendants can not escape performance under the Agreement.

The Court recognizes that September 11 was an extreme, unforeseeable occurrence which is of the magnitude to trigger a force majeure clause. Nonetheless, this does not absolve Defendants of the burden of proving that September 11 did in fact render performance under the agreement "inadvisable." The Court finds that, when looked at in the context of the Force Majeure clause, the events of September 11 did not render performance under the agreement in February of the following year objectively inadvisable. Defendants argue that holding the Power Jam 2002 event was "inadvisable" due to people's fear and uncertainty (Defs.' Opp., at 20), however, fear and uncertainty should not be enough to excuse performance under the Agreement. If such were the case, contracting would no longer provide any stability and predictability to commercial transactions.

Defendant's experts cite extensive evidence that the travel and tourism industries in Hawaii and elsewhere around the country were severely affected in the aftermath of September 11. (See Expert Reports of Lawrence W. Boyd, Ph.D., and Douglas H. Wheeler, SFX's Mem. Supp. Mot. Summ. J., Exs K, L.) Plaintiff does not argue this point, however, the effect on these industries does not prove that it was objectively "inadvisable" to travel. It merely demonstrates Americans' subjective feelings about post-September 11 travel, not whether there were objective threats to travel to Maui in February 2002 sufficient to make performance under the Agreement "inadvisable." In fact, according to the Air Transport Association, United States' airlines alone still carried 38.2 million passengers in October 2001 and 38.7 million passengers in November 2001. (Pl.'s CSF Supp. Mot. Summ. J., Ex. M, at 16.) Furthermore, Defendants have not presented evidence that the island of Maui faced any specific terrorist threat.

Based on the case law involving force majeure clauses and impracticability, Defendants have not presented sufficient evidence that terrorism presented travelers in February 2002 with circumstances so "extreme and unreasonable" as to excuse performance under the Agreement. See *Butler*, 354 P.2d at 244-45. Looking at the Force Majeure clause as a whole, and not merely consisting of the term "inadvisable," the Court finds that Defendant SFX Multimedia Group, LLC's performance under the Agreement was not excused by the Force Majeure provision.

Accordingly, the Court GRANTS Plaintiff's Motion for Summary Judgment with respect to this issue.

C.   Liquidated Damages Provision [Omitted]

II.   Defendant Clear Channel's Motion for Summary Judgment [Omitted]

III.   SFX Multimedia Group, LLC's Motion for Summary Judgment

A.   Force Majeure Clause

As the Court has granted Summary Judgment for Plaintiff on the issue of whether the Force Majeure clause excuses Defendant SFX's performance under the Agreement, the Court DENIES Defendant SFX Multimedia Group, LLC's Motion for Summary Judgment on the same issue.

IV.   Plaintiff's Motion to Strike Portions of Defendant SFX Multimedia Group, LLC's Summary Judgment Evidence ...

A.   Expert Report of Lawrence W. Boyd

Plaintiff seeks to exclude eight statements in Dr. Boyd's expert report that pertain to his opinions on how travel to Hawaii was affected in the months following September 11, 2001 as well as his opinions on whether holding the Power Jam 2002 event was "inadvisable" based on the economic after-effects of September 11. Plaintiff argues that such statements are inadmissible in that they lack foundation and are conclusory and speculative.

Federal Rule of Evidence 702 states that a witness qualified as an expert may testify "in the form of an opinion or otherwise, if (1) the testimony is based upon sufficient facts or data, (2) the testimony is the product of reliable principles and methods, and (3) the witness has applied the principles and methods reliably to the facts of the case." Unlike lay witnesses, expert witnesses do not need to have personal knowledge of the underlying facts. See Fed. R. Evid. 703. They may testify to opinions based on the facts perceived by or made known to the expert at or before the hearing. Id.; see Daubert v. Merrell Dow Pharmaceuticals, Inc., 509 U.S. 579, 592, 125 L. Ed. 2d 469, 113 S. Ct. 2786.

Dr. Boyd's statements are admissible in that they are not merely based on his "economic model" as Plaintiff contends. His opinion is based on numerous news reports, various Hawaii visitor, hotel occupancy, and convention data from the State of Hawaii Department of Business and Economic Development and the Center for Labor Education and Research, the Declaration of Miller London, and the Declaration of Carole Carper. Based on the information provided, Dr. Boyd's opinions that Plaintiff seeks to strike do have an adequate foundation and are thus appropriate summary judgment evidence. See Fed. R. Evid. 702, 703. Moreover, Dr. Boyd's experience and education in the fields of economics and economic behavior provide him with a sufficient background to form his expert opinions. See Fed. R. Evid. 702, 703.

B. Expert Report of Douglas H. Wheeler

Plaintiff also seeks to strike six statements from the expert report of Mr. Wheeler. These statements pertain to the effects of September 11 on the travel and tourism industry, the effects of September 11 on his clients, and his opinions as to whether it was reasonable and advisable for SFX to cancel the Power Jam 2002 event. Plaintiff objects to the statements on the grounds that they are speculative and lack foundation. For the reasons stated above with regard to Dr. Boyd's statements, Mr. Wheeler's testimony is admissible expert testimony. Based on his knowledge and experience, as well as the information he considered, Mr. Wheeler's statements are not inadmissible speculative statements. Furthermore, Plaintiff's assertion that the statements lack foundation as the record contains no specific facts concerning the circumstances surrounding the cancellation of Mr. Wheeler's client's events is without merit.

C. Declaration of Carole Carper [Omitted]

Conclusion

The Court GRANTS in part and DENIES in part Plaintiff's Motion for Summary Judgment. . . .

The Court also finds that in looking at the Force Majeure provision as a whole, and interpreting "inadvisable" by an objective standard in the context of the provision, that SFX Multimedia Group's performance under the Agreement was not excused by the Force Majeure clause. Thus the Court grants Plaintiff's Motion for Summary Judgment with respect to the issue of the Force Majeure clause. . . .

Questions

1.   How does the "force majeure" provision relate to the concept of frustration of purpose?

2.   What does the court say about the impracticability defense?

3.   What is the purpose of the expert's testimony in relation to the concept of frustration of purpose?

Werner v. Ashcraft Bloomquist, Inc.
10 S.W.3d 575 (Mo. App. 2000)

ABI entered into a contract with the owner of Fenton Plaza, Diversified Developers Realty Corp. (hereinafter Diversified), whereby it agreed to be the general contractor on a remodeling project for the shopping center. ABI entered into a subcontract with Werner to "remove and reinstall all store front signage with union labor" for a total price of $26,700.00. The contract was for labor only; no materials were included. Pursuant to the contract, Werner removed the signs and was paid $13,260.00 for that work.

Thereafter, Diversified determined that it wanted new signs and in accordance with its contract with ABI entered a change order to delete the reinstallation of the signs from its contract with ABI. ABI informed Werner that it was discontinuing its contract with him. Werner brought this action for, inter alia, breach of contract. The trial court found that ABI had breached the contract and awarded damages to Werner in the amount of $13,400.00.

Our standard of review in a court-tried case is enunciated in Murphy v. Carron, 536 S.W.2d 30, 32 (Mo. banc 1976).

In its first point on appeal, ABI challenges the trial court's finding that it breached its contract with Werner for the reason that the doctrines of impossibility of performance and/or commercial frustration excused its performance. ABI argues that because "Diversified exercised its right to enter a change order and removed all remaining signage work from ABI's contract," it "no longer had the right or ability to allow Werner to perform that work" under the contract at issue.

The doctrine of impossibility of performance excuses a party to a contract from performance when an Act of God, the law, or the other party renders performance impossible. Grannemann v. Columbia Ins. Group, 391 S.W.2d 502, 506 (Mo. App. W.D. 1996). If a party desires to be excused from performance in the event of contingencies arising after the formation of a contract, it is that party's duty to provide therefore in the contract. Stein v. Bruce, 366 S.W.2d 732, 734 (Mo. App. 1963).

The change order by Diversified is not the type of unexpected event warranting consideration of the application of the impossibility of performance doctrine. See, e.g., West Los Angeles Institute for Cancer Research v. Mayer, 366 F.2d 220 (9th Cir. 1966) (change in the law in the form of a revenue ruling); Lake Development Enterprises, Inc. v. Kojetinsky, 410 S.W.2d 361 (Mo. App. 1966) (Act of God in the form of freezing temperatures); Stein v. Bruce, 366 S.W.2d at 732 (death of a party). Furthermore, ABI made no provision for the termination of its obligation under its contract with Werner in the event Diversified entered a change order regarding the removal or reinstallation of the signs. See, e.g., Sanfillippo v. Oehler, 869 S.W.2d 159 (Mo. App. E.D. 1993) (because the non-competition agreement did not provide for termination of his obligation the death of the dentist from whom he purchased the assets of a dental practice, dentist-purchaser was not excused from paying under the non-compete agreement).

In addition, the ultimate question is whether or not the nature of the contract and the surrounding circumstances show that the risk of the subsequent events, whether or not foreseen, was assumed by the promisor. *West Los Angeles Institute for Cancer Research*, 366 F.2d at 225. In the case before us, it appears from the nature of ABI's contract with Werner and from the surrounding circumstances that ABI assumed the risk of a change order by Diversified after it contracted with Werner. As between ABI and Werner, ABI was in the better position to anticipate the frustrating event of a change order. ABI's failure to make provision for that contingency in its contract with Werner indicated its assumption of the risk that a change order might occur which could impair its contract with Werner.

ABI alternatively argues commercial frustration as a basis for discharging its performance under its contract with Werner. Under the doctrine of commercial frustration, if the happening of an event not foreseen by the parties and not caused by or under the control of either party has destroyed or nearly destroyed either the value of the performance or the object or purpose of the contract, then the parties are excused from further performance. Howard v. Nicholson, 556 S.W.2d 477, 482 (Mo. App. 1977). The doctrine of commercial frustration is close to but distinct from the doctrine of impossibility of performance. Id. Both concern the effect of supervening circumstances upon the rights and duties of the parties; but in cases of commercial frustration, performance remains possible but the expected value of performance in the party seeking to be excused has been destroyed by the fortuitous event which supervenes to cause an actual but not literal failure of consideration. Id.

If the event was reasonably foreseeable, however, the parties should have provided for its occurrence in the contract and the absence of such provision indicates an assumption of risk by the promisor. Id. Courts consider the relation of the parties, the terms of the contract, and the circumstances surrounding the formation of the contract in determining whether the supervening event was reasonably foreseeable. Id.

The doctrine of commercial frustration is not applicable in this case. It was foreseeable to ABI at the time ABI entered into its contract with Werner that Diversified might enter a change order to the original contract with

ABI that could impair performance under ABI's contract with Werner. In Conlon Group, Inc. v. City of St. Louis, 980 S.W.2d 37, 40-41 (Mo. App. E.D. 1998), *cert. denied*, 526 U.S. 1127, 143 L. Ed. 2d 814, 119 S. Ct. 1786 (1999), this court declined to find commercial frustration where the structural problems in a 100-year-old building were foreseeable. This court concluded that the purpose of the agreement with the city's redevelopment authority remained intact, despite the increased costs of redevelopment project. Id. In Shop 'N Save Warehouse Foods, Inc. v. Soffer, 918 S.W.2d 851, 863 (Mo. App. E.D. 1996), this court concluded that an instruction on commercial frustration was not warranted in a breach of contract action. This court reasoned that it was foreseeable to the lessor that a supermarket chain to which he leased property might bring an action to enforce the one-mile radius restriction in a lease with him and thus bar his leasing property located across the street from the supermarket chain to another grocery store. Id. Here, although the possibility of a change order in its contract with Diversified was foreseeable to ABI, ABI failed to provide for that contingency in its contract with Werner. Thus, the doctrine of commercial frustration does not excuse ABI's performance under its contract with Werner.

The doctrines of commercial frustration and of impossibility of performance are limited in applications so as to preserve the certainty of contracts. *Howard*, 556 S.W.2d at 483. ABI cannot in hindsight excuse its performance under its contract with Werner based on either doctrine. ABI's first point is denied.

In its second point, ABI asserts the trial court erred in enforcing the contract because the acts of a third party, i.e. Diversified, frustrated and prevented the performance of ABI's contractual obligations to Werner.

On the one hand, if the fulfillment of the contract depends on the act or consent of a third party, the contract is unenforceable until the third party so acts or consents. Cosky v. Vandalia Bus Lines, Inc., 970 S.W.2d 861, 866 (Mo. App. S.D. 1998). On the other hand, if a party to a contract unconditionally undertakes to perform an act that is not impossible, but merely requires a third party to acquiesce or perform a preceding act, the party's performance is not deemed to be conditioned on the third party's acquiescence or performance. Id. In the latter situation, the inability to secure the necessary permission or acts of the third party does not excuse performance of the contract. Id.

Here, ABI contracted with Werner to remove and reinstall the signs in the shopping center. There was no indication, either in its contract with Werner or by the parties' actions, that ABI's performance was conditioned on Diversified's acquiescence or performance. Thus, Diversified's acts did not excuse ABI's performance. ABI's second point is denied. The judgment of the trial court is affirmed.

Questions

1. What is the relationship between the doctrines of impossibility of performance and commercial frustration?

2. How does the court's interpretation of assumption of the risk affect its ultimate conclusion?

3. What role did Diversified play in bringing about this court action?

Suggested Case References

1. In a contract the parties have agreed to settle disputes by arbitration. A conflict arises regarding price, but the parties failed to set the arbitration process in motion. Is the action of not establishing the arbitration called for in the contract an example of mutual rescission by act of the parties? Read what the Louisiana court said in Shell Oil Co. v. Texas Gas Transmission Corp., 210 So. 2d 554 (La. App. 1968).

2. Does a new agreement between the parties that covers the matters in a disputed contract absorb the original contract into the new agreement? Is this new agreement a separate contract or an accord and satisfaction? Read what the North Dakota court held in First National Bank, Bismarck v. O'Callaghan, 143 N.W.2d 104 (N.D. 1966).

3. If a party to a contract refuses to complete performance without additional consideration and continues to delay performance for a month, does that conduct constitute anticipatory breach? Amberg Granite Co. v. Marinette County, 247 Wis. 36 (1945).

4. May a written contract be verbally rescinded without any additional consideration? Read the decision in Cowin v. Salmon, 244 Ala. 285, 13 So. 2d 190 (1943).

5. Does the fact that the contract has become overly expensive to complete discharge a party's obligations? Read Dunaj v. Glassmayer, 61 Ohio Misc. 2d 493, 580 N.E.2d 98 (1990).

11 Remedies

Learning Objectives

After studying this chapter you will be able to:

- Distinguish between legal and equitable remedies
- Define compensatory damages
- Discuss when punitive damages may be sought
- Explain what is meant by consequential damages
- Distinguish between liquidated damages and limitation of damages
- Define "injunction"
- Understand when specific performance may be sought as a remedy
- Explain the effect of rescission and restitution on a contract
- List the quasi-contractual remedies
- Discuss the effect of waivers on a breach of contract

CHAPTER OVERVIEW

The time has finally come to answer the question everyone usually wants to start with: "What can I get?" The contract itself is complete, it has met every requirement of the law, all of the parties with vested interests in the agreement have been properly identified, and all conditions have been met. At this point, the promiser does not perform. The promisee is now injured; he has not received his promised-for

consideration. What remedies are available to the injured party in a contractual relationship?

Historically, the judicial system was divided into **law** and **equity.**
Law and the law courts were based on statutes and judicial precedents,
and their purpose was to see that all citizens were treated equally and
fairly. Equity and the equity courts were established from the concept of
the sovereign's mercy and dealt with situations in which the legal out-
comes might be just but were not merciful. These are situations in which,
under legal principles, one party could "get away with something." To
rectify this potentially unjust situation, equity was established. Equity
prevents unjust enrichment that might result from a pure application of
legal principles. Although today both these systems are merged into
one, the theories proposed by the litigants follow the ancient concepts
and precedents of law and equity, and the remedies are different
depending on which theory, the legal or the equitable argument,
prevails.

With respect to contract law, the concepts of legal and equitable
remedies come into play whenever one party breaches her contractual
obligations. A breach of contract is a broken promise. The promiser has
failed to deliver what she had promised under the contract. When this
occurs, the nonbreaching or innocent party to the contract is permitted
to seek judicial relief to remedy the situation.

The injured party may seek *legal remedies* if her injury can be corrected
simply by money. Legal remedies are known as *damages*, which denotes
monetary relief. The type of damages available depends on the specific
nature of the contract, the breach, and the injury incurred.

Equitable remedies are nonmonetary relief. They are awarded in those
limited situations in which a monetary award would not compensate the
innocent party for the injury occasioned by the breach. Equitable remedies
are less frequently awarded than damages, and the circumstances must
clearly meet all of the requirements of equitable doctrines.

Because the legal and equitable systems are now merged into one
judicial process, an injured party may seek both legal and equitable remedies in the same action, and the court will determine which would be the
most appropriate for the particular injury involved.

Legal Remedies

Legal remedies, or **damages,** are monetary awards granted to an
injured party in a contractual dispute whenever money would be an appropriate method of rectifying the injury. The court awards four types of
damages:

1. compensatory damages;
2. punitive damages;

3. consequential damages; and
4. liquidated damages.

Compensatory Damages

Compensatory damages are monetary awards designed to put the injured party in the same position he would have been in had the contract been completed as originally planned. The court determines the amount of the monetary loss the injured party suffered because of the breach.

The formula the courts use to determine the exact amount of compensatory damages was outlined in a judicial case decided many decades ago. The events of the case occurred in a rural community. A farmer's son was injured in a fire, and the palm of his hand was severely burned. In a nearby community, a doctor had been experimenting with skin grafts on farm animals, and when he heard about the farm boy, he offered to try a skin graft on the child for a specified sum of money. The doctor promised that the boy would have a "perfectly good hand."

The farmer agreed, and the operation took place. The doctor grafted skin from the boy's thigh onto the hand. After surgery, the hand healed, and the farmer was delighted. Unfortunately, a few years later the boy entered puberty, and hair started growing on the palm of his hand. The skin the doctor used for the graft was from a hair-producing part of the body. The farmer sued for breach of contract.

In determining that the boy was entitled to compensatory damages, the court arrived at the following formula for making the dollar determination: Take the value of what the injured party started with, add to it the value of what he was promised, and then subtract or add what he was left with to determine whether there was an injury, and the amount of the damage. Compensatory damages are used to put the party in the position he would have been in if the contract had not been breached. If he ends up with more than he was promised, there are no damages. In the case of the farm boy, he started with a burned hand, was promised a perfectly good hand, and was left with a hand with a hairy palm. The amount of his damage is the difference between a "perfectly good hand" and a hand with a hairy palm.

EXAMPLES:

1. Alice purchases a pearl ring from Jean for $200. After the sale is complete, Alice discovers that the ring is phony and is only worth $2. The amount of Alice's compensatory damage would be $198, the difference between what she was promised (a genuine pearl ring worth $200) and what she actually received (a phony pearl ring worth $2).

2. Eatwell contracts to buy 100 bushels of Grade A plums from Farmer Grey at $10 per bushel. Farmer Grey delivers plums that are Grade B, worth $8 per bushel. Eatwell's compensatory damages are $2 per bushel, the difference between what it was promised and what it received.

To determine the amount of the compensatory damages, the courts have established certain guidelines depending on the type of contract in question. For instance, if the contract is for the sale of goods, compensatory damages are generally the difference between the market price and the contract price. If the buyer is the innocent party, she can recover the difference between the contract price and what she paid for substituted goods in mitigation. If the seller is the injured party, she can resell the goods and recover the difference from the buyer, or, if the goods cannot be resold, she is entitled to the full contract price.

For employment contracts, if the employer breaches, the employee gets the contract price; if the employee breaches, the employer can recover the cost of replacing the worker. Generally, in computing compensatory damages the court simply uses common sense under the given circumstance.

Compensatory damages are the most common remedy for breach of contract.

Punitive Damages

Punitive, or **exemplary, damages** are monetary awards granted by a court for a breach of contract that involves very unusual circumstances. Exemplary damages are intended not only to compensate the injured party but to punish the breaching party. Punishment is not a usual aspect of contract law. As a consequence, for a party to be entitled to punitive damages, there must be some statutory basis for the award under the state's law. Generally, punitive damages are only awarded by statute where the breach of contract is accompanied by some other violation of a breach of trust, such as fraud or antitrust. If a party is seeking punitive damages, he must be able to show the existence of a breach of contract as well as a statutory violation. The innocent party is awarded not only compensatory damages, but punitive damages as well.

 EXAMPLE:

Ira is induced to buy a table from Harry for $500. Harry is an antique dealer, and although he claims that it *is* an antique, he knows that the table is not. Because a fraud is involved as well as a breach of contract, Ira may be entitled to punitive as well as compensatory damages if the state statute permits.

Consequential Damages

Consequential damages are monetary awards beyond the standard measure (compensatory damages) due to the special circumstances and expenses incurred because of the injury. For the innocent party to be entitled to consequential damages, when entering into the contractual relationship, she must make the other party aware of special losses that might result from a breach of contract. In this manner, the promisor can decide whether or not to enter into the contractual relationship.

In a famous case, a mill owner had contracted with several farmers in the area to mill their grain during a bumper season. Unfortunately, the mill shaft broke right before the harvest. The miller brought the shaft to a repairman who promised to repair the shaft in a week. The miller made no mention of any special need for the shaft. After the repair, the shaft broke during the first day of use, and the miller sued the repairman, not only for the value of the shaft, but for all his lost profit as well. It seems that because the shaft was the only one the miller had, when it broke he had to cancel his contract with the farmers. The court held that the miller was not entitled to lost profits. This was a loss that could not be foreseen by the repairman when the contract was entered into, and so he could not be responsible for those types of losses. The repairman did have to return to the miller the price of the repairs as compensatory damages.

Therefore, to be entitled to consequential damages, the promisee must make the promisor aware of any unusual or unforeseen consequences that could result from a potential breach at the time the contract is entered into; otherwise the breaching part will only be liable for compensatory damages.

Consequential and punitive damages must be distinguished from the concept of **speculative damages.** Speculative damages are monetary injuries the injured party believes she suffered because of the breach, but they are not readily ascertainable, provable, or quantifiable. An example of speculative damages would be profit the injured party had hoped to make as a result of the contract. Speculative damages cannot be recovered under any circumstances.

 EXAMPLE:

Leane hires a limousine to take her to an important business meeting where she is to sign a million dollar contract. The limousine fails to appear, Leane cannot get to the meeting, and she loses the deal. She sues the limousine company for her lost profit of $300,000. Leane will not prevail. She would be entitled to the cost of the limousine, if she had paid for it, but her loss of a million dollar contract is not a foreseeable result of a car service failing to perform. Under these circumstances Leane would not be entitled to consequential damages. Also, her loss may be speculative; more information is needed to determine how realistic that contract was.

Liquidated Damages

Liquidated damages are reasonable damages that the parties themselves have agreed to in the contract itself. Normally, parties to a contract would specify liquidated damages if it would be difficult or impossible to compute compensatory damages because of the uncertain nature of the contract or the subject matter. When liquidated damages are specified, the court will usually award those damages, and the parties are generally precluded from arguing that the amount is too high or too low. Because liquidated damages are determined at the outset of the contract, in order to avoid lengthy litigation later on, the court will simply abide by the parties' agreement under the concept of freedom of contract. The parties never had to agree in the first place, so if they did, their agreement prevails.

However, for the liquidated damages provision of a contract to be enforced, it must be clear that the provision is in fact meant to ease recovery of hard-to-determine losses; if the liquidated damages clause is in fact meant as a punishment for the breaching party or to compensate for speculative damages, the court will not honor the provision.

EXAMPLE:

Gene and Elga have a contract to develop and patent an inexpensive process for creating a clotting agent. Because they don't know whether the idea is patentable or will be successful, they contract with a liquidated damages provision in the amount of $100,000. The contract is breached by Gene, and Elga sues. Regardless of the actual dollar amount of the loss, if Elga can show the existence of a valid contract and a breach by Gene, she will be awarded $100,000.

Liquidated damages should be distinguished from **limitation of damages,** another type of provision that can appear in contractual agreements. With limitation of damages, the parties agree when entering into the contract that, in case of breach, the breaching party will be liable for no more than the amount established as the ceiling, or limitation, in the contract. Unlike liquidated damages, with a limitation of damages provision the injured party must not only prove the contract and the breach, but must prove the actual damages as well. The financial award is limited to the amount contractually specified, but if the actual loss is less than that amount, the smaller sum is awarded. Liquidated damages set the amount of the recovery, regardless of actual loss, whereas a limitation of damages caps liability of actual loss to be no higher than the amount specified.

EXAMPLE:

Assume that instead of a liquidated damages provision, Gene and Elga insert a limitation of damages clause, setting the amount at

$100,000. When Gene breaches, Elga now has to prove her actual loss. If she can only show a loss of $75,000, that is all she will recover. If she can show a loss of $250,000, she will only get $100,000, because she has contracted to limit her recovery to that amount.

As discussed in the previous chapter, whenever the court is computing the value of the damages suffered by the injured party, the court also looks to see whether the injured party attempted to **mitigate damages.** It is the duty of every innocent party in a breach of contract to attempt to lessen the damages the breaching party may have to pay, provided that such attempts are not unreasonable or unduly burdensome for the innocent person. The promisee does not have to go out of his way to mitigate but must make some attempt, if possible, to remedy the situation himself. The ultimate award will thereby be reduced by the amount of the mitigation.

 EXAMPLES:

1. Ace Supermarkets has a contract to purchase 1000 bushels of oranges from Farmer Jones at $10 per bushel. Farmer Jones fails to deliver, and Ace is able to find another farmer to sell it the oranges at $11 per bushel. Ace has mitigated its damages, and now is only entitled to $1000 from Farmer Jones instead of $10,000 (the difference between the $10 per bushel it was to pay Farmer Jones and the $11 per bushel it actually had to pay).

2. In the same situation as above, Ace can find a farmer to sell it oranges at $9 per bushel. In this instance, Farmer Jones' breach has put Ace in a better position than it would have been in had the contract gone through, and so Ace is not entitled to any award from Farmer Jones.

3. Tiffany's contracts with a Thai mine to purchase a 50-carat sapphire for one of its customers. When the mine fails to deliver the jewel, Tiffany's cannot find a replacement stone. Because it is impossible for Tiffany's to mitigate, it is entitled to full compensatory damages.

Equitable Remedies

Whenever the legal remedy of damages is insufficient to compensate the injured party to a breach of contract, the innocent party can look for some equitable relief. **Equitable remedies** are designed to prevent unfairness and unjust enrichment. These largely nonmonetary awards are divided into five categories:

1. injunctions;
2. specific performance;
3. rescission and restitution;
4. reformation; and
5. quasi-contractual.

Injunction

An **injunction** is a court order to stop someone from engaging in a specific action. The verb is *to enjoin*, and the court will only order this when the innocent party could not otherwise be compensated.

 EXAMPLES:

1. Salim has a contract to purchase Whiteacre from Faruk, closing to take place in one month. Two weeks before the closing date, Salim discovers that Faruk is attempting to sell the property to someone else. Salim could go to court to have the court enjoin Faruk from selling the house to anyone other than Salim, pursuant to the contract. Although the injunction would stop Faruk from selling the property to anyone other than Salim, it does not mean that he will actually convey the property to Salim; he can still breach the contract by some other action later on.

2. Joe leaves Acme, Inc., after working there for 20 years. Joe and Acme have a contract in which Joe agreed that, should he leave Acme, he would not go into competition against them for 2 years. One week after Joe leaves Acme, he goes to work for Acme's biggest competitor. Acme can enjoin Joe from working for the competitor, pursuant to their contract.

Injunctions are permanent or temporary orders of the court to stop a particular action or activity. Because the courts do not usually order injunctions easily or without a full hearing (and only on a showing that irreparable harm would result from a refusal to order the injunction), until a full hearing can be arranged a litigant may be entitled to a **temporary restraining order (TRO)**. A TRO is only a temporary measure by the court until the hearing for full injunctive relief can take place. A TRO is for a short period of time; an injunction is more far reaching.

Specific Performance

Specific performance is a court order requiring the breaching party to perform exactly what she promised under the contract. Specific performance is only granted when the subject matter of the contract is considered unique and therefore not replaceable, or when no other remedy would rectify the injury to the innocent party. Unlike an injunction, in which the court orders a party to stop doing something, with specific performance the court is ordering a party to do something.

 EXAMPLES:

1. In the situation above with Salim and Faruk, on closing day Faruk refuses to convey the property to Salim. Because real estate is generally considered unique, Salim could go to court to seek specific performance. The court would order Faruk to convey Whiteacre to Salim, pursuant to the contract.

2. In the example with Joe and Acme, Acme could also have the court order specific performance of the contract provision. Joe would then have to abide by the agreement and not compete with Acme for two years. The injunction only stopped Joe from working for a specific competitor.

Rescission and Restitution

If a party to a contract finds that fulfillment of the contract would be unduly burdensome, he can ask the court for **rescission and restitution,** whereby the court will rescind, or revoke, the contract in the interest of fairness. It will then have each party restore to the other what the other has expended on the contract to date. If the parties can agree to this procedure by themselves, it is a form of discharge of obligation by a new agreement, as discussed in Chapter 10. If the parties cannot agree to terminate the relationship themselves, the court may do it for them.

Unlike the equitable remedies discussed previously, it is the party who wants to breach who is seeking relief from the court in the form of rescission and restitution. To be entitled to rescission and restitution, the party seeking the remedy must be able to demonstrate that fulfillment of the contract would be so burdensome as to be unjust. Mere economic loss, unless very substantial, is insufficient; economic loss is a risk of contract. What is deemed burdensome is determined by the court on a case-by-case basis.

EXAMPLE:

Chad and Jeremy have entered into a partnership agreement to publish a magazine. Chad has an independent income; Jeremy does not. After two years of operation, the publication is still losing money with no change likely in the foreseeable future. Jeremy has gone through his money, and he needs to get a paying job. Chad wants to continue the magazine pursuant to the agreement. Under these circumstances, Jeremy could have the court rescind the contract because its fulfillment would be unduly burdensome.

Reformation

Reformation can be considered a court-ordered accord and satisfaction. When the parties to a disputed contract cannot resolve the conflict, the court may do so for them while still keeping the contractual relationship intact. Under the rule of construction that contracts are to be upheld if at all possible (Chapter 7), if the dispute merely involves one of quantity or quality of subject matter, the court can reform the contract to correspond to what was actually delivered. In this manner, the contractual relationship can go forward, and neither of the parties will be in breach.

 EXAMPLE:

In the example discussed earlier in which Eatwell received the plums from Farmer Grey, Eatwell claimed the plums were Grade B, whereas Farmer Grey claimed they were in fact Grade A. The parties themselves could not resolve the dispute, but this was the first installment of a year's worth of deliveries. In court, instead of awarding damages, because of the long-term nature of the contract and the difficulty of proving grades of plums, the court could reform the contract to delete mention of the grade of plums and to change the price to $8.50 a bushel. In this manner, the contract between Eatwell and Farmer Grey can be maintained.

Quasi-contractual Remedies

The **quasi-contractual remedies** are the only equitable remedies that involve a monetary award. Quasi-contractual remedies are available in situations in which no contract exists, but there has been unjust enrichment to one of the parties of the dispute. To rectify the unjust enrichment, the court will order the injured party to be awarded the value of what she has lost (the value of the unjust enrichment). There are two types of quasi-contractual remedies:

1. *Quantum meruit* and
2. *Quantum valebant.*

Quantum Meruit

Quantum meruit means the value of the service rendered. If the defendant is unjustly enriched by receiving uncompensated-for services, she must pay the injured party the value of those services. Remember the paralegal who worked for her aunt with the expectation of receiving the aunt's property on the aunt's death (Chapter 1): Although no contract did in fact exist, the paralegal was entitled to the value of the services she performed for the aunt. This is *quantum meruit*.

Quantum Valebant

Quantum valebant means the value of the property received. If the injured party conveys property that unjustly enriches the recipient, the recipient is required to pay the innocent party for the value of the property. An example would be the newspaper that was left on the doorstep in Chapter 1. The person who kept accepting the newspaper is liable for the value of the paper to the publisher, who never intended to give the paper as a gift.

Both *quantum meruit* and *quantum valebant* are applied in cases involving quasi-contracts in the interests of justice.

Waivers and Their Effect

A party cannot be sued for breaching his obligation under a contract if the innocent party waives that breach. A **waiver** is the forgiveness by a party to a contract of the other side's failure to meet a contractual obligation. The waiver can be for a contractual covenant or for any condition specified in the contract.

A party can waive a contractual provision either expressly or implicitly. An **express waiver** occurs when the promisee specifically manifests that she intends to forgive the other side's breach. An **implied waiver** occurs, not by the words or manifestations of the promisee, but by the promisee's actions. In both instances, when a contractual provision has been waived, the other side is relieved of that specific obligation.

 EXAMPLES:

1. Leo contracts with Bob for the construction of an addition to his house. The contract states that Leo will only pay for the work when it is complete, and Bob gets an architect's certificate that the work meets all structural specifications. The work is done, and Leo pays Bob without having the architect's certificate. Leo has waived this condition of the contract by his actions.

2. Leona rents an apartment from ABC Realty, and the lease specifies that the apartment cannot be sublet. Leona has to go out of town for a long period of time and asks ABC if they would permit a short-term sublet to help her out. ABC agrees in writing to waive the nonsublet provision of the lease. Leona is now free to sublet without being in breach.

As a general rule, any party to a contract is free to waive any provision she wishes. However, the promisor cannot always rely on the waiver to relieve him of all liabilities, especially if the waiver waives an obligation that is an ongoing obligation, such as monthly rent during a two-year lease. To protect the parties, many contracts include a waiver provision in which it is specifically stated that waiving one provision of the contract does not necessarily waive any other provision, nor is a waiver at one time to be considered a continuing waiver of that contractual provision during the full term of the contract. Therefore, if one party to a contract is going to be unable to fulfill a particular contractual provision, it would behoove him to seek a waiver for the provision to avoid being in breach. The effect of an obligation being specifically waived is that the obligation cannot be reinstated or made the subject of a suit for breach of contract. The party who waives the provision is estopped, or barred, from raising that provision as the grounds of a lawsuit.

Arbitration Provisions

Despite the foregoing, many contracts specify that disputes will be decided not by going to court, but by having the matter resolved by **arbitration.** Arbitration is a nonjudicial method of settling legal disputes in which both sides agree to submit the claim to an agreed-on arbitrator for relief. Arbitration is usually a faster and less expensive method of resolving disputes than litigation.

Arbitrators are not bound by evidentiary rules and are free to determine liabilities and relief as they see fit. In most instances, the decision of the arbitrator is final and binding, precluding the parties from seeking further judicial relief. Examples of arbitration clauses appear in Chapter 12, Drafting Simple Contracts.

Because arbitration is now so popular, it must be considered when determining appropriate remedies for a contractual disagreement.

SAMPLE CLAUSES

1

The failure of the lessor to insist upon the strict performance of the terms, covenants, agreements and conditions herein contained, or any of them, shall not constitute or be construed as a waiver or relinquishment of the lessor's right to thereafter enforce any such term, covenant, agreement or condition, but the same shall continue in full force and effect.

The above is an example of a waiver provision in a lease. By these words, the promisee is stating that he may, if he so desires, forgive enforcement of a contract promise, but that waiver is not to be considered a continuing waiver, or a waiver of all his rights. What he forgives once he may not forgive a second time, and the promisor is still contractually bound for all covenants and conditions not waived. Typically contracts will specify that waivers must be in writing; this protects both sides to the agreement. Remember, a promisor is not obligated to fulfill any promise that the promisee has waived. Failure to fulfill a waived obligation is *not* a breach of contract.

2

Should Seller breach any of the provisions of the agreement, Seller shall be liable for liquidated damages in the amount of $X.

The preceding is an example of a liquidated damages clause. The contracting parties, when entering into the agreement, have specified what the damages shall be in the case of breach. In this instance, the seller would be liable for $X, provided the buyer could prove the contract was breached. No evidence need be given with respect to the actual damages involved; damages have already been contractually determined.

3

In the event of breach of any of the provisions of this agreement, damages shall be limited to $X, exclusive of attorneys' fees and court costs.

In the above example, the parties have set a limitation to their potential liability. In this case, the injured party not only has to prove breach but must also prove the amount of damages. Regardless of what can be proven, damages will not exceed the amount stipulated by the parties in their contract.

CHAPTER SUMMARY

Remedies are the awards the injured party in a contractual dispute can receive from the party who has breached her obligation. The type and the amount of the award depends on the nature of the injury occasioned by the breach; the purpose is to put the injured party in the same position she would have been in had there been no breach.

Legal remedies, known as damages, are monetary awards based on the injury suffered. The standard measure of damages is compensatory damages, which attempts to put the innocent party in the same position he would have been in had the contract been fulfilled as planned. In unusual circumstances, the injured party may be entitled to a monetary award different from the standard measure. If the nonbreaching party makes the promisor aware of some special losses that would be occasioned by a breach, he may be entitled to consequential damages to compensate him for this extraordinary loss. If the breach is accompanied by some other wrongdoing (such as fraud), the court, under statutory authority, may punish the breaching party. In this case, punitive, or exemplary, damages are awarded in addition to the standard measure.

When negotiating the agreement, the parties to the contract are always free to agree on liquidated damages or a limitation of liability. With liquidated damages, the parties agree that, in case of breach, the amount recovered by the nonbreaching party will be an amount established in the contract itself. With a limitation of liability provision, damages must be proven but cannot exceed the amount stipulated in the agreement.

If monetary awards would be insufficient, or inappropriate, to compensate the injured party, under the court's equitable jurisdiction the innocent party may be entitled to some nonmonetary relief. Examples of these equitable remedies are injunctions, to stop the breaching party from engaging in a specific action; specific performance, ordering the breaching party to fulfill the specific obligations of the contract; rescission and restitution, in which the court will rescind the contract and put the parties in the same position they were in before the contract was entered into; and reformation, in which the court will alter the terms of the agreement to keep the total contract in effect. In addition to these nonmonetary awards, if the source of the dispute is a quasi-contractual relationship, the court may order some monetary relief for the value of the unjust enrichment.

A promisee may waive any provision of a contract that she wishes, and the waiver relieves the promisor of that contractual provision without being in breach of contract. However, the waiver of one provision is usually not considered to be a waiver of any other provision, and except for the specifically waived obligation, the promisor remains contractually bound.

In court, the injured party may ask for as many different types of remedies as seem appropriate to the action. The court will make the ultimate decision as to which remedies to award.

SYNOPSIS

Legal remedies
>Damages (money)
>>1. Compensatory
>>2. Punitive
>>3. Consequential

Equitable remedies (nonmonetary)
>1. Injunction
>2. Specific performance
>3. Rescission and restitution
>4. Reformation
>5. Quasi-contractual

Contract clauses
>1. Liquidated damages
>2. Limitation of damages
>3. Waivers
>4. Arbitration

Key Terms

Arbitration: nonjudicial method of resolving legal disputes

Compensatory damages: standard measure of damages; puts injured party in the position he would have been in had the contract been fulfilled

Consequential damages: damages above the standard measure due to special losses occasioned by the breach

Damages: legal remedies; monetary awards

Equitable remedies: nonmonetary awards

Equity: area of law concerned with preventing unfairness and unjust enrichment

Exemplary damages: additional monetary award designed to punish the breaching party

Express waiver: a waiver occurring when the promisee specifically manifests an intention to forgive the other side's breach

Implied waiver: a waiver occurring when the promisee's actions imply an intention to forgive the other side's breach

Injunction: court order to stop engaging in a specific action

Law: division of law concerned with historical legal principles designed to provide equal treatment to all persons

Legal remedies: monetary awards

Limitation of damages: contractual provision placing a ceiling on the amount of potential liability for breach of the contract

Liquidated damages: contractual provision providing a specified dollar amount for breach of the contract

Mitigation of damages: duty imposed on innocent party to make reasonable attempts to lessen the liability of the breaching party

Punitive damages: exemplary damages
Quantum meruit: quasi-contractual award; value of the service performed
Quantum valebant: quasi-contractual award; value of the good given
Quasi-contractual remedy: an equitable remedy involving a monetary
    award
Reformation: a court-ordered accord and satisfaction
Rescission and restitution: a court order revoking a contract that would be
    unduly burdensome to fulfill
Specific performances: court order to perform contractual promise
Speculative damages: damages that are not specifically provable
Temporary restraining order (TRO):   preliminary step to an injunction
Waiver: forgiveness of a contract obligation

EXERCISES

1. Give an example of a situation in which punitive damages would
   be possible.
2. Your school decides to disband the paralegal program before you
   complete your studies. What damage would you claim, and how
   could you substantiate that claim?
3. What is the effect of a disclaimer on consequential damages?
4. Argue that a limitation of damages provision should not be considered valid.
5. Give two examples not discussed in the chapter in which quasi-
   contractual remedies would be appropriate.

Cases for Analysis

The following case summaries highlight the concepts of when specific
performance may be granted, Morabito v. Harris, and when exemplary
damages may or may not be awarded under a breach of warranty claim,
Salter v. Al-Hallaq.

Morabito v. Harris
2002 Del. Ch. LEXIS 27

This action arises out of an unsuccessful real estate transaction in
which the disappointed buyer seeks specific performance. The Master in
Chancery, after a full evidentiary hearing, issued a Final Report that
rejected the buyer's request to compel conveyance of the property. Specific
performance is a remedy predicated upon the exercise of equitable discretion and the Master recommended that, in the circumstances of this case, a
court of equity should withhold such relief. Having carefully reviewed the
record and having read the entire transcript of the hearing before the

Master, I conclude that the Master correctly balanced the equitable interests in conflict and that his determination is free from error.

I. Standard of Review

The standard of review applicable here is the *de novo* standard both with respect to the facts of the matter and the conclusions of law. Nevertheless, it is well established that "even where the parties except to one or more of the master's factual findings, a new hearing may not be required." Instead, "the court may read the portion of the record relevant to the exception raised and draw its own factual conclusions."

II. Facts

The facts are as follows. On April 13, 2000, Mr. Morabito (the promisee buyer) and Mr. and Mrs. Harris (the promisor sellers) agreed by contract that Morabito would purchase the Harrises' house and lot located at 306 David Hall Road in Rodney Village, Dover for a price of $82,000. The contract of sale contemplated that Morabito would satisfy two contingencies for the contract to become effective. First, he was obliged to apply for mortgage financing within ten days. Second, before the closing date, that is, "on or before" June 30, 2000, Morabito was to obtain a commitment to assume the mortgage encumbering the Harrises' house (approximately $4,400 for a term of 27.5 years).

The Harrises intended to sell their Rodney Village house so as to acquire a larger home near Magnolia. At the same time they negotiated with Morabito, the Harrises sought a financing commitment sufficient to effectuate their Magnolia house purchase. Because closing on the Magnolia house was tentatively scheduled for June, the Harrises and Morabito sought to coordinate closing on the Rodney Village property. Thus, in order to enable the Harrises to satisfy the mortgage on their Rodney Village home before they acquired the new home in Magnolia, the parties agreed to schedule the Rodney Village settlement in the morning and the Magnolia house settlement in the afternoon, both on the same day (June 30).

As the agreement between the parties obliged Morabito to assume the Harrises' FHA mortgage, Morabito contacted the lender and requested the documents necessary for the mortgage assumption. To prepare the documents for the mortgage assumption, Morabito had to do two things: First, he had to obtain the sellers' authorization and, second, he had to provide the mortgage company with the exact closing date. To this end, Morabito contacted the real estate agent, Robert Gaston, who was a "dual agent" representing both the buyer and the sellers. Gaston told Morabito that because the Harrises had encountered problems with respect to the purchase of the new home in Magnolia, that he (Morabito) could postpone applying for the mortgage assumption on the Rodney Village property until a closing date had been determined. When told of this problem,

Morabito advised Gaston that he would be willing to extend the Rodney Village settlement, even beyond the agreed June 30 settlement date.

In late May or early June, the Harrises' lender discovered that their income (in part) consisted of an annuity, which was about to expire. As a result, the Harrises' total income would soon be insufficient to support a mortgage on the Magnolia property. The lender promptly revoked its financing commitment. Unable to finance the purchase, the Harrises advised Morabito, via Gaston, that they no longer could afford to sell their Rodney Village home. Morabito nonetheless went forward and obtained his own financing commitment for the Rodney Village property.

When the Harrises refused to go forward with settlement, Morabito filed this action, seeking specific performance of the sales contract. After a trial, the Master in Chancery recommended that the request for specific performance be denied and that Morabito be left to pursue his remedy in a court of law. Exceptions were taken and the matter is now before me.

III. Analysis

Having reviewed the trial transcript in light of the parties' contentions, I agree with the Master's conclusions and recommendations. The parties entered into a valid contract for the sale of the Rodney Village property. The Harrises repudiated the contract after they learned that they could not afford a new home. In the special circumstances here, I agree with the Master that the equities weigh against specific performance. In this case, the remedy of specific performance inflicts a burden far more onerous upon the Harrises than the benefits such a remedy would confer upon Morabito. For that reason, Morabito should pursue the standard legal remedies available for breach of contract.

The Court of Chancery has jurisdiction to enforce contracts for the sale of land where the remedy at law appears to be inadequate. To grant specific performance, there must be proof of a valid contract to purchase real property and proof that plaintiff was ready, willing and able to perform his contractual obligations. In addition, the Court must determine whether the "balance of equities" tips in favor of specific performance. This case turns on this last requirement — considerations of equity.

The balance of equities issue "reflect[s] the traditional concern of a court of equity that its special processes not be used in a way that unjustifiably increases human suffering." In some circumstances, when the specific enforcement of a validly formed contact would cause even greater harm than it would save, courts of equity will decline a petition for specific enforcement. Thus, the remedy of specific performance is limited to instances where the presence of special equities calls for it.

The record evidence in this case shows that each party can appeal to equity on its behalf. But in the end, enforcing the contract specifically will be far more onerous for the Harrises than for Morabito.

Morabito insists that the Rodney Village property is unique. It has an attractive assumable mortgage (6.5%), a large backyard for garage building purposes, close proximity to his place of work and to his mother-in-law's home (across the street), a basement and a wood-burning stove. To Morabito, no doubt these were important characteristics of the property.

For the Harrises, however, a decree of specific performance will impose significant hardships. The Harrises have modest financial prospects, coupled with the need to support a child. Specific performance of the contract will equate to homelessness for the Harrises, given the change in their financial situation. In addition, they point to the fact that Morabito could find comparable houses for sale in Rodney Village, many that are similar in design and construction to the Harrises' home.

I agree with the Master that the housing development in question is composed of architecturally similar homes. It also appears from the record that, at the time that the Master issued his report, a number of alternative vacant lots were available for sale. The existence of alternative homes or building lots in Rodney Village reduces the force of Morabito's "uniqueness of this property" argument. Moreover, the existence of an assumable mortgage at uniquely favorable conditions also is a contention lacking persuasive force. At present, Morabito could take advantage of real estate mortgage financing under equally favorable (or even superior) terms, so that factor does not tip the equities in his favor either.

Ultimately, the Master concluded that a valid contract of sale existed, but that Morabito should pursue his legal remedies for its breach because to enforce it specifically would cause more harm, in this particular case, than it would avoid. The evidence clearly supports the Master's conclusion. Although Morabito can obtain comparable housing in the same housing development, the evidence indicates that the Harrises' financial condition had deteriorated significantly and they effectively will be made homeless if this Court orders specific enforcement. I conclude, in these circumstances, that the balance of equities strongly favors the Harrises. Accordingly, I approve the Master's Report. Although Morabito is free to pursue his legal remedies for breach of contract, he is not entitled to specific performance in light of the special circumstances of this case.

Morabito's final argument is that refusing specific performance will signal promisors that they can evade their contractual obligations. This argument proceeds from a false premise, since refusing specific performance does not mean the breaching party will not have to pay damages for the breach. But the argument raises the larger question of the appropriate remedy for contract breach—money damages versus specific performance. This question has provided much grist for the academic mill over the past three decades.

Our jurisprudence, however, is best reflected in Oliver Wendell Holmes' famous line: "The only universal consequence of a legally binding promise is, that the law makes the promisor pay damages if the promised event does not come to pass." Holmes' approach to contractual remedies would later evolve into the "efficient breach" theory of contract law, which urges expectation damages as a remedy in order to encourage a promisor's breach where resulting profits to the promisor exceed the loss to the promisee. As a result, today a damages remedy is routinely available, but specific performance is considered extraordinary, awarded on a discretionary basis by courts of equity. Thus, contrary to Morabito's belief, there is no "entitlement" to specific performance, even when a contract breach involving unique goods is admitted. Specific performance is available when it is equitable, and in this case specific enforcement (to repeat) would be inequitable. In addition, I note that nothing suggests that the promisor is in breach because of an effort by the promisor to exploit the promisee (Morabito). Rather the promisor (Harrises) cannot afford to sell their home, and have no other place to live. I also note that there is no allegation that the promisee expended any monies on the property, aside from incidental out-of-pocket expenses and the related transaction costs of time and effort. Such incidental expenses are generally recoverable, however, in an action at law. In short, I do not agree that denying specific performance in these circumstances is inconsistent with this Court's traditional approach to contract remedies in the land sale context. Each specific performance action turns on its own special facts and equities, which is the case here.

IT IS SO ORDERED.

Questions

1. Under what circumstances will the court award specific performance?

2. What is the requisite proof as a condition precedent to the court awarding specific performance?

3. What is your opinion of this decision?

Salter v. Al-Hallaq
2003 U.S. Dist. LEXIS 6136 (D. Kan. 2003)

This breach of warranty and fraud action stems from plaintiff's purchase of a used car. In addition to asserting several state law claims, plaintiff, a citizen of Kansas, asserts a claim against defendants, also citizens of Kansas, pursuant to the Magnuson-Moss Warranty Act, 15 U.S.C. §2301 *et seq.* ("Magnuson-Moss" or "the Act"). Defendants move to dismiss plaintiff's complaint for lack of subject matter jurisdiction (doc. #11). Specifically, defendants maintain that plaintiff has failed to meet the Act's requirement that the amount in controversy be at least $50,000. As set forth below, defendants' motion is granted and plaintiff's complaint is dismissed in its entirety.

Magnuson-Moss confers federal jurisdiction only when the amount in controversy is at least $50,000. See 15 U.S.C. §2310(d)(1)(B) & (d)(3)(B). To justify dismissal of the claim for lack of jurisdiction, it must appear to a legal certainty that the claim is really for less than the jurisdictional amount. St. Paul Mercury Indemnity Co. v. Red Cab Co., 303 U.S. 283, 289, 82 L. Ed. 845, 58 S. Ct. 586 (1938). On the other hand, if, from the face of the pleadings, it is apparent, to a legal certainty, that the plaintiff cannot recover the amount claimed, the suit must be dismissed. *Id.* In determining whether the jurisdictional amount is satisfied, the court looks to the face of plaintiff's complaint, as plaintiff's claim for damages controls if that claim is apparently made in good faith. *See* Miera v. Dairyland Ins. Co., 143 F.3d 1337, 1340 (10th Cir. 1998) (citing *St. Paul Mercury,* 303 U.S. at 288-89).

In her complaint, plaintiff asserts that she has sustained actual damages in excess of $25,000. Specifically, plaintiff claims that she purchased a 2000 Toyota Echo from defendants for the sum of $9000. According to plaintiff, defendants represented to her that the vehicle was worth more than $9000 (she states that the previous owners of the vehicle were paid $12,500 as the "full value" of the vehicle after it was "totaled" in a collision) when, in fact, the vehicle was worth virtually nothing in light of prior extensive damage to the vehicle that defendants failed to disclose to plaintiff. Plaintiff also claims that defendants told her that the vehicle was covered by a 36-month warranty which would cover all repair costs when, in fact, the vehicle is not covered by the warranty. According to plaintiff, she has suffered damages in the amount of $1054.99 for repair costs and she continues to incur monthly expenses for the vehicle. In sum, plaintiff claims that the actual value of the vehicle, coupled with the value of the 36-month warranty and other damages that plaintiff continues to incur, puts plaintiff's actual damages beyond $25,000. Plaintiff also seeks punitive damages in excess of $75,000.

In their motion to dismiss, defendants urge that plaintiff's complaint reveals, at the very most, a claim for $15,000 in actual damages and, thus, that plaintiff can satisfy the amount-in-controversy requirement only if her claim for punitive damages may be counted along with her claim for actual damages. According to defendants, plaintiff's claim for punitive damages cannot be used in calculating the jurisdictional amount because the relevant state law does not allow for the recovery of punitive damages for a breach of warranty. Plaintiff contends that state law does permit the recovery of punitive damages for a breach of warranty and, thus, her claim for punitive damages can be used in calculating the jurisdictional amount.

Both parties apparently agree that punitive damages may not be included in the calculation of the jurisdictional amount for purposes of Magnuson-Moss unless the pertinent state law permits punitive damages for a breach of warranty action. *See* Boyd v. Homes of Legend, Inc., 188 F.3d 1294, 1298 (11th Cir. 1999) (court must look to state law, rather than federal law, to determine whether punitive damages are available under Magnuson-Moss); Boelens v. Redman Homes, Inc., 748 F.2d 1058, 1069 (5th Cir. 1984) (punitive damages are recoverable under Magnuson-Moss for breach of warranty only if they may be recovered in a breach of warranty action brought under the governing state law); In re General Motors Corp. Engine Interchange Litigation, 594 F.2d 1106, 1132 n.44 (7th Cir. 1979) (although not deciding the issue, surmising that punitive damages would be available under Magnuson-Moss to the extent authorized by state law). Both parties also agree that the relevant state law in this case is that of

Kansas. The question, then, is whether Kansas law permits the recovery of punitive damages for breach of warranty.

Under Kansas's version of the Uniform Commercial Code (UCC), which appears to govern the transaction in this case, punitive damages are not recoverable. Specifically, K.S.A. §84-1-106(1) states that:

> The remedies provided by this act shall be liberally administered to the end that the aggrieved party may be put in as good a position as if the other party had fully performed but neither consequential or special nor penal damages may be had except as specifically provided in this act or by other rule of law.

See also *Boyd*, 188 F.3d at 1299 (looking to Alabama's identical provision of the UCC and concluding that it did not permit recovery of punitive damages and, thus, district court erred when it considered punitive damages in calculation of jurisdictional amount under Magnuson-Moss). The court finds nothing in other Kansas statutes or in the Kansas common law that would authorize an award of punitive damages under Magnuson-Moss in this case. Under Kansas common law, punitive damages are not recoverable for breach of contract, even if the breach is intentional and unjustified. See Farrell v. General Motors Corp., 249 Kan. 231, 247, 815 P.2d 538 (1991). However, punitive damages are allowable if there is some independent tort present, id. (citing Equitable Life Leasing Corp. v. Abbick, 243 Kan. 513, 516, 757 P.2d 304 (1988)), and it is this rule upon which plaintiff relies.

It is evident from a review of the cases, however, that Kansas law awards punitive damages for the accompanying tort, not for the breach of contract itself. See, e.g., W-V Enterprises, Inc. v. Federal Sav. & Loan Ins. Corp., 234 Kan. 354, 369, 673 P.2d 1112 (1983) (noting that jury's finding of fraud was what supported the award of punitive damages in breach of contract case); Guarantee Abstract & Title Co. v. Interstate Fire & Casualty Co., 232 Kan. 76, 79-80, 652 P.2d 665 (1982) (punitive damages must be predicated on an independent tort that results in additional injury). To recover punitive damages, an independent tort must be separately pleaded and proved. See *Equitable Life Leasing*, 243 Kan. at 516 ("Breach of contract, standing alone, does not call for punitive damages, but such damages are allowed if an independent tort of fraud is proven."); Bowman v. Doherty, 235 Kan. 870, 882, 686 P.2d 112 (1984) (punitive damages may be recovered for a breach of contract when an independent tort is proven).

Thus, Kansas law does not permit the recovery of punitive damages for a breach of warranty per se. Plaintiff therefore may not count her claim for punitive damages toward satisfaction of the jurisdictional amount in controversy. See *Boelens*, 748 F.2d at 1070-71 (even though Texas law permitted recovery of punitive damages for breach of contract if the breach is accompanied by an independent tort, those damages were for the tort and not the breach itself; plaintiffs could not recover punitive damages for breach of warranty per se and thus were not permitted to count their claim for punitive damages toward satisfaction of the jurisdictional amount). Because plaintiff claims only $25,000 in actual damages, then, she has failed to meet the requisite amount in controversy for federal jurisdiction under Magnuson-Moss and her complaint must be dismissed.

IT IS THEREFORE ORDERED BY THE COURT THAT defendants' motion to dismiss plaintiff's complaint for lack of subject matter jurisdiction (doc. #11) is granted and plaintiff's complaint is dismissed in its entirety.

IT IS SO ORDERED.

Questions

1. According to the court, under what circumstances would punitive damages be allowed under a breach of warranty claim?

2. Does your state's version of the UCC permit punitive damages under the circumstances appearing in this case?

3. What is your opinion of the appropriateness of exemplary damages for breach of contract actions?

Suggested Case References

1. Read the requirements needed to be granted punitive damages in North Carolina. Process Components v. Baltimore Aircoil Co., Inc., 89 N.C. App. 649, 366 S.E.2d 907 (1988).

2. Who has the burden of proving mitigation of damages, the breaching party or the injured party? Cobb v. Osman, 83 Nev. 415 (1967).

3. What circumstances are necessary before a court may order specific performance? Mann v. Golub, 182 W. Va. 523, 389 S.E.2d 734 (1990); In re Estate of Hayhurst, 478 P.2d 343 (Okla. 1970).

4. Does a party's actual performance under a contract in which performance was subject to a condition precedent constitute a waiver of the condition? See what the Montana court said in Hein v. Fox, 126 Mont. 514, 254 P.2d 1076 (1954).

5. Under what circumstances will a court award punitive damages for breach of contract? Read Edens v. Goodyear Tire & Rubber Co., 858 F.2d 198 (4th Cir. 1988).

12 Drafting Simple Contracts

Learning Objectives

After studying this chapter you will be able to:

- Deconstruct a basic contract
- Create a tickler of important contractual clauses
- Know how to describe the consideration in a contract
- Understand when certain provisions are appropriate for a contract
- List the special provisions and clauses that appear in most contracts
- Discuss the grounds for terminating a contract that could appear in the agreement
- Distinguish between the choice of law and submission to a particular jurisdiction
- Explain the effect of arbitration clauses on contract enforcement

CHAPTER OBJECTIVE

This chapter incorporates all of the principles and ideas discussed in the previous chapters into one complete contract. Many people are daunted at the prospect of creating a contractual relationship, but in fact the process is quite interesting and challenging.

There are three keys to creating a contract that will truly reflect the parties' wishes: 1) start with a thorough understanding of the precise wishes of the contracting parties; 2) use a checklist of clauses, or topics, that should be covered; and 3) create the agreement by referring to existing contracts covering the same or similar subject matter. No lawyer or paralegal is expected to devise a contract out of whole cloth, and to this end there are many sources of sample contracts available to the drafter.

Before attempting to draft a contract, make sure that you have a clear idea of the precise nature of the relationship the parties intend. This must include all of the six major requirements of every valid contract (Chapter 1). Additionally, every industry has its own special terminology and relationships that must be included in an industry contract. To ascertain what those areas might be, use the library to read books about the particular area involved. Not only law libraries, but regular public libraries have innumerable volumes covering every conceivable industry, and this should always be a first reference before drafting a contract. These sources not only will indicate special areas of concern but usually will include sample agreements that can be used as models.

Always ask the parties themselves and the attorney whether they have old contracts that they wish to have used as a basis for the new agreement. This is usually the best source of a sample because the parties have already used, and presumably have been happy with, that format. Just bear in mind that these former contracts are usable only as samples; it is exceedingly rare that one contract will be perfect for several different parties. There is always going to be a need to make certain changes in the contractual provisions to reflect the current contractual relationship. And finally, always check the appropriate state law, both common and statutory, to insure compliance with any particular requirements.

The following section of this chapter will discuss many of the most typical types of clauses that appear in contracts. This section can be used as a checklist in preparing a draft contract. By going through the list, the paralegal will be able to determine that all of the important provisions have been discussed. Of course, the list is hardly exhaustive, but it does provide the basic guidelines for simple contract drafting. Additionally, sample contracts have been included that cover many different areas of law and that can be used as models by the novice drafter. After a while, attorneys and paralegals develop their own samples from the contracts they have drafted. To build an excellent resource for samples, paralegals should develop the habit of keeping copies of all legal documents that they come in contact with for future use, deleting the parties' names and identifying information. As long as a person has sample format to follow, drafting contracts becomes an easy process.

Always bear in mind that each clause in a sample contract must be read to determine whether its wording is in the best interests of a given client; if not, simple changes in the language can be made. To this end, it is always a good idea to use more than one sample contract; by having multiple samples, clauses can be compared and contrasted, and sentences can be taken from different contracts to create a clause that would suit the given client.

Reviewing existing contracts and contract interpretation should also be mentioned here. There will be many instances in which the paralegal must analyze an existing contract to determine the rights and liabilities of a client. The process of interpretation is the exact reverse of drafting. Simply read the contract to determine what is said in each clause, and use the checklist to make sure no major areas have been deleted or ignored. Pretend that the contract to be analyzed is a sample and go through it the same way you would if you were drafting the contract.

Checklist of Clauses

The following clauses are presented in an order most often followed in drafting contracts, but, of course, changes in the order can always be made.

Description of the Parties

The first clause of every contract usually contains a description of the parties to the agreement. The term *description* means the legal names and aliases of the parties, type of entity each party is, and the manner in which the parties will be referred to throughout the remainder of the contract.

 EXAMPLE:

This agreement is made this _____ day of _____, 20____, between Acme Realty, Inc., a New York corporation (hereinafter "Corporation"), and Lyle Roberts, an individual resident in the State of Pennsylvania (hereinafter "Roberts").

It is necessary to note the exact legal names of the parties and the type of entity each party is — corporation, limited partnership, individual, and so forth — in case of a potential dispute with respect to the agreement. When commencing a lawsuit and serving process, it is necessary to know exactly how the parties are legally designated. To this end, the introductory clause may also include the parties' addresses. Addresses usually appear at the end of a contract below the parties' signatures or may appear in provisions providing for notice to the parties.

Indicating a nomenclature for the parties other than their legal names is for the purpose of achieving simplicity throughout the remainder of the agreement. Many times, especially if the contract is a form contract used by one of the parties, this designation may indicate the roles the parties play in the agreement, such as Buyer, Seller, or Landlord. Any designation agreed on is appropriate. Simply make sure that the same designation is used throughout the remainder of the agreement. Be consistent.

Description of the Consideration

For the purpose of contract law, this section of the agreement assumes primary importance. In this clause, the offer, acceptance, and consideration coalesce into a binding contract. As indicated in the first four chapters of this book, it is mandatory that the consideration be specifically described, indicating a mutuality of consideration. This means the description must specify what each party to the contract is giving and receiving. It must include such terms as price, quantity, quality, and time of performance. This clause is generally the first covenant of the contract.

In addition to the specifics of the consideration, any conditions the parties wish to attach to their performances should be included in this clause. Such conditions could include such items as provisions for installment purchases, if and how the agreement may be modified, and how payments may be accelerated. It is important to ascertain exactly what covenants and conditions the parties expect to have placed on their performances.

Also remember that whereas most contracts make payment of money the consideration for a good or service received, a contract is just as valid if the consideration is a good for a good, a service for a service, or a service for a good. The concept of barter is a legal one.

 EXAMPLE:

In consideration of Five Hundred Dollars ($500), Seller agrees to sell to Buyer the following: one used CD player.

Note that dollar amounts are usually written out as well as indicated numerically to avoid confusion and mistakes.

EXAMPLE:

It is agreed that Vendor will sell and Purchaser will buy all of the oranges growing at the farm of Vendor located at _____, during the year of _____, for the sum of Ten Thousand Dollars ($10,000.00), of which Four Thousand Dollars ($4,000.00) shall be paid upon the signing of this Agreement, Three Thousand Dollars ($3,000.00) shall be paid upon completion of the harvest, and Three Thousand Dollars ($3,000.00) shall be paid no later than one month after delivery of said oranges to Purchaser.

Purchaser shall, at his own expense, gather and harvest said fruit when it is sufficiently mature, and Purchaser and his employees shall have free access to the above-mentioned farm for the sole and exclusive purpose of harvesting said fruit.

In the above example, an output contract, the parties have agreed to an installment sale for the purchase of the oranges. All of the requisite terms and conditions have been specified.

 ## EXAMPLE:

Seller agrees to convey to Buyer, for the sum of Eight Thousand Dollars ($8,000.00), upon the conditions set forth below, the following personal property:

(Exact description of the property)

The Buyer hereby agrees to pay to the Seller the sum of Two Thousand Dollars ($2,000) upon delivery of the above mentioned goods to the Buyer's place of business, and the sum of One Thousand Dollars ($1,000) on the first day of each month following the date of this agreement until the full amount is paid. It is further agreed that, in the event of failure by the Buyer to make any installment as it becomes due, the whole of the sum then outstanding shall immediately become due and payable. If the Buyer so wishes, he may accelerate payments. No modification of this agreement shall be effective unless executed in writing and signed by both parties.

The above example indicates an installment sales contract that provides for remedies if an installment is not made on time, and further permits acceleration of the payment schedule as well as a method of modifying the agreement.

 ## EXAMPLE:

In consideration of Attorney drafting and executing the Last Will and Testament of Dentist, Dentist hereby agrees to perform root canal work on Attorney's number 18 tooth. All services shall be completed no later than two months from the date of this agreement.

This is an example of a contract clause in which each side performs services for the other, indicating exactly what services are to be performed and the timing of the performances.

In drafting the consideration clause, be sure to include the following:

1. A complete description of the consideration:
   a. for *money*, indicate the exact amount;
   b. for *real estate*, give a complete legal description or street address;
   c. for *personal property*, give as many identifying adjectives as are necessary to avoid confusion;
   d. for *services*, specify the service to be performed.
2. Indicate a mutuality of consideration.
3. Indicate the time of performance.
4. Specify any conditions or timing elements that attach to the performance.
5. Use words of present tense; don't use conditional words when indicating the covenants.
6. If the contract is covered by the UCC, determine whether a UCC form exists by checking the state statute book or legal stationery store.

Security Agreement

As discussed in Chapter 8, The Uniform Commercial Code, if a party to the agreement wishes to create a security interest in some property in the case of default, one of the requirements is to have a security agreement specifying that a secured interest is being created. Typically, the contract between the parties will satisfy this requirement of Article IX of the Code, provided that the contract indicates words to that effect. To this end, it becomes encumbent on the drafter to include such a clause in the contract.

 EXAMPLE:

We grant to you a security interest in, and the right of set-off with respect to, all receivables as defined above, all present and future instruments, documents, chattel paper, and general intangibles (as defined in the Uniform Commercial Code), and all proceeds thereof. All of the foregoing shall secure payment and performance of all our obligations at any time owing to you, fixed or contingent, whether arising out of this agreement or by operation of law.

The preceding example constitutes a security agreement for receivables and intangibles under the UCC. This clause would read the same regardless of the collateral specified.

Warranties

As discussed in Chapter 8, The Uniform Commercial Code, whenever the agreement involves the sale of goods, certain warranties attach. Obviously the implied warranties exist regardless of what the contract says, but the contract itself is one method of creating express warranties between the parties. If the parties intend specific guarantees with respect to the subject goods, it is recommended to include provisions concerning these express warranties. These clauses may be part of the Description of the Consideration or may follow those provisions as indicated by the order given here. All express warranties become covenants of the seller.

EXAMPLE:

Seller hereby warrants that the (good) is in good and merchantable condition, and is free and clear of all liens, security interests and encumbrances. Seller further warrants that the (good) meets all of the following specifications: (specifications).

The preceding clause not only creates express warranties based on particular specifications of the parties but also makes express warranties of the implied warranty of merchantability and title.

Title

Title to the property indicates ownership, right of control, possession, and transfer, and the right to insure the property. As a consequence, it becomes important to indicate in a contract the moment at which title transfers from the seller to the buyer. In any transaction where the mutual consideration is exchanged at the same time, title is transferred simultaneously. Problems arise only when there is to be a delay in full payment for the property conveyed or a lag time due to delivery. Some examples of these situations would be installment sales or mortgaging real estate. In these instances, it is necessary to insert a clause in the contract indicating the condition that gives rise to the transfer of the title.

EXAMPLES:

1. Seller hereby agrees to convey all his right, title, and interest in and to the aforementioned property upon receipt of a certified check from the Buyer in the amount of _____.

2. In an installment sale:
   When the full sum above mentioned is fully paid, title to said property shall vest in the vendee, but until then title shall remain in the vendor.

The parties themselves are always free to determine the exact moment title passes; however, there are three timing elements that are typically used: (1) when the contract is signed; (2) when the goods are fully paid for; or (3) for installment sales, at the moment an agreed-on percentage of the total selling price has been paid. Simply insert the timing element the parties have agreed on into the contract.

Risk of Loss

Risk of loss, as discussed in Chapter 8, The Uniform Commercial Code, comes into play whenever there is some delay in having the goods transferred from the seller to the buyer, either because of a conditional sales agreement or because of transportation of the items. As exemplified in Chapter 8, there are several standard clauses that can be inserted into the contract to cover this contingency; simply refer to that chapter to find and use the appropriate description.

Waivers

See Chapters 7 and 8 for a discussion of waivers and their effects on a contract. There are certain standard clauses with respect to waivers that are usually inserted into contracts, examples of which appear below.

 EXAMPLES:

1. This Agreement shall constitute the entire Agreement between the parties, and no variance or modification shall be valid except by a written agreement, executed in the same manner as this Agreement.

2. No delay or failure on the part of _____ to fulfill any of these provisions shall operate as a waiver of such or of any other right, and no waiver whatsoever shall be valid unless in writing and signed by the parties, and only to the extent therein set forth.

3. The waiver of any one provision of this Agreement shall not constitute a continuing waiver.

Assignments

Most contracts are assignable (see Chapter 9, Third Party Contracts), but usually parties insert clauses into contracts specifically covering this topic, either by stating that the contract may not be assigned or, if assignable, by indicating the method of effectuating the transfer of rights. It is generally a good idea to have such a clause in every contract to avoid problems later on.

EXAMPLES:

1. The rights herein permitted to _____ may be assigned, and upon such assignment, such Assignee shall have all of _____'s rights with respect thereto.

2. This contract is not transferable or assignable.

3. No assignment of this contract shall be effective unless executed in writing and signed by all parties.

In addition to specific assignment clauses, if a contract refers to assignees, that reference is sufficient to indicate that the contract is assignable. An example would be the phrase "the Agreement shall be binding on _____, his heirs, executors, assigns, etc." Also be aware that many states have specific case and statutory law with respect to the assignability of commercial leases, and for such contracts each jurisdiction's law must be specifically checked.

Delegation

Just as with assignments discussed above, many contracts may be delegated, unless performance depends on personal services or confidence. (See Chapter 9.) Once again, a provision may be inserted into the agreement specifically covering this point.

EXAMPLES:

1. The obligations specified in this Agreement may not be delegated by the parties.

2. _____ may delegate his obligation to _____.

Terminology

Unless otherwise indicated, all contractual terms are construed in their ordinary meaning. Consequently, if the contracting parties expect specific words, terms, or designations to be defined in a particular manner, it is necessary to indicate that definition in the contract itself. Because many terms are peculiar to particular industries, it becomes imperative that the meaning the parties want to attach to those terms be stated. Also, because "custom and usage" is the standard under the UCC for interpreting sales contracts, it would best serve the parties to have the custom and usage delineated in the agreement so that it does not become a problem of interpretation later on.

It is impossible to give a detailed list of terms because terms are particular to each contracting party; however, some of the sample contracts that follow will have a terminology section that can be used as a model. Simply remember to define any important term in the agreement itself.

Special Provisions and Clauses

In the same way that terminology will be peculiar to particular industries, so will special contractual covenants and conditions. There are certain matters that must be contractually agreed on by the parties, but these clauses are dependent on the nature of the contract and the industry involved. Following is merely a sample of the types of special provisions that may appear in various agreements.

Covenant Not to Compete

"Employee hereby covenants and agrees that in the event of the termination of this Agreement for any reason, with or without cause, that Employee will not compete directly or indirectly with Employer on his own account or as an employee of any other person or entity in _____ for a period of _____ years."

Duties

In an employment or personal services contract, every one of the duties of the employee should be specified, including details of the authority of the employee, any limitations on her authority, and any special accounting methods that may be used to determine compensation. In addition, all other employee benefits to which the employee will be entitled should either be specified, or, if part of a general employee benefit and compensation package, should be incorporated by reference in the main body of the agreement.

Pronouns

"Any masculine personal pronoun as set forth in this Agreement shall be considered to mean the corresponding feminine or neuter personal pronoun, as the case may be."

Severability

"If, for any reason, any provision hereof shall be inoperative, the validity and effect of all other provisions shall not be affected thereby."

Successors

"This Agreement and all provisions hereunder shall inure to the benefits of and shall be binding upon the heirs, executors, legal representatives, next of kin, transferees, and assigns of the parties hereto."

Time of the Essence

Time in all respects is of the essence of this contract.

Trade Secrets

"_____ further covenants not to divulge, during the term of this Agreement, or at any time subsequently, any trade secrets, processes, procedures, or operations, including, but not limited to, the following: _____."

Work Product

"Employee hereby agrees that all inventions, improvements, ideas, and suggestions made by him and patents obtained by him severally or jointly with any other person or persons during the entire period of his employment, are and shall be the sole property of the Employer, free from any legal or equitable title of the Employee, and that all necessary documents for perfecting such title shall be executed by the Employee and delivered to the Employer."

It is usually a good idea to specify the type of property involved.

Duration and Termination

Every contract should specify the duration of its provisions. This is established in two ways: First, the contract should have a specific statement indicating the intended termination date. Second, the contract should specify grounds for terminating the agreement prior to the intended termination date without causing the parties to be in breach. The duration clause is usually as simple as a one-sentence statement indicating the number of years of duration from the date indicated in the contract, or indicating that the agreement shall terminate on a specified date or on the occurrence of a specified event.

Clauses involving grounds for termination are a bit more problematical. The usual grounds given for termination are

1. failure of a party to fulfill a covenant;
2. failure of a condition specified in the contract;

3. dissolution of one or more of the contracting entities;
4. bankruptcy;
5. death, illness, or disability of one or both of the parties;
6. destruction of the subject matter;
7. commission of a felony by one of the parties;
8. incarceration of one of the parties; or
9. change in circumstance (such changes must be delineated in the agreement).

All of the foregoing indicate grounds for terminating the agreement for cause. However, the parties may also provide that the contract may be terminated without cause by one or both of the parties by giving appropriate notice to the other party.

All properly drafted contracts should contain some provision with respect to duration and termination of the agreement; the specifics are dependent on the wishes of the parties to the contract.

Notice of Default

If a party fails to fulfill a contractual obligation, thereby being in default, the agreement should provide for notice by the injured party of the default. The notice provision should specify how such notice is to be given, and whether the defaulting party may be given the opportunity to cure the default.

EXAMPLE:

In the event of a default of any of these provisions, _____ shall notify _____ in writing by first class mail or fax, of such default. Should _____ fail to cure such default within _____ days, he or she shall be deemed to be in breach.

Remedies

A contract should contain some provision with respect to remedies available to the innocent party in the case of a breach.

In contracts that include a provision for a security interest, the security holder, in addition to rights granted to her under the UCC, usually specifies the right to dispose of the collateral so as to satisfy the default. Any money the injured party receives from the disposition of the property above the amount owed belongs to the defaulting party.

EXAMPLE:

Should the Buyer in any way default upon his obligation under this agreement, the Seller shall be at full liberty, at any time thereafter, to resell the _____(property)_____, either by public auction or by private contract, and the expenses attending thereto shall be borne by the Buyer, but any excess in the price obtained shall belong to the Buyer.

As discussed and exemplified in Chapter 11, Remedies, the parties may specify liquidated damages, or include a limitation of damages clause. Any cost incurred in proceeding against the breaching party may be specified as being the breaching party's obligation.

EXAMPLE:

All costs, including reasonable attorney's fees, resulting from any dispute or controversy arising out of or under this Agreement shall be borne by _____.

Choice of Law

As a rule, contracts specify the state law that will govern its provisions and application.

EXAMPLE:

This Agreement shall be construed in accordance with and governed in all respects by the law of the State of _____.

Arbitration

Nowadays, to avoid the time and expense of judicial litigation for problems arising out of a contract, many parties include an arbitration clause by which the parties agree to submit disputes to an arbitrator instead of to the courts.

EXAMPLE:

All disputes, differences, and controversies arising under and in connection with this Agreement shall be settled and finally determined by arbitration according to the rules of the American Arbitration Association now in force or hereafter adopted.

Submission to Jurisdiction

Many contracts specify that the parties agree to submit to the jurisdiction of a particular court.

EXAMPLE:

The parties hereto agree that, in the case of any dispute or controversy arising under or out of this Agreement, to submit to the jurisdiction of the courts of the State of _____ for a settlement of said dispute or controversy.

Many contracts contain what is known as a *cognovit* provision, or a *confession of judgment*, whereby one party agrees to have the other party, in the case of a dispute, hire an attorney to represent and plead the alleged breaching party guilty. Many states do not favor these clauses, although they have been upheld by the U.S. Supreme Court, and so each jurisdiction should be researched to determine the appropriateness of such clauses.

Signatures

The final part of every contract is the signature of the parties. The signatures are usually introduced by the standard phrase: "IN WITNESS WHEREOF, the parties hereto, have hereunder signed this Agreement the day last above written." Following this introductory phrase, the parties sign above their typewritten names. If any of the parties is signing in a representative capacity, the full name of the organization should appear along with the signatory's name and title indicating the authority to sign the contract. If the party is a corporation, occasionally the corporate seal may be affixed as well.

CHAPTER SUMMARY

There are three preliminary rules of drafting a well-written contract:

1. Be conversant with the parties' wishes.
2. Use a checklist of clauses and topics incident to the subject matter involved.
3. Use several sample contracts to establish the format.

Most important in drafting a contractual agreement, be extremely precise in the choice of words. Do not be afraid to draft long clauses; precision requires words of limitation that may appear long-winded but that in fact create precision. For instance, the words "my house" are not nearly as precise as "my house located in Sunapee, New Hampshire," nor is that as precise as giving an exact street address or legal description. Laypersons confuse "lengthy" with "precise." Never be afraid of being wordy if the words create precision and avoid confusion. However, always scrutinize each clause you intend to use to make sure that it serves a useful purpose. Never insert a meaningless clause simply because it appears in a sample format.

After you have drafted a contract, go back over it to interpret what you have written, just as opposing counsel will do. Determine exactly what has been stated in each clause, whether anything has been left out, how each clause affects each party, whether the words are capable of multiple interpretations, and whether it truly reflects the parties' intent. If you are satisfied with what has been written, you now have a sample contract for your next assignment.

EXERCISES

1. Draft an employment contract for yourself as a paralegal working for the firm of Pratt & Chase, a partnership of 25 attorneys working in your town. The contract is for a two-year period.
2. Go to the library and find two more sales contracts. Compare them to the samples in the Appendix. How would you use these contracts to create a new model for your own use?
3. What clauses would you include in a complex Antenuptial Agreement? Why?
4. Analyze the following draft of a contract:

Marketing Agreement

This document will outline the agreed to understanding between __(Credit Union)__ and __(Group)__; or any client of associate relationships presented to Credit Union and accepted in the membership of said Credit Union.

The Group will present said Credit Union with individuals and employer institutions that may wish to become members of Credit Union and become eligible to participate in said Credit Union benefits. It is understood by the management of said Credit Union that the Group is a life and health organization.

It is the intention of the Group to offer its insurance products to these marketed organizations, and any individuals within these organizations on a voluntary basis. The Credit Union may not enter into an agreement with any competing organization as it pertains to any group marketed by the Group, its clients or any of its associate organizations. The Credit Union will not impose any administrative fees to be paid by the Group on this block of premium production. The Credit Union may not directly compete against the Group.

The Credit Union will remit premiums to the selected insurance carriers from the Credit Union accounts of any individual who chooses to participate in said life and health plans provided proper documentation is presented to said Credit Union in a timely manner.

It is also understood that the Group will be responsible to provide said Credit Union members with sales and service and be accountable to the Board of Directors of the Credit Union as it pertains to their practices. Should the Group not sufficiently provide service to, or engage in unethical practices, the Credit Union may require that the Group be presented to the Board of the Credit Union to state its case. Should said inquiry result in the desire not to have the Group represent the Credit Union, this agreement can be terminated within 90 days, providing that the following items are enacted at the point of said termination:

The Group will secure an agreement with a properly bonded "third party administrator" that will assume the responsibility of collecting insurance premiums marketed by the Group or any of its clients and/or associate organizations, from the Credit Union in the form of a list bill.

The Credit Union will be given the option of keeping said Group marketed individuals in its membership with written request during said 90-day transition period, and may continue to provide benefits to said members. However, the Credit Union may not introduce a competitive insurance organization to this block of members. Should the Board of the Credit Union impose this clause, the Group will not represent to any Credit Union member that we are being sponsored by, or have any involvement with, the Credit Union.

The Credit Union will remit said insurance premiums to the "third party administrator" of the Group's choice, and will impose no administrative charge to either the Group or the third party administrator for this fee. The Credit Union will continue to provide the Group with any documentation pertaining to policy service on this block of business.

This Agreement between the Credit Union and the Group governs that block of business that is marketed by the Group.

There will be another Agreement that will govern premiums that were not introduced to the Credit Union and the Group.

_____

The Credit Union

_____

The Group

Date: _____
Witness: _____
Witness: _____

Cases for Analysis

The following two decisions have been included to underscore the problems that may be associated with drafting a contract. Walsh v. Nelson concerns interpretation of a lease agreement, and American Express Travel Related Services, Inc., v. Weppler discusses contract construction.

Walsh v. Nelson
622 N.W.2d 499 (Iowa Sup. 2001)

This is a declaratory judgment action to determine the parties' rights under a commercial lease.

I. Background Facts and Proceedings

In July 1997, plaintiff James Walsh, Jr. brought a declaratory judgment action against Donna and Verner Nelson (the Nelsons) to determine his right, as tenant, to terminate an eighteen-year commercial lease prior to the end of the lease term. The final lease, signed in 1985, was the product of four drafts and nearly eighteen months of negotiations between Walsh and the Nelsons. The negotiations concerned the amount of rent, the length of the lease, and issues involved in financing the Nelsons' restoration of the building and Walsh's eligibility for an historic building tax credit.

The lease provision in dispute is paragraph 35, titled "Modification of Term." The paragraph provides:

> This lease is terminable at tenants['] option if, *at the end of the first six year term, but not sooner,* any of the members of the Clark, Butler, Walsh & McGivern law firm are deceased or permanently retired from practice of law or are disabled. A determination of what constitutes disability for purposes of this paragraph shall be made solely by the tenant. Tenant shall give landlord 30 days notice of any intent to terminate pursuant to the provisions of this paragraph. (Emphasis added.)

Walsh did not attempt to terminate the lease until June 1996, nearly five years after the end of the first six-year term. Two of Walsh's partners had retired. The Nelsons, however, refused to let Walsh out of the lease, so he filed this action, contending that the language highlighted above permitted him to terminate the lease at any time after the first six years. The Nelsons argued in the district court, and urge on appeal, that the language gave Walsh only one "out"—at the end of the first six-year term, but not after.

The Nelsons also filed a counterclaim alleging that Walsh owed $51,224.85 in unpaid rent under paragraph 30 of the lease. Paragraph 30(a) set the rent for the first six years. From July 1991 until December 1994, the parties argued about the proper method for recalculating this base rent. In December 1994, they agreed that Walsh would pay $9.40 per square foot for rent up to that point in time, and would continue to pay $9.40 per square foot until the next scheduled rent adjustment on July 1, 1996, the beginning of the lease's twelfth year. The parties failed to recalculate the base rent at the beginning of the twelfth year, and Walsh continued to pay $9.40 per square foot. At trial Walsh argued that after July 1, 1996 he paid too much; the Nelsons insisted he paid too little.

The district court, after considering the evidence tendered by each party, concluded that the lease gave Walsh only one opportunity to terminate before the end of the eighteen-year term. In the court's words, "the language of paragraph 35 is clear and unambiguous." The court also found that Walsh overpaid rent in the sum of $7226.34.

Walsh appealed, and we transferred the case to the court of appeals. That court reversed in part and affirmed in part. It first determined, contrary to the district court, that the termination provision of the contract was ambiguous as a matter of law. It then resolved the ambiguity in Walsh's favor and affirmed his judgment against the Nelsons for excess rental payments.

The Nelsons sought, and this court granted, further review. They claim that once the court of appeals determined the disputed lease term was ambiguous, it engaged in an improper de novo review of the record to determine the parties' intent. They also contend the court of appeals incorrectly calculated the amount of rent owed by Walsh. We shall consider the arguments in turn.

II.   Scope of Review [Omitted]

III.   Issues on Appeal

A.   Lease Interpretation

The main thrust of the Nelsons' argument is that the court of appeals disregarded the applicable standard of review when it substituted its judgment for the trial court's on the question of whether paragraph 35 of the lease is ambiguous. Walsh counters that because the language of paragraph 35 is ambiguous as a matter of law, the court of appeals' use of extrinsic evidence to reverse the district court's judgment for the Nelsons was proper. Fundamental rules guide our consideration of these competing theories.

1.   Applicable Rules

Because leases are contracts as well as conveyances of property, ordinary contract principles apply. Dickson v. Hubbell Realty Co., 567 N.W.2d 427, 430 (Iowa 1997). Where, as here, the dispute centers on the meaning of certain lease terms, we engage in the process of *interpretation*, rather than *construction*. See Fausel v. JRJ Enters., Inc., 603 N.W.2d 612, 618 (Iowa 1999) (interpretation is process of determining meaning of contract terms while construction is process of determining legal effect of such terms).

The primary goal of contract interpretation is to determine the parties' intentions at the time they executed the contract. See Hartig Drug Co., 602 N.W.2d at 797. Interpretation involves a two-step process. First, from the words chosen, a court must determine "what meanings are reasonably possible." Restatement (Second) of Contracts §202 cmt. a, at 87 (1981). In so doing, the court determines whether a disputed term is ambiguous. A term is not ambiguous merely because the parties disagree about its meaning. *Hartig Drug Co.*, 602 N.W.2d at 797. A term is ambiguous if, "after all pertinent rules of interpretation have been considered," "a genuine uncertainty exists concerning which of two reasonable interpretations is proper." Id.

Once an ambiguity is identified, the court must then "choose among possible meanings." Restatement (Second) of Contracts §202 cmt. a, at 87. If the resolution of ambiguous language involves extrinsic evidence, a question of interpretation arises which is reserved for the trier of fact. *Fausel*, 603 N.W.2d at 618.

As the foregoing discussion reveals, rules of interpretation are "used both to determine what meanings [of disputed terms] are reasonably possible as well as to choose among two reasonable meanings." *Hartig Drug Co.*, 602 N.W.2d at 797 (*citing* Restatement (Second) of Contracts §202 cmt. a, at 87). Put another way, the disputed language and the parties' conduct must be interpreted "in the light of all the circumstances" regardless of whether the language is ambiguous. *Fausel*, 603 N.W.2d at 618.

This idea is expressed in Restatement (Second) of Contracts section 212 comment b:

> Any determination of meaning or ambiguity should only be made in the light of the relevant evidence of the situation and relations of the parties, the subject matter of the transaction, preliminary negotiations and statements made therein, usages of trade, and the course of dealing between the parties. But after the transaction had been shown in all its length and breadth, *the words of an integrated agreement remain the most important evidence of intention.* (Emphasis added.) (Citations omitted.)

In short, although other evidence may aid the process of interpretation, the words of the contract remain the key to determining whether the lease terms are ambiguous.

2.   Analysis

Applying these principles to the case before us, we are convinced from the words of the contract as well as the surrounding circumstances that the meaning of paragraph 35 is ambiguous as a matter of law. It is evident from the contract language that Walsh had an option to terminate the lease at some point after the first six years but before the end of the eighteen-year term. The language "at the end" suggests that the option to terminate would occur at a specific time. The next phrase, "but not sooner," makes clear that Walsh could not terminate the lease during the first six years.

The difficulty arises in determining if "at the end ... but not sooner" means at midnight on July 1, 1991 or at some other time during or near the end of the sixth year or, as Walsh suggests, anytime thereafter. The nature of the conditions for termination — retirement, death or disability of a law partner — suggests a reasonable need for flexibility. Such events are not within Walsh's control. If the "end of the sixth year" must be precisely determined, it could be urged that the provision gives Walsh such a limited time to exercise his options as to make it meaningless. See Am. Soil Processing, Inc. v. Iowa Comprehensive Petroleum Underground Storage Tank Fund Bd., 586 N.W.2d 325, 334 (Iowa 1998) (because agreements interpreted as a whole, interpretation that gives meaning to all terms preferred to one rendering a part unreasonable).

The circumstances surrounding Walsh's and Nelsons' agreement further support a finding of ambiguity. The context in which the lease was negotiated and signed is evidenced by multiple draft leases, correspondence between the parties concerning the lease, and each party's testimony. Each draft contained a provision allowing Walsh some option for early termination. Walsh expressed concern over the length of the lease in a letter to Nelsons' architect, a concern which Donna Nelson confirmed at trial. The letter states, in part:

> It has also been suggested that a 15 year lease is enough for historic buildings. If that is true perhaps we could work out a 15 year lease arrangement that provided us with appropriate "escape hatches" and provided you with adequate notice of our intentions so that while it would be a 15 year lease it could be flexible enough to look and act like a 5 year lease.

Walsh's claim of ambiguity is further supported by a letter to the Nelsons in which he directly addressed an earlier version of paragraph 35. He stated that he was concerned that "it was too lenient in terms of not continuing for the whole 16 years" and that the IRS would question its suitability for favorable tax treatment. Walsh went on to state that "at any rate, it shouldn't affect you one way or the other," citing his understanding that the Nelsons were not concerned with the length of the lease beyond the five to six years needed for financing.

Donna Nelson countered Walsh's recollection of events by indicating that she needed a long-term lease to secure financing. While she produced no documents to support this contention, she testified that her finance company insisted on a long-term lease because she could not develop a project of this size on the basis of short-term leases.

Based on this evidence of conflicting expectations, we are convinced — as was the court of appeals — that the district court erred as a matter of law when it determined paragraph 35 was unambiguous. We are further convinced, however, that the court of appeals erred when it leaped to the second step of contract interpretation — choosing among possible meanings for the ambiguous terms. Reweighing the evidence, it found that the facts supported Walsh's interpretation. In making this finding, it exceeded the limits of its appellate review. See 5 Am. Jur. 2d *Appellate Review* §662, at 337 (1995) ("Generally speaking, except in review of cases in equity, or matters of constitutional law, an appellate court does not reweigh the evidence presented in the court below.").

We must, therefore, vacate the decision of the court of appeals, reverse the decision of the district court, and remand to allow the district court, as the trier of fact, to interpret the contract anew based on the record already made. See *Fausel*, 603 N.W.2d at 618 ("When the meaning of an agreement depends on extrinsic evidence, a question of interpretation is left for the trier of fact. . . ."); see also 17A Am. Jur. 2d *Contracts* §339, at 346 (1991) ("If the language in a contract is ambiguous, evidence may be admitted as to the intent of the parties, *and the determination of the parties' intent is a question of fact*." (Emphasis added.)).

Because the district court will be interpreting the contract on remand, we turn to the disputed issue of rent calculation under the terms of the lease.

B.   Rent Dispute

The Nelsons claim that both the court of appeals and the district court erred as a matter of law in determining that Walsh overpaid rent in the sum of $7226.34. The disputed figure rests on a calculation of $9.04 per square foot from July 1996 until the time Walsh filed this action. The Nelsons contend that the district court erroneously calculated the base rent under paragraph 30(b), and failed to calculate the Consumer Price Index (CPI) adjustment according to paragraph 30(c), errors the court of appeals repeated on appeal.

The thrust of Nelsons' claim is that, while the court of appeals acknowledged that paragraph 30(c) called for a rent increase at the beginning of the twelfth year based on the CPI, it found the Nelsons presented no evidence of the CPI for January 1996. It therefore affirmed the district court's calculations. Nelsons claim such a finding is not supported by the record. We agree.

Paragraph 30(d) details how rent shall be calculated after the set payments for the lease's first six years. It provides that the base rent must be recalculated at the end of the eleventh lease year to "reflect the average rate of the building excluding the athletic club" according to paragraph 30(b). The district court correctly calculated the base rent according to plaintiff's exhibit 36, titled "Rent Roll-River Plaza — 1996." This figure remains the base rent for the remainder of the lease. But in addition, starting on July 1, 1996 (the beginning of the twelfth lease year) the rent was to be increased according to a CPI adjustment provided in paragraph 30(c).

Contrary to the court of appeals' finding, the record does present evidence from which to determine the appropriate CPI adjustment. Defendant's Exhibit F, although misnumbered, shows that the CPI increase at the beginning of the twelfth lease year was 8.2%. The record reveals no objection by Walsh to this evidence. Thus, on remand, the district court should consider this evidence as it applies to the rent calculation under paragraph 30 to determine the proper rent for the twelfth lease year and thereafter.

For the reasons stated above, we vacate the decision of the court of appeals, reverse the district court and remand the case for further proceedings consistent with this opinion.

Questions

1.   How does the court differentiate between contract interpretation and contract construction?
2.   What is the alleged ambiguity in this contract?
3.   Why was this case remanded?

American Express Travel Related Services, Inc. v. Weppler
2003 Conn. Super. LEXIS 115

This is an action instituted by the plaintiff, American Express Travel Related Services, Inc., against the defendant, Jay Weppler, claiming money damages for the failure to pay amounts due from the purchase of commodities and services made under a credit agreement. The matter was tried to the court on September 11, 2002 and post-trial briefs were filed by the parties. The plaintiff's brief was filed on September 25, 2002 and the defendant's brief was filed on October 7, 2002. After consideration of the evidence and the issues as presented, the court enters a verdict in favor of the defendant.

The dispositive facts of this matter are undisputed. As part of a solicitation by the plaintiff, the defendant signed an application requesting the plaintiff to issue two credit cards, to himself and another employee of UNICO, Inc. The defendant was the president and employee of the company UNICO, Inc. The court finds on the basis of the defendant's testimony that the amounts sought by the plaintiff were for charges incurred by the defendant for the benefit of UNICO. Neither the plaintiff nor UNICO paid for the charges at issue which total $42,315.39.

The terms and conditions for the use of this card were contained in an "Agreement Between Corporate Cardmember and American Express Travel Related Services Company, Inc." The plaintiff relies on the following provisions in this agreement to support its claim against the defendant:

> You, as the Corporate Cardmember, are solely and personally liable to us for all Charges made in connection with Corporate Card issued to you. The company is not responsible to us for payment of such Charges. You should notify us immediately of any change in your billing address. Valid business expenses charged to the Corporate Card will be reimbursable by the company under the Company's expense reimbursement procedures applicable to you. This agreement has no effect on such procedures or your right to reimbursement by the Company.
>
> No other person is permitted to use this Corporate Card for charges, for identification, or any other reasons. We will look to you for payment of all Charges made with the Corporate Card issued to you, even if you have let someone else use the Corporate Card or relinquished physical possession of the Corporate Card.

The defendant, on the other hand, relies on a later provision of the agreement to support his defense that he is not personally liable for the charges. This provision is contained in what appears to be an addendum or a rider to the primary agreement:

> The Corporate Cardmember will be solely liable for all Charges on the Corporate Card Account except that the Company will be responsible to Amexco for Charges which benefitted the Company directly or indirectly and for which the Company has not reimbursed the Cardmember; and for any charges centrally billed to the Company.

In summary, one provision of the agreement indicates that "Cardmember" is solely responsible for all charges on the account and the company is not responsible for any of the payments, whereas another provision indicates that the company will be responsible for payments for those unreimbursed charges that are incurred for the benefit of the company. The courts agree with the defendant's position regarding the interpretation of this agreement. The plaintiff's view that the defendant is primarily and solely liable for the charges is rejected because it would construe the agreement in a manner which would make the later provision superfluous and meaningless.

The court finds that the latter language relied on by the defendant qualifies the earlier provisions of the Agreement so that the defendant was made responsible for charges on the card for his personal benefit; and the company, UNICO, was made responsible for charges on the card for UNICO's benefit for which UNICO failed to reimburse the defendant. This construction of the contract is the most reasonable interpretation of these provisions which appear facially inconsistent. The agreement consists of form documents created by the plaintiff, and the law is established that an ambiguity such as the one presented here must be construed against the drafter. Hartford Electric Applicators of Thermalux, Inc. v. Alden, 169 Conn. 177, 182, 363 A.2d 135 (1975) ("When there is ambiguity, we must construe contractual terms against the drafter").

Therefore, for the foregoing reasons, judgment shall enter in favor of the defendant, Jay Weppler, and against the plaintiff, American Express Travel Related Services, Inc.

So ordered.

Questions

1. What are the terms of the conflicting provisions of the contract in question?
2. Why is the contract construed against the drafter?
3. What could have been done to avoid this problem of interpretation when the agreement was drafted?

APPENDIX A

Sample Contracts

Antenuptial Agreement (Simple Form)
Consulting Agreement
Employment Contract (Simple Form)
Employment Contract
Equipment Lease Agreement
General Partnership Agreement (Simple Form)
Limited Partnership Agreement
Real Estate Lease
Retainer Agreement
Shareholders Agreement
Subscription Agreement (Limited Partnership)
Work for Hire Agreement

Antenuptial Agreement (Simple Form)

Agreement entered into this _____ day of _____, 20 _____, by and between _____ and _____.

Whereas the parties agree to enter into the marriage relationship and hereafter live together as husband and wife,

NOW THEREFORE, in consideration of the marriage to be entered into by the parties they do hereby agree to the following:

1.   That all manner of property hereafter acquired or accumulated by them, or either of them, shall be held in joint or equal ownership.

2.   That each of the parties hereby grants, bargains, sells and conveys to the other an undivided one-half interest in all the property, real and personal, which he or she now owns, for the purpose and with the intent of vesting in both parties the joint ownership of all property at this date owned in severalty by either of them.

3.   In case of the death of one of the above mentioned parties, all said property shall, subject to the claims of creditors, vest absolutely in the survivor.

4.   That in the case of divorce of the above mentioned parties, all rights to property shall be equally divided between them pursuant to the terms of this Agreement.

IN WITNESS WHEREOF, the parties have executed this Agreement the day and year first above written.

_____

_____

Consulting Agreement

This Agreement is made this _____ day of _____, 20 ____, by and between _____ (X), an individual residing at _____, and _____ (Consultant), an individual doing business at _____.

Consultant agrees to act as a financial consultant to X with respect to the development, production, and promotion of _____. Consultant shall meet and consult with X as the need arises, and shall perform services consistent with the duties of a financial consultant.

As full compensation for the services to be performed by Consultant, X agrees to pay Consultant 10% (ten percent) of the gross profit derived from the sale and marketing of the _____. The determination of the amount of said profit shall be made by an independent accounting firm should the parties to this Agreement disagree as to the amount of said profit.

Reasonable expenses actually incurred by Consultant incidental to the services performed shall be paid by X once money is received from the sale and marketing of _____ upon submission of a voucher of expenses to X by Consultant.

Should X willfully fail to develop, produce, and promote the _____, X shall pay Consultant reasonable compensation for work actually performed by Consultant on X's behalf.

Consultant, with respect to the services performed under this Agreement, is acting as an independent contractor and is not an employee. Consultant may be employed by other persons, firms, associations, or corporations not in conflict of interest with the terms of this Agreement during the term of this Agreement. Any employee or other personnel engaged by Consultant not for the express and direct benefit of X shall be under the exclusive direction and control of Consultant.

This Agreement is effective from the date above written and shall terminate when X no longer has any rights or title, direct or indirect, in _____.

This Agreement constitutes the entire Agreement between the parties relating to the subject matter contained in it, and supersedes all prior and contemporaneous representations, agreements, or understandings between the parties. No amendment or supplement of this Agreement shall be binding unless executed in writing by the parties. No waiver of one provision of this Agreement shall constitute a waiver of any other provision, nor shall any one waiver constitute a continuing waiver. No waiver shall be binding unless executed in writing by the party against whom the waiver is asserted.

This Agreement shall be construed and interpreted in accordance with, and governed by, the laws of the State of _____.

This Agreement may not be assigned by either party without the written consent of the other party.

If any provision of this Agreement is held by a court of competent jurisdiction to be invalid or unenforceable, the remainder of this Agreement shall remain in full force and shall in no way be impaired.

Any controversy or claim arising out of or relating to this Agreement, or the breach thereof, shall be settled by arbitration in accordance with the Rules of the American Arbitration Association, and judgment upon the award rendered by the arbitrator(s) may be entered in any court having jurisdiction thereof.

IN WITNESS WHEREOF, the parties have executed this Agreement on the date first above written.

X _____

_____
Consultant

Employment Contract (Simple Form)

Agreement made this _____ day of _____, 20 _____, between X of _____ (X), and Y, Inc., a corporation with principal offices at _____ (Y).

WHEREAS X is a well-known _____; and

WHEREAS Y is a well-known _____; and

WHEREAS Y wishes to make use of X's expertise; and

WHEREAS X accepts such employment,

NOW THEREFORE, in consideration of the mutual covenants herein contained, and other good and valuable consideration, it is agreed between the parties as follows:

1. Services

X shall provide Y with (describe specific services).

2. Compensation

Y shall compensate X in the sum of _____ Dollars ($ _____), payable in equal weekly installments.

3. No Further Obligations

All obligations with respect to the services to be performed by X shall cease upon _____.

4. Arbitration

Any controversy or claim arising out of or relating to this Agreement shall be settled by arbitration in the City of _____ in accordance with the Rules of the American Arbitration Association, and judgment upon the award rendered in such arbitration may be entered in any court having jurisdiction thereof.

5. Controlling Law

This Agreement shall be governed by the laws of the State of _____.

6. Entire Agreement

This Agreement expresses the whole Agreement between the parties hereto as of the date hereof. This Agreement shall not be changed, modified, terminated, or discharged except by a writing signed by the parties hereto.

7. Binding Effect

This Agreement shall be binding upon and ensure to the benefit of each of the parties hereto, their heirs, executors, administrators, or assigns.

IN WITNESS WHEREOF, the parties have executed this Agreement on the day and year first above written.

X _____

Y _____

By:_____

Employment Contract

Agreement dated _____, 20 _____, between X, Inc., a _____ corporation with principal offices at _____ (the Company), and Y, residing at _____ (Y).

WITNESSETH:

WHEREAS the Company is doing business as a _____ and wishes to avail itself of the services of Y; and

WHEREAS Y has substantial expertise and experience and is willing to perform services for the Company, all in accordance with the following terms and conditions;

NOW THEREFORE, it is agreed as follows:

1. Employment

The Company agrees to hire Y, and Y agrees to serve the Company as its _____, with overall responsibility for _____.

2. Term

The term of employment shall be for one (1) year, commencing on the _____ day of _____, 20 ____, and ending as of the _____ day of _____, 20 _____ (Termination Date). Sixty (60) days' written notice prior to the Termination Date must be given by either party if the intention of either party is not to negotiate a new Agreement.

3. Compensation

As compensation for the services hereunder, the Company shall pay Y a total of (i) _____ Dollars ($ _____), payable in equal semimonthly installments; and (ii) a sum equal to one-half (1/2) percent of the gross sales volume accrued during the term of this Agreement, payable in one installment not later than thirty (30) days after the Termination Date.

4. Records

The Company shall cause to be made available to Y, at least monthly, whatever figures are necessary to ascertain accurate records as to the gross volume of the Company.

5. Expenses

Y shall be reimbursed for all reasonable and necessary expenses incurred hereunder, upon the presentation of paid vouchers, or, as the case may be, the Company shall pay directly such expenses as may be determined in advance.

6. Travel

The Company agrees that it will consent to send Y at least twice yearly to the _____ in connection with the furtherance of his employment, and it is further agreed that Y will make two trips to _____ on behalf of the Company to introduce the Company's line.

7. Incidental Services

The Company shall make available to Y the various incidental services he deems necessary to successfully carry out his employment.

8. Responsibility

The Company intends that Y assume full responsibility for _____, maintaining a climate of maximum creativity within the Company's _____. It therefore agrees that Y shall be given substantial decision-making power in hiring and firing of all personnel.

9. Benefits

Y shall be entitled to receive those benefits which the Company provides for its key executive employees, including, without limiting the foregoing, hospitalization, major medical insurance, and disability insurance.

10. Life Insurance

The Company shall provide Y with life insurance of at least _____ Dollars ($ _____) during the term of this Agreement. Said insurance shall be convertible upon termination.

11. Vacation

Y shall be entitled to at least three (3) weeks' paid vacation per year, it being understood that said vacation shall be taken at times which are mutually convenient for the parties and shall not be taken consecutively.

12. Representation and Warranty

Y represents and warrants that he is not bound by any covenant or agreement, oral or written, which prohibits him from entering into this employment and from being employed by the Company.

13. Restrictive Covenant

Y will, during the term of this Agreement, devote his entire time, attention, and energies to the performance of his duties hereunder, and he will not directly or indirectly, either as a shareholder, owner, partner, director, officer, employee, consultant, or otherwise, be engaged in or concerned with any other commercial duties or pursuits whatsoever.

It is expressly understood and agreed that:

(a) All inventions, patents, copyrights, developments, and ideas and concepts developed by Y during the course of his employment under this Agreement shall be the exclusive property of the Company.

(b) Y shall have no right, either during or after employment under this Agreement, to use, sell, copy, transfer, or otherwise make use of, either for himself or for any other person other than the Company, any of the confidential information and trade secrets of the Company.

14. Illness or Disability

If during the term of this Agreement, Y becomes disabled or incapacitated by reason of illness, physical or mental, as to be unable to perform all duties to be performed hereunder, he shall be paid by the Company his salary during the first three (3) months of such disability, less a sum equal to the amount received by him under a disability insurance policy. In addition, Y shall be entitled to a sum equal to one-half (1/2) percent of the gross volume of the sales during said disability. Said sum shall be paid at the end of the three (3) months.

15. Severability

If any one or more of the provisions hereof shall be held to be invalid, illegal or unenforceable, the validity and enforceability of its other provisions shall not be affected thereby.

16. Notice

Any notice required to be given pursuant to the provisions of this Agreement shall be in writing and mailed prepaid to the parties at the addresses given at the beginning of this Agreement, by certified or registered mail, return receipt requested.

17. Arbitration

Any controversy or claim arising out of or relating to this Agreement, or the breach thereof, shall be settled by arbitration in the city _____ in accordance with the Rules of the American Arbitration Association, and the judgment upon the award rendered by the arbitrator(s) may be entered in any court having jurisdiction thereof.

18. Governing Law

This Agreement shall be governed by and construed according to the laws of the State of _____.

19. Modification

This Agreement contains the entire understanding of the parties and may not be amended, supplemented, or discharged except by an instrument in writing signed by the parties hereto.

20. Binding Effect

This Agreement shall enure to the benefit of and shall be binding upon the Company, its successors, and assigns.

IN WITNESS WHEREOF, the parties hereto have executed this Agreement as of the date and year first above written.

_____

Company

By:_____

_____

Y

Equipment Lease Agreement

Agreement made the _____ day of _____, 20 _____, between _____, Inc., with a place of business at _____ (Lessor) and _____ Inc. with a place of business at _____ (Lessee).

1. The Lessor hereby leases to the Lessee, and the Lessee hereby hires from the Lessor, subject to the terms and conditions hereinafter set forth, the following property consisting of _____ (Equipment).

2. The lease is for _____ months commencing on the _____ day of _____, 20 ____, and ending on the _____ day of _____, 20 _____. The total rent for said initial term is the sum of _____ Dollars ($ _____), plus sales tax payable as follows:

(a) _____ Dollars ($ _____) upon execution of the lease.

(b) The balance of the total rental of _____ Dollars ($ _____), i.e., $ _____, shall then be payable in equal monthly installments from and after payment of the initial $ _____ rental sum plus sales tax.

3. Lessee shall have the right and option to renew the said lease by the giving of ninety (90) days' advance written notice to the Lessor of its intention to do so. Lessee may renew the Lease for _____ terms (_____) of two (2) years each, with each term being renewed by the giving of the same ninety (90) days' advance written notice. Rent for each remaining term shall be as follows:

4. This Agreement creates a lease only of the Equipment and not a sale thereof or the creation of a security interest therein. The Lessor shall remain the sole owner of the Equipment, and nothing contained herein or the payment of rent hereunder shall enable the Lessee to acquire any right, title, or other interest in or to the Equipment.

5. Lessor agrees that neither it nor any principal or shareholder therein, nor any affiliate or entity in any way associated with Lessor, shall compete with the Lessee at any time during the term of this lease.

6. Upon delivery of the said Equipment by Lessor or Lessee, Lessor warrants that the same shall be in proper working order and fit for the purpose for which it was intended. The monthly rental payments by Lessee to Lessor specifically include consideration for Lessor's maintenance of the said Equipment, and during the term of the lease it shall be Lessor's responsibility to repair and maintain the same at Lessor's expense, provided that such repair and maintenance is for ordinary wear and tear.

7. (a) The Lessor shall pay all use taxes, personal property taxes, or other direct taxes imposed on the ownership, possession, use or operation of the Equipment or levied against or based upon the amount of rent to be paid hereunder or assessed in connection with the execution, filing, or recording of this Agreement. The term "direct taxes" as used herein shall include all taxes (except income taxes), charges, and fees imposed by any federal, state, or local authority.

(b) The Lessee assumes all responsibility and the cost and expense as may be required for the lawful operation of the Equipment. All certificates of title or registration applicable to the Equipment shall be applied for, issued, and maintained in the name of the Lessor, as Owner.

(c) The Lessee shall observe all safety rules and other requirements of regulatory bodies having jurisdiction and shall pay all fines and similar charges that may be duly and lawfully imposed or assessed by reason of the Lessee's failure to comply with the rules, regulations, and orders of regulatory bodies having jurisdiction.

(d) If the taxes, fines, or other charges, with the exception of permit fees, that the Lessee is responsible for under this Paragraph are levied, assessed, charged, or imposed against the Lessor, it shall notify the Lessee in writing of such fact. The Lessor shall have the option, but not the obligation, to pay any such tax, fine, or other charge, whether levied, assessed, charged, or imposed against Lessor or Lessee. In the event such payment is made by the Lessor, the Lessee shall reimburse the Lessor within seven (7) days after receipt of an invoice therefor, and the failure to make such reimbursement when due shall be deemed a default within Paragraph 8 hereof.

8. The Equipment shall be delivered by the Lessor to the Lessee at the Lessee's place of business. The Lessor shall have the right to place and maintain conspicuously on the side of the Equipment during the term of this lease the inscription _____, indicating the name of the owner of the Equipment or words of similar import in the event the lease is assigned by the Lessor, and the Lessee shall not remove, obscure, deface, or obliterate such inscription or suffer any other person to do so. Lessor can only assign its rights in this lease subject to all of the terms and conditions and rights that vest in Lessee herein.

9. The Lessee shall pay all operating expenses. The Lessee shall at all times provide suitable storage facilities and appropriate services for the Equipment including washing, polishing, cleaning, inspection, and storage space, and at the end or other expiration of this lease shall return the Equipment to the Lessor at the address above set forth in operating order and in the same condition and state of repair as it was at the date of delivery, ordinary wear and tear excepted.

10. The Lessee hereby indemnifies and shall hold the Lessor harmless from all loss and damage the Lessor may sustain or suffer by reason of the death of or injury to the person or property of any third person as a result, in whole or in part, of the use or maintenance of the Equipment during the term of this lease; and the Lessee shall procure, at the Lessee's cost and expense, a policy or policies of insurance issued by a company satisfactory to the Lessor with premiums prepaid thereon, insuring the Lessee against the risks and hazards specified above to the extent of the full value of the equipment and in the minimum amounts of _____ Dollars ($ _____) personal injury liability, together with fire and casualty loss. Such policy or policies shall name the Lessor as loss payee and not as co-insured. It shall be delivered to the Lessor simultaneously and prior to the delivery of the Equipment leased hereunder and shall carry an endorsement by the insurer either upon the policy or policies issued by

it or by an independent instrument that the Lessor will receive thirty (30) days' written notice of the alteration or cancellation of such policy or policies. Failure by the Lessee to procure such insurance shall not affect the Lessee's obligations under the terms, covenants and conditions of this lease, and the loss, damage to, or destruction of the Equipment shall not terminate the lease nor, except to the extent that the Lessor is actually compensated by insurance paid for by the Lessee, as herein provided, relieve the Lessee from the Lessee's liability hereunder. Should the Lessee fail to procure or maintain the insurance provided for herein, the Lessor shall have the option, but not the obligation, to do so for the account of the Lessee. In the event payment for procuring or maintaining such insurance is made by the Lessor, the Lessee shall reimburse the Lessor within seven (7) days after receipt of an invoice therefor, and the failure to make such reimbursement when due shall be deemed a default hereof.

11. The Lessee shall employ and have absolute control and supervision over the operator or operators of the Equipment and will not permit any person to operate the equipment unless such person is licensed.

12. In the event the Lessee fails to perform any material term, condition, and covenant contained herein in the manner and at the time or times required hereunder, including, but not limited to, the payment in full of any rental payment or the reimbursement of the Lessor for a disbursement made hereunder, or if any proceedings in bankruptcy or insolvency are instituted by or against the Lessee, or if reorganization of the Lessee is sought under any statute, state or federal, or a receiver appointed for the goods and chattels of the Lessee, or the Lessee makes an assignment for the benefit of creditors or makes an attempt to sell, secrete, convert, or remove the Equipment, or if any distress, execution, or attachment be levied thereon, or the Equipment be encumbered in any way, or if, at any time, in the Lessor's judgment (reasonable standard is applicable), its rights in the Equipment shall be threatened or rendered insecure, the Lessee shall be deemed to be in default under this Agreement, and the Lessor shall have the right to exercise either of the following remedies:

(a) To declare the balance of the rental payable hereunder to be due and payable whereupon the same shall become immediately due and payable, but Lessor shall use due diligence to release all Equipment covered in this Agreement; or

(b) To retake and retain the Equipment with demand on five (5) days' notice or legal process free of all right of the Lessee, in which case the Lessee authorizes the Lessor or its agents to enter upon any premises where the Equipment may be found for the purpose of repossessing the same, and the Lessee specifically waives any right of action it might otherwise have arising out of such entry and repossession, whereupon all rights of the Lessee in the Equipment shall terminate immediately. If the Lessor retakes possession of the Equipment and at the time of such retaking there shall be in, upon, or attached to the Equipment any property, goods, or things of value belonging to the Lessee or in the custody or under the control of the Lessee, the Lessor is hereby authorized to take possession of such property, goods, or things of value and hold the same for the Lessee or place such property, goods, or things of value in public storage for the account of and at the expense of the Lessee.

13. Forbearance on the part of the Lessor to exercise any right or remedy available hereunder upon the Lessee's breach of the terms, conditions, and covenants of this Agreement, or the Lessor's failure to demand the punctual performance thereof, shall not be deemed a waiver:

    (a) Of such right or remedy;
    (b) Of the requirement of punctual performance; or
    (c) Of any subsequent breach or default on the part of the Lessee.

14. Neither this lease nor the Lessee's rights hereunder shall be assignable by the Lessee without any prior written consent of the Lessor, which consent shall not unreasonably be withheld.

15. The Lessee shall make available to the Lessor the Equipment for inspection as required by any governmental agency. The Equipment shall be available on forty-eight (48) hours' notice to Lessee at Lessee's place of business. Failure to make the Equipment available for said inspection shall be a substantial breach of this Agreement, and the operator will surrender the Equipment immediately upon notice.

16. The Lessee shall be responsible for obeying all laws, rules, and regulation of the State of _____ and the City of _____, and any other governmental authority having jurisdiction. Further, any fines or penalties imposed because of the Lessee's failure to obey such laws, rules, and regulations shall be the sole responsibility of the Lessee, and paid for solely by him or her.

17. The Lessee acknowledges that he or she is not in the employ of the Lessor but is an independent contractor responsible for his or her own acts. Further, the Lessee shall maintain records and be responsible for the payment of any and all taxes and fees as previously mentioned. Any substantial violation by the Lessee to this Agreement shall render the entire Agreement in default, and the Lessee will be responsible to return the Lessor's Equipment within forty-eight (48) hours.

18. All notification from one party to the other as set forth in this Agreement must be in writing and forwarded by certified mail at the address specified on the first page of this lease.

19. Lessor represents that the permits and/or licenses it has in order to effectuate the said terms and conditions of this lease are in good standing and that the Lessor has the authority to enter into the within lease. Lessor further warrants that there are no assessments, taxes, levies, charges, encumbrances, liens, security interests, or other rights presently outstanding that would in any way interfere with or affect Lessee's intended operation.

20. The parties hereto specifically agree that Lessee has the right to cure any default provided the same occurred within ten (10) days' of written notification by Lessor to Lessee of the same.

21. This instrument contains the entire Agreement between the parties and shall be binding on their respective heirs, executors, administrators,

legal representatives, successors, and assigns. This Agreement may not be amended or altered except by a writing signed by both parties.

22. This Agreement is subject to the laws of the State of _____.

IN WITNESS WHEREOF, the parties hereto have executed this Agreement on the day and year first above written.

_____
Lessor
By:_____

_____
Lessee
By:_____

General Partnership Agreement (Simple Form)

This Agreement, made this _____ day of _____, 20 ____, by and between _____, First Party, _____, Second Party, and _____, Third Party, witnesses as follows:

That the said parties hereby agree to become partners in the business of _____ under the firm name of _____ for the term of _____ years from the date hereof, upon the terms and conditions hereinafter stated:

1. That the business shall be carried on at _____ or at any other place that may hereinafter be mutually agreed upon by the parties.

2. That proper books of account shall be kept, and therein shall be duly entered, from time to time, all dealings, transactions, matters, and things whatsoever in or relating to the said business; and each party shall have full and free access thereto at all times, but shall not remove the same from the premises.

3. That the capital requirements for carrying on the said business shall be borne by said partners in equal parts, and the said capital, and all such stock, implements, and utensils in trade purchased out of the partnership funds as well as the gains and profits of the said business, shall belong to the said partners in equal parts.

4. That each partner shall be at full liberty to have _____ Dollars ($ _____) monthly for his own private use, on account, but not in excess of his presumptive share of the profits, so long as the said business shall be found profitable.

5. That an account of the stock, implements, and utensils belonging to the said business, and of the book debts and capital, shall be taken, and a statement of the affairs of the said partnership to be made yearly, to be computed from the date hereof, when the sums drawn by each partner during the preceding year shall be charged to his share of the profits of said business; but, if, at the end of any one year of the said partnership it shall be found to be unprofitable, the said partnership shall thereupon be dissolved, unless it shall be occasioned by some accidental circumstances.

6. That each party shall sign duplicate copies of each of such statement of affairs, and shall retain one of these for his own use, and another copy shall be written in one of the partnership books, and likewise signed by each of them.

7. That all partners of the same class shall have identical and equal rights except as herein otherwise provided: _____. Each partner shall devote his best efforts to the firm and its clients and customers, and each partner shall follow the rules and policies of the business that may from time to time be adopted by them.

8. That no partner may be added to the firm unless each additional partner be unanimously elected by all of the existing partners.

9. That the death of a partner shall terminate all his interest in the partnership, its property and assets. The continuing firm shall pay in cash to his estate, or to his nominee, the following amounts to be paid in installments at the times indicated: _____.

10. That any partner may voluntarily withdraw from the partnership at any time on notice of thirty (30) days to the other partners. At the expiration of the thirty (30) day period, or sooner if mutually agreed upon, the withdrawal shall become effective. The withdrawing partner's rights, title, and interests in the firm shall be extinguished in consideration of the payments to him by the continuing firm on the following basis: _____.

11. That any partner may be expelled from the firm for cause when it has been determined by a vote of the partners that any of the following reasons for his expulsion exist:

    (a) Loss of professional license;
    (b) Professional misconduct;
    (c) Insolvency;
    (d) Breach of any of the provisions of this Agreement;
    (e) Any other reason that the other partners unanimously agree warrants expulsion.

Upon expulsion, the expelled partner shall have no further rights, duties, or interest in the firm or any of its assets, records, or affairs. He shall immediately remove himself and his personal effects from the firm's offices. A partner so expelled shall be entitled to the same rights, the same payments by, and be subject to the same duties to the continuing firm as if he were voluntarily withdrawing from the firm.

12. That all provisions of this Agreement shall be construed and shall be enforced according to the laws of the State of _____.

13. That any controversy or claim arising out of or relating to any provision of this Agreement or the breach thereof shall be settled by arbitration in accordance with the Rules then in effect of the American Arbitration Association, to the extent consistent with the laws of the State of _____.

14. That no partner may assign or in any way transfer his interest in the partnership, all such rights and interests being personal to him.

15. That the invalidity or unenforceability of any one provision of this Agreement shall not affect the validity or enforceability of the other provisions of this Agreement.

IN WITNESS WHEREOF, the parties hereto have executed this Agreement on the day and year first above written.

_____
First Party

_____
Second Party

_____
Third Party

Limited Partnership Agreement

Agreement of Limited Partnership (the Agreement) of _____ (the Partnership), entered into this _____ day of _____, 20 _____, by and among _____, Inc. (the General Partner), and each of the persons executing this Agreement (the Limited Partners). Reference herein to "Partners" without designation to "General" or "Limited" includes the General Partner and the Limited Partners except as the context otherwise requires.

PREAMBLE

The Partnership has been organized as a Limited Partnership under the laws of the State of _____ for the purpose of _____.

NOW THEREFORE, in consideration of the promises and mutual covenants hereinafter set forth, the parties hereto do hereby agree and certify as follows:

Article I

Definitions

1.0 Whenever used in this Agreement, the following terms shall have the following meanings:

(a) "Affiliate" shall mean (i) any person directly or indirectly controlling, controlled by or under common control with another person, (ii) a person owning or controlling ten percent (10%) or more of the outstanding voting securities of such other person, (iii) any officer, director, or partner of such person, and (iv) if such other person is an officer, director, or partner, any company for which such person acts in any such capacity.

(b) "Capital Account" means with respect to each partner his Capital Contribution, to the extent contributed, *increased* by: (i) any additional contributions and (ii) his distributive share of Partnership income and gains, and *decreased* by (i) cash and the Partnership's adjusted basis of property distributed to him and (ii) his distributive share of Partnership losses.

(c) "Capital Contribution" means the capital contributed by the General Partner and Limited Partners as set forth in Article IV and as hereinafter contributed to the Partnership by any Partner.

(d) "Cash Flow" means cash form revenues to the Partnership available for distribution after payment of Partnership expenses, advances made by the General Partner and others, and after amounts reserved to meet future contingencies as determined in the sole discretion of the General Partner.

(e) "Closing Date" shall mean the date the offering of the Units is complete.

(f) "Code" shall mean the Internal Revenue Code of 1986, as amended.

(g) "General Partner's Contribution" shall mean the contribution of the General Partner pursuant to Section 4.2 hereof.

(h) "Interest" shall mean the individual interest of each Partner in the Partnership.

(i) "Limited Partners' Contributions" shall mean the aggregate cash contributors of the Limited Partners.

(j) "Original Limited Partner" shall mean the Limited Partner who executed the original Certificate of Limited Partnership of the Partnership.

(k) "P&L Percentage" shall mean the percent of Profits and Losses allocable to each Partner.

(l) "Partnership Property" or "Partnership Properties" shall mean all interest, properties and rights of any type owner or leased by the Partnership.

(m) "Permitted Transfer" shall mean a transfer by a Limited Partner of his Interest to: (i) his spouse, unless legally separated, child, parent, or grand-parent; or (ii) a corporation, partnership, trust or other entity, fifty-one percent (51%) of the equity interest of which is owned by such Limited Partner individually or with any of the persons specified in subparagraph (i) hereof.

(n) "Profits and Losses" shall mean the Profits and Losses of the Partnership as reflected on its Federal Partnership Income Tax Return.

(o) "Unit" shall have the same meaning ascribed to such a term in a Private Placement Memorandum of the Partnership and any and all amendments thereto (the Memorandum).

Article II

Organization

2.1 *Addition of Limited Partners.* Promptly following the execution hereof, the General Partner, on behalf of the Partnership, shall execute or cause to be executed an Amended Certificate of Limited Partnership reflecting the withdrawal of the Original Limited Partner and the addition of the Limited Partners to the Partnership and all such other certificates and documents conforming thereto and shall do all such filing, recording, publishing and other acts, as may be necessary or appropriate from time to time to comply with all requirements for the operation of a limited partnership in the State of _____ and all other jurisdictions where the Partnership shall desire to conduct business. The General Partner shall cause the Partnership to comply with all requirements for the qualification of the Partnership as a Limited Partnership (of a partnership in which the Limited Partners have limited liability) in any jurisdiction before the Partnership shall conduct any business in such jurisdiction.

2.2 *Withdrawal of Original Limited Partner.* Upon execution of this Agreement by the Limited Partners, the Original Limited Partner shall withdraw as a Limited Partner and acknowledge that he shall have no interest in the Partnership as a Limited Partner and no rights to any of the profits, losses, or other distributions of the Partnership from the inception of the Partnership.

2.3 *Partnership Name.* The name of the Partnership shall be _____.

2.4 *Purposes of the Partnership.* The purposes of the Partnership shall be to acquire, own and continue to acquire, own, lease, and deal in or with real and personal property, securities, and investments of every kind, nature and description consistent with the best interests of the Limited Partners.

2.5 *Principal Place of Business and Address.* The principal office of the Partnership shall be maintained as _____, or such other address or addresses as the General Partner may designate by notice to Limited Partners. The Partnership may maintain offices and other facilities from time to time at such locations, within or without the State of _____, as may be deemed necessary or advisable by the General Partner.

2.6 *Term.* The Partnership shall dissolve on December 31, 20_____, unless sooner terminated or dissolved under the provisions of this Agreement.

Article III

Operation of the Partnership

3.1 *Powers and Duties of the General Partner.* Except as set forth in Section 3.2 below, the General Partner (if more than one, then such General Partners shall act by any one of the General Partners with the consent of the majority of the General Partners) shall have full, exclusive, and irrevocable authority to manage and control the Partnership and the Partnership Properties, and to do all reasonable and prudent things on behalf of the Partnership including, but not limited to, the following:

(a) To acquire any additional Partnership Property, including all property ancillary thereto and obtain rights to enable the Partnership to renovate, construct, alter, equip, staff, operate, manage, lease, maintain, and promote the Partnership Property, as well as all of the equipment and any other personal or mixed property connected therewith, including, but not limited to, the financial arrangements, development, improvement, maintenance, exchange, trade, or sale of such Property (including, but not limited to, all real or personal property connected therewith) at such price or amount for cash, securities, or other property, and upon such terms as it deems in its absolute discretion to be in the best interests of the Partnership;

(b) To sell or otherwise dispose of the Partnership Property and terminate the Partnership;

(c) To borrow or lend money for operation and/or for any other Partnership purpose, and, if security is required therefor, to mortgage or subject to any other security device any portion of the Partnership Property, to obtain replacements of any mortgage or other security device, and to prepay, in whole or in part, refinance, increase, modify, consolidate, or extend any mortgage or other security device, all of the foregoing at such terms and in such amounts as it deems, in its absolute discretion, to be in the best interest of the Partnership;

(d) To enter into contracts with various contractors and subcontractors for the maintenance of the Property;

(e) To enter into employment or other agreements to provide for the management and operation of the Partnership Property (including the right to contract with affiliates of the General Partner on behalf of the Partnership for such services);

(f) To place record title to, or the right to use, Partnership assets in the name or names of a nominee or nominees for any purpose convenient or beneficial to the Partnership;

(g) To acquire and enter into any contract of insurance that the General Partner deems necessary and proper for the protection of the Partnership, for the conservation of its assets, or for any other purpose, convenience, or benefit of the Partnership;

(h) To employ persons in the operation and management of the Partnership business, including, but not limited to, supervisory managing agents, consultants, insurance brokers, and loan brokers on such terms and for such compensation as the General Partner shall determine;

(i) To employ attorneys and accountants to represent the Partnership in connection with Partnership business;

(j) To pay or not pay rentals and other payments to lessors;

(k) To sell, trade, release, surrender, or abandon any or all of the Partnership Properties, or any portion thereof, or other assets of the Partnership;

(l) To settle claims, prosecute, defend, and settle and handle all matters with governmental agencies;

(m) To purchase, acquire, lease, construct, and/or operate equipment and any other type of tangible, real or personal property;

(n) To open bank accounts for the Partnership and to designate and change signatories on such accounts;

(o) To invest the funds of the Partnership in certificates of deposit or evidence of debt of the United States of America or any state, or commonwealth thereof, or any instrumentality of either;

(p) To enter into any other partnership agreement whether general or limited, or any joint venture or other similar agreement; and

(q) Without in any manner being limited by the foregoing, to execute any and all other agreements, conveyances, and other documents and to take any and all other action which the General Partner in its sole discretion deems to be necessary, useful, or convenient in connection with the Partnership Properties or business.

In accomplishing all of the foregoing, the General Partner may, in its sole discretion, but shall not be required to, use its own personnel, properties, and equipment, and may employ on a temporary or continuing basis outside accountants, attorneys, brokers, consultants, and others on such terms as he deems advisable. Any or all of the Partnership Properties, and any or all of the other Partnership assets, may be held from time to time, at the General Partner's sole discretion, in the name of the General Partner, the Partnership, or one or more nominees; and any and all of the powers of the General Partner may be exercised from time to time, at the General Partner's sole discretion, in the name of any one or more of the foregoing.

3.2 *Limitations of the Powers of the General Partner.* The General Partner may not act for or bind the Partnership without the prior consent of the holders of fifty-one percent (51%) of Limited Partnership Interests on the following matters:

(i) Amendment of the Partnership Agreement (except as set forth in Section 12.4); or

(ii) A change in the general character or nature of the Partnership's business.

3.3 *Powers and Liabilities of the Limited Partners.* No Limited Partner shall have any personal liability or obligation for any liability or obligation of the Partnership or be required to lend or advance funds to the Partnership for any purpose. No Limited Partner shall be responsible for the obligations of any other Limited Partner. No Limited Partner shall take part in the management of the business of the Partnership or transact any business for the Partnership, and no Limited Partner shall have power to sign for or bind the Partnership. No Limited Partner shall have a drawing account. No Limited Partner shall be entitled to the return of his capital contribution, except to the extent, if any, that distributions are made or deemed to be made to such Limited Partner otherwise than out of Profits pursuant to this Agreement. No Limited Partner shall receive any interest on his capital account. Upon the consent of fifty-one percent (51%) in interest of the Limited Partners, the Limited Partners shall have a right to call a meeting of the Partnership upon written notice to all of the Partners of the time, date, and place of such meeting. Upon the written request of twenty-five percent (25%) in interest of the nonaffiliated Limited Partners, the General Partner shall promptly call an informational meeting of the Partnership upon written notice to all of the Partners of the time, date, and place of such meeting.

3.4 *Exculpation and Indemnification of the General Partner.* (a) The Limited Partners recognize that there are substantial risks involved in the Partnership's business. The General Partner is willing to continue to serve as General Partner only because the Limited Partners hereby accept the speculative character of the Partnership business and the uncertainties and hazards which may be involved, and only because the Limited Partners hereby agree, that despite the broad authority granted to the General Partner by Section 3.1, the General Partner shall have no liability to the Partnership or to the Limited Partners because of the failure of the

General Partner to act as a prudent operator, or based upon errors in judgment, negligence, or other fault of the General Partner in connection with its management of the Partnership, so long as the General Partner is acting in good faith. Accordingly, the Limited Partners, for themselves, their heirs, distributees, legal representatives, successors, and assigns, covenant not to assert or attempt to assert any claim or liability as against the General Partner for any reason whatsoever except for gross negligence, fraud, bad faith, or willful misconduct in connection with the operation of the Partnership. It shall be deemed conclusively established that the General Partner is acting in good faith with respect to action taken by him on the advice of the independent accountants, legal counsel, or independent consultants of the partnership.

(b) In the event of any action, suit, or other legal proceeding, including arbitration, instituted or threatened against the General Partner or in which he (or if more than one, any of them) may be a party, whether such suit, action, or proceeding is brought on behalf of third parties or Limited Partners, individually or as a class, or in a derivative or representative capacity, the General Partner shall have the right to obtain legal counsel and other expert counsel at the expense of the Partnership and to defend or participate in any such suit, action, or proceeding at the expense of the Partnership, and he shall be reimbursed, indemnified against, and saved harmless by the Partnership for and with respect to any liabilities, costs, and expenses incurred in connection therewith. It is understood and agreed that the reimbursement and indemnification herein provided for shall include and extend to any suit, action, or proceeding based upon a claim of misrepresentation or omission to reveal any act of substance in any document pursuant to which the Limited Partnership Interests have been offered. It is expressly agreed that any claim of the nature referred to in the preceding sentences is and shall be subject to the provisions of this Subsection 3.4(b), other provisions of this Section, and other provisions of this Agreement relating to the nonliability, reimbursement, and indemnification of the General Partner. This Agreement is part of the consideration inducing the General Partner to accept the Limited Partners as members of the Partnership. The foregoing provisions for the indemnification and reimbursement of the General Partner shall apply in every case except in which it is affirmatively determined in any proceeding that the General Partner shall not be entitled to have indemnification or reimbursement by reason of his having been guilty of gross negligence, fraud, bad faith, or willful misconduct.

(c) Nothing herein shall be deemed to constitute a representation or warranty by the General Partner with respect to the title to or value of any Partnership Property or with respect to the existence or nonexistence of any contracts or other encumbrances with regard thereto, whether as against its own acts in the normal course of business or otherwise.

3.5 *Power of Attorney.* (a) Each Limited Partner by the execution of this Agreement does irrevocably constitute and appoint the General Partner or any one of them, if more than one, with full power of substitution, as his true and lawful attorney in his name, place, and stead to execute, acknowledge, deliver, file, and record all documents in connection with the Partnership, including but not limited to (i) the original Certificate of Limited Partnership and all amendments thereto required by law or the provisions of this Agreement, (ii) all certificates and other instruments necessary to qualify or continue the Partnership as a limited partnership or partnership wherein the Limited Partners have limited liability in the states or provinces where the partnership may be doing its business, (iii) all instruments necessary to effect a change or modification of the Partnership in accordance with this Agreement, (iv) all conveyances and other instruments necessary to effect the dissolution and termination of the Partnership, and (v) all election under the Internal Revenue Code governing the taxation of the Partnership. Each Limited Partner agrees to be bound by any representations of the attorney-in-fact under this power of attorney, and hereby ratifies and confirms all acts which the said attorney-in-fact may take as attorney-in-fact hereunder in all respects as though performed by the Limited Partner.

(b) The Power of attorney granted herein shall be deemed to be coupled with an interest and shall be irrevocable and survive the death of a Limited Partner. In the event of any conflict between this Agreement and any instruments filed by such attorney-in-fact pursuant to the power of attorney granted in this Section, this Agreement shall control, and no power granted herein shall be used to create any personal liabilities on the part of the Limited Partners.

(c) By virtue of the power of attorney granted herein, the General Partner, or any one of them, if more than one, shall execute the Certificate of Limited Partnership and any amendments thereto by listing all of the Limited Partners and executing any instrument with the signature of the General Partner(s) acting as attorney-in-fact for all of them. Each Limited Partner agrees to execute with acknowledgement of affidavit, if required, any further documents and writings which may be necessary to effectively grant the foregoing power of attorney to the General Partner(s).

Article IV

Capitalization and Capital Contribution

4.1 *Capitalization.* The total initial capital of the Partnership shall be a minimum of _____ ($ _____) and a maximum of _____ ($ _____), exclusive of any capital contribution by the General Partner.

4.2 *General Partner's Contribution.* The General Partner has contributed _____ ($ _____) in cash to the capital of the Partnership and will be reimbursed at Closing for amounts that he has expended on behalf of the Partnership prior to Closing.

4.3 *Limited Partner's Contribution.* Each Limited Partner has made the contribution of capital to the Partnership in the amount set forth on

Schedule A annexed hereto. Subscription for a Unit shall be made upon the execution hereof by the payment of ($ _____) in cash on subscription.

4.4 *Capital Accounts.* A separate Capital Account shall be maintained for each Partner and shall be credited with his Capital Contribution and his allocable share of all revenues, income, or gain and shall be debited with his allocable share of costs, expenses, deductions, and losses of the Partnership and any distributions made to him.

Article V

Fees and Compensation

In consideration of various services to be rendered to the Partnership by the General Partner, the General Partner will receive the compensation and fees as described in the Memorandum.

In furtherance of the provisions of Article III hereof, the General Partner may contract with any person, firm, or corporation (whether or not affiliated with the General Partner) for fair value and at reasonable competitive rates of compensation, for the performance of any and all services which may at any time be necessary, proper, convenient, or advisable to carry on the business of the Partnership.

Article VI

Distribution of Proceeds from Operations and Profit and Loss Allocations

6.1 *Distribution of Cash Flow.* Subject to the right of the General Partner to retain all or any portion of the annual cash flow for the anticipated needs of the Partnership, the net annual cash flow of the Partnership available for distribution from operations will be allocated ninety-nine percent (99%) to the Limited Partners (pro rata among them in the proportion that each Unit owned by a Limited Partner bears to the total number of Units owned by all Limited Partners) and one percent (1%) to the General Partner, until such time as the Limited Partners shall have received their capital contributions (Payout) and thereafter, fifty percent (50%) to the Limited Partners, pro rata, and fifty percent (50%) to the General Partner.

6.2 *Allocation of Profits and Losses.* Profits and losses of the Partnership from operation will be allocated ninety-nine percent (99%) to the Limited Partners (pro rata among them in proportion that each Unit owned by a Limited Partner bears to the total number of Units owned by all Limited

Partners) and one percent (1%) to the General Partner until Payout. After Payout, profits and losses will be allocated fifty percent (50%) to the Limited Partners, pro rata, and fifty percent (50%) to the General Partner.

6.3 *Allocation of Income for Certain Tax Purposes*. (a) Anything contained in this Agreement to the contrary notwithstanding, in the event an allocation of income in any calendar year pursuant to Section 6.2 above would cause the General Partner to have a positive Capital Account at the end of such year at a time when the Limited Partners have negative Capital Accounts, the amount of such income which would have been allocated to the General Partner pursuant to Section 6.2 in excess of the aggregate negative Capital Accounts of the Limited Partners shall instead be allocated to the Capital Accounts of the Limited Partners on a pro rata basis. For purposes of computing what a Partner's Capital Account would be at the end of a year, any cash available for distribution at such time which is intended to be distributed shall be deemed to have been distributed to such Partner on the last day of such year.

(b) Anything contained in this Agreement to the contrary notwithstanding, a Partner or Partners with deficit Capital Account balances resulting, in whole or in part, from an interest or other expense accrual, shall be allocated income resulting from the forgiveness of indebtedness of such deficit Capital Account balances no later than the time at which the accrual is reduced below the sum of such deficit Capital Account balances.

(c) If any Partner is, for income tax purposes, allocated additional income or denied a loss because of Section 6.3(b) above, a compensating allocation shall be made, for income tax purposes, at the first time such an allocation would be permissible thereunder.

Article VII

Allocation of Profits and Losses on a Sale or Other Taxable Disposition of Partnership Property

7.1 Any gain realized by the Partnership in connection with the sale or other taxable disposition of the Partnership Property shall be allocated to the Partners in the following order of priority:

(a) If any Partner has a negative Capital Account, any gain from the sale or other disposition of the Partnership Property shall be allocated to such Partners in the amount of their respective negative account balances, until the balance of each such Partner's Capital Account is equal to zero; and

(b) Any remaining gains shall be allocated ninety-nine percent (99%) to the Limited Partners, pro rata, and one percent (1%) to the General Partner until Payout, and thereafter fifty percent (50%) to the Limited Partners, pro rata, and fifty percent (50%) to the General Partner.

7.2 Any loss realized by the Partnership in connection with the sale or other taxable disposition of the Partnership Property shall be allocated to the Partners in the following order of priority:

(a) If any of the Partners has a positive Capital Account, any loss from the sale or other disposition of the Partnership Property shall be allocated to such Partners in the amount of their respective positive account balances, until the balance of each such Partner's Capital Account is equal to zero; and

(b) Any remaining losses shall be allocated to the Partners as set forth in Section 7.1(b) above.

7.3 It is the intention of the General Partner that the allocation set forth herein have "substantial economic effect" within the meaning of regulations promulgated under Internal Revenue Code Section 704. In the event such allocations are deemed by the Internal Revenue Service or the courts not to have substantial economic effect, the General Partner reserves the right to modify allocations of profits and losses, after consulting with counsel, to achieve substantial economic effect. Nothing herein shall be construed to require the General Partner to so modify the allocation as set forth herein.

Article VIII

Limited Partners' Covenants and Representation with Respect to Securities Act

8.1 *Investment Representations.* Each of the Limited Partners, by signing this Agreement, represents and warrants to the General Partner and to the Partnership that he (a) is acquiring his Interest in the Partnership for his own personal account for investment purposes only and without any intention of selling or distributing all or any part of the same; (b) has no reason to anticipate any change in personal circumstances, financial or otherwise, which would cause him to sell or distribute, or necessitate or require any sale or distribution of such Interest; (c) is familiar with the nature of and risks attending investments in securities and the particular financial, legal, and tax implications of the business to be conducted by the Partnership, and has determined on his own or on the basis of consultation with his own financial and tax advisors that the purchase of such Interest is consistent with his own investment objectives and income prospects; (d) has received a copy of the Private Placement Memorandum, to which a copy of this Agreement is attached as Exhibit A, and has had access to any and all information concerning the Partnership which he and his financial, tax, and legal advisors requested or considered necessary to make proper evaluation of this investment; (e) is aware that no trading market for Interests in the Partnership will exist at any time and that his Interest will at no time be freely transferable or be transferable with potential adverse tax consequences; and (f) is aware that there is a substantial risk that the federal partnership tax returns will be audited by the Internal Revenue Service and that, upon such audit, a part of the deductions allocated to the Limited Partners could be disallowed, thereby reducing the tax benefits of investing in the Partnership.

8.2 *Covenant Against Resale.* Each of the Limited Partners agrees hereby that he will, in no event, sell or distribute his Interest in the Partnership or any portion thereof unless, in the opinion of counsel to the Partnership, such Interest may be legally sold or distributed without registration under the Securities Act of 1933, as amended, or registration or qualification under then applicable state or federal statutes, or such Interest shall have been so registered or qualified and an appropriate prospectus shall then be in effect. *Notwithstanding the foregoing, no Limited Partner will be permitted to sell, distribute, or otherwise transfer his Interest in the Partnership or any portion thereof without the written consent of the General Partner (except as otherwise provided in Paragraph 9.1(b) below), the granting of which consent is in the absolute discretion of the General Partner.*

8.3 *Reliance on Private Offering Exemption.* Each of the Limited Partners represents and warrants hereby that he is fully aware that his Interest in the Partnership is being issued and sold to him by the Partnership in reliance upon the exemption provided for by Section 4(2) of the Securities Act of 1933, as amended, and Regulation D promulgated under such Act, and exemptions available under state securities laws, on the grounds that no public offering is involved, and upon the representations, warranties, and agreements set forth in this Article VIII.

Article IX

Transfer of Partnership Interests

9.1 *Limited Partnership Interest.* (a) No transfer of all or any part of a Limited Partner's Interest (including a transferee by death or operation of law and including a transferee in a Permitted Transfer) shall be admitted to the Partnership as a Limited Partner without the written consent of the General Partner, which consent may be withheld in the complete discretion of the General Partner. In no event shall the General Partner consent to the admission of the transferee as a Limited Partner unless the transferee executes this Agreement and such other instruments as may be required by law, or as the General Partner shall deem necessary or desirable to confirm the undertaking of such transferee to: (i) be bound by all the terms and provisions of this Agreement; and (ii) pay all reasonable expenses incurred by the Partnership in conjunction with the transfer, including, but not limited to, the cost of preparation, filing, and publishing such amendments to the Certificate as may be required by law of such other instruments as the General Partner may deem necessary and desirable.

A sale, assignment, or transfer of a Limited Partner's Interest will be recognized by the Partnership when it has received written notice of such sale or assignment, signed by both parties, containing the purchaser's or assignee's acceptance of the terms of the Partnership Agreement and a representation by the parties that the sale or assignment was lawful. Such sale or assignment will be recognized as of the date of such notice, except that if such date is more than thirty (30) days prior to the time of filing of such notice, such sale or assignment will be recognized as of the time the notice was filed with the Partnership. For purposes of allocating Profits and Losses, the assignee will be treated as having become a Limited Partner as of the date of which the sale, assignment, or transfer was recognized by the Partnership.

(b) Except for: (i) a Permitted Transfer and/or transfer by operation of law other than transfers in excess of the "forty percent (40%) limitation" (see subsection (c) below); or (ii) a transfer by gift, bequest, or inheritance, on Limited Partner may transfer all or any part of his Interest without first giving written notice of the proposed transfer to the General Partner (setting forth the terms thereof and the name and address of the proposed transferee) and obtaining the written consent of the General Partner to such transfer. Such consent shall be within the complete discretion of the General Partner and subject to such conditions, if any, as it shall determine.

(c) Anything else to the contrary contained herein notwithstanding:

(i) in any period of twelve (12) consecutive months, no transfer of an Interest may be made which would result in increasing the aggregate Profit and Loss Percentages of Partnership Interests previously transferred in such period above forty percent (40%). This limitation is herein referred to as the "forty percent (40%) limitation";

(ii) a Permitted Transfer is fully subject to the forty percent (40%) limitation;

(iii) subparagraph (i) hereof shall not apply to a transfer by gift, bequest, or inheritance, or a transfer to the Partnership, and for the purposes of the forty percent (40%) limitation, any such transfer shall not be treated as such;

(iv) if, after the forty percent (40%) limitation is reached in any consecutive twelve- (12-) month period, a transfer of a Partnership Interest would otherwise take place by operation of law (but not including any transfer referred to in subparagraph (iii) hereof), then such Partnership Interest shall be deemed sold by the transferor to the Partnership immediately prior to such transfer for a price equal to the fair market value of such interest on such date of transfer. The price shall be paid within ninety (90) days after the date of the sale out of the assets of the Partnership and the General Partner. If the Partnership and the transferor do not agree upon the fair market value of the Partnership Interest, then the purchase prices shall be determined in accordance with Section 9.3. The purchase price shall be paid by the Partnership out of its assets in cash within ten (10) days after such determination.

9.2 *Events Requiring Sale of Partnership Interest.* (a) The Interest of a Limited Partner shall be deemed offered for sale to a person designated by the General Partner upon the happening of any of the following events:

(i) a petition in bankruptcy having been filed by or against a Limited Partner and not discharged within ninety (90) days from the date of such filing; or

(ii) a receiver or committee having been appointed to manage a Limited Partner's property; or

(iii) a creditor of a Limited Partner having attached his Interest and such attachment not being discharged or vacated within ninety (90) days from the date it became effective.

The General Partner shall have ninety (90) days after the occurrence of any of the foregoing within which to accept such offer, designate such a purchaser (including the General Partner), and transmit written notice thereof to such Limited Partner. If the General Partner fails to make such designation within ninety (90) days as aforesaid, the offer shall be deemed withdrawn. The purchase price for such Interest shall be its appraised value as determined in accordance with Section 9.3. The purchaser shall pay over to the selling Limited Partner the purchase price in cash within ten (10) days after such determination. Upon payment of the purchase price to the selling Limited Partner, his Interest shall be deemed transferred to the aforesaid designated person.

(b) If any of the events described in Subsection 10.1(a)(v) should occur to the General Partner, or any one of them if more than one, and the Partnership shall not thereafter be dissolved but shall continue as a successor Limited Partnership with a successor General Partner, then upon the happening of any of such events the Interest of such General Partner shall be deemed offered for sale to the successor General Partner at its appraised value determined in accordance with Section 9.3 (except in the case of a voluntary withdrawal by a General Partner, in which event the value shall be determined by the withdrawing General Partner and the proposed successor General Partner, as selected by the withdrawing General Partner). The successor General Partner shall not become a General Partner of the Partnership until such former General Partner's Interest has been paid for in full in cash.

9.3 *Appraisal.* For the purpose of this Agreement, the appraised value of an Interest shall be the average of the values determined by three appraisers who are experts in evaluating property similar to the Partnership Property selected at the request of the General Partner. The appraisal made by such appraisers shall be binding and conclusive as between the selling Partner or Partners and the persons purchasing such Interest. The cost of such appraisal shall be borne equally by the selling and purchasing parties, and by each set of parties, among themselves, in proportion to their respective shares.

9.4 *Death, Bankruptcy, Incompetence, or Dissolution of a Limited Partner.* (a) Upon the death, bankruptcy, or legal incompetency of an individual

Limited Partner, his legally authorized personal representative shall have all of the rights of a Limited Partner for the purpose of settling or managing his estate, and shall have such power as the decedent, bankrupt, or incompetent possessed to make an assignment of his Interest in the Partnership in accordance with the terms hereof and to join with such assignee in making application to substitute such assignee as a Limited Partner.

(b) Upon bankruptcy, insolvency, dissolution, or other cessation to exist as a legal entity of any Limited Partner which is not an individual, the authorized representative of such entity shall have all of the rights of the Limited Partner for the purpose of effecting the orderly winding up and disposition of the business of such entity, and such power as such entity possessed to make an assignment of its Interest in the Partnership in accordance with the terms hereof and to join with such assignee in making application to substitute such assignee as a Limited Partner.

9.5 *Voluntary Withdrawal or Transfer by a General Partner.* (a) A General Partner may resign as General Partner at any time, but only upon compliance with the following procedures:

(i) The General Partner shall give notification to all Limited Partners that he proposes to withdraw and that he proposes that there be substituted in his place a person designated and described in such notification.

(ii) Enclosed with such notification shall be (a) an opinion of counsel to the Partnership that the proposed General Partner qualifies to serve as a General Partner under federal law, and (b) a certificate, duly executed by or on behalf of such proposed successor General Partner, to the effect that he is experienced in performing (or employs sufficient personnel who are experienced in performing) functions of the type then being performed by the resigning General Partner.

(iii) The consent of the remaining General Partner and the holders of at least fifty-one percent (51%) in interest of the Limited Partner shall be required for the appointment of the proposed successor General Partner pursuant to this Section 9.5(a). If the proposed successor General Partner shall not receive such consent within sixty (60) days after the date of the withdrawing General Partner's notification, then, at the sole option of the General Partner seeking to withdraw, the Partnership may be terminated and dissolved and its assets liquidated in accordance with Article VIII of this Agreement.

(iv) The General Partner who has withdrawn pursuant to this Section shall cooperate fully with the successor General Partner so that the responsibilities of such withdrawn General Partner may be transferred to such successor General Partner with as little disruption of the Partnership's business and affairs as is practicable.

(b) Except as part of a transfer to a successor General Partner pursuant to Section 9.5(a), the General Partner shall not have the right to retire or to transfer or assign his General Partner's Interest.

9.6 *Removal of a General Partner.* (a) A General Partner may be removed as General Partner only without his consent or the consent of the other General Partners only for cause upon the consent of 51% in Interest of the Limited Partners, such removal to be effective upon the service of written notice upon the General Partner to be removed by posting said notice in the United States mails. Upon such removal, the Partnership shall continue and the remaining General Partners shall continue the Partnership. If all the General Partners are removed, then the Partnership shall be dissolved unless 51% in Interest of the Limited Partners vote to continue the Partnership as a successor limited partnership and appoint a successor General Partner who (i) in the opinion of counsel to the Partnership qualifies to serve as General Partner under federal law, and (ii) agrees to purchase the Interest of the other General Partners in accordance with Sections 9.2(b) and 9.3 hereof.

(b) Any successor General Partner appointed by the Limited Partners to replace the General Partner shall, beginning on the effective date of such replacement, have the same rights and obligations under this Agreement as the General Partner would have had subsequent to such date if the General Partner continued to act as General Partner.

9.7 *Death, Retirement, Bankruptcy, Legal Incapacity, etc. of a General Partner.* Upon the death, retirement, or legal incapacity of a General Partner, or the filing by or against a General Partner of a petition in bankruptcy, the adjudication of the General Partner as a bankrupt, or the making by the General Partner of an assignment for the benefit of creditors, the remaining General Partners shall continue the Partnership unless all of the General Partners are subject to the foregoing events, in which case the Partnership shall terminate unless fifty-one percent (51%) in Interest of the Limited Partners (or one hundred percent (100%) in the case of the death, retirement, or insanity of a General Partner) vote to continue the Partnership as a successor Limited Partnership and appoint a successor General Partner, who (i) in the opinion of counsel to the Partnership qualifies to serve as General Partner under federal law, and (ii) agrees to purchase the Interest of the General Partner in accordance with Sections 9.2(b) and 9.3 hereof.

9.8 *Admission of a Successor General Partner.* The admission of a successor General Partner shall be effective only if the Interests of the Limited Partners shall not be affected by the admission of such successor General Partner.

9.9 *Liability and Rights of Replaced General Partner.* Any General Partner who shall be replaced as General Partner shall remain liable for his portion of any obligation and liabilities incurred by him as General Partner prior to the time such replacement shall have become effective, but he shall be free of any obligation or liability incurred on account of the activities of the Partnership from and after such time. Such replacement shall not affect any rights of the General Partner which shall mature prior to the effective date of such replacement.

Article X

Dissolution, Liquidation, and Termination

10.1 *Dissolution.* (a) The Partnership shall be dissolved upon the earliest of:

(i) the expiration of its term as provided in this Agreement;

(ii) the sale of all or substantially all of the Partnership Property;

(iii) the occurrence of any event which causes the dissolution of a limited partnership under the laws of the State of _____;

(iv) the written election of Limited Partners owning eighty percent (80%) of the Limited Partnership Interests; or

(v) except as otherwise provided herein, the withdrawal or removal of, the death, retirement, or legal incapacity of, or the filing of a petition in bankruptcy, the adjudication as a bankrupt, or the making of an assignment for the benefit of creditors by the last remaining General Partner, unless fifty-one percent (51%) in Interest of the Limited Partners (or one hundred percent (100%) in the case of the death, retirement, or legal incapacity of the General Partner) appoint a successor General Partner and vote to continue the Partnership as a successor Limited Partnership.

(b) The Partnership shall not be dissolved upon the death of a Limited Partner.

(c) In the event of such dissolution, the assets of the Partnership shall be liquidated and the proceeds thereof distributed in accordance with Section 7.1 hereof.

10.2 *Liquidating Trustee.* Upon the dissolution of the Partnership, the liquidating trustee (which shall be those General Partners which are not subject to any of the events set forth in subparagraph 10.1(a)(v), or, in the event all General Partners are subject to such events, a trustee appointed by the Limited Partners representing a majority in interest of the profit and loss percentages of the Limited Partners), shall proceed diligently to wind up the affairs of the Partnership and distribute its assets in accordance with Section 7.1 hereof. All saleable assets of the Partnership may be sold in connection with any liquidation at public or private sale, at such price and upon such terms as the liquidating trustee in his sole discretion may deem advisable. Any Partner and any partnership, corporation, or other firm in which any Partner is in any way interested may purchase assets at such sale. Distributions of Partnership assets may be made in cash or in kind, in the sole and absolute discretion of the liquidating trustee. The liquidating trustee shall make a proper accounting to each Limited Partner of his Capital Account and of the net profit or loss of the Partnership from the date of the last previous accounting to the date of dissolution.

Article XI

Accounting, Records, Reports, and Taxes

11.1 *Fiscal Year and Reports.* The fiscal year of the Partnership for both accounting and federal income tax purposes shall be the calendar year. At all times during the continuance of the Partnership, the General Partner shall keep or cause to be kept full and faithful books of account in which shall be entered fully and accurately each transaction of the Partnership. All of the books of account shall be open to the inspection and examination of the Limited Partners or their duly authorized representatives upon reasonable notice during normal business hours. Annual financial statement of the Partnership shall be transmitted by the General Partner to each Limited Partner. The General Partner shall further transmit to each Limited Partner annually, within a reasonable time after the end of each calendar year (but in no event later than seventy-five (75) days after the end of the calendar year or as soon as practicable thereafter), a report setting forth the Limited Partner's share of the Partnership's Profits or Losses for each such year, and such Limited Partner's allocation of cash receipts. The reports and statements delivered in accordance herewith may be changed from time to time to cure errors or omission and to give effect to any retroactive costs or adjustments. All costs and expenses incurred in connection with such reports and statements shall constitute expenses of Partnership operation.

11.2 *Income Tax Elections.* (a) No elections shall be made by the Partnership, the General Partner or any Limited Partner to be excluded from the application of the provision of Subchapter K of Chapter I of Subtitle A of the Code or from the application of any similar provisions of state tax laws.

(b) All other elections required or permitted under the Code shall be made by the General Partner in such manner as will, in the opinion of the Partnership's accountants, be most advantageous to a majority in Interest of the Limited Partners.

11.3 *Tax Matters Partner.* The General Partner shall be designated the tax matters partner of the Partnership pursuant to Section 6231(7) of the Internal Revenue Code.

Article XII

General

12.1 *Notices.* Any notice, communication, or consent required or permitted to be given by any provision of this Agreement shall, except as otherwise expressly provided herein, be deemed to have been sufficiently given or served for any purpose only if in writing, delivered personally, or sent by registered mail, postage and charges prepaid, or by standard pre-paid telegram.

12.2 *Further Assurances*. Each of the Partners agrees hereafter to exe-cute, acknowledge, deliver, file, record, and publish such further certifi-cates, instruments, agreements and other documents and to take all such further actions as may be required by law or deemed by the General Partner to be necessary or useful in furtherance of the Partnership's pur-poses and the objectives and intentions underlying this Agreement and not inconsistent with the terms hereof.

12.3 *Banking*. All funds shall be deposited in the Partnership's name in such checking accounts as shall be designated by the General Partner. All withdrawals therefrom shall be made upon checks signed by the General Partner.

12.4 *Amendment of Certificate of Limited Partnership*. The General Part-ners may amend the Certificate of Limited Partnership and the Agreement when any one of the following events occur: (a) there is a change in the name of the Partnership, or the amount of character of the contribution of any Limited Partner; (b) a person is substituted as a Limited Partner; or (c) an additional Limited Partner is admitted.

12.5 *Voting Rights of Limited Partners*. This Agreement may not be mod-ified or amended in any manner whatsoever except with the written consent of the General Partner and the written consent of Limited Partners whose Profit and Loss percentages at that time are sixty-six and two-thirds percent (66^2/$_3$%) of the total Profit and Loss Percentages of all Limited Partners.

12.6 *Meetings*. Any vote of the Limited Partners on any matters upon which Limited Partners are entitled to vote hereunder may be accom-plished at a meeting of Limited Partners called for such purposes by the General Partner or by the nonpromoted, nonaffiliated Limited Partners whose Profit and Loss Percentages at that time exceed fifty-one percent (51%) of the total Profit and Loss Percentages of all such Limited Partners, upon not less than ten (10) days' prior notice or, in lieu of a meeting, by the written consent of the required percentage of Limited Partners.

12.7 *Access to Records*. The Limited Partners and their designated repre-sentatives shall be permitted access to all records of the Partnership at the office of the Partnership during reasonable hours. The Partnership records shall include a list of the names and addresses of the Limited Partners.

12.8 *Miscellaneous*. (a) Except as otherwise expressly provided herein, the headings in this Agreement are inserted for convenience of reference only and are in no way intended to describe, interpret, define, or limit the scope, extent, or intent of this Agreement or any provision hereof.

(b) Every provision of this Agreement is intended to be severable. If any term or provision hereof is illegal or invalid for any reason whatsoever, such illegality or invalidity shall not affect the validity of the remainder of this Agreement.

(c) This Agreement, and the application and interpretation hereof, shall be governed exclusively by the terms hereof and by the laws of the State of _____.

(d) The rights and remedies provided by this Agreement are cumulative, and the use of any one right or remedy by any party shall not preclude or waive its right to pursue any or all other remedies. Such rights and remedies are given in addition to any other rights the parties may have by law, statute, ordinance, or otherwise.

(e) This Agreement may be executed in any number of counterparts with the same effect as if the parties had all signed the same instrument. All counterparts shall be construed together and shall constitute one Agreement. Limited Partners may become parties to this Agreement by executing and delivering to the General Partner a signature page hereto in the form approved by the General Partner.

(f) Time is of the essence hereof.

(g) Each and all of the covenants, terms, provisions and agreements therein contained shall be binding upon and inure to the benefit of each party and, to the extent permitted by this Agreement, the respective successors and assigns of the parties.

(h) No person, firm, or corporation dealing with the Partnership shall be required to inquire into the authority of the General Partner to take any action or to make any decision.

(i) This instrument incorporates the entire agreement between the parties hereto, regardless of anything to the contrary contained in any certificate of limited partnership or other instrument or notice purporting to summarize the terms hereof, whether or not the same shall be recorded or published.

(j) The General Partner shall prepare or cause to be prepared and shall file on or before the due date (or any extension thereof) any federal, state, or local tax returns required to be filed by the Partnership. The General Partner shall cause the Partnership to pay any taxes payable by the Partnership.

IN WITNESS WHEREOF, the undersigned have executed this Agreement as of the day and year first above written.

_____
General Partner

_____
Limited Partner

Real Estate Lease

Agreement made this _____ day of _____, 20_____, between X, Inc., a _____ corporation (Lessor), and _____, an individual (Lessee).

The Lessor hereby devises and lets to the Lessee the premises known as _____ for the term of one year, commencing on the _____ day of _____, 20_____, and ending on the _____ day of _____, 20_____, for which the Lessee agrees to pay the Lessor, at his place of business, promptly on the first day of each month, in advance, a monthly rental of _____ Dollars ($ _____). On the failure of the Lessee to pay said rent when due, all further rent under this contract shall immediately become due and payable, and the Lessor has the right, at his option, to declare this lease void, cancel the same, enter and take possession of the premises.

It is further agreed that:

(Indicate all specific covenants the parties agree to, for example:
Allocation of cost of repairs
Maintenance of premises
Right of Lessor to enter
Subletting
Destruction of property due to fire or act of God
Alteration of premises
Payment of damages due to negligence
Notice to quit
Security deposit)

All of the aforementioned agreements, covenants, and conditions shall apply to and be binding upon the parties hereto, their heirs, executors, administrators, and assigns.

IN WITNESS WHEREOF, the parties hereto have set their hands and seals this _____ day of _____, 20 _____.

_____
Lessor

By:_____

_____
Lessee

Retainer Agreement

Names and Addresses of the Parties

THIS AGREEMENT FOR LEGAL SERVICES by and between

Client, and

, Esq.

Attorney

constitutes a binding legal contract and should be reviewed carefully.

Nature of the Services to Be Rendered

The Client authorizes the Attorney to take any steps which, in the sole discretion of the Attorney, are deemed necessary or appropriate to protect Client's interest in the matter.

Amount of the Advance Retainer, If Any, and What It Is Intended to Cover

In order for Attorney to begin the representation, Client agrees to pay Attorney and Attorney has agreed to accept a retainer payment of $_____. This retainer payment does not necessarily represent the amount of the overall fee which may be incurred by virtue of Attorney's services. This retainer constitutes a Minimum Fee and is non-refundable. This retainer shall entitle Client to up to _____ hours of Attorney's time. The amount of Attorney's eventual fee will be based upon Attorney's regular schedule of established hourly time charges, along with any out-of-pocket disbursements (such as court costs, messenger services, transcripts of proceedings, long distance telephone calls, faxes, process service fees, mileage, deposition and court transcripts, and excess postage) which are incurred on Client's behalf.

The Client further understands that the hourly rates apply to all time expanded relative to the Client's matter, including but not limited to, office meetings and conferences, telephone calls and conferences, either placed by or placed to the Client, or otherwise made or had on the Client's behalf or relative to the Client's matter, preparation, review and revision of correspondence, pleadings, motions, disclosure demands and responses, affidavits and affirmations, or any other documents, memoranda, or papers relative to the Client's matter, legal research, court appearances, conferences, file review, preparation time, travel time, and any other time expended on behalf of or in connection with the Client's matter.

Client's Right to Cancel This Agreement

Client has the absolute right to cancel this agreement at any time. Should Client exercise this right, Client will be charged only the fee expenses (time charges and disbursements) incurred within that period that exceeds the amount of the Earned Retainer, based upon the hourly rates set forth in the Retainer Agreement.

Client's Duty to Pay Fee

Client agrees to pay Attorney amounts that may be due not later than ten (10) days from the date that Attorney shall submit a bill to Client for the same. If an amount due is not paid within ten (10) days after Attorney's statement to Client for the amount due, interest at the rate of 10% per annum shall be added to the balance due to Attorney.

Hourly Fee

Client shall be charged an hourly fee of $_____. In addition, Client is responsible for direct payment or reimbursement of Attorney for disbursements advanced on Client's behalf.

The hourly fee set forth in this Retainer Agreement shall remain in effect throughout this period of Attorney's representation for the matter set forth in this Retainer Agreement, unless changed by mutual consent of Client and Attorney, in which event any modification of this Retainer Agreement will be reduced to writing and signed by Attorney and Client.

Frequency of Billing

Client will be billed periodically, generally each month but in no event less frequently than 60 days. Included in the bill will be a detailed explanation of the services rendered and the disbursements incurred in connection with Client's matter. Upon receipt of the bill Client is expected to review the bill and promptly bring to Attorney's attention any objection Client may have to the bill. While Attorney strives to keep perfectly accurate time records, Attorney recognizes the possibility of human error and Attorney shall discuss with Client any objection raised with respect to the bill. Client will not be charged for time expended in discussing any aspect of the bill rendered to Client.

Client's Right to Copies of Documents and to Be Apprised of the Status of the Case

Attorneys shall keep Client informed of the status of the case and agrees to explain the laws pertinent to Client's situation, the available course of action, and the attendant risks. Attorney shall notify Client promptly of any development in Client's case, and will be available for meetings and telephone conversations with Client at mutually convenient times. Copies of all papers will be supplied to Client unless Client requests the contrary, and Client will be billed reasonable photocopy charges for these materials which will be included in the periodic bill.

Attorney's Right to Withdraw

Client is advised that if, in the judgment of Attorney, Attorney decides that there has been an irretrievable breakdown in the attorney-client relationship, or a material breach of the terms of his Retainer Agreement, Attorney may decide to make application to the court in which Client's action is pending, or by letter to Client in the situation in which no case is pending before a court, to be relieved as Clients' Attorney. In such event, Client will be provided with notice of such application and an opportunity to be heard. Should any fees be due and owing to Attorney at the time of such discharge or withdrawal, Attorney shall have the right, in addition to any other remedy, to seek a charging lien, i.e., a lien upon the property that is awarded to Client as a result of any conclusion of this matter.

In the event that any bill from Attorney remains unpaid beyond a 90 day period, Client agrees that Attorney may withdraw his representation, at the option of the Attorney. In the event that an action is pending, and absent Client's consent, an application must be made to the Court for such withdrawal. Where the fee is unpaid for the period set forth above, the Client acknowledges that in connection with any such withdrawal application, that the account delinquency shall be good cause for withdrawal.

Arbitration

Should a dispute arise with respect to this agreement, the parties agree to submit such dispute to arbitration for resolution pursuant to Article 75 of the CPLR.

Acknowledgment and Understanding

Client acknowledges that he or she has read this Retainer Agreement in its entirety, has had full opportunity to consider its terms, and has had full and satisfactory explanation of same, and fully understands its terms and agrees to such terms.

Client fully understands and acknowledges that there are no additional or different terms or agreements other than those expressly set forth in the Retainer Agreement.

Client acknowledges that he or she was provided with and read the Statement of Client's Rights and Responsibilities, a copy of which is attached hereto.

Certifications

Attorney has Informed Client that pursuant to court rules, Attorney may be required to certify court papers submitted by Client which contain statements of fact and specificity to certify that Attorney has no knowledge that the substance of such submission is false. Accordingly, Client agrees to provide Attorney with complete and accurate information which forms the basis for court papers and to certify in writing to Attorney, prior to the time the papers are actually submitted to the court, the accuracy of the court submission which Attorney prepares on Client's behalf, and which Client shall review and sign.

No Guarantees

It is specifically acknowledged by Client that Attorney has made no representations, express or implied, concerning the outcome of this representation. Client further acknowledges that the Attorney has not guaranteed and cannot guarantee the success of any action taken by Attorney on Client's behalf.

Other Matters

Closing

Client acknowledges that no guarantees have been made with respect to any phase of this representation.

Dated:

_____
, Attorney

I have read and understand the above, received a copy and accept all of its terms.

_____
, Client

Statement of Client's Rights and Responsibilities

Your attorney is providing you with this document to inform you of what you, as a client, are entitled to by law or by custom. To help prevent any misunderstanding between you and your attorney please read this document carefully.

If you ever have any questions about these rights, or about the way your case is being handled, do not hesitate to ask your attorney. He or she should be readily available to represent your best interests and keep you informed about your case.

An attorney may not refuse to represent you on the basis of race, creed, color, sex, sexual orientation, age, national origin or disability.

You are entitled to an attorney who will be capable of handling your case; show you courtesy and consideration at all times; represent you zealously; and preserve your confidences and secrets that are revealed in the course of the relationship.

You are entitled to a written retainer agreement which must set forth, in plain language, the nature of the relationship and the details of the fee arrangement. At your request, and before you sign the agreement, you are entitled to have your attorney clarify in writing any of its terms, or include additional provisions.

You are entitled to fully understand the proposed rates and retainer fee before you sign a retainer agreement, as in any other contract.

You may refuse to enter into any fee arrangement that you find unsatisfactory.

Your attorney may not request a fee that is contingent on the securing of a divorce or on the amount of money or property that may be obtained.

Your attorney may not request a retainer fee that is nonrefundable. That is, should you discharge your attorney, or should your attorney withdraw from the case, before the retainer is used up, he or she is entitled to be paid commensurate with the work performed on your case and any expenses, but must return the balance of the retainer to you. However, your attorney may enter into a minimum fee arrangement with you that provides for the payment of a specific amount below which the fee will not fall based upon the handling of the case to its conclusion.

You are entitled to know the approximate number of attorneys and other legal staff members who will be working on your case at any given time and what you will be charged for the services of each.

You are entitled to know in advance how you will be asked to pay legal fees and expenses, and how the retainer, if any, will be spent.

At your request, and after your attorney has had a reasonable opportunity to investigate your case, you are entitled to be given an estimate of approximate future costs of your case, which estimate shall be made in good faith but may be subject to change due to facts and circumstances affecting the case.

You are entitled to receive a written, itemized bill on a regular basis, at least every 60 days.

You are expected to review the itemized bills sent by counsel, and to raise any objections or errors in a timely manner. Time spent in discussion or explanation of bills will not be charged to you.

You are expected to be truthful in all discussions with your attorney, and to provide all relevant information and documentation to enable him or her to competently prepare your case.

You are entitled to be kept informed of the status of your case, and to be provided with copies of correspondence and documents prepared on your behalf or received from the court or your adversary.

You have the right to be present in court at the time that conferences are held.

You are entitled to make the ultimate decision on the objectives to be pursued in your case, and to make the final decision regarding the settlement of your case.

Your attorney's written retainer agreement must specify under what circumstances he or she might seek to withdraw as your attorney for non-payment of legal fees. If an action or proceeding is pending, the court may give your attorney a "charging lien," which entitles your attorney to payment for services already rendered at the end of the case out of the proceeds of the final order or judgment.

You are under no legal obligation to sign a confession of judgment or promissory note, or to agree to a lien or mortgage on your home to cover legal fees. Your attorney's written retainer agreement must specify whether, and under what circumstances, such security may be requested. In no event may such security interest be obtained by your attorney without prior court approval and notice to your adversary. An attorney's security interest in the marital residence cannot be foreclosed against you.

You are entitled to have your attorney's best efforts exerted on your behalf, but no particular results can be guaranteed.

If you entrust money with an attorney for an escrow deposit in your case, the attorney must safeguard the escrow in a special bank account. You are entitled to a written escrow agreement, a written receipt, and a complete record concerning the escrow. When the terms of the escrow agreement have been performed, the attorney must promptly make payment of the escrow to all persons who are entitled to it.

In the event of a fee dispute, you may have the right to seek arbitration. Your attorney will provide you with the necessary information regarding arbitration in the event of a fee dispute, or upon your request.

Receipt Acknowledged:

Attorney's signature:

Client's signature:

Date:

Shareholders Agreement

Agreement made this _____ day of _____, 20 _____,
by and between _____, residing at _____ (hereinafter X), and _____, residing at _____ (hereinafter Y).

IN CONSIDERATION OF the mutual covenants and conditions
contained herein, it is hereby agreed as follows:

1. Organization of the Corporation

1.1 The parties agree that upon the execution of this Agreement, they
will cause a corporation to be formed under the laws of the State
of _____ to be named _____ (hereinafter called
the Corporation). The Corporation shall be authorized to issue _____
shares of common voting stock, all with(out) a par value (of $ _____).

1.2(a) Each party hereto agrees that he will subscribe for and purchase
shares of the common stock of the Corporation as follows:

X — _____ shares
Y — _____ shares

(b) Each party agrees that in consideration of the shares of the Corporation's stock to be purchased by him he will pay to the Corporation the
sum of $ _____.

1.3 The parties hereto shall vote (as shareholders or directors, as the
case may be) as follows:

(a) To elect the following as Directors of the Corporation so long as
they are stockholders thereof: X and Y.

(b) To elect the following as Officers of the Corporation so long as they
are stockholders, directors, and/or employees thereof:

X — President
Y — Secretary-Treasurer

(c) To cause the Corporation to become a party to this Agreement by
adopting same after the Corporation has been organized and to take all
necessary action to carry out the terms of this Agreement.

2. Operation of the Corporation

2.1 The business of the Corporation shall be _____.

2.2 X and Y each agrees to make available to the Corporation, as additional working capital, up to $ _____ each, upon such terms as they and
the Corporation may from time to time agree.

2.3 It is agreed by the parties hereto that no action shall be taken with respect to any of the following matters except by a unanimous vote of all of the stockholders and directors:

(a) Sale of all or substantially all of the assets of the Corporation;

(b) The merger, consolidation, or reorganization of the Corporation;

(c) The issuance or sale, or the offer to sell, any additional shares of stock to existing shareholders or third parties;

(d) The commitment of the Corporation to any lease or distributorship;

(e) The creation of indebtedness on behalf of the Corporation to any one person or firm in excess of $ _____.

The Bylaws of the Corporation shall set out and include a statement of the foregoing action requiring the unanimous consent of the directors and/ or shareholders, as the case may be.

2.4 The Corporation shall select as its depository the _____ Bank. The resolution authorizing the opening and maintenance of such bank account shall provide that all checks, notes, drafts, and other evidence of indebtedness, etc., drawn on the account of the Corporation at such bank, shall be executed by the President and the Secretary-Treasurer.

2.5 The Corporation shall enter into an employment agreement with X in the form annexed hereto, which shall also contain the following terms:

(a) X shall be paid a salary of $ _____ per week during the first five (5) years of his employment or until its earlier termination, plus _____ % of the net profits of the Corporation.

(b) X agrees that he shall devote all of his business time to the Corporation and agrees that so long as he is an employee and a stockholder of the Corporation and for such further period of two (2) years thereafter, he will not directly or indirectly, engage as a principal, owner, stockholder, employee, officer, or director, or in any other capacity in any business venture or enterprise which deals directly or indirectly, or by association, in the business from time to time conducted by the Corporation or by any wholly owned subsidiary corporation or affiliate.

(c) The salary of X shall from time to time be increased as determined by the Board of Directors of the Corporation.

(d) The parties hereto shall each be entitled to receive as benefits under their respective employment with the Corporation, at the expense of the Corporation, health insurance coverage and such other benefits as the Corporation from time to time may determine.

3. Transfer for Shares

3.1 No share of stock of the Corporation, whether preferred or common, and whenever issued, shall be sold, assigned, transferred or otherwise disposed of, encumbered, pledged or hypothecated except as hereinafter provided. A stockholder desiring to sell all (and not a part) of his stock shall offer to sell all of his shares in the Corporation in writing, which offer shall be mailed to the Corporation and to each of the stockholders. The Corporation shall have the first option to accept or reject the offer. Such option must be exercised within thirty (30) days and no longer from the date of receipt of the offer, which acceptance must be in writing and mailed to the offeror. Failure on the part of the Corporation to respond to the offer shall constitute rejection as of the end of the thirtieth day following receipt of the offer. If the Corporation rejects the offer (and any partial acceptance or partial rejection shall constitute a total rejection), the other stockholders or stockholder, as the case may be, shall pro rata to their then shareholdings in the Corporation, have second option to accept or reject the offer. Such option must be exercised within fifteen (15) days (and no longer) from the date of the rejection and must be exercised in writing and mailed to the offeror. Failure to timely respond by such other stockholders (or any of the stockholders) shall likewise constitute a total rejection. Thereafter, for an additional fifteen (15) days (and no longer) the remaining stockholders who have not rejected the offer made to them, may, in proportion to their shareholdings, accept the entire offer of all such offered shareholdings. If all of the offered shares are not wholly accepted as provided above, all of the shares of the offeree stockholders shall, without further act, be automatically deemed counteroffered for sale to the original offeror, which counteroffer must be accepted by the original offeror within fifteen (15) days (and no longer) from the making of the counteroffer. Such counteroffer shall be deemed to have been made as of the date of the rejection by the remaining stockholders as provided above. Failure to timely respond to such original offeror shall likewise constitute a total rejection of such counteroffer. In all cases a partial acceptance or a partial rejection shall constitute a total rejection.

If all of the offered shares are not wholly accepted as provided above, the parties covenant to and shall take immediate steps thereafter to dissolve and liquidate the Corporation and its assets; and for such purposes, the offeror is hereby, without further act or document, constituted, appointed, and delegated as attorney-in-fact and as irrevocable agent (which agency shall be deemed to be "coupled with an interest") with all proxy rights in connection therewith, to dissolve and liquidate the Corporation on behalf and at the pro rata cost and expense of all of the then shareholders.

The price and terms of any offer shall be as a hereinafter set forth. Closing shall take place on the 15th business day following the receipt of the acceptance at the Corporation's then principal office at 10:00 A.M. of that day.

(a) The stockholders, simultaneously herewith, have executed a "Certificate of Agreed Value," setting forth the total net value of the Corporation as of this date. They agree to execute new such Certificates semiannually or more often. The term "total net value" as used herein shall be deemed to mean the agreed total value of all of the assets of the Corporation, after deducting therefrom any and all liabilities, howsoever characterized.

(b) The price for the offered shares in the Corporation shall be computed as follows:

The total number of common shares of stock then issued and outstanding in such Corporation shall be divided into the total net value set forth in such Certificate of Agreed Value, and the quotient shall be the price for each share of common stock of the Corporation sold, subject to no adjustments, except as hereinafter provided. The latest dated such Certificate of Agreed Value shall control, except that if any such Certificate, at the time of any total acceptance by any offeree is dated prior to one year from the date of such total acceptance, there shall be added to or subtracted from the total net value set forth in the last dated such Certificate of Agreed Value the difference between the "book value" of the Corporation (as hereinafter defined) as of the date of the last dated such Certificate and such "book value" as of the date of the total acceptance. In computing book value, if necessary, as hereinbefore provided, the established accounting practices, including, but not limited to, Reserves for Bad Debts, Contingent Liabilities, Depreciation, and Amortization, theretofore employed by the Corporation, shall be applied, subject to and in accordance with the following rules:

1. Goodwill, franchises, trademarks, and trade names shall in no way be considered assets for the purpose of determining the "book value";

2. The value of the fixed assets and merchandise inventory shall be fixed by agreement amongst the parties or, if the parties cannot agree, by arbitration, as hereinafter provided;

3. All other assets and liabilities shall be taken at the net figures at which they appear on the books of account;

4. Any life insurance policy owned by the Corporation shall be valued at its cash surrender value.

(c) The price, as hereinbefore determined, shall be adjusted as follows: (i) by subtracting therefrom all personal debts and interest thereon, if any, owed by the offeror to the Corporation, whether or not due; and (ii) by adding thereto all debts and interest thereon, if any, owed by the Corporation to the offeror, whether or not due. If the purchaser is another stockholder, and not the Corporation, an assignment without recourse shall be delivered to him at the closing by the offeror of such corporate debt due to the offeror; and likewise, such other stockholder-purchaser shall be liable (in such same percentage) for debts due to the Corporation from the offeror if an adjustment was made therefor in computing the price, as aforesaid, and the offeror and the Corporation shall execute and deliver unto the offeror a Release in connection with such obligation.

(d) If any offering stockholder shall be indebted to any other stockholder of the Corporation, such selling-stockholder shall, at the closing hereinabove provided for, discharge any such indebtedness by payment thereof to such other stockholder, with all interest due thereon, whether or not such debt is then due. Furthermore, should any offering-stockholder have monies or other collateral deposited as security for any corporate indebtedness, such monies or collateral shall be returned in full at such closing. In addition, and at the same time, the Corporation and each purchasing-stockholder thereof shall indemnify the selling-stockholder and agree to hold him harmless against any and all claims, losses, demands, and expenses of every nature, arising out of or which may result from or be based upon any guarantee executed or given by the selling-stockholder with respect to any corporate obligation.

(e) The price, as adjusted, shall be paid as follows: 25% in cash or by good, certified check, at the closing, and the balance in twelve (12) equal monthly installments, with interest as set forth below. The installments shall be evidence by a series of twelve (12) negotiable promissory notes to be made by the offeree as "Maker" to the order of the offerer as "Payee," dated the date of the closing, the first note being due one month after the closing and monthly consecutively thereafter; each of the notes to bear interest at the rate of _____ percent (_____%) per annum and contain a grace period of ten (10) days, and shall be payable at the bank of the Maker. The notes shall contain an acceleration clause, but failure to assert such right of acceleration shall not be deemed a waiver thereof. If the Corporation is the Maker, the other stockholders shall, jointly and severally, endorse each note and guarantors.

(f) The notes may be prepaid without penalty on any installment date, upon thirty (30) days' prior written notice, in inverse order, with all accrued interest on each note so prepaid; provided, however, that at the option of the offeror: (i) no prepayment shall be allowed in the same calendar year of the closing; and (ii) the payment of all or any part of the notes ordinarily due in such calendar year shall be deferred (and all interest thereon shall run) to January 2 of the next calendar year.

(g) Should the surplus and/or the net assets of the Corporation be insufficient to authorize the purchase of all of the stock so offered in accordance with the provisions of the __(State corporation law)__ as the same is or may be from time to time amended, and should the Corporation exercise the option to purchase, then and in such event, the Corporation shall purchase so much as it is authorized by law and the other stockholders shall purchase (such obligation being mandatory upon such other stockholders) the balance of such offered shares, which obligation shall be joint and several.

3.2 In the event of the death of X or Y, his estate or his personal representative shall sell his stock to the Corporation. The Corporation shall purchase the same upon the following terms: the price per share shall be as determined in paragraph 3.1 and shall be payable as therein set forth, except as may be hereinafter provided. Should there be insurance on the life of such deceased stockholder (of which insurance the Corporation shall be the beneficiary in whole or in part), then, upon the death of X or Y, the Corporation shall proceed immediately to collect the proceeds of such insurance on his life and upon such collection of all such proceeds and the qualification of a legal representative of such deceased stockholder, the Corporation shall use such insurance proceeds by payment thereof in cash against the purchase price; provided, however, that if the insurance proceeds be greater than the purchase price, the entire price shall be paid in cash at the closing, and the Corporation may retain the balance of the proceeds for its own corporate purposes, but if the purchase price is greater than the insurance proceeds, the entire proceeds shall be applied as the cash deposit against the price and the balance of the price shall be paid in twelve (12) equal monthly installments, the first such installment to be due thirty (30) days after the closing and each installment to bear interest at the rate of _____ percent (_____ %) per annum and which said installments are to be evidenced by a series of promissory notes as hereinabove provided in paragraph 3.1, and the same provisions as therein set forth shall apply herein with respect to such notes, except that the said notes may be prepaid in inverse order in whole or in part at any time with all accrued interest on any notes so prepaid.

4. Escrow

At the option of the seller, all of the documents required to be delivered at the closing by the seller shall be retained in escrow with his attorneys, pending full payment of the "adjusted" price. Should the escrowee receive notice of a default, he shall forthwith deliver the documents to the seller of his representative, who shall, upon ten (10) days' written notice to the defaulting purchaser, by certified or registered mail, return receipt requested, sell the shareholdings at public or private sale, at which sale the seller or his representative may purchase. Any sales proceeds received in excess of the unpaid balance due and interest, and the expenses of the sale, shall forthwith be turned over to the defaulting purchaser, who shall be liable for any deficiency. There shall be included as a cost of sale legal fees calculated on the unpaid balance and interest, at _____ percent (_____%), together with the costs and disbursements of the sale. Upon the escrowee receiving written notice from the seller of full payment, he shall forthwith deliver the escrowed documents to the purchaser or purchasers. At the closing, the seller and the purchasers shall execute general releases, excepting therefrom the provisions of this Agreement applicable to the purchaser and the provisions of all Agreements and notes executed at the closing provided for deferred payments and indemnification by the purchaser.

5. Endorsement of Stock Certificates

The Certificates of Stock of the Corporation shall be endorsed as follows:
"The shares of stock represented by this Certificate are subject to all the terms and conditions of an Agreement made on the _____ day

of _____, 20 _____ , a copy of which is on file in the office of the Corporation."

6. Voting

At any stockholders' meeting called by the Corporation, for the purpose of accepting or rejecting any offer made by a stockholder to sell his shares in accordance with this Agreement, such stockholder shall be deemed to have voted for the Corporation's purchasing or redeeming the offered shares.

7. Equity

The provisions of this Agreement may be enforced in a court of equity by injunction or specific performance. Such remedies shall be cumulative and not exclusive and shall be in addition to any other remedies which the parties may have. Should any part or parts of this Agreement be determined to be void by a court of competent jurisdiction, the remaining provisions hereof shall nevertheless be binding.

8. Notices

All notices, options, offers, and acceptances hereunder (unless deemed to have been made by the operation of the terms of this Agreement) shall be in writing and served by certified or registered mail, return receipt requested and, unless otherwise herein specified, shall be deemed to have been made as of the date of mailing.

9. Arbitration

Any question or controversy with respect to any question arising hereunder shall be resolved by arbitration in accordance with the laws of the State of _____ and pursuant to the Rules of the American Arbitration Association.

10. Entire Agreement

This Agreement constitutes the entire understanding of the parties concerning the subject matter herein contained. No modification of any provision of this Agreement shall be valid, and the same may not be terminated or abandoned except by a writing signed by the parties to this Agreement.

IN WITNESS WHEREOF, the parties have hereunto set their hands and seals the day and year first above written.

X _____

Y _____

Subscription Agreement (Limited Partnership)

   1. The undersigned hereby subscribes for the number of Units of limited partnership interests set forth below in _____, a _____ limited partnership (the Partnership), each Unit of _____ Dollars ($ _____) payable in full on subscription.

   2. The undersigned understands that the General Partner will notify him prior to _____, 20 _____, as to whether this subscription has been accepted or rejected. If rejected, the check tendered by him will be returned to him forthwith without interest or deduction. The undersigned understands that the payments made under this Subscription Agreement will be held in escrow by the Partnership for his benefit at a commercial bank in _____ with assets of at least $10,000,000. If accepted, the check tendered by the undersigned will be applied in accordance with the use of proceeds description set forth in the Private Placement Memorandum relating to the Partnership (the Memorandum).

   3. The undersigned had been furnished with and has carefully read the Memorandum relating to the Partnership and the documents attached as Exhibits thereto, including the Partnership Agreement. The undersigned is aware that:

   (i) The Partnership has no financial or operating history;

   (ii) There are substantial risks incident to an investment in the Partnership, as summarized under "Risks" and "Tax Risks" in the Memorandum;

   (iii) No federal or state agency has passed upon the Units or made any finding or determination as to the fairness of the investment;

   (iv) The discussion of the tax consequences arising from investment in the Partnership set forth in the Memorandum is general in nature, and the tax consequences to the undersigned of an investment in the Partnership depend upon his particular circumstances;

   (v) There can be no assurance that the Internal Revenue Code or the regulations thereunder will not be amended in such manner as to deprive the Partnership and its Partners of some of the tax benefits they might now receive; and

   (vi) The books and records of the Partnership will be available for inspection of the undersigned at the Partnership's place of business.

   4. The undersigned understands that investment in the Partnership is an illiquid investment. In particular, the undersigned recognizes that:

   (i) The undersigned must bear the economic risk of investment in the Units for an indefinite period of time since the Units have not been registered under the Securities Act of 1933, as amended, and, therefore, cannot be sold unless either they are subsequently registered under said Act or an exemption from such registration is available and a favorable opinion of counsel for the Partnership to such effect is obtained;

   (ii) There will be no established market for the Units and it is not likely that any public market for the Units will develop; and

   (iii) The undersigned's rights to transfer his Units will be restricted, as provided for in the Partnership Agreement.

5. The undersigned represents and warrants to the Partnership and to the General Partner that:

(i) The undersigned has carefully reviewed and understands the risks of, and other considerations relating to, a purchase of Units, including the risks set forth under "Risk Factors" and "Tax Risks" in the Memorandum and the considerations described under "Federal Income Tax Consequences" in the Memorandum;

(ii) The undersigned has been furnished with all materials relating to the Partnership and its proposed activities, the offering of Units, or anything set forth in the Memorandum which he has requested, and has been afforded the opportunity to obtain any additional information necessary to verify the accuracy of any representations or information set forth in the Memorandum;

(iii) The General Partner has answered all inquiries of the undersigned concerning the Partnership and its proposed activities, the offering of Units, or any other matter relating to the business of the Partnership as set forth in the Memorandum;

(iv) The undersigned has not been furnished any offering literature other than the Memorandum and the documents attached as Exhibits thereto, and the undersigned has relied only on the information contained in the Memorandum and such Exhibits and the information furnished or made available by the Partnership or the General Partner, as described in subparagraphs (ii) and (iii) above;

(v) The undersigned is acquiring the Units for which he hereby subscribes for his own account, as principal, for investment and not with a view to the resale or distribution of all or any part of such Units;

(vi) The undersigned, if a corporation, partnership, trust, or other form of business entity, is authorized and otherwise duly qualified to purchase and hold Units in the Partnership, such entity has its principal place of business as set forth on the signature page hereof and such entity has not been formed for the specific purchase of acquiring Units in the Partnership;

(vii) The undersigned has adequate means of providing for his current needs and personal contingencies and has no need for liquidity in this investment;

(viii) All the information which the undersigned has heretofore furnished the General Partner, or which is set forth in his Purchase Questionnaire and elsewhere with respect to his financial position and business experience, is correct and complete as of the date of this Agreement and, if there should be any material change in such information prior to the completion of the Offering, the undersigned will immediately furnish such revised or corrected information to the General Partner;

(ix) The undersigned further agrees to be bound by all of the terms and conditions of the Offering made by the Memorandum and Exhibits thereto, and by all of the terms and conditions of the Partnership Agreement and to perform any obligations therein imposed upon a Limited Partner thereof.

6. In order to facilitate the admission of the undersigned and other subscribers into the Partnership, the undersigned hereby irrevocably

constitutes and appoints the General Partner, or any one of them if more than one, as his agent and attorney-in-fact, in his name, place and stead, to make, execute, acknowledge, swear to, file, record, and deliver the Amended Certificate of Limited Partnership of the Partnership to admit the undersigned into the Partnership, and any and all other instruments which may be required to effect the admission of the undersigned into the Partnership as a Limited Partner thereof or otherwise comply with applicable law. It is expressly understood and intended by the undersigned that the grant of the foregoing power of attorney is coupled with an interest, and such grant shall be irrevocable. Said power of attorney shall survive the death, bankruptcy, or mental incapacitation of the undersigned, to the extent he may legally contract for such survival, or the assignment or transfer of all or any part of the undersigned's interest in the Partnership. Any person dealing with the Partnership may conclusively presume and rely upon the fact that any instrument referred to above, executed by such agents and attorneys-in-fact, is authorized, regular, and binding without further inquiry. If required, the undersigned shall execute and deliver to the General Partner, within five (5) days after the receipt of a request therefor, such further designations, powers of attorney, or other instruments as the General Partner shall reasonably deem necessary for the purpose of this provision.

   7. This subscription is not transferable or assignable by the undersigned.

   8. If the undersigned is more than one person, the obligations of the undersigned shall be joint and several and the representations and warranties herein contained shall be deemed to be made by and be binding upon each such person and his heirs, executors, administrators, successors, and assigns.

   9. This subscription, upon acceptance by the Partnership, shall be binding upon the heirs, executors, administrators, successors, and assigns of the undersigned.

   10. This Subscription Agreement shall be construed in accordance with and governed in all respects by the laws of the State of _____.

   11. Any masculine personal pronoun as set forth in this Subscription Agreement shall be considered to mean the corresponding feminine or neuter personal pronoun, as the context requires.

   12. The undersigned represents that the information furnished in the Purchaser Questionnaire is true and complete as of the date hereof, and the undersigned agrees to notify the Partnership of any changes in the information prior to completion of the Offering.

   13. The undersigned is subscribing for the following number of Units:
   Number of Units subscribed for: _____
   Amount of check enclosed: $_____

                                        Dated:_____
                                        /s/_____

                                        _____
                                        Printed Name:

                                        Address:_____

                                        _____

Work for Hire Agreement

This Agreement is made and entered into this _____ day of _____ 200_____ by and between Jones (Jones) whose address is _____ and Smith (Smith) whose address is _____, and Brown whose address is _____.

Whereas the parties to this Agreement are collaborating on a musical entitled "_____" (hereinafter known as "Musical") in which each of the parties has made a unique contribution and for which parties have composed the music and lyrics for the Musical.

Now, therefore, the parties do agree as follows:

1. The parties acknowledge that Composers have composed the music for the Musical, and the parties are engaging the services of Brown as an arranger (Brown will hereinafter be referred to as "Arranger") for the Musical.

2. Arranger, for good and valuable consideration of thirty percent (30) of any royalties received by the parties for the use of said music, said payment not to exceed a maximum of fifty thousand dollars ($50,000.00), (which sum Arranger may be entitled), certifies and agrees that all of the results and proceeds of the services of every kind heretofore rendered by and hereafter to be rendered by Arranger in connection with the Musical are and shall be deemed works "made-for-hire" for Composers and/or works assigned to Composers, as applicable. Accordingly, Arranger further acknowledges, certifies and agrees that Composers shall be deemed the authors and/or exclusive owners of the music for the Musical throughout the world, and of all the rights comprised in the copyright thereof (expressly including the copyrights in and to the "sound recordings" and any renewal or extension rights in connection therewith and of any and all other rights thereto), and that Composers shall have the right to exploit any or all of the foregoing in any and all media, now known or hereafter devised, throughout the universe, in perpetuity, in all configurations as Composers determine.

3. Arranger hereby agrees not to make any claim against Composers or any party authorized by Composers to exploit said Musical based on such moral or like rights.

4. Composers warrant that all lyrics and other material, including, without limitation, so-called "samples" and all compositions, ideas, designs and inventions of Composers, furnished by Composers in connection with the Musical are or will be original or in the public domain throughout the world or used with the consent of the original owner thereof, and shall not infringe upon or violate any copyright of, or infringe upon or violate the right or privacy or any other right of, any person.

5. Composers agree that Arranger shall have billing credit as arranger on all programs, billings, posters, advertisements, and so forth connected with a production of the Musical.

6. Arranger agrees to hold Composers and their respective successors, licensees and assigns harmless from and against all damages, losses, costs and expenses (including reasonable attorneys' fees and costs) which Arranger and their respective successors, licensees or assigns may suffer or incur by reason by the breach of any of the warranties made in this Agreement.
7. This Agreement shall be deemed to have been made in New York, New York and shall be construed, interpreted and enforced in accordance with the laws of the State of New York applicable to agreements executed, delivered and to be performed wholly within such State.
8. This Agreement shall be the complete and binding agreement between the parties and arranger and may not be amended except by an agreement in writing signed by the arranger and the parties hereto.

IN WITNESS WHEREOF, the parties have duly executed this Agreement on the day and year first above written.

_____

Jones

_____

Smith

_____

Brown

APPENDIX B

Supplemental Cases

The following cases are presented to highlight certain material discussed in the text:

1. *Don King Productions, Inc. v. Douglas*: discusses the concept of consideration and what may be legally valuable at the time of contract
2. *Matter of Baby M*: concerns the legality of relinquishing certain parental rights
3. *Hong v. Marriott Corp.*: highlights, in an amusing fashion, the concept of warranties under UCC Article II
4. *In re Peregrine Entertainment, Ltd*: details the method of perfecting a securities interest under Article IX of the UCC

Don King Productions, Inc. v. Douglas
742 F. Supp. 741 (S.D.N.Y. 1990)

... Indefiniteness of Consideration

According to Johnson and Douglas, the Promotion and Bout Agreements are unenforceable because they are indefinite as to the essential term of consideration. The facts are undisputed: the Promotion Agreement provided for payment of $25,000 to Douglas in return for his granting DKP the exclusive right to promote his bouts for a stated term. Compensation for the individual bouts that were contemplated by the Promotion Agreement (numbering no fewer than three per year, with the exception of the first contract year) was made subject to further negotiation and agreement, with the agreed-to terms to be set forth in the individually-negotiated bout agreements. The Promotion Agreement specified a floor level of compensation of $25,000, plus $10,000 in training expenses, for these fights, except that in the case of a title bout or defense of such a bout, no floor (or ceiling) was provided, the purse to be "negotiated and mutually agreed upon between us."

One such subsequent agreement as to Douglas' purse for a title fight was reached, as set forth in the Bout Agreement executed for the match with then-world champion Tyson. The Bout Agreement stated that "in full consideration of [Douglas'] participation in the [Tokyo] Bout and for all of the rights herein granted to Promoter," Douglas would be paid $1.3 million. That agreement further provided that with respect to Douglas' first three fights post-Tokyo, upon which DKP was given an exclusive option, the purse per fight would be $1 million, unless Douglas was the winner in Tokyo, in which case the amount would be subject to negotiation with that sum of $1 million as a floor.

In the face of this contractual language, Douglas and Johnson are forced to take the position that "although a minimum purse of $1,000,000 was specified, this is insufficient to render the contract sufficiently definite for enforcement" because "the 'minimum' consideration is obviously a token, at best." The factual predicate for the argument is that the market at present values the world champion heavyweight fighter at considerably more than one million dollars a pop (Johnson states he has received offers as high as $50 million for Douglas to fight, and King apparently offered him $15 million plus a percentage of gross receipts). Therefore, the contractually-specified million dollar compensation floor is asserted to be nothing other than the proverbial "peppercorn" of consideration.

Assuming the factual premise as to Douglas' present value, the argument, nevertheless, suffers once one considers that the appropriate yard-stick for making the judgment. Whether one million dollars is token consideration must be assessed by reference to Douglas' expected future value as a fighter at the time the agreement was entered into, i.e., before his unexpected defeat of Tyson. No one has contended on this record that $1 million was a "mere token" vis-a-vis Douglas' value at the time he, Johnson and their lawyer Enz, negotiated the Bout Agreement, and, in fact, the parties, after such negotiations, fixed a figure reasonably proximate to that—$1.3 million—for services to be rendered in a title fight with an undefeated heavy-weight champion. Thus, when Douglas and Johnson signed the Bout Agreement they evidently did not regard one million dollars as a "peppercorn," even if they did not regard it as the full (as opposed to minimum) value to be affixed to Douglas' services when defending a championship. The subsequent change in Douglas' relative fortunes does not provide a legal basis now to disregard his prior agreement as to the reasonable floor at which to begin discussion of the value of his services as defending heavyweight champion.

It is standard contract law that a contract, to be binding, must address without "impenetrable vagueness" the terms material to its subject matter. Joseph Martin, Jr. Delicatessen, Inc. v. Schumacher, 52 N.Y.2d 105, 109, 436

N.Y.S.2d 247, 249, 417 N.E.2d 541, 543 (1981). Just as well settled is the proposition that

> to render a contract enforceable, absolute certainty is not required; it is enough if the promise or agreement is sufficiently definite and explicit so that the intention of the parties may be ascertained "to a reasonable certainty." Varney v. Ditmars, 217 N.Y. 223, 228, 111 N.E. 822, 824, Ann. Cas. 1916B, 758. A contract cannot be ignored as meaningless, except as a last resort. "Indefiniteness must reach the point where construction becomes futile." Cohen & Sons v. M. Lurie Woolen Co., 232 N.Y. 112, 114, 133 N.E. 370, 371.

Here, the Promotional Agreement and Bout Agreement addressed their essential subject matter in a manner that is far from impenetrable. While leaving certain terms open to future negotiation, the contracts were explicit and definite about Douglas' commitment to fight only for DKP during the life of those contracts and about the minimum consideration he could receive for making that commitment. Thus, the contracts, at least with respect to their exclusivity terms, are much more than "mere agreements to agree." Joseph Martin, Jr. Delicatessen, 52 N.Y.2d at 109, 436 N.Y.S.2d at 249, 417 N.E.2d at 543.

The parties agreed to leave open the compensation that would be payable under certain contingencies, such as after Douglas' becoming world champion (in contrast to the fixed purse for title fights against another champion, which were priced at $1 million a bout) and this may have repercussions as to Douglas' obligation to fight a particular title defense at a particular price named by King, since no separate bout agreement has been executed for such fight pursuant to the process of negotiation contemplated by the Promotion Agreement for fights to be held under its provisions. Nevertheless, the writing manifests in definite language Douglas and DKP's agreement to deal exclusively with one another with respect to title defenses and to negotiate in an effort to reach a mutual understanding as to the open price term for such a defense.

For that reason, the exclusivity provisions of the Agreements are not void *ab initio* on grounds of price indefiniteness. See R.S. Stokvis & Sons v. Kearney & Trecker Corp., 58 F. Supp. 260, 267 (S.D.N.Y. 1944) (agreement containing definite grant of "exclusive representation" valid as to that term, notwithstanding that agreement contained "no provisions with respect to quantities, prices, deliveries, payments, or even discounts," all of which were "left 'to be arranged separately.'"). Whether $1 million turns out to be a definite default price — or merely a minimum price — simply does not control the question of whether Douglas and Johnson have violated the definite right they granted to DKP to exclusively "secure and arrange all [of Douglas'] professional boxing bouts" and their definite duty under the Agreement to refrain from "render[ing][ ] services as a professional boxer to any person, firm or entity" other than DKP. That is because the minimum price terms, together with DKP's upfront payment of $25,000 and its commitments to hold a set number of bouts, clearly did provide an expectancy of compensation for Douglas that was sufficiently definite to induce his promise to fight exclusively for DKP. Accordingly, Douglas/Johnson fail to sustain their burden as movants seeking dismissal of the complaint on the ground that the underlying instruments are too illusory to be breached.

Adequacy of the Term

Douglas and Johnson next urge that this case is an appropriate one for application of the maxim that "an option actually intended by the parties to run for an unlimited time, i.e., forever is void." Mohr Park Manor, Inc. v. Mohr, 83 Nev. 107, 424 P.2d 101 (1967).

The Promotional Agreement and Bout Agreement do not fall into that class of contracts, as both contain clauses explicitly addressing duration and neither contemplates an indefinite term. The former provides that it shall run for three years and shall be "automatically extended to cover the entire period [Douglas is] world champion and a period of two years following the date on which [Douglas] thereafter cease[s], for any reason, to be so recognized as world champion." So extensive a commitment of one's services might be questioned as excessive, but clearly does not suffer from indefiniteness or ambiguity. Nor does the Bout Agreement: it grants DKP an exclusive option on the promotion of Douglas' "next three fights," which must be exercised within thirty days of the Tokyo bout.

Both are contracts "of the type . . . which do provide for termination or cancellation upon the occurrence of a specified event," Payroll Express Corp. v. Aetna Casualty & Sur. Co., 659 F.2d 285, 291 (2d Cir. 1981), and are therefore not jeopardized by the void-for-indefiniteness rule. Id. Contracts which "provide no fixed date for the termination of the promisor's obligation but condition the obligation upon an event which would necessarily terminate the contract" remain in force until that event occurs. Warner-Lambert Pharmaceutical Co. v. John J. Reynolds, Inc., 178 F. Supp. 655 (S.D.N.Y. 1959), aff'd, 280 F.2d 197 (2d Cir. 1960) (upholding contract entered into in 1881 that lacked termination date but which obligated pharmaceutical manufacturer to pay royalties on every gross of "Listerine" made and sold by it as long as it continued to manufacture the product); Ketcham v. Hall Syndicate, Inc., 37 Misc. 2d 693, 236 N.Y.S.2d 206, 212-213 (Sup. Ct. 1962) (agreement for syndication of cartoons sufficiently definite as to term where duration of contract was made subject to termination in event artist's share of revenue fell below stipulated amount), aff'd, 19 A.D.2d 611, 242 N.Y.S.2d 182 (1st Dep't 1963). . . .

The Unconscionable Contracts Defense

Douglas and Johnson plead as an affirmative defense that the contracts they entered into with DKP are unconscionable. Under New York law, a determination of unconscionability requires a showing that the contract was both procedurally and substantively unconscionable *when made* — i.e., "some showing of an 'absence of meaningful choice on the part of one of the parties together with contract terms which are unreasonably favorable to the other party.'"

Gillman v. Chase Manhattan Bank, N.A., 73 N.Y.2d 1, 10, 537 N.Y.S.2d 787, 791, 534 N.E.2d 824, 828 (1988) (citations omitted and emphasis supplied). The factual contentions set forth in the Douglas/Johnson interrogatories to support the unconscionability defense — that the Tokyo conduct of King was unconscionable, that King is a powerful promoter, and that exclusive, extendable terms of the contracts are unreasonably favorable to King — are as a matter of law insufficient.

The Douglas/Johnson contention that the contracts "became unconscionable" *after* their inception owing to King's conduct during the Tokyo fight is unavailing, as the underlined language in Gillman illustrates. The doctrine of unconscionability implicates the circumstances and terms of a contract at the time of formation — not the parties' subsequent performance under it. See State v. Avco Financial Service of New York, Inc., 50 N.Y.2d 383, 390, 429 N.Y.S.2d 181, 185, 406 N.E.2d 1075, 1079 (1980) (referring to "circumstances existing at the time of the making"). The Tokyo performance by King is, of course, relevant to whether King breached his obligations of good faith and fair dealing under the contracts, an issue discussed at length in the May 18 Opinion and which has been reserved for trial to a jury. That conduct has, however, absolutely no bearing on the defense of unconscionability, which relates to substantive and procedural fairness of a contract "when made." *Gillman*, 73 N.Y.2d at 10, 537 N.Y.S.2d at 791, 534 N.E.2d at 828.

Douglas/Johnson next contend that King so dominates promotion of heavyweight fights that the Douglas-King contracts are inherently procedurally unconscionable. That assertion, if true, sounds more probative of an antitrust claim for monopolization than it is demonstrative of the particularized showing of an unfair bargaining process that is requisite to the defense of unconscionability. Douglas/Johnson make no allegation here that deceptive or high-pressure tactics were employed in concluding the contracts, that contract terms were concealed in fine print, or that there was a gross asymmetry in the experience and education of the parties, each of whom was represented by counsel throughout the course of their arms-length negotiations. See May 18 Opinion at 747; cf. *Gillman*, 73 N.Y.2d at 11, 537 N.Y.S.2d at 791, 534 N.E.2d at 828 (identifying relevance of these and other factors to establishment of procedural unfairness).

At least as stated in the responses to the contention interrogatories, the unconscionability defense does not here implicate its primary use as "a means with which to protect the commercially illiterate consumer beguiled into a grossly unfair bargain by a deceptive vendor or finance company." Marvel Entertainment Group, Inc. v. Young Astronaut Council, No. 88-5141, 1989 WL 129504 (S.D.N.Y. October 27, 1989). Without some definite allegation of a defect in the contract negotiation process apart from King's stature in the boxing field, which alone does not suggest "inequality so strong and manifest as to shock the conscience and confound the judgment," id. (quoting Christian v. Christian, 42 N.Y.2d 63, 71, 396 N.Y.S.2d 817, 823, 365 N.E.2d 849, 855 (1977)), defendants have failed to create an issue of procedural unconscionability requiring resolution by jury.

The contention that the contracts require Douglas to fight exclusively for DKP for the extendable terms of such contracts, which could amount to the rest of the boxer's professional life, equally fails to satisfy the requirement of substantive unconscionability. Only in "exceptional cases" is "a provision of [a] contract . . . so outrageous as to warrant holding it unenforceable on the ground of substantive unconscionability alone." *Gillman*, 73 N.Y.2d at 12, 537 N.Y.S.2d at 792, 534 N.E.2d at 829 (omitting citations); see also *Marvel Entertainment* (citing Christian v. Christian, 42 N.Y.2d 63, 71, 396 N.Y.S.2d 817, 823, 365 N.E.2d 849, 855 (1977)) (terms must be "such as no [person] in his senses and not under delusion would make on one hand, and no honest and fair [person] would accept on the other").

Douglas and Johnson fail to make any proffer as to what makes this term of their contract so exceptional as to fit within the line of cases referred to in *Gillman*, and they cite to no case considering or holding an exclusive services contract unconscionable on grounds of duration. . . . The court therefore declines to revisit its prior legal determinations that the contract durational terms were definite in nature and the contracts were supported by sufficiently-definite price consideration to induce Douglas' promise to fight exclusively for DKP. See May 18 Opinion at 761-764. The unconscionability defense accordingly shall be stricken, there having been no proffer or allegation sufficient to establish either its procedural or substantive elements. . . .

Matter of Baby M
109 N.J. 396 (1988)

WILENTZ, C. J.

In this matter the Court is asked to determine the validity of a contract that purports to provide a new way of bringing children into a family. For a fee of $10,000, a woman agrees to be artificially inseminated with the semen of another woman's husband; she is to conceive a child, carry it to term, and after its birth surrender it to the natural father and his wife. The intent of the contract is that the child's natural mother will thereafter be forever separated from her child. The wife is to adopt the child, and she and the natural father are to be regarded as its parents for all purposes. The contract providing for this is called "surrogacy contract," the natal mother inappropriately called the "surrogate mother."

We invalidate the surrogacy contract because it conflicts with the law and public policy of this State. While we recognize the depth of the yearning of infertile couples to have their own children, we find the payment of money to a "surrogate" mother illegal, perhaps criminal, and potentially degrading to women. Although in this case we grant custody to the natural father, the evidence having clearly proved such custody to be in the best interests of the infant, we void both the termination of the surrogate mother's parental rights and the adoption of the child by the wife/step-parent. We thus restore the "surrogate" as the mother of the child. We remand the issue of the natural mother's visitation rights to the trial court, since that issue was not reached below and the record before us is not sufficient to permit us to decide it *de novo*.

We find no offense to our present laws where a woman voluntarily and without payment agrees to act as a "surrogate" mother, provided that she is not subject to a binding agreement to surrender her child. Moreover, our holding today does not preclude the Legislature from altering the current statutory scheme, within constitutional limits, so as to permit surrogacy contracts. Under current law, however, the surrogacy agreement before us is illegal and invalid. . . .

Invalidity and Unenforceability of Surrogacy Contract

We have concluded that this surrogacy contact is invalid. Our conclusion has two bases: direct conflict with existing statutes and conflict with the public policies of this State, as expressed in its statutory and decisional law.

One of the surrogacy contract's basic purposes, to achieve the adoption of a child through private placement, though permitted in New Jersey "is very much disfavored." Sees v. Baber, 74 N.J. 201, 217 (1977). Its use of money for this purpose—and we have no doubt whatsoever that the money is being paid to obtain an adoption and not, as the Sterns argue, for the personal services of Mary Beth Whitehead—is illegal and perhaps criminal. N.J.S.A. 9:3-54. In addition to the inducement of money, there is the coercion of contract: the natural mother's irrevocable agreement, prior to birth, even prior to conception, to surrender the child to the adoptive couple. Such an agreement is totally unenforceable in private placement adoption. *Sees*, 74 N.J. at 212-214. Even where the adoption is through an approved agency, the formal agreement to surrender occurs only *after* birth (as we read N.J.S.A. 9:2-16 and 9:2-17, and similar statutes), and then, by regulation, only after the birth mother has been offered counseling. N.J.A.C. 10:121A-5.4(c). Integral to these invalid provisions of the surrogacy contract is the related agreement, equally invalid, on the part of the natural mother to cooperate with, and not to contest, proceedings to terminate her parental rights, as well as her contractual concession, in aid of the adoption, that the child's best interests would be served by awarding custody to the natural father and his wife—all of this before she has even conceived, and, in some cases, before she has the slightest idea of what the natural father and adoptive mother are like.

The foregoing provisions not only directly conflict with New Jersey statutes, but also offend long-established State policies. These critical terms, which are at the heart of the contract are invalid and unenforceable; the conclusion therefore follows, without more, that the entire contract is unenforceable.

Conflict with Statutory Provisions

The surrogacy contract conflicts with: (1) laws prohibiting the use of money in connection with adoptions; (2) laws requiring proof of parental unfitness or abandonment before termination of parental rights is ordered or an adoption is granted; and (3) laws that make surrender of custody and consent to adoption revocable in private placement adoptions.

(1) Our law prohibits paying or accepting money in connection with any placement of a child for adoption. N.J.S.A. 9:3-54a. Violation is a high misdemeanor. N.J.S.A. 9:3-54c. Excepted are fees of an approved agency (which must be a non-profit entity, N.J.S.A. 9:3-38a.) and certain expenses in connection with childbirth. N.J.S.A. 9:3-54b.

Considerable care was taken in this case to structure the surrogacy arrangement so as not to violate this prohibition. The arrangement was structured as follows: the adopting parent, Mrs. Stern, was not a party to the surrogacy contract; the money paid to Mrs. Whitehead was stated to be for her services — not for the adoption; the sole purpose of the contract was stated as being that "of giving a child to William Stern, its natural and biological father"; the money was purported to be "compensation for services and expenses and in no way . . . a fee for termination of parental rights or a payment in exchange for consent to surrender a child for adoption"; the fee to the Infertility Center ($7,500) was stated to be for legal representation, advice, administrative work, and other "services." Nevertheless, it seems clear that the money was paid and accepted in connection with an adoption.

The Infertility Center's major role was first as a "finder" of the surrogate mother whose child was to be adopted, and second as the arranger of all proceedings that led to the adoption. Its role as adoption finder is demonstrated by the provision requiring Mr. Stern to pay another $7,500 if he uses Mary Beth Whitehead again as a surrogate, and by ICNY's agreement to "coordinate arrangements for the adoption of the child by the wife." The surrogacy agreement requires Mrs. Whitehead to surrender Baby M for the purposes of adoption. The agreement notes that Mr. *and* Mrs. Stern wanted to have a child, and provides that the child be "placed" with Mrs. Stern in the event Mr. Stern dies before the child is born. The payment of the $10,000 occurs only on surrender of custody of the child and "completion of the duties and obligations" of Mrs. Whitehead, including termination of her parental rights to facilitate adoption by Mrs. Stern. As for the contention that the Sterns are paying only for services and not for an adoption, we need note only that they would pay nothing in the event the child died before the fourth month of pregnancy, and only $1,000 if the child were stillborn, even though the "services" had been fully rendered. Additionally, one of Mrs. Whitehead's estimated costs, to be assumed by Mr. Stern, was an "Adoption Fee," presumably for Mrs. Whitehead's incidental costs in connection with the adoption.

Mr. Stern knew he was paying for the adoption of a child; Mrs. Whitehead knew she was accepting money so that a child might be adopted; the Infertility Center knew that it was being paid for assisting in the adoption of a child. The actions of all three worked to frustrate the goals of the statute. It strains credulity to claim that these arrangements, touted by those in the surrogacy business as an attractive alternative to the usual route leading to an adoption, really amount to something other than a private placement adoption for money.

The prohibition of our statute is strong. Violation constitutes a high misdemeanor, N.J.S.A. 9:3-54c, a third-degree crime, N.J.S.A. 2C:43-1b, carrying a penalty of three to five years imprisonment. N.J.S.A. 2C:43-6a(3). The evils inherent in baby-bartering are loathsome for a myriad of reasons. The child is sold without regard for whether the purchasers will be suitable parents. N. Baker, Baby Selling: The Scandal of Black Market Adoption 7 (1978). The natural mother does not receive the benefit of counseling and guidance to assist her in making a decision that may affect her for a lifetime. In fact, the monetary incentive to sell her child may, depending on her financial circumstances, make her decision less voluntary. Id. at 44. Furthermore, the adoptive parents may not be fully informed of the natural parents' medical history.

Baby-selling potentially results in the exploitation of all parties involved. Ibid. Conversely, adoption statutes seek to further humanitarian goals, foremost among them the best interests of the child. H. Witmer, E. Herzog, E. Weinstein, & M. Sullivan, Independent Adoptions: A Follow-Up Study 32 (1967). The negative consequences of baby-buying are potentially present in the surrogacy context, especially the potential for placing and adopting a child without regard to the interest of the child or the natural mother. . . .

The provision in the surrogacy contract stating that Mary Beth Whitehead agrees to "surrender custody . . . and terminate all parental rights" contains no clause giving her a right to rescind. It is intended to be an irrevocable consent to surrender the child for adoption — in other words, an irrevocable commitment by Mrs. Whitehead to turn Baby M over to the Sterns and thereafter to allow termination of her parental rights. The trial court required a "best interests" showing as a condition to granting specific performance of the surrogacy contract. 217 N.J. Super. at 399-400. Having decided the "best interests" issue in favor of the Sterns, that court's order included, among other things, specific performance of this agreement to surrender custody and terminate all parental rights.

Mrs. Whitehead, shortly after the child's birth, had attempted to revoke her consent and surrender by refusing, after the Sterns had allowed her to have the child "just for one week," to return Baby M to them. The trial court's award of specific performance therefore reflects its view that the consent to surrender the child was irrevocable. We accept the trial court's construction of the contract; indeed it appears quite clear that this was the parties' intent. Such a provision, however, making irrevocable the natural mother's consent to surrender custody of her child in a private placement adoption, clearly conflicts with New Jersey law.

Our analysis commences with the statute providing for surrender of custody to an approved agency and termination of parental rights on the

suit of that agency. The two basic provisions of the statute are N.J.S.A.
9:2-14 and 9:2-16. The former provides explicitly that

> [e]xcept as otherwise provided by law or by order or judgment of a court of
> competent jurisdiction or by testamentary disposition, no surrender of the
> custody of a child shall be valid in this state unless made to an approved
> agency pursuant to the provisions of this act. . . .

There is no exception "provided by law," and it is not clear that there could
be any "order or judgment of a court of competent jurisdiction" validating a
surrender of custody as a basis for adoption when that surrender was not in
conformance with the statute. Requirements for a voluntary surrender to
an approved agency are set forth in N.J.S.A. 9:2-16. This section allows an
approved agency to take a voluntary surrender of custody from the parent
of a child but provides stringent requirements as a condition to its validity.
The surrender must be in writing, must be in such form as is required for
the recording of a deed, and, pursuant to N.J.S.A. 9:2-17, must

> be such as to declare that the person executing the same desires to relinquish
> the custody of the child, acknowledge the termination of parental rights as to
> such custody in favor of the approved agency, and acknowledge full
> understanding of the effect of such surrender as provided by this act.

If the foregoing requirements are met, the consent, the voluntary
surrender of custody

> shall be valid whether or not the person giving same is a minor and shall be
> irrevocable except at the discretion of the approved agency taking such
> surrender or upon order or judgment of a court of competent jurisdiction,
> setting aside such surrender upon proof of fraud, duress, or misrepresenta-
> tion. [N.J.S.A. 9:2-16.]

The importance of that irrevocability is that the surrender itself gives the
agency the power to obtain termination of parental rights — in other words,
permanent separation of the parent from the child, leading in the ordinary
case to an adoption. N.J.S.A. 9:2-18 to 9:2-20.

This statutory pattern, providing for a surrender in writing and for
termination of parental rights by an approved agency, is generally followed
in connection with adoption proceedings and proceedings by DYFS to
obtain permanent custody of a child. Our adoption statute repeats the
requirements necessary to accomplish an irrevocable surrender to an
approved agency in both form and substance. N.J.S.A. 9:3-41a. It provides
that the surrender "shall be valid and binding without regard to the age of
the person executing the surrender," ibid.; and although the word "irrevocable" is not used, that seems clearly to be the intent of the provision. The
statute speaks of such surrender as constituting "relinquishment of such
person's parental rights in or guardianship or custody of the child *named
therein* and consent by such person to adoption of the child." Ibid. (emphasis supplied). We emphasize "named therein," for we construe the statute

to allow a surrender only after the birth of the child. The formal consent to surrender enables the approved agency to terminate parental rights.

Similarly, DYFS is empowered to "take voluntary surrenders and releases of custody and consents to adoption[s]" from parents, which surrenders, releases, or consents "when properly acknowledged . . . shall be valid and binding irrespective of the age of the person giving the same, and shall be irrevocable except at the discretion of the Bureau of Children's Services [currently DYFS] or upon order of a court of competent jurisdiction." N.J.S.A. 30:4C-23. Such consent to surrender of the custody of the child would presumably lead to an adoption placement by DYFS. See N.J.S.A. 30:4C-20.

It is clear that the Legislature so carefully circumscribed all aspects of a consent to surrender custody — its form and substance, its manner of execution, and the agency or agencies to which it may be made — in order to provide the basis for irrevocability. It seems most unlikely that the Legislature intended that a consent not complying with these requirements would also be irrevocable, especially where, as here, that consent falls radically short of compliance. Not only do the form and substance of the consent in the surrogacy contract fail to meet statutory requirements, but the surrender of custody is made to a private party. It is not made, as the statute requires, either to an approved agency or to DYFS.

These strict prerequisites to irrevocability constitute a recognition of the most serious consequences that flow from such consents: termination of parental rights, the permanent separation of parent from child, and the ultimate adoption of the child. See Sees v. Baber, supra, 74 N.J. at 217. Because of those consequences, the Legislature severely limited the circumstances under which such consent would be irrevocable. The legislative goal is furthered by regulations requiring approved agencies, prior to accepting irrevocable consents, to provide advice and counseling to women, making it more likely that they fully understand and appreciate the consequences of their acts. N.J.A.C. 10:121A-5.4(c).

Contractual surrender of parental rights is not provided for in our statutes as now written. Indeed, in the Parentage Act, N.J.S.A. 9:17-38 to 59, there is a specific provision invalidating any agreement "between an alleged or presumed father and the mother of the child" to bar an action brought for the purpose of determining paternity "[r]egardless of [the contract's] terms." N.J.S.A. 9:17-45. Even a settlement agreement concerning parentage reached in a judicially-mandated consent conference is not valid unless the proposed settlement is approved beforehand by the court. N.J.S.A. 9:17-48c and 9:17-48d. There is no doubt that a contractual provision purporting to constitute an irrevocable agreement to surrender custody of a child for adoption is invalid.

In Sees v. Baber, supra, 74 N.J. 201, we noted that a natural mother's consent to surrender her child and to its subsequent adoption was no longer *required* by the statute in private placement adoptions. After tracing the statutory history from the time when such a consent had been an essential prerequisite to adoption, we concluded that such a consent was now neither necessary nor sufficient for the purpose of terminating parental rights. Id. at 213. The consent to surrender custody in that case was in writing, had been executed prior to physical surrender of the infant, and had been explained to the mother by an attorney. The trial court found that the consent to surrender of custody in that private placement adoption was knowing, voluntary, and deliberate. Id. at 216. The physical surrender of the child took place four days after its birth. Two days thereafter the natural mother changed her mind, and asked that the adoptive couple give her baby back to her. We held that she was entitled to the baby's return. The effect of our holding in that case necessarily encompassed our conclusion that "in an unsupervised private placement, since there is no statutory obligation to consent, there can be no legal barrier to its retraction." Id. at 215. The only possible relevance of consent in these matters, we noted, was that it *might* bear on whether there had been an abandonment of the child, or a forsaking of parental obligations. Id. at 216. Otherwise, consent in a private placement adoption is not only revocable, but, when revoked early enough, irrelevant. Id. at 213-215.

The provision in the surrogacy contract whereby the mother irrevocably agrees to surrender custody of her child and to terminate her parental rights conflicts with the settled interpretation of New Jersey statutory law. There is only one irrevocable consent, and that is the one explicitly provided for by statute: a consent to surrender of custody and a placement with an approved agency or with DYFS. The provision in the surrogacy contract, agreed to before conception, requiring the natural mother to surrender custody of the child without any right of revocation is one more indication of the essential nature of this transaction: the creation of a contractual system of termination and adoption designed to circumvent our statutes.

Public Policy Considerations

The surrogacy contract's invalidity, resulting from its direct conflict with the above statutory provisions, is further underlined when its goals and means are measured against New Jersey's public policy. The contract's basic premise, that the natural parents can decide in advance of birth which one is to have custody of the child, bears no relationship to the settled law that the child's best interests shall determine custody. See Fantony v. Fantony, 21 N.J. 525, 536-537 (1956); see also Sheehan v. Sheehan, 38 N.J. Super. 120, 125 (App. Div. 1955) ("Whatever the agreement of the parents, the ultimate determination of custody lies with the court in the exercise of its supervisory jurisdiction as *parens patriae*."). The fact that the trial court remedied that aspect of the contract through the "best interests" phase does not make the contractual provision any less offensive to the public policy of this State.

The surrogacy contract guarantees permanent separation of the child from one of its natural parents. Our policy, however, has long been that to the extent possible, children should remain with and be brought up by both of their natural parents. That was the first stated purpose of the previous adoption act, L. 1953, c. 264, §1, codified at N.J.S.A. 9:3-17 (repealed): "it is necessary and desirable (a) to protect the child from unnecessary separation from his natural parents. . . ." While not so stated in the present adoption law, this purpose remains part of the public policy of this State. See, e.g., Wilke v. Culp, 196 N.J. Super. 487, 496 (App. Div. 1984), *certif. den.*, 99 N.J. 243 (1985); In re Adoption by J.J.P., supra, 175 N.J. Super. at 426. This is not simply some theoretical ideal that in practice has no meaning. The impact of failure to follow that policy is nowhere better shown than in the results of this surrogacy contract. A child, instead of starting off its life with as much peace and security as possible, finds itself immediately in a tug-of-war between contending mother and father.

The surrogacy contract violates the policy of this State that the rights of natural parents are equal concerning their child, the father's right no greater than the mother's. "The parent and child relationship extends equally to every child and to every parent, regardless of the marital status of the parents." N.J.S.A. 9:17-40. As the Assembly Judiciary Committee noted in its statement to the bill, this section establishes "the principle that regardless of the marital status of the parents, all children *and all parents* have equal rights with respect to each other." Statement to Senate No. 888, Assembly Judiciary, Law, Public Safety and Defense Committee (1983) (emphasis supplied). The whole purpose and effect of the surrogacy contract was to give the father the exclusive right to the child by destroying the rights of the mother. . . .

The only legal advice Mary Beth Whitehead received regarding the surrogacy contract was provided in connection with the contract that she previously entered into with another couple. Mrs. Whitehead's lawyer was referred to her by the Infertility Center, with which he had an agreement to act as counsel for surrogate candidates. His services consisted of spending one hour going through the contract with the Whiteheads, section by section, and answering their questions. Mrs. Whitehead received no further legal advice prior to signing the contract with the Sterns. . . .

Under the contract, the natural mother is irrevocably committed before she knows the strength of her bond with her child. She never makes a totally voluntary, informed decision, for quite clearly any decision prior to the baby's birth is, in the most important sense, uninformed, and any decision after that, compelled by a pre-existing contractual commitment, the threat of a lawsuit, and the inducement of a $10,000 payment is less than totally voluntary. Her interests are of little concern to those who controlled this transaction.

Although the interest of the natural father and adoptive mother is certainly the predominant interest, realistically the *only* interest served, even they are left with less than what public policy requires. They know little about the natural mother, her genetic makeup, and her psychological and medical history. Moreover, not even a superficial attempt is made to determine their awareness of their responsibilities as parents.

Worst of all, however, is the contract's total disregard of the best interests of the child. There is not the slightest suggestion that any inquiry will be made at any time to determine the fitness of the Sterns as custodial parents, of Mrs. Stern as an adoptive parent, their superiority to Mrs. Whitehead, or the effect on the child of not living with her natural mother.

This is the sale of a child, or, at the very least, the sale of a mother's right to her child, the only mitigating factor being that one of the purchasers is the father. Almost every evil that prompted the prohibition on the payment of money in connection with adoptions exists here.

The differences between an adoption and a surrogacy contract should be noted, since it is asserted that the use of money in connection with surrogacy does not pose the risks found where money buys an adoption. Katz, "Surrogate Motherhood and the Baby-Selling Laws," 20 Colum. J.L. & Soc. Probs. 1 (1986).

First, and perhaps most important, all parties concede that it is unlikely that surrogacy will survive without money. Despite the alleged selfless motivation of surrogate mothers, if there is no payment, there will be no surrogates, or very few. That conclusion contrasts with adoption; for obvious reasons, there remains a steady supply, albeit insufficient, despite the prohibitions against payment. The adoption itself, relieving the natural mother of the financial burden of supporting an infant, is in some sense the equivalent of payment.

Second, the use of money in adoptions does not *produce* the problem — conception occurs, and usually the birth itself, before illicit funds are offered. With surrogacy, the "problem," if one views it as such, consisting of the purchase of a woman's procreative capacity, at the risk of her life, is caused by and originates with the offer of money.

Third, with the law prohibiting the use of money in connection with adoptions, the built-in financial pressure of the unwanted pregnancy and the consequent support obligation do not lead the mother to the highest paying, ill-suited, adoptive parents. She is just as well-off surrendering the child to an approved agency. In surrogacy, the highest bidders will presumably become the adoptive parents regardless of suitability, so long as payment of money is permitted.

Fourth, the mother's consent to surrender her child in adoptions is revocable, even after surrender of the child, unless it be to an approved agency, where by regulation there are protections against an ill-advised surrender. In surrogacy, consent occurs so early that no amount of advice would satisfy the potential mother's need, yet the consent is irrevocable.

The main difference, that the unwanted pregnancy is unintended while the situation of the surrogate mother is voluntary and intended, is really not significant. Initially, it produces stronger reactions of sympathy for the mother whose pregnancy was unwanted than for the surrogate mother, who "went into this with her eyes wide open." On reflection, however, it appears that the essential evil is the same, taking advantage of a woman's circumstances (the unwanted pregnancy or the need for money) in order to take away her child, the difference being one of degree.

In the scheme contemplated by the surrogacy contract in this case, a middle man, propelled by profit, promotes the sale. Whatever idealism may have motivated any of the participants, the profit motive predominates, permeates, and ultimately governs the transaction. The demand for children is great and the supply small. The availability of contraception, abortion, and the greater willingness of single mothers to bring up their children has led to a shortage of babies offered for adoption. See N. Baker, Baby Selling: The Scandal of Black Market Adoption supra; Adoption and Foster Care, 1975; Hearings on Baby Selling Before the Subcomm. On Children and Youth of the Senate Comm. on Labor and Public Welfare, 94th Cong. 1st Sess. 6 (1975) (Statement of Joseph H. Reid, Executive Director, Child Welfare League of America, Inc.). The situation is ripe for the entry of the middleman who will bring some equilibrium into the market by increasing the supply through the use of money.

Intimated, but disputed, is the assertion that surrogacy will be used for the benefit of the rich at the expense of the poor. See, e.g., Radin, "Market Inalienability," 100 Harv. L. Rev. 1849, 1930 (1987). In response it is noted that the Sterns are not rich and the Whiteheads not poor. Nevertheless, it is clear to us that it is unlikely that surrogate mothers will be as proportionately numerous among those women in the top twenty percent income bracket as among those in the bottom twenty percent. Ibid. Put differently, we doubt that infertile couples in the low-income bracket will find upper income surrogates.

In any event, even in this case one should not pretend that disparate wealth does not play a part simply because the contrast is not the dramatic "rich versus poor." At the time of trial, the Whiteheads' net assets were probably negative—Mrs. Whitehead's own sister was foreclosing on a second mortgage. Their income derived from Mr. Whitehead's labors. Mrs. Whitehead is a homemaker, having previously held part-time jobs. The Sterns are both professionals, she a medical doctor, he a biochemist. Their combined income when both were working was about $89,500 a year and their assets sufficient to pay for the surrogacy contract arrangements.

The point is made that Mrs. Whitehead *agreed* to the surrogacy arrangement, supposedly fully understanding the consequences. Putting aside the issue of how compelling her need for money may have been, and how significant her understanding of the consequences, we suggest that her consent is irrelevant. There are, in a civilized society, some things that money cannot buy. In America, we decided long ago that merely because conduct purchased by money was "voluntary" did not mean that it was good or beyond regulation and prohibition. West Coast Hotel Co. v. Parrish, 300 U.S. 379, 57 S. Ct. 578, 81 L. Ed. 703 (1937). Employers can no longer buy labor at the lowest price they can bargain for, even though that labor is "voluntary," 29 U.S.C. §206 (1982), or buy women's labor for less money than paid to men for the same job, 29 U.S.C. §206(d), or purchase the agreement of children to perform oppressive labor, 29 U.S.C. §212, or purchase the agreement of workers to subject themselves to unsafe or unhealthful working conditions, 29 U.S.C. §§651 to 678. (Occupational Safety and Health Act of 1970). There are, in short, values that society deems more important than granting to wealth whatever it can buy, be it labor, love, or life. Whether this principle recommends prohibition of surrogacy, which presumably sometimes results in great satisfaction to all of the parties, is not for us to say. We note here only that, under existing law, the fact that Mrs. Whitehead "agreed" to the arrangement is not dispositive.

The long-term effects of surrogacy contracts are not known, but feared — the impact on the child who learns her life was bought, that she is the offspring of someone who gave birth to her only to obtain money; the impact on the natural mother as the full weight of her isolation is felt along with the full reality of the sale of her body and her child; the impact on the natural father and adoptive mother once they realize the consequences of their conduct. Literature in related areas suggests these are substantial considerations, although, given the newness of surrogacy, there is little information. See N. Baker, Baby Selling: The Scandal of Black Market Adoption, supra; Adoption and Foster Care, 1975: Hearings on Baby Selling Before the Subcomm. on Children and Youth of the Senate Comm. on Labor and Public Welfare, 94th Cong. 1st Sess. (1975).

The surrogacy contract is based on principles that are directly contrary to the objectives of our laws. It guarantees the separation of a child from its mother; it looks to adoption regardless of suitability; it totally ignores the child; it takes the child from the mother regardless of her wishes and her maternal fitness; and it does all of this, it accomplishes all of its goals, through the use of money.

Beyond that is the potential degradation of some women that may result from this arrangement. In many cases, of course, surrogacy may bring satisfaction, not only to the infertile couple, but to the surrogate mother herself. The fact, however, that many women may not perceive surrogacy negatively but rather see it as an opportunity does not diminish its potential for devastation to other women.

In sum, the harmful consequences of this surrogacy arrangement appear to us all too palpable. In New Jersey the surrogate mother's agreement to sell her child is void. . . .

We have found that our present laws do not permit the surrogacy contract used in this case. Nowhere, however, do we find any legal prohibition against surrogacy when the surrogate mother volunteers, without any payment, to act as a surrogate and is given the right to change her mind and to assert her parental rights. Moreover, the Legislature remains free to deal with this most sensitive issue as it sees fit, subject only to constitutional constraints. . . .

The judgment is affirmed in part, reversed in part, and remanded for further proceedings consistent with this opinion.

Hong v. Marriott Corp.
656 F. Supp. 445 (D. Md. 1987)

Smalkin, District Judge.

The plaintiff, Yong Cha Hong, commenced this case in a Maryland court with a complaint alleging counts of negligence and breach of warranty against defendants, the proprietor of a chain of fast food restaurants called Roy Rogers Family Restaurants (Marriott) and the supplier of raw frying chicken to the chain (Gold Kist). The case was removed to this Court on diversity grounds. It seems that the plaintiff was contentedly munching away one day on a piece of Roy Rogers take-out fried chicken[1] (a wing) when she bit into something in the chicken that she perceived to be a worm. She suffered, it is alleged, great physical and emotional upset from her encounter with this item, including permanent injuries, in consequence of which she prays damages in the amount of $500,000.00.

The defendants moved for summary judgment on plaintiff's warranty count, and also, later, as to the entire complaint, on the ground that there is no genuine dispute of material fact and that, as a matter of law, there was no breach of warranty or negligence. If they are right, they are entitled to summary judgment. Fed. R. Civ. P. 56(c); Anderson v. Liberty Lobby, Inc., 106 S. Ct. 2505 (1986).

It appears that the item encountered by plaintiff in the chicken wing was probably not a worm or other parasite, although plaintiff, in her deposition, steadfastly maintains that it was a worm, notwithstanding the expert analysis. If it was not in fact a worm, i.e., if the expert analysis is correct, it was either one of the chicken's major blood vessels (the aorta) or its trachea, both of which (the Court can judicially notice) would appear worm-like (although not meaty like a worm, but hollow) to a person unschooled in chicken anatomy. The Court must presume plaintiff to be inexpert as to chickens, even though she admits some acquaintance with fresh-slaughtered chickens. See Ross v. Communications Satellite Corp., 759 F.2d 355, 364 (4th Cir. 1985). For the purposes of analyzing the plaintiff's warranty claim, the Court will assume that the item was not a worm. Precisely how the aorta or trachea wound up in this hapless chicken's wing is a fascinating, but as yet unanswered (and presently immaterial), question.

Thus, the warranty issue squarely framed is, does Maryland law[2] provide a breach of warranty[3] remedy for personal injury flowing from an unexpected encounter with an inedible[4] part of the chicken's anatomy in a piece of fast food fried chicken? Defendants contend that there can be no warranty recovery unless the offending item was a "foreign object," i.e., not a part of the chicken itself.

In Webster v. Blue Ship Tea Room, Inc., 347 Mass. 421, 198 N.E.2d 309 (1964), a favorite of commercial law teachers,[5] the plaintiff was injured when a fish bone she encountered in a bowl of New England fish chowder, served in a "quaint" Boston restaurant, became stuck in her throat. She was denied warranty recovery (on a theory of implied warranty of merchantability) on grounds that are not altogether clear from the court's opinion. The opinion can be read in several ways: (1) There was no breach because

---

1. The court takes judicial notice (because it is so well-known in this jurisdiction) that Roy Rogers specializes in fried chicken, to eat in or take out. Fed. R. Evid. 201.

2. Of course, Maryland law applies in this diversity case. Erie Railroad v. Tompkins, 304 U.S. 64 (1938).

3. The relevant warranty is found in Md. Comm. Law Code Ann. [UCC] §2-314(2) (1975). The Maryland UCC warranty of merchantability applies to sales of food in restaurants, including take-out sales. UCC §2-1314(1).

4. Although perhaps digestible, the aorta and the trachea of a chicken would appear indisputably to belong to the realm of the inedible in that fowl's anatomy.

5. Of which this Judge is one (part-time).

the bone was not extraneous, but a natural substance; (2) There was no breach because New England fish chowder always has bones as an unavoidable contaminant; or (3) The plaintiff, an undoubted Yankee, should have expected to find a bone in her chowder and should have slurped it more gingerly.

In their respected hornbook, UCC, §9-7 (2d Ed. 1979) at 351, Professors White and Summers classify *Webster* in a category of warranty cases involving "the presence of unexpected objects," along with several other cases illustrative of that genre. Id. at n.96. In DeGraff v. Myers Foods, 19 Pa. D&C2d 19, 1 UCC Rep. 110 (C.P. 1958), the unexpected object was a chicken bone in a chicken pot pie. (The plaintiff won.) In Flip-po v. Mode O'Day Frock Shops, 248 Ark. 1, 449 S.W.2d 692 (1970), the unexpected object was a poisonous spider lurking in a newly bought pair of trousers. (It bit plaintiff. Plaintiff lost.)

Unlike New England Fish Chowder, a well-known regional specialty, fried chicken (though of Southern origin) is a ubiquitous American dish. Chicken, generically, has a special place in the American poultry pantheon:

> The dream of the good life in America is embodied in the promise of "a chicken in every pot." Domestic and wild fowl have always been abundant and popular, and each wave of immigrants has brought along favorite dishes—such as paella and chicken cacciatori—which have soon become naturalized citizens.

The Fannie Farmer Cookbook (Knopf: 1980) at 228.

Indeed, as to fried chicken, Fannie Farmer lists recipes for three varieties of fried chicken alone—pan-fried, batter-fried, and Maryland Fried chicken.[6] Id. at 238-239. As best this Judge can determine (and he is no culinary expert) the fast-food chicken served in Roy Rogers most resembles Fannie Farmer's batter-fried chicken. That is, it is covered with a thick, crusty (often highly spiced) batter, that usually conceals from inspection whatever lurks beneath. There is deposition testimony from plaintiff establishing that she saw the offending item before she bit into it, having torn the wing asunder before eating it. A question of fact is raised as to just what she saw, or how carefully she might reasonably be expected to have examined what she saw before eating. It is common knowledge that chicken parts often harbor minor blood vessels. But, this Judge, born and raised south of the Mason-Dixon Line (where fried chicken has been around longer than in any other part of America), knows of no special heightened awareness chargeable to fried chicken eaters that ought to caution them to be on the alert for tracheas or aortas in the middle of their wings.[7]

6. Oddly enough, Maryland Fried Chicken is seldom encountered in Maryland restaurants, though this Judge has seen it on restaurant menus in Ireland and England.

7. Of course, if as a matter of fact and law plaintiff abandoned her reliance on defendants' warranty by eating the wing with "contributory negligence," the defendants would have a good warranty defense, as well as a good negligence defense, under Maryland law. Erdman v. Johnson Bros. Radio & Television, 260 Md. 190, 271 A.2d 744 (1970). But this is quintessentially a question of fact for the jury. Id. at 303-304, 271 A.2d at 751.

Certainly, in *Webster* and many other cases that have denied warranty recovery as a matter of law, the injurious substance was, as in this case, a natural (though inedible) part of the edible item consumed. Thus, in Shapiro v. Hotel Statler Corp., 132 F. Supp. 891 (S.D. Cal. 1955), recovery was denied for a fish bone in "Hot Barquette of Seafood Mornay." And in Allen v. Grafton, 170 Ohio St. 249, 164 N.E.2d 167 (1960), recovery was denied for oyster shell in fried oysters.[8] But in all these cases, the natural item was, beyond dispute, reasonably to be expected in the dish by its very nature, under the prevailing expectation of any reasonable consumer. Indeed, precisely this "reasonable expectation" test has been adopted in a number of cases. See, e.g., Morrison's Cafeteria of Montgomery, Inc. v. Haddox, 431 So. 2d 975, 35 UCC 1074 (Ala. 1983); Battiste v. St. Thomas Diving Club, 26 UCC 324 (D.V.I. 1979); Jeffries v. Clark's Restaurant Enterprises, Inc., 20 Wash. App. 428, 580 P.2d 1103, 24 UCC 587 (1978); Williams v. Braum Ice Cream Stores, Inc., 534 P.2d 700, 15 UCC 1019 (Okla. App. 1974); Stark v. Chock Full O'Nuts, 77 Misc. 2d 553, 356 N.Y.S.2d 403, 14 UCC 51 (1974). The "reasonable expectation" test has largely displaced the natural/foreign test adverted to by defendants. In the circumstances of this case and many others, it is the only one that makes sense. In the absence of any Maryland decisional law, and in view of the expense and impracticality of certification of the question to the Court of Appeals of, Maryland in this case, this court must decide the issue by applying the rule that that Court would likely adopt some time in the future. See, e.g., Wilson v. Ford Motor Co., 656 F.2d 960 (4th Cir. 1981). This court is confident that Maryland would apply the "reasonable expectation" rule to this warranty case, especially in view of the Court of Appeals' holding in Bryer v. Rath Packing Co., 221 Md. 105, 156 A.2d 442 (1959), recognizing a negligence claim for the presence in a prepared food item of "something that should not be there" which renders the food unfit. Id. at 112, 156 A.2d at 447.

Applying the reasonable expectation test to this case, the court cannot conclude that the presence of a trachea or an aorta in a fast food fried chicken wing is so reasonably to be expected as to render it merchantable, as a matter of law, within the bounds of UCC §2-314(2). This is not like the situation involving a 1 cm. bone in a piece of fried fish in *Morrison's Cafeteria*. Everyone but a fool knows that tiny bones may remain in even the best filets of fish. This case is more like *Williams*, where the court held that the issue was for the trier of fact, on a claim arising from a cherry pit in cherry ice cream. Thus, a question of fact is presented that precludes the grant of summary judgment. See Celotex Corp. v. Catrett, 106 S.Ct. 2548 (1986). The jury must determine whether a piece of fast food fried chicken is merchantable if it contains an inedible item of the chicken's anatomy. Of course, the jury will be instructed that the consumer's reasonable expectations form a part of the merchantability concept (under the theory of ordinary fitness, UCC §2-314(2)(c)), as do trade quality standards (under UCC §2-214(2)(a)).

---

8. Although the item encountered by plaintiff in this case does not carry the same potential for physical harm as do fish bones and oyster shells, plaintiff alleges compensable personal injury damage under UCC §2-715(2)(b).

In short, summary judgment cannot be awarded defendants on plaintiff's warranty count, and their motion for partial summary judgment is, accordingly, denied.

Defendants' motion for summary judgment as to the entire complaint is mainly predicated upon plaintiff's insistence at her deposition that the offending item was in fact a worm, notwithstanding the independent analysis showing it not to be a worm. It is true that a party having the burden of proof cannot carry that burden by "evidence which points in both directions," see N.L.R.B. v. Patrick Plaza Dodge, Inc., 522 F.2d 804, 809 (4th Cir. 1975), but it is also the undoubted common law of all American jurisdictions that a plaintiff can advance alternative legal theories of recovery. Here, the negligence and breach of warranty counts (as interpreted by this court's preceding discussion of the scope of the warranty) would permit recovery whether the item was worm or non-worm. Of course, plaintiff's credibility may be severely damaged by her insistence (on deposition and perhaps even at trial) that the item was a worm, despite the contrary expert analysis, which stands unimpugned by contrary expert evidence. This, however, is a risk that plaintiff must assume as part of her right to have the issues of fact tried by a jury under the Seventh Amendment, and summary judgment cannot be used to foreclose that right under the state of this record.

Finally, the court perceives genuine, material disputes of fact and law on plaintiff's negligence count, precluding summary judgment thereon. Fed R. Civ. P. 56(c). Neither expert testimony nor other direct evidence of any sort is needed (except in professional malpractice cases) to prove negligence under Maryland law; negligence can be inferred. Western Md. R. Co. v. Shivers, 101 Md. 391, 393, 61 A. 618, 619 (1905). Although perhaps weak, all inferences, including inferences establishing negligence, must be taken in plaintiff's favor at this stage of the proceedings. Ross v. Communications Satellite Corp., 759 F.2d at 364.

For these reasons, the defendant's motion for summary judgment *in toto* is also denied.

In re Peregrine Entertainment, Ltd.
116 Bankr. 194 (C.D. Cal. 1990)

This appeal from a decision of the bankruptcy court raises an issue never before confronted by a federal court in a published opinion: Is a security interest in a copyright perfected by an appropriate filing with the United States Copyright Office or by a UCC-1 financing statement filed with the relevant secretary of state?

I

National Peregrine, Inc. (NPI) is a Chapter 11 debtor in possession whose principal assets are a library of copyrights, distribution rights and licenses to approximately 145 films, and accounts receivable arising from the licensing of these films to various programmers. NPI claims to have an outright assignment of some of the copyrights; as for the others, NPI claims it has an exclusive license to distribute in a certain territory, or for a certain period of time.

In June 1985, Capitol Federal Savings and Loan Association of Denver (Cap Fed) extended to American National Enterprises, Inc., NPI's predecessor by merger, a six million dollar line of credit secured by what is now NPI's film library. Both the security agreement and the UCC-1 financing statements filed by Cap Fed describe the collateral as "[a]ll inventory consisting of films and all accounts, contract rights, chattel paper, general intangibles, instruments, equipment, and documents related to such inventory, now owned or hereafter acquired by the Debtor." Although Cap Fed filed its UCC-1 financing statements in California, Colorado and Utah, it did not record its security interest in the United States Copyright Office.

NPI filed a voluntary petition for bankruptcy on January 30, 1989. On April 6, 1989, NPI filed an amended complaint against Cap Fed, contending that the bank's security interest in the copyrights to the films in NPI's library and in the accounts receivable generated by their distribution were unperfected because Cap Fed failed to record its security interest with the Copyright Office. NPI claimed that, as a debtor in possession, it had a judicial lien on all assets in the bankruptcy estate, including the copyrights and receivables. Armed with this lien, it sought to avoid, recover and preserve Cap Fed's supposedly unperfected security interest for the benefit of the estate.

The parties filed cross-motions for partial summary judgment on the question of whether Cap Fed had a valid security interest in the NPI film library. The bankruptcy court held for Cap Fed. See Memorandum of Decision re Motion for Partial Summary Adjudication (Nov. 14, 1989) [hereinafter "Memorandum of Decision"] and Order re Summary Adjudication of Issues (Dec. 18, 1989). NPI appeals.

II

A. Where to File

The Copyright Act provides that "[a]ny transfer of copyright ownership or other document pertaining to a copyright" may be recorded in the United States Copyright Office. 17 U.S.C. §205(a); see Copyright Office Circular 12: Recordation of Transfers and Other Documents (reprinted in 1 Copyright L. Rep. (CCH) ¶15,015) [hereinafter "Circular 12"]. A "transfer" under the Act includes any "mortgage" or "hypothecation of a copyright," whether "in whole or in part" and "by any means of conveyance or by operation of law." 17 U.S.C. §§101, 201(d)(1); see 3 Nimmer on Copyright §10.05[A], at 10-43–10-45 (1989). The terms "mortgage" and "hypothecation" include a pledge of property as security or collateral for a debt. See Black's Law Dictionary 669 (5th ed. 1979). In addition, the Copyright Office has defined a "document pertaining to a copyright" as one that has a direct or indirect relationship to the existence, scope, duration, or identification of a copyright, or to the ownership, division, allocation, licensing, transfer, or exercise of rights under a copyright. That relationship may be past, present, future, or potential.

37 C.F.R. §201.4(a)(2); see also Compendium of Copyright Office Practices II ¶¶1602-1603 (identifying which documents the Copyright Office will accept for filing).

It is clear from the preceding that an agreement granting a creditor a security interest in a copyright may be recorded in the Copyright Office. See G. Gilmore, Security Interests in Personal Property §17.3, at 545 (1965). Likewise, because a copyright entitles the holder to receive all income derived from the display of the creative work, see 17 U.S.C. §106, an agreement creating a security interest in the receivables generated by a copyright may also be recorded in the Copyright Office. Thus, Cap Fed's security interest *could* have been recorded in the Copyright Office; the parties seem to agree on this much. The question is, does the UCC provide a parallel method of perfecting a security interest in a copyright? One can answer this question by reference to either federal or state law; both inquiries lead to the same conclusion.

1

Even in the absence of express language, federal regulation will preempt state law if it is so pervasive as to indicate that "Congress left no room for supplementary state regulation," or if "the federal interest is so dominant that the federal system will be assumed to preclude enforcement of state laws on the same subject," Hillsborough County v. Automated Medical Laboratories, Inc., 471 U.S. 707, 713, 105 S. Ct. 2371, 2375, 85 L. Ed. 2d 714 (1985) (internal quotations omitted). Here, the comprehensive scope of the federal Copyright Act's recording provisions, along with the unique federal interests they implicate, support the view that federal law preempts state methods of perfecting security interests in copyrights and related accounts receivable.

The federal copyright laws ensure "predictability and certainty of copyright ownership," "promote national uniformity" and "avoid the practical difficulties of determining and enforcing an author's rights under the differing laws and in the separate courts of the various States." Community for Creative Non-Violence v. Reid, ____ U.S. ____ , 109 S. Ct. 2166, 2177, 104 L. Ed. 2d 811 (1989); H.R. Rep. No. 1476, 94th Cong., 2d Sess. 129 (1976), U.S. Code Cong., & Admin. News 1976, p. 5659. As discussed above, section 205(a) of the Copyright Act establishes a uniform method for recording security interests in copyrights. A secured creditor need only file in the Copyright Office in order to give "all persons constructive notice of the facts stated in the recorded document." 17 U.S.C. §205(c). Likewise, an interested third party need only search the indices maintained by the Copyright Office to determine whether a particular copyright is encumbered. See Northern Songs, Ltd. v. Distinguished Productions, Inc., 581 F. Supp. 638, 640-641 (S.D.N.Y 1984); Circular 12, at 8035-4.

A recording system works by virtue of the fact that interested parties have a specific place to look in order to discover with certainty whether a particular interest has been transferred or encumbered. To the extent there are competing recordation schemes, this lessens the utility of each; when records are scattered in several filing units, potential creditors must conduct several searches before they can be sure that the property is not encumbered. See Danning v. Pacific Propeller, Inc., (In re Holiday Airlines Corp.), 620 F.2d 731 (9th Cir.), *cert. denied*, 449 U.S. 900, 101 S. Ct. 269, 66 L. Ed. 2d 130 (1980); Red Carpet Homes of Johnstown, Inc. v. Gerling (In re Knapp), 575 F.2d 341, 343 (2d Cir. 1978); UCC §9401, Official Comment ¶1. It is for that reason that parallel recordation schemes for the same types of property are scarce as hens' teeth; the court is aware of no others, and the parties have cited none. No useful purposes would be served — indeed, much confusion would result — if creditors were permitted to perfect security interests by filing with either the Copyright Office or state offices. See G. Gilmore, Security Interests in Personal Property §17.3, at 545 (1965); see also 3 Nimmer on Copyright §10.05[A] at 10-44 (1989) ("a persuasive argument . . . can be made to the effect that by reasons of Sections 201(d)(1), 204(a), 205(c) and 205(d) of the current Act . . . Congress has preempted the field with respect to the form and recordation requirements applicable to copyright mortgages").

If state methods of perfection were valid, a third party (such as a potential purchaser of the copyright) who wanted to learn of any encumbrances thereon would have to check not merely the indices of the U.S. Copyright Office, but also the indices of any relevant secretary of state. Because copyrights are incorporeal — they have no fixed situs — a number of state authorities could be relevant. See, e.g., note 4 supra. Thus, interested third parties could never be entirely sure that all relevant jurisdictions have been searched. This possibility, together with the expense and delay of conducting searches in a variety of jurisdictions, could hinder the purchaser and sale of copyrights, frustrating Congress's policy that copyrights be readily transferable in commerce.

This is the reasoning adopted by the Ninth Circuit in Danning v. Pacific Propeller. *Danning* held that 49 U.S.C. App. §1403(a), the Federal Aviation Act's provision for recording conveyances and the creation of liens and security interests in civil aircraft, preempts state filing provisions. 620 F.2d at 735-736. According to *Danning*,

> [t]he predominant purpose of the statute was to provide one central place for the filing of [liens on aircraft] and thus eliminate the need, given the highly mobile nature of aircraft and their appurtenances, for the examination of State and County records.

620 F.2d at 735-736. Copyrights, even more than aircraft, lack a clear situs; tangible, movable goods such as airplanes must always exist at some physical location; they may have a home base from which they operate or where they receive regular maintenance. The same cannot be said of intangibles. As noted above, this lack of an identifiable situs militates

against individual state filings and in favor of a single, national registration scheme.

Moreover, as discussed at greater length below, see pp. 205-207 infra, the Copyright Act establishes its own scheme for determining priority between conflicting transferees, one that differs in certain respects from that of Article Nine. Under Article Nine, priority between holders of conflicting security interests in intangibles is generally determined by who perfected his interest first. UCC §9312(5). By contrast, section 205(d) of the Copyright Act provides:

> As between two conflicting transfers, the one executed first prevails if it is recorded, in the manner required to give constructive notice under subsection (c), *within one month after its execution in the United States or within two months after its execution outside the United States*, or at any time before recordation in such manner of the later transfer. . . .

17 U.S.C. §205(d) (emphasis added). Thus, unlike Article Nine, the Copyright Act permits the effect of recording with the Copyright Office to relate back as far as two months.

Because the Copyright Act and Article Nine create different priority schemes, there will be occasions when different results will be reached depending on which scheme was employed. The availability of filing under the UCC would thus undermine the priority scheme established by Congress with respect to copyrights. This type of direct interference with the operation of federal law weighs heavily in favor of preemption. See generally Bonito Boats, Inc. v. Thunder Craft Boats, Inc., 489 U.S. 141, 109 S. Ct. 971, 103 L. Ed. 2d 118 (1989).

The bankruptcy court below nevertheless concluded that security interests in copyrights could be perfected by filing either with the copyright office or with the secretary of state under the UCC, making a tongue-in-cheek analog to the use of a belt and suspenders to hold up a pair of pants. According to the bankruptcy court, because either device is equally useful, one should be free to choose which one to wear. With all due respect, this court finds the analogy inapt. There is no legitimate reason why pants should be held up in only one particular manner: Individuals and public modesty are equally served by either device, or even by a safety pin or a piece of rope; all that really matters is that the job gets done. Registration schemes are different in that the *way* notice is given is precisely what matters. To the extent interested parties are confused as to which system is being employed, this increases the level of uncertainty and multiplies the risk of error, exposing creditors to the possibility that they might get caught with their pants down.

A recordation scheme best serves its purpose where interested parties can obtain notice of all encumbrances by referring to a single, precisely defined recordation system. The availability of parallel state recordation systems that could put parties on constructive notice as to encumbrances on copyrights would surely interfere with the effectiveness of the federal recordation scheme. Given the virtual absence of dual recordation schemes in our legal system, Congress cannot be presumed to have contemplated such a result. The court therefore concludes that any state recordation system pertaining to interests in copyrights would be preempted by the Copyright Act.

2

State law leads to the same conclusion. Article Nine of the Uniform Commercial Code establishes a comprehensive scheme for the regulation of security interests in personal property and fixtures. By superseding a multitude of pre-Code security devices, it provides "a simple and unified structure within which the immense variety of present-day secured financing transactions can go forward with less cost and greater certainty." UCC §9101, Official Comment. However, Article Nine is not all encompassing; under the "step back" provision of UCC §9104, Article Nine does not apply "[t]o a security interest subject to any statute of the United States to the extent that such statute governs the rights of parties to and third parties affected by transactions in particular types of property."

For most items of personal property, Article Nine provides that security interests must be perfected by filing with the office of the secretary of state in which the debtor is located. See UCC §§9302(1), 9401(1)(c). Such filing, however, is not "necessary of effective to perfect a security interest in property subject to . . . [a] statute or treaty of the United States which provides for a national or international registration . . . or which specifies a place of filing different from that specified in [Article Nine] for filing of the security interest." UCC §9302(3)(a). When a national system for recording security interests exists, the Code treats compliance with that system as "equivalent to the filing of a financing statement under [Article Nine,] and a security interest in property subject to the statute or treaty can be perfected only by compliance therewith. . . ." UCC §9302(4).

As discussed above, section 205(a) of the Copyright Act clearly does establish a national system for recording transfers of copyright interests, and it specifies a place of filing different from that provided in Article Nine. Recording in the Copyright Office gives nationwide, constructive notice to third parties of the recorded encumbrance. Except for the fact that the Copyright Office's indices are organized on the basis of the title and registration number, rather than by reference to the identity of the debtor, this system is nearly identical to that which Article Nine generally provides on a statewide basis. And, lest there be any doubt, the drafters of the UCC specifically identified the Copyright Act as establishing the type of national registration system that would trigger the §9302(3) and (4) step back provisions.

> Examples of the type of federal statute referred to in [UCC §9302(3)(a)] are the provisions of [Title 17] (copyrights). . . .

UCC §9302, Official Comment ¶8; see G. Gilmore, Security Interests in Personal Property §17.3, at 545 (1965) ("[t]here can be no doubt that [the Copyright Act was] meant to be within the description of §9-302(3)(a)").

The court therefore concludes that the Copyright Act provides for national registration and "specifies a place of filing different from that specified in [Article Nine] for filing of the security interest." UCC §9302(3)(a). Recording in the U.S. Copyright Office, rather than filing a financing statement under Article Nine, is the proper method for perfecting a security interest in a copyright.

In reaching this conclusion, the court rejects City Bank & Trust Co. v. Otto Fabric, Inc., 83 B.R. 780 (D. Kan. 1988), and In re Transportation Design & Technology Inc., 48 B.R. 635 (Bankr. S.D. Cal. 1985), insofar as they are germane to the issues presented here. Both cases held that, under the UCC, security interests in patents need not be recorded in the U.S. Patent and Trademark Office to be perfected as against lien creditors because the federal statute governing patent assignments does not specifically provide for liens:

> Applications for patent, patents, or any interest therein, shall be assignable in law by an instrument in writing. The applicant, patentee, or his assigns or legal representatives may in like manner grant and convey an exclusive right under his application for patent, or patents, to the whole or any specified part of the United States. . . .
>
> An assignment, grant or conveyance shall be void as against *any subsequent purchaser or mortgagee* for a valuable consideration, without notice, unless it is recorded in the Patent and Trademark Office within three months from its date or prior to the date of such subsequent purchase or mortgage.

35 U.S.C. §261 (emphasis added).

According to *In re Transportation*, because section 261's priority scheme only provides for a "subsequent purchaser or mortgagee for valuable consideration," it does not require recording in the Patent and Trademark Office to perfect against lien creditors. See 48 B.R. at 639. Likewise, *City Bank* held that "the failure of the statute to mention protection against lien creditors suggests that it is unnecessary to record an assignment or other conveyance with the Patent Office to protect the appellant's security interest against the trustee." 83 B.R. at 782.

These cases misconstrue the plain language of UCC section 9104, which provides for the voluntary step back of Article Nine's provisions *"to the extent* [federal law] governs the rights of [the] parties." UCC §9104(a) (emphasis added). Thus, when a federal statute provides for a national system of recordation or specifies a place of filing different from that in Article Nine, the methods of perfection specified in Article Nine are supplanted by that national system; compliance with a national system of recordation is equivalent to the filing of a financing statement under Article Nine. UCC §9302(4). Whether the federal statute also provides a priority scheme different from that in Article Nine is a separate issue, addressed below. Compliance with a national registration scheme is necessary for perfection regardless of whether federal law governs priorities. Cap Fed's security interest in the copyrights of the films in NPI's library and the receivables they have generated therefore is unperfected.

B. Effect of Failing to Record with the Copyright Office

Having concluded that Cap Fed should have, but did not, record its security interest with the Copyright Office, the court must next determine whether NPI as a debtor in possession can subordinate Cap Fed's interest and recover it for the benefit of the bankruptcy estate. As a debtor in possession, NPI has nearly all of the powers of a bankruptcy trustee, see 11 U.S.C. §1107(a), including the authority to set aside preferential or fraudulent transfers, as well as transfers otherwise voidable under applicable state or federal law. See 11 U.S.C. §§544, 547, 548.

Particularly relevant is the "strong arm clause" of 11 U.S.C. §544(a)(1), which, in respect to personal property in the bankruptcy estate, gives the debtor in possession every right and power state law confers upon one who has acquired a lien by legal or equitable proceedings. If, under the applicable law, a judicial lien creditor would prevail over an adverse claimant, the debtor in possession prevails; if not, not. Wind Power Systems, Inc. v. Cannon Financial Group, Inc. (In re Wind Power Systems, Inc.), 841 F.2d 288, 293 (9th Cir. 1988); Angeles Real Estate Co. v. Kerxton (In re Construction General Inc.), 737 F.2d 416, 418 (4th Cir. 1984). A lien creditor generally takes priority over unperfected security interests in estate property because, under Article Nine, "an unperfected security interest is subordinate to the rights of . . . [a] person who becomes a lien creditor before the security interest is perfected." UCC §9301(1)(b). But, as discussed previously, the UCC does not apply to the extent a federal statute "governs the rights of parties to and third parties affected by transactions in particular types of property." UCC §9104. Section 205(d) of the Copyright Act is such a statute, establishing a priority scheme between conflicting transfers of interests in a copyright:

> As between two conflicting *transfers*, the one executed first prevails if it is recorded, in the manner required to give constructive notice under subsection (c), within one month after its execution in the United States or within two months after its execution outside the United States, or at any time before recordation in such manner of the later transfer. Otherwise, the later *transfer* prevails if recorded first in such manner, and if taken in good faith, for valuable consideration or on the basis of a binding promise to pay royalties, and without notice of the earlier *transfer*.

17 U.S.C. §205(d) (emphasis added). The federal priority scheme preempts the state priority scheme.

Section 205(d) does not expressly address the rights of lien creditors, speaking only in terms of competing transfers of copyright interests. To determine whether NPI, as a hypothetical lien creditor, may avoid Cap Fed's unperfected security interest, the court must therefore consider whether a judicial lien is a transfer as that term is used in the Copyright Act.

As noted above, the Copyright Act recognizes transfers of copyright ownership "in whole or in part by any means of conveyance or by operation of law." 17 U.S.C. §201(d)(1). Transfer is defined broadly to include any "assignment, mortgage, exclusive license, or any other conveyance, alienation, or hypothecation of a copyright . . . whether or not it is limited in time or place of effect." 17 U.S.C. §101. A judicial lien creditor is a creditor who has obtained a lien "by judgment, levy, sequestration, or other legal or equitable process or proceeding." 11 U.S.C. §101(32). Such a creditor typically has the power to seize and sell property held by the debtor at the time of the creation of the lien in order to satisfy the judgment or, in the case of general intangibles such as copyrights, to collect the revenues generated by the intangible as they come due. See, e.g., Cal. Civ. P. Code §§701.510, 701.520, 701.640. . . . Thus, while the creation of a lien on a copyright may not give a creditor an immediate right to control the copyright, it amounts to a sufficient transfer of rights to come within the broad definition of transfer under the Copyright Act. See Phoenix Bond & Indemnity Co. v. Shamblin (In re Shamblin), 890 F.2d 123, 127 n.7 (9th Cir. 1989) (under the Bankruptcy Code, "[t]his court has consistently treated the creation of liens on the debtor's property as a transfer").

Cap Fed contends that, in order to prevail under 17 U.S.C. §205(d), NPI must have the status of a bona fide purchaser, rather than that of a judicial lien creditor. See Pistole v. Mellor (In re Mellor), 734 F.2d 1396, 1401 n.4 (9th Cir. 1984) (judicial lien creditor does not have the same rights as a bona fide purchaser); cf. 11 U.S.C. §544(a)(3) (for real estate in the bankruptcy estate, debtor in possession has the rights of a bona fide purchaser). Cap Fed, in essence, is arguing that the term transfer in section 205(d) refers only to consensual transfers. For the reasons expressed above, the court rejects this argument. The Copyright Act's definition of transfer is very broad and specifically includes transfers by operation of law. 17 U.S.C. §201(d)(1). The term is broad enough to encompass not merely purchasers, but lien creditors as well. NPI therefore is entitled to priority if it meets the statutory good faith, notice, consideration and recording requirements of section 205(a). As the hypothetical lien creditor, NPI is deemed to have taken in good faith and without notice. See 11 U.S.C. §544(a). The only remaining issues are whether NPI could have recorded its interest in the Copyright Office and whether it obtained its lien for valuable consideration.

In order to obtain a lien on a particular piece of property, a creditor who has received a money judgment in the form of a writ of execution must prepare a notice of levy that specifically identifies the property to be encumbered and the consequences of that action. See Cal. Civ. P. Code §699.540. If such a notice identifies a federal copyright or the receivables generated by such a copyright, it and the underlying writ of execution, constitute "document[s] pertaining to a copyright" and, therefore, are capable of recordation in the Copyright Office. See 17 U.S.C. §205(a); Compendium of Copyright Office Practices II ¶¶1602-1603 (identifying which documents the Copyright Office will accept for filing). Because these documents could be recorded in the Copyright Office, NPI as debtor in possession will be deemed to have done so.

Finally, contrary to Cap Fed's assertion, a trustee or debtor in possession is deemed to have given valuable consideration for its judicial lien. Section 544(a)(1) provides:

> The trustee [or debtor in possession] shall have, as of the commencement of the case . . . the right and powers of, or may avoid any transfer of property of the debtor or any obligation incurred by the debtor that is voidable by . . . a creditor *that extends credit to the debtor at the time of the commencement of the case*, and that obtains, at such time and with respect to such credit, a judicial lien on all property on which a creditor on a simple contract could have obtained such a judicial lien. . . .

11 U.S.C. §544(a)(1) (emphasis added). The act of extending credit, of course, constitutes the giving of valuable consideration. See First Maryland Leasecorp v. M/V Golden Egret, 764 F.2d 749, 753 (11th Cir. 1985); United States v. Cahall Bros., 674 F.2d 578, 581 (6th Cir. 1982). In addition, the trustee's lien — like that of any other judgment creditor — is deemed to be in exchange for the claim that formed the basis of the underlying judgment, a claim that is extinguished by the entry of the judgment.

Because NPI meets all of the requirements for subsequent transferees to prevail under 17 U.S.C. §205(b) — a transferee who took in good faith, for valuable consideration and without notice of the earlier transfer — Cap Fed's unperfected security interest in NPI's copyrights and the receivables they generated is trumped by NPI's hypothetical judicial lien. NPI may therefore avoid Cap Fed's interest and preserve it for the benefit of the bankruptcy estate.

Conclusion

The judgment of the bankruptcy court is reversed. The case is ordered remanded for a determination of which movies in NPI's library are the subject of valid copyrights.

GLOSSARY

Acceptance: manifestation of assent in the manner requested or authorized by the offeror.

Accord and satisfaction: a special agreement in which the parties to a disputed contract agree to new terms in exchange for forbearing to sue under the original contract.

Antenuptial agreement: contract entered into prior to marriage determining the parties' rights on dissolution of the marriage; must be in writing to be enforceable.

Anticipatory breach: positive, unconditional, and unequivocal words that a party intends to breach his contractual obligations.

Arbitration: nonjudicial method of resolving legal disputes.

Assignee: transferee of contractual rights.

Assignment: transference of contractual rights by the promisee to a third party.

Assignor: transferor of a contractual right.

Attachment: the time a security interest becomes an inchoate right under Article IX of the UCC.

Auction with reserve: parties have the right to revoke any time before gavel comes down.

Auction without reserve: property owner relinquishes the right to revoke.

Battle of the forms: difference in forms used by merchants for sales agreements pursuant to Article II of the UCC.

Bilateral contract: a promise for a promise.

Breach of contract: failure of a promisor to fulfill a contractual obligation.

Caveat emptor: let the buyer beware.

Caveat venditor: let the seller beware.

Charitable subscription: promise to donate to a charity, given the enforceability of a contract under law.

Children of tender years: children between the ages of 7 and 14.

CIF: cost of insurance and freight.

Class: a group of persons identified as a group rather than as named individuals.

COD: cost on delivery, the moment when risk passes to the buyer.

Collateral: property subject of a security agreement under Article IX of the UCC.

Compensatory damages: standard measure of damages; puts the injured party in the same position he would have been in had the contract been fulfilled.

Condition: fact or event, the happening or nonhappening of which creates or extinguishes an absolute duty to perform.

Condition concurrent: promise to perform and performance occur simultaneously.

Condition precedent: fact or event that creates an absolute duty to perform.

Condition subsequent: fact or event that extinguishes as absolute duty to perform.

Conditional promise: a promise dependent on the happening or non-happening of some event.

Consequential damages: damages above the standard measure due to special losses occasioned by the breach.

Consideration: a benefit conferred or a detriment incurred; a basic requirement of every valid contract.

Consignment contract: agreement whereby risk of loss to the subject goods remains with the seller until the buyer resells the goods.

Constructive condition: an implied-in-fact condition.

Contract: a legally enforceable agreement between two or more parties in which each agrees to give and receive something of legal value.

Contract of adhesion: a contract entered into where one party has an unfair bargaining advantage; voidable.

Contractual capacity: the legal ability to enter into a contractual relationship.

Contractual intent: the purposefulness of forming a contractual relationship.

Co-signer: person who agrees to be equally liable with a promisor under a contract.

Counteroffer: a variance in the terms of an offer that constitutes a rejection of the original offer and results in a new offer by the offeree to the original offeror.

Covenant: an absolute, unconditional promise to perform.

Cover: remedy whereby the buyer can purchase goods in substitution for the goods designated in a breached contract.

Cross-offer: see Counteroffer.

Damages: legal remedies; monetary awards.

Delegation: promisor having assistance in fulfilling contractual duties.

Divisible contract: contract capable of being broken down into several equal agreements.

Duress: force or coercion used to induce agreement to a contract.

Economic duress: threatening the loss of an economic benefit if the person refuses to contract.

Emancipation: a minor no longer under the legal care of an adult.

Equitable remedies: nonmonetary awards.

Equity: the branch of the legal system that deals with fairness and mercy.

Estoppel: equitable term; the doctrine bars certain actions in the interest of fairness.

Executed contract: a contract that is complete and final with respect to all of its terms and conditions.

Executory contract: a contract in which one or both of the parties still have obligations to perform.

Exemplary damages: additional monetary award designed to punish the breaching party.

Express condition: a condition created by the words of the parties.

Express contract: a contract manifested in so many words, oral or written.

Express waiver: a waiver occurring when the promisee specifically manifests an intention to forgive the other side's breach.

Express warranty: a guarantee created by words or conduct of the seller.

Ex ship: risk passes to buyer of the goods when the goods are offloaded from the means of conveyance.

FAS: free alongside; risk passes to buyer when goods are placed alongside the vessel used for transportation.

Financing statement: document filed in government office to protect a security interest under Article IX of the UCC.

Firm offer: Offer made by a merchant under the provisions of the UCC that cannot be revoked for a period of time.

Floating lien: security interest in after-acquired property.

FOB: free on board; risk passes to buyer when the goods are loaded on the vessel used to transport the goods.

Formal contract: historically, a written contract under seal; currently, any contract so designated by a state statute.

Fraud: a misrepresentation of a material fact made with the intent to deceive, relied on by the other party to his or her detriment.

Frustration of purpose: the purpose for which the contract was formed no longer exists.

Guarantee: promise to answer for the debts of another; must be in writing.

Guarantor: person who agrees to be responsible to answer for the debts of another should the debtor default.

Implied-in-fact condition: condition created by the reasonable expectation of the parties.

Implied-in-fact contract: a contract in which the promises of the parties are inferred from their actions as opposed to specific words.

Implied-in-law condition: a condition imposed by law in the interests of fairness.

Implied-in-law contract: see Quasi-contract.

Implied waiver: a waiver occurring when the promisee's actions imply an intention to forgive the other side's breach.

Implied warranty: guarantee created by operation of law.

Impossibility of performance: promisor's performance cannot be fulfilled due to outside forces.

Incidental beneficiary: person who benefits tangentially from a contract.

Informal contract: any nonformal contract.

Injunction: court order to stop engaging in a specific action.

Intended beneficiary: third party beneficiary.

Iron clad offer: offer under the UCC whose terms cannot be modified by the offeree.

Law: division of the legal system concerned with historical legal principles designed to provide equal treatment to all persons.

Legal remedies: monetary awards.

Limitation of damages: a contractual provision placing a ceiling on the amount of potential liability for breach of the contract.

Liquidated damages: a contractual provision providing a specified dollar amount for breach of the contract.

Mailbox rule: the acceptance of a bilateral contract is effective when properly dispatched by an authorized means of communication.

Majority: adulthood; above the legal age of consent.

Malum in se: bad in and of itself, against public morals.

Malum prohibitum: regulatory wrong; violates a statute.

Material breach: breach of contract that goes to the heart of the agreement.

Mechanic's lien: security interest given under common law to persons who repair property.

Mental duress: psychological threats used to induce a person to contract.

Merchant: under the UCC, any person who regularly trades in goods or who holds himself out as having knowledge peculiar to a specific good.

Minor breach: breach of contract that goes to an insignificant aspect of the agreement.

Minority: persons under the legal age of consent.

Mirror image rule: an acceptance must correspond exactly to the terms of the offer.

Misrepresentation: mistakes of a material fact relied on by the other party to his or her detriment; no intent to defraud.

Mistake: misconception of the subject matter of the contract.

Mitigation of damages: duty imposed on injured party to lessen, by reasonable means, the breaching party's liability.

Mutual assent: a meeting of the minds; agreeing to the same terms at the same time; the offer and acceptance combined.

Mutual mistake: misconception of the subject matter of a contract by both parties; makes the contract unenforceable.

Mutual rescission: agreement by both contracting parties to do away with the contract.

Mutuality of consideration: the bargain element of the contract; that each side must give and receive something of legal value.

Natural infant: a child under the age of seven.

Necessaries: food, clothing, shelter, and medical aid.

No arrival, no sale: risk passes to the buyer when the goods are tendered to the buyer.

Nominal consideration: consideration of insufficient legal value to support a contract.

Novation: substitution of a party to a contract; novated person takes over all rights and obligations under the contract.

Offer: a proposition made by one party to another manifesting a present intention to enter into a valid contract and creating a power in the other person to create a valid contract by making an appropriate acceptance.

Offeree: the person to whom an offer is made; the party who has the power to create a valid contract by making an appropriate acceptance.

Offeror: the person who initiates a contract by proposing the offer.

Operation of law: a manner in which rights and obligations devolve on a person without the act or cooperation of the party himself.

Option: a contract to keep an offer open for a specified time.

Output contract: an agreement whereby one person agrees to buy or sell all the goods produced by the other party.

Palimony: payment made to a person under certain circumstances pursuant to the break-up of a nonmarital relationship.

Parol evidence rule: oral testimony may not be used to vary the terms of a writing.

Perfect tender: Under the UCC the buyer's right to complete, not substantial, performance.

Perfection: method of creating and protecting a security interest under Article IX of the UCC.

Physical duress: threatening physical harm to force a person to contract.

Preexisting duty rule: promises to do what one is already legally bound to do is not consideration.

Prenuptial agreement: antenuptial agreement.

Principal-agent: an agent is one who acts for and on behalf of another, the principal, for the purpose of entering into contracts with third persons.

Promisee: the one who receives consideration in a bilateral contract.

Promisor: the one who gives consideration in a bilateral contract.

Promissory estoppel: doctrine in which promises not supported by consideration are given enforceability if the promisee had detrimentally relied on the promises.

Promissory note: promise to pay money; repayment of a loan.

Punitive damages: exemplary damages.

Purchase money security interest: security interest created in the person whose money was used to buy the collateral.

Quantum meruit: quasi-contractual award; value of the service performed.

Quantum valebant: quasi-contractual award; value of the good given.

Quasi-contract: a legal relationship that the courts, in the interests of fairness and equity, treat in a manner similar to a contractual relationship, but one in which no contract exists.

Quasi-contractual remedy: an equitable remedy involving a monetary award.

Quid pro quo: this for that; the mutuality of consideration.

Real party in interest: person with enforceable contractual rights.

Reformation: a court-ordered accord and satisfaction.

Rejection: to refuse an offer.

Release: contract relieving the promisor from an obligation under an existing contract.

Replevin: quitable remedy in which buyer reclaims property previously rejected.

Requirements contract: agreement whereby one person agrees to buy all his supplies from the other person.

Rescission and restitution: a court order revoking a contract that would be unduly burdensome to fulfill.

Reverse unilateral contract: a contract in which the performer, rather than the promisor, makes the offer.

Revocation: to recall an offer.

Rules of construction: guidelines used by the courts to interpret contractual provisions.

Sale on approval: risk passes to the buyer when the buyer receives and approves the goods.

Sale or return: risk passes to the buyer when the buyer receives the goods, but the buyer bears the cost of returning any goods of which she does not approve.

Secured transaction: any transaction, regardless of form, that intends to create a security interest in personal property or fixtures.

Security agreement: document signed by debtor and creditor naming the collateral and creating a security interest in said collateral.

Security interest: right acquired by a creditor to attach collateral in case of default by the debtor.

Severability: the ability to separate a contract into its legal and illegal portions.

Sham consideration: legally insufficient consideration used to mask a gift in words of contract.

Shipment contract: agreement whereby risk passes from seller to buyer when goods are transported by a third person under Article II of the UCC.

Specific performance: court order to perform contractual promises.

Speculative damages: damages that are not specifically provable.

Statute of Frauds: statute mandating that certain contracts must be in writing to be enforceable.

Strict liability: no standard of care; automatic liability if properly used goods do not meet warranties.

Substituted agreement: a new contract that incorporates the original contract in the new provisions.

Sufficiency of the consideration: doctrine that each party to a contract must contribute something of legal value for which he has bargained.

Supervening illegality: change in law that makes the subject matter of the contract illegal.

Temporary restraining order (TRO): preliminary step to an injunction.

Tender complete performance: being ready, willing, and able to perform.

Third party beneficiary contract: contract entered into for the purpose of benefiting someone not a party to the contract.

Third party creditor beneficiary: person who receives the benefit of a contract in order to extinguish a debt owed to him by the promisee.

Third party donee beneficiary: person who receives the benefit of a contract in order to receive a gift from the promisee.

Time of the essence clause: contractual clause in which a specified time for performance is made a key element of the contract.

Token chose: item of symbolic, rather than monetary, significance.

Undisclosed principal: a person, represented by an agent, who is party to a contract but has not revealed his or her identity to the other party.

Undue influence: mental duress by a person in a close and particular relationship to the innocent party.

Unenforceable contract: a contract that is otherwise valid but for breach of which there is no remedy at law.

Uniform Commercial Code (UCC): statutory enactment codifying certain areas of contract law, specifically with respect to sales contracts and security agreements.

Unilateral contract: a promise for an act.

Unilateral mistake: misconception of the subject matter of a contract by only one party to the contract; may be enforceable.

Usury: rate of interest higher than the rate allowed by law.

Valid contract: an agreement that meets all six contractual requirements.

Vested: having a legally enforceable right.

Void contract: a situation in which the parties have attempted to create a contract, but because one or more of the requisite elements are missing no contract exists.

Voidable contract: a contract that one party may avoid at his option without being in breach of contract.

Voluntary disablement: volitional act by a promisor making her obligation virtually incapable of being performed.

Waiver: forgiveness of a contractual obligation.

Warranty: guarantee made by the manufacturer or seller with respect to the quality, quantity, and type of good being sold.

Warranty of fitness for a particular use: guarantee that goods can be used for a specified purpose.

Warranty of merchantability: guarantee that goods can be used in their current condition.

Warranty of title: guarantee that seller has a title sufficient to transfer the goods to the buyer.

Index